W9-BZA-681

# COLORADO

A HISTORY OF THE CENTENNIAL STATE

v

"Smelting Works at Denver" (1892) by Thomas Moran.

# COLORADO

## A HISTORY OF THE CENTENNIAL STATE

THIRD EDITION

Carl Abbott ■ *Portland State University*

Stephen J. Leonard ■ *Metropolitan State College of Denver*

David McComb ■ *Colorado State University*

UNIVERSITY PRESS OF COLORADO

© 1982, 1994, University Press of Colorado

Third Edition

Published by the University Press of Colorado
P.O. Box 849
Niwot, Colorado 80544

Cover photograph: Mount Sneffels. Courtesy of the STATE
HISTORICAL SOCIETY OF COLORADO.

The University Press of Colorado is a cooperative publishing enterprise
supported, in part, by Adams State College, Colorado State University,
Fort Lewis College, Mesa State College, Metropolitan State College of
Denver, University of Colorado, University of Northern Colorado, University of Southern Colorado, and Western State College of Colorado.

Abbott, Carl.
    Colorado, a history of the Centennial State / Carl Abbott, Stephen
  J. Leonard, David McComb. — 3rd ed.
        p.   cm.
    Includes bibliographical references (p.     ) and index.
    ISBN 0-87081-343-9 (cloth) — ISBN 0-087081-344-7 (paper)
    1. Colorado—History.   I. Leonard, Stephen J.   II. McComb, David
  G.   III. Title.
  F776.A22   1994
  978.8—dc20                                              94-9340
                                                            CIP

The paper used in this publication meets the minimum requirements of the American National Standard for Information Sci-
ences—Permanence of Paper for Printed Library Materials.
ANSI Z39.48–1984

10   9   8   7   6   5   4   3   2

# CONTENTS

# MAPS

# INTRODUCTION

The United States is a plural society. From the seventeenth to the twentieth centuries, its peoples have defined themselves as members of groups within a larger national system. They have given allegiance to their particular colony, state, or section. They have identified themselves as members of the leisured or laboring classes and as representatives of specific industries. They have led their lives more as members of particular ethnic groups than as "Americans" in the abstract sense. The nation's history, in large measure, has been made by the interaction of such groups — their conflicts, their cooperation, their gradual blending in recent decades under the unifying pressures of modern commerce and communication.

As much as any state, Colorado has grown within this multicultural framework. For nearly three hundred years there have been deep divisions among Native Americans, Spanish-speaking Americans, and English-speaking Americans. The split between entrepreneurs and working people and the divisions among economic regions on the basis of geographical differences from mountains to plains have been equally important. The politics of the state have revolved around the appearance and partial resolution of conflicts among its various social and economic groups.

Throughout the United States, cities have been the natural focus for group interaction. From the earliest years of colonization to the present, cities have been the dynamic centers of U.S. growth. As commercial and manufacturing centers they have been indispensable for organizing the nation's economic activities and for tying its people together into metropolitan regions. Economic growth has, in turn, attracted a variety of ethnic groups to the major cities and promoted the differentiation of social classes. The pace of change and the mixing of peoples have also made U.S. cities the centers for cultural and intellectual life in which the future of the nation is debated.

The role of cities has been especially obvious on the American frontier. In every new region during the initial years of settlement, urban centers grew more rapidly than the surrounding countryside. During the years of pioneering, the frontier city was an advance base of supply, furnishing food, clothing, and tools. When settlers began to produce a surplus of goods, the city provided credit and transportation and found outside buyers. Because the interregional and international exchange of agricultural and mineral products for manufactured goods was the foundation of U.S. economic growth for the first three centuries of settlement, the frontier city was vital not only to the surrounding area but also to the development of the nation as a whole.

Certainly in the trans-Mississippi West, the urban frontier and the frontier of settlement were nearly synonymous. Credit, capital, and supplies for the development of the plains and mountains came initially from the peripheral cities of St. Louis, Chicago, and San Francisco. Within the new territory were cattle towns, farm-market centers, and mining towns established simultaneously with the activities they were designed to serve. Even after the initial excitement of settlement, it was the new towns and cities that provided the money and leadership that exploited new resources and brought them to market.

Within Colorado, Denver has monopolized these metropolitan functions since 1859. In 1990 the Denver-Boulder metropolitan area counted a population nearly five times that of Colorado Springs, ten times that of Fort Collins, fourteen times that of Greeley, and fifteen times that of Pueblo. In Asia and Africa such a pattern of size relations is usually found in countries long subject to European rule, where urban development has centered on a single seaport capital such as Manila or Lagos. Denver served similarly as a channel for eastern capital and influence during Colorado's development as a supplier of raw materials for eastern consumption. If Colorado and other western states have been economic colonies of the East, as numerous writers have complained, then Denver has been one of the colonial capitals.

Another characteristic plays a role in the history of Colorado, apart from the cities and the citizens — the land itself. The opportunities and constraints offered by the land have regulated the growth of mining, tourism, and agriculture. Those who chronicle the history of Colorado must view their subject with the perspectives of geologist, geographer, botanist, and zoologist, among others, to trace the plains and peaks, to sample the air and measure the rainfall, and to count the elk and analyze the grasses. They are also called upon to discover the ways in which Coloradans have reacted to their land. At the least, it is necessary to note the deep affection for the topography most residents have shared. In the nineteenth century, there was true excitement in exploring the land and learning how to appreciate the scenery. In the twentieth century, there has been a fierce desire to hold fast to a landscape threatened by rapid development.

A historian of Colorado must also examine changes in the ways in which Coloradans have perceived both their environment and themselves. Men and women in the 1820s or 1890s did not react to problems and choices in the same way as citizens in the 1990s. Each generation views the world with different perspectives and operates on the basis of different assumptions. Over the years Coloradans have valued different elements of their scenery. They have approached the natural resources with changing ideas about their proper uses. They have faced changing attitudes about the proper spheres of activity for men and women and with a slowly evolving appreciation of the contributions of the differing cultures, both previously and today.

A number of the following chapters trace single themes through several stages of development. In so doing, this book since its first edition in 1976 has focused on many of the themes that are central to the "new western history" as developed in the 1980s and 1990s. Topical organization shows clearly how Coloradans have reacted to particular problems over time. It also allows emphasis on the diversity of Colorado's growth with individual chapters on Native Americans, Hispanic settlers, the evolution of ethnic patterns, and twentieth-century racial minorities. It permits focused consideration of mining entrepreneurs and mine laborers, city dwellers and farmers. It singles out the varied contributions of mining, agriculture, tourism, and urban finance to the economic growth of the state. It looks at Colorado's development as it has been affected by decisions in world capitals and New York board rooms.

The book also follows a broad chronological pattern. Chapters 1 through 5 cover the period of exploration and initial settlement ending in the 1870s. Chapters 6 through 12 deal with the era of rapid economic growth from the 1870s through 1920. The remaining chapters describe the emergence of the modern state. For this third edition, Stephen Leonard took primary responsibility for Chapter 10, "The People of Colorado," and Chapter 13 on the 1920s and 1930s. David McComb took particular responsibility for Chapter 16, recounting the events of the 1970s and 1980s as Coloradans attempted to cope with the problems of rapid growth, the Western Slope energy boom and bust, and such disasters as the Big Thompson Flood of 1976.

The movement of Anglo-Americans westward across the continent was the central experience of U.S. nation-building. When we examine the process from a century's vantage, we can still feel the sense of possibility on each new frontier. However, historians also need to recapture the conflicts as well as the excitement. Economic and personal success for some Coloradans has come at the expense of others. Native Americans, Hispanos, European immigrants, and women have all struggled to assert control over facets of their own lives. Historic decisions have also closed off possibilities never tried, narrowing as well as expanding the American future through conscious and unconscious choices. Mission, betrayal, and continued hope are mixed in the evaluation of our past. For a sense of the changes, we turn to poet Vachel Lindsay, who tried to reconcile for himself the contradictions of change in "The Flower-fed Buffaloes":

> The flower-fed buffaloes of the spring
> In the days of long ago,
> Ranged where the locomotives sing
> And the prairie flowers lie low;
> The tossing, blooming, perfumed grass
> Is swept away by wheat,
> Wheels and wheels and wheels spin by
> In the spring that still is sweet.
> But the flower-fed buffaloes of the spring
> Left us long ago.
> They gore no more, they bellow no more,
> They trundle around the hills no more —
> With the Blackfeet lying low,
> With the Pawnees lying low.

# COLORADO

A HISTORY OF THE CENTENNIAL STATE

# CHAPTER 1

# MOUNTAINS AND PLAINS

"When our small party arrived on the hill they with one accord gave three *cheers* to the *Mexican mountains*."[1] It was 2:30 in the afternoon on Saturday, November 5, 1806. Zebulon Pike and his fifteen companions had just glimpsed the peaks of the Rockies appearing in the distance like small blue clouds. Since the expedition had left Missouri four months earlier, the men had toiled slowly westward along the rivers — first the Missouri, then the Osage, then the Kansas, and finally the Arkansas. Late in October, Pike had dispatched half a dozen of his party of twenty-two down the Arkansas to return to the United States before winter descended. With his remaining companions, he intended to continue his search for the sources of the Red River and the boundaries of the Louisiana Territory. To every man, from Pike himself to Privates Thomas Dougherty and John Sparks, the sight of the mountains meant that the first stage of their journey was nearly over, that the barrier of the empty plains had been successfully crossed.

The cheers Pike's band gave the mountains are the first recorded response of west-moving Anglo-Americans to the Colorado Rockies. They have set the tone for travelers since. Like Pike, most Anglo-Americans have entered Colorado from the east. Few have been impressed by their first view. To natives of the humid East Coast, the dry plains where the Kansas rivers fade into their beds are bare, brown, and tiresome.

In the summer of 1820, for example, Major Stephen H. Long of the United States Topographical Engineers led a scientific expedition of twenty people up the Platte River from its junction with the Missouri. Like the expedition of Lewis and Clark in the previous decade, these explorers were looking to see what the West held of value to the United States. The terrain was grim. Botanist Edwin James compared the plains of western Nebraska to the "dreary solitude of the ocean," finding it "tiresome to the eye and fatiguing to the spirit." His account of the journey refers repeatedly to the "inhospitable deserts of the Platte," a "barren and ungenial district" of "naked sand." The country up-river, in the northeast corner of present-day Colorado, was even worse — more sterile, more monotonous. In Long's report of the exploration appears the famous evaluation of the entire central plains as a Great American Desert:

> In regard to this extensive section of country, I do not hesi-tate in giving the opinion that it is almost wholly unfit for cultivation, and of course uninhabitable by a people depend-ing upon agriculture for their subsistence. Although tracts of fertile land, considerably extensive, are occasionally to be met with, yet the scarcity of wood and water, almost uni-formly present, will prove an insuperable obstacle in the way of settling the country.[2]

Long's party was the first official reconnaissance of the area at the head of the South Platte and Arkansas since 1807, when a Spanish patrol had captured Pike at his winter quarters on the Conejos River and taken him as a prisoner to Santa Fe and then deeper into Mexico. More than two more decades passed before John Charles Fremont set out on a third series of government ex-plorations. His first expedition in 1842 took him up the North Platte to the Wind River Range of Wyoming. The next year, he crossed Kansas to Fort St. Vrain near the site of modern-day Greeley. From there he detoured southward along the base of the Rockies to Pueblo before returning to pick his way through the Wyoming mountains and South Pass. During the remainder of 1843 and the spring of the following year, his expedition toured Utah, Idaho, Oregon, Nevada, and California before returning through the mountains of central Colorado in June 1844.

Like Long and Pike before him, Fremont disliked the plains of Colorado, finding only a "parched country" of sand hills with an "appearance of general sterility." In his reaction he echoed Tho-mas Farnham, a Vermont lawyer who had threaded his way across Colorado in 1839. To Farnham, the "Great Prairie Wilder-ness" was a "scene of desolation scarcely equaled on the conti-nent." As interest in Oregon and the Mexican border provinces increased in the mid-1840s, such travelers as Francis Parkman and Rufus Sage repeated the description of sandy, arid wastes. A dozen years later, fortune hunters and journalists trying the shortcut to the Pikes Peak gold fields across the plains of western Kansas and eastern Colorado raised the same bitter complaint.

"We seem to have reached the acme of barrenness and desolation," wrote Horace Greeley, the famous editor of the *New York Tribune*. "Wood and water fail, and we are in a desert indeed."[3]

To travelers in this frame of mind, the first sight of the Rocky Mountains could only be welcome. The "grand outline" of the immense mountain wall cheered the men in Long's party and delighted Fremont with its beauty. As it emerged into view from a vast pile of thunderheads, the sight of Longs Peak staggered Parkman. The same sight filled Albert Richardson with joy and astonishment after 600 miles of "naked prairie." "No vision could be more grand and inspiring," wrote Samuel Bowles; "none was more welcome to eyes weary with the monotony of plains."[4] Even in the railroad age, when powerful locomotives cut the travel time from a long week to a long day, the sight was still inspiring. Firstview, a whistlestop on the Kansas Pacific, was named to capitalize on the excitement generated.

By the 1860s the contrast between the two terrains had become an artistic cliché. Illustrators of books on the West emphasized the sublime, the grand, the picturesque, and the uplifting in woodcuts of mountain lakes and forests. In engravings of the plains they tended to show the hardships of travel — buffalo skulls, storms, digging for water. Journalists who filled the first chapters of their travel books with complaints about the monotony of the American desert exercised their full talents for overblown rhetoric when they wrote of the mountains. Their "snowcapped peaks, their deep ravines and narrow gorges, their purpling shadowed sides and tops" were the record of cosmic forces. They were "monuments of Creation and History" upon which rested the "Finger of Silence."[5]

By the time Congress drew the boundaries of Colorado Territory in 1861, no one believed the dotted lines on the map outlined a natural unit. The difficulties of early travel and the prejudgments of early visitors had together confirmed in the American mind the difference between two landscapes. As Horace Greeley reported from Denver to his avid *New York Tribune* readers, there were

> few greater contrasts than between the region which stretches hundreds of miles eastward from this spot toward the Missouri, and is known as *The Plains,* and that which overlooks us to the west and, alike by its abrupt and sharp-ridged foothills seeming just at hand and its glittering peaks of snow in the blue distance, vindicates its current designation, *The Mountains*.[6]

For any practical use of the new territory, a simple division into flat Colorado and jagged Colorado was scarcely sufficient. What were the differences from place to place within the plains? Were some areas more fertile, others more barren, some well watered, and others not? Where were the valleys behind the mountain rampart? Above all, where did the rivers rise? In an age fascinated by the search for the source of the Nile, the great practical problem of U.S. geography was to determine the headwaters of the Mississippi, Columbia, Missouri, Yellowstone, and Rio Grande del Norte rivers, as well as myriad smaller streams. Pike's instructions in 1806 impressed the need to "ascertain the direction, extent and navigation of the Arkansas and Red Rivers."[7] Long and Fremont hoped to map the sources of the Platte. In a later generation, John Wesley Powell was to make his reputation as a man of science and courage by solving the final question of the route and tributaries of the Colorado River.

The desire to discover and delimit Colorado's river basins, to subdivide the plains and mountains into smaller and smaller units, was a typical expression of the nineteenth-century urge to categorize. Although it was the century of Darwin and Maxwell, the more common scientist was the classifier. Naturalists discovered new species of frogs and fungi and fitted each into its proper slot in the Linnaean system, and political economists worked out their taxonomies: three types of socialism, ten types of government. Alexander von Humboldt and Herbert Spencer published influential compendiums that attempted to outline the entire body of human knowledge about nature and society. Recognizing and naming regions and subregions was also an exacting intellectual enterprise, a product of the same impulse. In every travel account and government report, explorers and scientists organized their data and made their experiences and observations intelligible to themselves and others by preparing geographically oriented catalogs. Every report — in systematic fashion or not — selected certain prominent features of topography, vegetation, wildlife, and soils and described their distribution over the landscape, building regional classifications in the process.

Then, as now, westward-headed travelers disliked the level landscape and the lack of trees on the central plains. The short buffalo grass that forms the natural cover accentuates the appearance of sterility, showing bare gravel between its clumps and bunches. Yet, variations have always been there for anyone willing to look. Modern tourists speeding along Interstate 70 fail

Red Rock Lake.

to notice because they have neither time nor need, but earlier visitors knew wood and water as necessities for survival. For such travelers, the major river valleys not only refreshed the eye but relieved unspoken fears of death. In the spring, budding cottonwoods, flowers, and rich grass made the bottomlands of the Arkansas and South Platte into elongated gardens one-half to two miles wide. In 1846 the grass along the Arkansas was rich enough to sustain the horses of Stephen Watts Kearny's entire army en route to occupy New Mexico and California. The letters of prospectors who followed the courses of the rivers in 1859 reported none of the hardships suffered by those who struck directly across the plains.

Nor are the Colorado plains uniformly flat. On the eastern edge of the state — the high plains to the modern geographer — the land is relatively level, the uneroded surface of debris washed from the Rockies. Early travelers noticed, however, that the terrain became more broken as they worked their way westward. In present-day Douglas, Elbert, and El Paso counties, they discovered that the Rockies throw out a wedge of high land to divide the basins of the South Platte and Arkansas rivers. South of Pueblo, as early users of Raton Pass were well aware, a similar salient of rough land breaks the Colorado piedmont with lava-capped mesas and buttes, eroded plateaus, and mountain spurs covered with ponderosa pine and juniper. Local residents call this area the Eastern Slope and consider it distinct from the plains.

Visitors who have taken the trouble to look twice have seen that there is more to the plains than brown grass and gray soil. Many have found the "softened, genial, finished, smooth outline of a cooling sea of land" far more agreeable than the jagged landscape of the mountains. In 1933 the view from the train approaching Denver reminded British diplomat Harold Nicolson of the Middle East: "The foreground is tawny like the Persian biaban. . . . It is exactly like Persia and we are delighted." Two generations before, artist Worthington Whittredge had been equally impressed. "Whoever crossed the plains at that period," he later wrote, "could hardly fail to be impressed with its vastness and silence and the appearance everywhere of an innocent, primitive existence." In his work the purple mountains are little more than a backdrop for the appreciative portrayal of the natural richness of the lower lands.[8]

The exploration and evaluation of differences within the mountains of Colorado were more difficult tasks than the description of obvious dissimilarities on the plains. Pike and Long were among the first to take mistaken ideas about the relations of streams and ranges behind the mountain wall back to civilization. Trappers and mountain men had crossed and recrossed the Colorado mountains in the 1830s and 1840s from centers of activity in New Mexico and Wyoming. Although their knowledge might be available on the streets and in the bars of St. Louis to anyone who asked the right questions or bought enough drinks, it was not public information. It spread by rumor and word of mouth. Reliable facts found their way from older to younger travelers and from friend to friend but seldom into published maps. The most expert mountain men kept their reports in their heads; consequently, much of the information reaching the East was third-hand and inaccurate. Because good Spanish maps of the eighteenth century were unknown to Anglo-Americans, Albert Gallatin in 1836 used guesswork to fill in the details of the Rockies on his map of the West. A few years later, Fremont could still say of the Colorado mountains that "the coves, the heads of the rivers, the approximations of their waters, the practicability of the mountain passes . . . although well-known to hunters and trappers, were unknown to science and to history."[9]

Trappers, for example, had long hunted and named the high, wild mountain valleys or parks that hide behind the Front Range and the Sangre de Cristo Range — San Luis Park or Valley, Bayou Salado or South Park, Old Park or Middle Park, New Park or North Park. Not until Fremont turned southward on his return from California in 1844, however, were the great parks fixed in the public mind and represented on a published map. His description of beautiful high valleys "walled in all around with snowy mountains, rich in water and with grass, fringed with pine," and his somewhat misleading map showing perfectly level basins surrounded by narrow mountain palisades, molded the popular image.[10] For the next twenty years, maps of commercial publishers and army engineers emphasized the contrast between smooth basin floors and impassable mountains.

By the early 1860s, the range and park system of Colorado was well-known. By then, prospectors had closely inspected the valleys and ridges. The Front Range, the Park Range, the Sawatch, the fringes of the San Juans — this entire central section was cut by trails and dotted with mining camps or their recently abandoned shells. Parties of gentlemen and ladies had begun to take summer camping trips to Hot Sulphur Springs and South Park, and topographical survey parties in the early 1870s often found empty whiskey bottles on high peaks.

The western third of Colorado was the last to be explored thoroughly. Its general features were known in a hazy fashion, but as late as 1867 local writers claimed ignorance of the vast area "over the range." Indeed, it took systematic, scientific survey work by government explorers to fill in the blanks that still appeared on the best maps. Between 1867 and 1869, John Wesley Powell traced the drainage system of the Western Slope from Middle Park, following the paths of the Grand, the White, and the Yampa rivers through their canyons and valleys and locating their intersections with the Green River of Utah. In the early 1870s, the entire area was covered more thoroughly by the U.S. Geological and Geographical Survey of the Territories. Parties of surveyors, artists, and scientists directed by Ferdinand V. Hayden covered all of Rocky Mountain Colorado, measuring heights and distances, climbing peaks, photographing natural features,

"The Rocky Mountains," a print of 1871 taken from a painting by
Worthington Whittredge.

describing the geology, evaluating the resources, fixing contour
lines, and sketching the topography. *The Geological and Geographical Atlas of Colorado and Portions of Adjacent Territory*,
in which the survey summarized its work in 1877, was of immense value to railroads, mining companies, and real estate
promoters.

Two decades after the Hayden survey, Powell climaxed this
activity by publishing a description of "The Physiographic Regions of the United States" in 1895. Drawing on his own experience and on the work of a century of explorations, Powell divided
the entire country into sixteen regions on the basis of geology
and topography. Within Colorado, he gave a sort of seal of approval to the three great divisions that had been obvious since
the 1860s — the Great Plains, the Park and Mountain belt, and
the Colorado Plateau. Powell's classification of regions has remained the basis for more refined topographical classifications
into the twentieth century. Although geographers have adjusted
regional boundaries and incorporated more data, subdividing
the flatlands into the High Plains and Piedmont and separating
the Wyoming Basin in the state's northwest corner from the
western plateau, it is clear that by the end of the nineteenth century the geography of Colorado was well-known and well understood. In 1921 a portion was renamed when Congressman

Edward Taylor of Glenwood Springs convinced Congress and President Harding to officially designate what was then known as the Grand River as the upper reach of the *Colorado* River.

The interpretation of the Colorado landscape was a prerequisite for its development. The state's natural environment has been the foundation on which settlers over the past century and a half have built a superstructure of human activities. The state's resources, its natural corridors for communication, and its topographical divisions have all influenced its growth. Different sections have received people at different times, from different places, and for different reasons. The result has been a progressive evolution of a system of human regions, areas sharing common problems of economic development, common groupings of peoples, and common patterns of settlement. To use Lewis Mumford's phrase, the state's cultural regions are "collective works of art," the products of human decisions and actions working upon the base of the Colorado environment.[11]

Colorado is, in fact, the meeting point for three major sections within the American West. Historians have long been accustomed to writing U.S. history in terms of sectional differences between North and South, Atlantic Coast and Mississippi Valley, Massachusetts and Virginia. The trans-Mississippi West invites the same theme, for the lines of contact between distinct and competing regions within the West have had as much importance as have the state borders. Colorado's boundaries overlap three of these historic regions. East, south, and west, its sections follow the great rivers as they diverge from its mountains. The Rio Grande ties the state to the Southwest, the Colorado to the range and plateau country of the Mountain West, the South Platte and Arkansas to the Great Plains.

Farmers in eastern Colorado, for example, turn their backs on the mountains, finding compatriots in the vast sweep of grassland between Texas and the Dakotas. For the past century, the common theme of the plains has been the problems of agriculture, in particular adjustment to the scarce rainfall and the inability of the land to support more than a scattered population. From 1850 to 1920, Americans viewed the plains as an area unified by unique opportunities. Since that time, however, the area's slow growth, its lack of manufacturing, and the absence of cities have caused both outsiders and residents to think of it as a region defined by a peculiar set of social and economic problems.

Mount Sneffels in the San Juans is one of more than fifty Colorado peaks exceeding 14,000 feet.

Today, as ninety years ago, the eastern edge of Colorado is a country of small towns stretching along the railroad tracks and highways, of ranches and wheat fields bathed in dry wind. The South Platte River runs through the northern edge of the Colorado plains and the Arkansas River through the southern edge. Both rivers support bands of irrigated farms whose sugar beets and vegetables are marketed through Fort Morgan, Sterling, Rocky Ford, La Junta, and Lamar. Flanking the valleys is a land where grain elevators stand as sentries guarding the march of civilization. The plains were the last part of Colorado to be settled, and their patterns of population still preserve the character of the nineteenth-century Middle West. Population has declined since 1920 in the eastern quarter of the state. A traveler crossing from north to south finds Las Animas County drier than Phillips or Washington, the ground more broken, sheep more in evidence, and wheat fields scarcer, but the general impression is the same. In settled areas visitors see a brown land that hesitates to welcome the farmer; in the Pawnee National Grassland in Weld

County or the Comanche Grassland in Otero and Baca counties they can see something like the orginal landscape.

Western Colorado has shared its problems and opportunities with Utah, Nevada, Idaho, Wyoming, and Montana. This is an area where the rural population totals little more than two persons per square mile, the historian's standard shorthand for defining a frontier region. Except for scattered oases, it is a vast expanse of mountain and desert with a thin overlay of human activities. At the turn of the century, Theodore Roosevelt described Garfield County as "a great, wild country. In the creek bottoms there were a good many ranches; but we only occasionally passed by these, on our way to our hunting grounds in the wilderness along the edge of the snowline. The mountains crowded close together in chain, peak, and tableland; all the higher ones were wrapped in an unrent shroud of snow."[12] A generation later, the northwestern Colorado ranch children in Jean Stafford's novel *The Mountain Lion* faced the same environment in which human activities looked like accidents:

> Once they found an empty whiskey bottle covered over with pine needles in a place so far from everything that they could not imagine what sort of person had put it there. From a favorite cliff they looked down into the valley. . . . A cattle train, puffing out a clean-lined cloud of white smoke, burrowed through the red banks like a mole, disappeared, and sent back a faint, protesting valedictory. There was always the possibility that they might see a mountain lion; they never did, but often they saw eagles.[13]

The Western Slope is an area in which the federal government still owns over half the land and where history has been the study of human intrusion threatening the precarious ecological balance. The spread of grazing in the twentieth century found an economic use for much of the snowmelt from the western slopes of the Rockies but failed to take up all of the slack caused by the decline of mining. Within Colorado, the population of the Front Range, the three mountain parks, and the Sawatch, Elk, and San Juan mountains fell between 1940 and 1960. Population has since turned upward, because the back-to-nature boom that began in the 1960s has made it possible to harvest dollars from gas pumps and ski lifts. The effects are especially marked along the Interstate 70 corridor through Summit, Eagle, Garfield, and Mesa counties. The irrigated lands along the Yampa, Gunnison,

The Pawnee National Grassland, Weld County.

and Colorado rivers grow peaches, apples, sugar beets, vegetables, and winter fodder, making the towns of Grand Junction, Montrose, and Durango larger and more diversified than any of the mountain towns.

The valleys flanking both sides of the Sangre de Cristo Range form the northern fringe of the American Southwest. In historic terms this great arc of land curving from Monterey on the Pacific to Corpus Christi on the Gulf of Mexico constituted the Spanish borderlands — the northernmost provinces of Mexico held by Spain in the eighteenth century. In the twentieth century it can be defined as a zone of cultural contact, the place where the nation's dominant Anglo-American culture has been forced into grudging acknowledgment of the social patterns of Native Americans and Spanish-speaking peoples. The region's common problems are less those of growth than of social adjustment and accommodation.

Certainly within Colorado the southern counties form a third region. The people alone set it apart, for the descendants of last century's Hispano migrants still form substantial minorities of 25 percent on the east and nearly 50 percent on the west. The San Luis Valley, despite the prosperity of its irrigated potato farms and recent land developments, is economically the poorest area in the state. The entire upper Rio Grande basin, from Poncha Pass to Santa Fe, has been an island of poverty with one of the lowest per capita income levels west of the Mississippi. The coal and iron belt stretching from Trinidad through Pueblo has similarly been a depressed area, in which automation and the decline of the soft coal industry removed the primary livelihood of thousands. In 1965 the entire area was combined with Hispanic New Mexico and the canyonlands of Arizona and Utah into the Four Corners Economic Development Region, one of six areas in the country singled out by the federal government for special aid to counteract low income, high unemployment, poor housing, and lack of growth. The thirteen counties of historic Hispanic Colorado, including the San Luis Valley and the southern parts of the Arkansas Valley, gained fewer than 1,000 people between 1970 and 1990 compared with gains of nearly 900,000 in the metropolitan corridor from Colorado Springs to Fort Collins and 150,000 on the Western Slope.

Colorado's division among several larger regions has made it a fragmented state. As if charged with static electricity, its sections seem to be constantly trying to avoid each other. All parts of Colorado share the same legal code, highway department, tax system, state universities, governor, and gold-covered state house dome, but they do not share the same needs and interests. Differences between the economic needs of the Eastern and Western Slopes have appeared repeatedly as the source of bitter disputes over currency inflation, political representation, water diversion, and conservation. Hispano versus Anglo has also been a recurring theme in Colorado politics, and the sectional power bases Democrats and Republicans established in the 1860s persist more than a century later.

Division among several regions has also meant that Colorado's growth has epitomized much of the history of the American West. Although the early historian who argued that the state's history displayed "all the problems of Democracy and Civilization" was perhaps carried away by his enthusiasm, it does display most of the patterns found in U.S. frontier expansion and most of the trends found in the growth of the West.[14] Its history is interesting for its own sake and is important because of its applicability to other parts of the West. In a sense, within its borders Colorado sums up the growth of the entire area between Spokane and Fargo, Sacramento and Fort Worth.

# CHAPTER 2

# THE FIRST COLORADANS

Americans have long been accustomed to talking about the westward movement of the frontier and its role in the advancement of the nation. National spokespersons have seen the growth of the West as the guarantee for the success and prosperity of the American republic. In Colorado, however, the westbound Anglo-Americans of the nineteenth century were late arrivals. For eleven millennia before, its history was made by two other great migrations — the southward movement of Native American peoples over thousands of years and the northward movement of the Spanish-American empire from the sixteenth to the nineteenth centuries.

The first Americans may have appeared in Colorado approximately fifteen thousand years ago. The earliest reliable dated site of human occupancy is located in Weld County, where a band of hunters left flint points along an old channel of the South Platte River in the years around 9200 B.C. The earliest Coloradans lived as small groups of roving foragers and hunters on both the plains and the western plateau. On the Western Slope, the lives of members of the Desert Culture revolved around deer, rabbits, and other small game. The earliest inhabitants of the plains could hunt mammoths, mastodons, and other huge animals until a change of climate around 8500 B.C. altered the region's ecology and turned the hunters to bison and smaller game.

Techniques of settled agriculture penetrated Colorado from two directions between 5000 B.C. and A.D. 500. As the climate of the high plains grew drier, peoples in the valleys of the South Platte, Arkansas, Purgatoire, and Republican rivers learned farming from more prosperous regions near the Mississippi. They built earth-lodge villages, planted gardens in the bottomlands along the streams, wandered in search of game and wild plants during the summer, and returned to harvest their crops in the fall. Horticulture also spread from the west up the Colorado River and its tributaries, the Yampa, White, and Gunnison

Cliff Palace, Mesa Verde, in a photograph taken by pioneer
photographer William Henry Jackson.

rivers. The "Fremont" peoples of western Colorado, who farmed,
foraged, and hunted, are known to us from the abundant art
they left on rocks and canyon walls.

The most highly developed culture in pre-European Colorado
was that of the Anasazi, the "ancient ones" who filled the Four
Corners region with multistoried stone and adobe houses. The
Anglo-Americans who first encountered the ruins, remarkably
preserved by the dry air of the Southwest, let their imaginations
run with speculation about the identity of the builders and gave
the structures names like Cliff Palace, Aztec Ruins, and Montezuma's Castle. In fact, the ancestors of the Anasazi were a gar-
dening and gathering people such as those of the Fremont
culture, living for centuries in the same parts of Colorado, New
Mexico, Arizona, and Utah in which the ruins are found. As the
influence of the higher culture of central Mexico slowly filtered
north, these "basketmaker" people learned to grow beans in addition to corn and squash, to make crude pottery, and to hunt

with bow and arrow. At about the same time — A.D. 450 or 500 — they began to construct villages with storage bins and pit houses arranged in a regular pattern. The latter structures, the remains of which dot the Four Corners area today, were sunk about four feet into the ground. A conical roof supported by vertical posts extended the same distance above the surface, and a tunnel usually provided the entrance to the house.

An expansion of Anasazi territory and a change in their style of living both occurred around A.D. 750–900. Instead of pit houses they built surface dwellings of rooms clustered in a block or an arc. In front of the structure were one or more *kivas,* circular subterranean rooms that had evolved from pit houses and were used for ceremonial purposes. Some of these cluster villages were built in river valleys, others on the tops of mesas such as Mesa Verde in Colorado. There are smaller ruins by the thousands along small streams throughout much of western Colorado, the northern part of New Mexico, the extreme southern part of Utah, and northern Arizona. Each was the home of one or two families who had come from larger villages in search of farmland.

The most extensive development of the Anasazi culture dates from the middle of the eleventh century. Several distinct subgroups are evident in the Four Corners area — the Kayenta Anasazi of Canyon de Chelly and other sites in northern Arizona, the Chaco Anasazi of Pueblo Bonito and other communities in northwestern New Mexico, and the San Juan Anasazi of Mesa Verde and other sites in southwestern Colorado and southeastern Utah. Throughout the Four Corners, the Anasazi built great stonework towns. Mesa Verde's Cliff Palace, which dates from about 1175, had space for four hundred people in its two hundred rooms. Other centers on Mesa Verde included Spruce Tree House and Balcony House. Each village was a complex of small, boxlike rooms assembled over decades into a structure sprawling hundreds of feet.

The modern archaeologist is almost overwhelmed by the variety of artifacts that survive from the height of the Anasazi culture in the twelfth and thirteenth centuries. The villagers planted their crops both on the mesa tops and on terraces along the canyon beds below. In some places they built small dams to store water for irrigation, and at others they dug ditches to channel water to their fields. Their pottery was of good quality and was highly decorated, the cotton textiles often elaborately woven. In their work they used tools of bone, stone, and wood. They

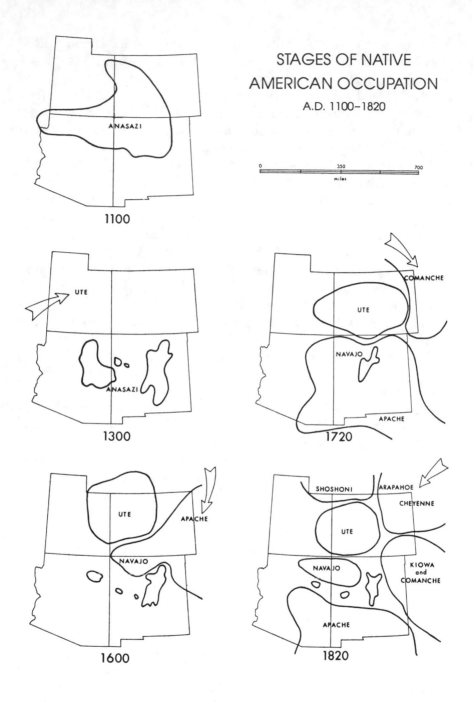

STAGES OF NATIVE
AMERICAN OCCUPATION
A.D. 1100–1820

wore woven sandals and ornaments of beads and turquoise; they used woven blankets, mats, baskets, and bags. The richness of material possessions indicates a culture with a large population and an economic surplus. The plastering and painting of some of their interior walls suggest the same conclusion. There was clearly trade between the Mesa Verde and the Chaco Canyon complexes in the years around 1100. There is evidence of Mesa Verde influences in Chaco Canyon, and there are a number of Colorado sites, such as Chimney Rock Pueblo, Lowry Ruin, Escalante Ruin, and Yucca House, that seem to have been Chaco culture outliers.

In the last quarter of the thirteenth century, the Anasazi abandoned most of their lands. Unstable rainfall over the preceding decades had already forced occasional migrations within the Four Corners region. Now in the 1270s, 1280s, and 1290s, climatic change may have forced more massive population shifts. Probably it was a combination of soil exhaustion, deforestation, drought seasons, and summer flooding and gullying that pushed the Mesa Verde people southward. In any event, by A.D. 1300 the Anasazi were gone from Colorado and Utah. Three centuries later, Spanish explorers encountered the descendants of these early Coloradans as the pueblo-dwelling Indians of the Hopi mesas of Arizona and perhaps of the Rio Grande Valley.

Replacing the Anasazi as the dominant people of southern Utah and Colorado were the Ute Indians, a tribe earlier located in the Great Basin of Nevada. Individual families spent each summer and fall hunting deer and elk in the mountains and gathering nuts and berries. Usually wintering in the river valleys of western Colorado, they assembled briefly into larger bands each spring before fanning out again in their search for food. Although the early Utes were probably not a military threat sufficient to drive out the Anasazi through open warfare, their competition for scarce natural resources during the extended drought and their raids on valuable food caches may have hastened the Anasazi's abandonment of their cliff and mesa villages.

At approximately the same time the Utes were moving eastward into Colorado, Indians speaking a variety of Athapascan dialects began to move south from their homeland along the Mackenzie River in northern Canada. Following the base of the Rockies, various Apache bands or tribes reached the plains of Colorado, Kansas, and northeastern New Mexico by the early 1500s. A related tribe, whom the Spanish were to call the "Apache de Navajo," turned westward in the same years to occupy parts of southern Colorado and northern New Mexico, particularly along the San Juan River. Navajos and Apaches lived in an uneasy balance with the agricultural descendants of the Anasazi.

In some years they raided the pueblos for maize and squash and for the luxury goods that filled the houses — cotton cloaks, featherwork, jewelry, and pottery. In other years they traded for the same goods, camping outside the village walls and offering dried meat, deer, buffalo, and antelope skins.

It was Spain that disturbed the uneasy equilibrium. Between 1540 and 1580, the silver-mining frontier in Mexico had crept slowly north. Through their meetings with the nomadic Indians they called *Chichimecas,* the Spaniards had learned how to fight nomadic hunters and how to pacify them with treaties, subsidies, and agricultural missions. Although little silver was found north of Parral and Monterey in Mexico, Spanish officials were intrigued by the stories of settled villages Coronado had seen along the Rio Grande between 1540 and 1542. To the viceroys in Mexico City and the bureaucrats in Madrid, the reports were an open invitation for Spanish colonization and missionary efforts. The result was the expedition Juan de Onate led north in 1598 to establish a new province deep in the continental interior. The colony of Nuevo Mexico lay fifteen hundred miles from Mexico City and seven hundred miles from the nearest Spanish settlements. Its only contact with the outside was a biennial caravan from the south.

The Spanish conquest of New Mexico directly changed the lives of the people who were the descendants of the Anasazi. Because the province held little other opportunity for profit, the Spanish governors extorted labor and confiscated much of the surplus of the pueblos. Missionaries built churches adjacent to the pueblos and interfered with the lives of the Indians, for Madrid had determined that the major purpose of the colony was to spread Christianity. The response was one of the most successful Native American revolts in North America. The tribes of the Rio Grande villages rose against the Spaniards in 1680, killed four hundred, and drove the refugees south to the site of El Paso.

Spanish reconquest between 1693 and 1696 ended the danger of local rebellion but scarcely broke the isolation that had invited it. European settlement was confined to the Rio Abajo, or "lower river" (a ten-mile strip along the Rio Grande from Socorro to Bernalillo), and to the mountain valleys of the Rio Arriba, the "upper river" country around Taos and Santa Fe. Commerce southward to Chihuahua remained dangerous, and New Mexicans traveled south only in annual trading caravans of several hundred persons under military escort. Occasional messages and orders from officials in Mexico City did little to change the situation of a province left to itself and to the protection of a handful of soldiers.

If Spanish conquest of New Mexico directly changed the lives of the pueblo dwellers, it indirectly changed the culture of every Native American tribe in the central valley of North America. The spread of the use of horses from northern Mexico and New Mexico in the late 1500s and the 1600s transformed dozens of peoples. The dates at which different groups adopted the horse are obscure, for "the use of the horse spread much faster than exploration, so that in many cases our first actual view of a tribe is as a horse user."[1] Horses were in use throughout Texas and as far north as Idaho by 1700 and as far north as Canada by 1750. Arikara, Hidatsa, Kansa, Iowa, Mandan, Missouri, Osage, Pawnee, Ponca — all of these tribes that previously had farmed on the eastern fringes of the plains now spent more and more time following the buffalo on horseback. Other Native Americans in the later 1600s and 1700s moved out of the woodlands around the Great Lakes; forsaking pottery and corn fields, the Arapahos, Cheyennes, Crows, and Dakotas took to the new lifestyle of mounted nomads.

On the western edge of the plains the horse was known long before it reached the Crows or the Pawnees. By the 1660s and 1670s the Navajos and the Apaches were mounted tribes whose new military superiority allowed them to raid the Rio Grande villages at will, although the Apaches also farmed in the river valleys of the plains. Their attacks may have helped to pressure the Pueblos into their revolt; their continued raids certainly helped to weaken the river tribes for Spanish reconquest. Apaches also used the decade of turmoil to move into central Texas, southern New Mexico, and southern Arizona while holding their previous territory. Raiding along the extended borders of this *Gran Apacheria,* the Apaches killed hundreds of Spaniards and settled Native Americans yearly. George E. Hyde described the change the horse brought to the Apaches:

> From the beginning of their history in the south they had always come to the Pueblo towns — twice each year, in the early summer and late autumn — and in the early times when they were afoot and very poor, they had come humbly . . . to beg or barter for a few simple needs; but now, after the Pueblo Revolt of 1680–92, these Apaches came to the

trading fairs at Pecos, Taos, and Picuris in strong mounted bands, haughty and fierce . . . and demanded of the Pueblos and Spaniards, first of all, metal weapons: long, ugly Spanish daggers, hatchets, and sword blades, which they used as points on their lances.[2]

Horses also changed the lives of the Utes in the mountains north of New Mexico. By 1675 the hunters who went out every autumn traveled on horseback. Now they could pursue the buffalo across the plains of Colorado and return in the early winter with more than enough meat and skins to feed and clothe their families. The creation of an economic surplus through more efficient hunting made it possible for scattered families to group together in larger bands under stronger leadership. Indeed, the early 1700s were a golden age for the Utes, with seven prosperous bands fixed in the territories they were to hold until the 1860s and 1870s — the Mouache band in southeastern Colorado; the Capote and Weeminuche bands in the San Luis Valley and the San Juan Valley of southwestern Colorado on the edge of Navajo country; the Tabegauche or Uncompahgre band along the Gunnison and Uncompahgre rivers; and the Grand River, Yampa, and Uintah bands in northern Colorado and Utah.

North of the Utes were their distant kin, the Shoshones and Comanches. Mountain Indians like the Utes in previous centuries, these tribes accepted use of the horse in the late 1600s. The Shoshones moved from Idaho onto the plains of Wyoming and Montana. The Comanches migrated southward from Wyoming into the Apache lands of eastern Colorado. They are clearly identified in Spanish records as early as 1705, occupying the territory north of the Arkansas River. In part, the Comanches may have moved under pressure from eastern tribes who were also pushing onto the plains. Just as important, however, was the desire to follow the buffalo herds on the relatively empty southwestern plains and to move closer to the supply of horses. As Rupert N. Richardson wrote, the fully mounted Comanches visited the Colorado-Texas plains region, "found that it was well suited to their mode of existence, and proceeded to fight for it and take it."[3]

Utes and Comanches on horseback added to Spanish problems. In 1675 the Utes had pledged friendship to New Mexico Governor Otermin at Santa Fe. Within twenty years, however, they were raiding Spanish villages and Indian pueblos for food, horses, and slaves. The Comanches began to raid New Mexico from the east in 1704. For the next three generations, New Mexican farmers were in constant danger of attack. At the same time, French activity along the Mississippi posed a threat to the integrity of New Spain. Traders from the Illinois country and from Louisiana worked westward among the Comanches and other nomadic peoples of the plains who bridged the gap between French Louisiana and Spanish New Mexico. As early as 1695 and 1698, reports reached New Mexico of Frenchmen in what is now Nebraska, Kansas, and Oklahoma. Sitting in low adobe rooms smoky from piñon fires and sputtering candles, New Mexican officials must have pondered maps and rumors nightly, wondering about a French-Pawnee alliance and speculating on the spread of firearms among the tribes.

Spanish reaction to both dangers was to try to play European-style power politics, maneuvering through war and negotiation to establish a balance of forces on New Mexico's periphery. To meet military threats and to carry their influence into the wilderness, the Spanish used the tactic of reconnaissance in force. With scores of isolated villages and pueblos in constant danger of attack from mounted nomads, static defense would have required vastly more resources than were available. As an alternative, strategists in Santa Fe hoped that periodic military expeditions could hold southern Colorado as a buffer, defeating or overawing Native American enemies and replying to French influence. Always their attention returned to the country of the upper Arkansas as the core for an extended zone of Spanish influence.

The Arkansas Valley witnessed a first New Mexican expedition in 1706. Over the Sangre de Cristo Range from Taos, north through the foothills of the Rockies, across the Arkansas near the site of present-day Pueblo — in his report Juan de Ulibarri described the route of his forty Spanish soldiers in such detail that accurate reconstruction of the route is possible. In his dust trudged a hundred Indian auxiliaries from the pueblos of New Mexico. Approximately sixty miles downstream from the ford he found his goal, the group of Jicarilla Apache villages called El Cuartelejo. Here were threescore refugees from Picuris Pueblo who had fled after the reconquest but who now wanted to return to New Mexico. Here, too, were tribes of plains Apaches still friendly with the Spanish. Occupying at least a dozen small villages, or *rancherias*, along the Arkansas, they grew crops and had begun to learn the arts of building, pottery, and irrigation. Because permanent settlement and the accumulation of stores of food made the rancheria Apaches attractive targets for raids, they were eager for Spanish protection. Ulibarri nominated one of their chiefs as a representative of Spanish authority, heard worrisome reports of French traders among the Pawnees, and claimed formal possession of the Arkansas Valley. One bright day he mounted a low hill to intone the formula, "Knights, Companions, and Friends: Let the broad new province of San Luis, the great settlement of Santa Domingo of El Cuartelejo be pacified by the arms of us who are the vassals of our monarch, king and natural lord, Don Philip V — may he live forever."[4]

In the following decade, Colorado became familiar ground to New Mexico's soldiers. Expeditions penetrated its mountains in 1714 and 1719 to make war on the Utes. In the latter year Governor Valverde also led 60 soldiers from Santa Fe, 45 Spanish settlers, 465 Pueblo warriors, and 165 Apaches against the Comanches, roughly retracing Ulibarri's route. Although he failed to catch the raiders, Valverde re-established contact with the Apaches of the Arkansas Valley and again assured them of Spanish support against the Comanches. He also heard reports of increased French activity among the plains tribes, of the building of French trading posts, and of depredations against the Jicarilla by their Pawnee allies. Although Spanish officials responded by suggesting a presidio at El Cuartelejo, Valverde dispatched a follow-up expedition to seek further evidence of intruders. Crossing the plains of Colorado in June 1720 under the leadership of Pedro de Villasur, the 42 soldiers and 60 Indians found a village of Pawnees along the Platte in western Nebraska. Because he was eager to arrange a parley with the Frenchmen suspected to be in the village, Villasur failed to post night sentries. Only 13 Spaniards survived to report the Pawnee attack after a frightened, hasty retreat across the prairie. Mexico City officials, hearing of the disaster, put their plans for an isolated fort on the Arkansas on the shelf — together with Valverde's career.

Spain left El Cuartelejo and the plains it controlled to the buffalo and the Comanches for the next two decades. The Colorado road was not reopened to Europeans until 1739, when the Mallet party of French traders followed the Platte River to the base of the mountains and made their way south to Taos. Spanish authorities were so surprised that they allowed the Frenchmen a safe return after holding them in hospitable captivity for several months. Other French merchants appeared in 1749, 1750, 1751, and 1752 — some by way of the Arkansas River through the country of their Comanche allies, some by way of the northerly route from the Missouri. The Spaniards prevented these later visitors from returning to the French settlements along the Mississippi but did little else to block the approaches to New Mexico. Perhaps the Comanches and their new French firearms foreclosed any effective long-range military operations. Perhaps also the province's hunger for imports caused New Mexicans in isolated villages to open their doors to contraband trade with half-wild Frenchmen who came one night and left the next.

Beginning in the 1720s, Spanish authorities authorized annual trade fairs at Pecos and Taos. One of the purposes was to attract the mounted tribes from the eastern frontier away from their French connections. The mounted tribes could exchange meat, hides, and captives for corn, horses, weapons, and luxuries imported from Mexico. Spanish officials kept a careful eye on the commerce with the *indios barbaros*, hoping honest trade would keep the Comanches within the economic orbit of New Mexico.

The Utes were nearly as important as the Comanches in the plans of New Mexican authorities. After defeat by Spanish troops in the late 1740s, Ute bands turned to peaceful trade with Taos and Abiquiu. They had been at war with the Comanches since 1727. When the Comanches drove the Jicarilla Apaches off the Colorado plains, the Utes befriended those remaining and continued to fight the Comanches for control of the Arkansas basin. The name "Comanche" comes from the Ute word *Komantcia*, meaning "anyone who wants to fight me all the time."

European diplomats finally eliminated the French interest in New Mexico by transferring title to Louisiana from France to Spain at the end of the Seven Years' War in 1763. New lines on European maps, however, did nothing to calm the Comanches. The record from the 1750s onward shows recurrent Comanche raids on Taos and other exposed towns and repeated forays by the Spanish into the lands south of the Arkansas River. In 1768 a Comanche chief wearing a leather headdress with a green horn (*cuerno verde* in Spanish) led an attack on the New Mexico town of Ojo Caliente, in which he was killed. The chief's son adopted the same headdress, and New Mexicans learned to fear the raids of Cuerno Verde. In search of a long-range solution, Mexican officials turned to one of the few great captains of their eighteenth-century frontier — Juan Bautista de Anza, founder of San Francisco, explorer of California, and then governor of New Mexico. In 1779 he led several hundred men northward from Taos through the San Luis Valley and South Park, adding Ute and Apache allies on the way. They met the Comanches and Cuerno Verde in the foothills between Walsenburg and Pueblo. Where Greenhorn Mountain now overlooks the plains, the Spaniards ambushed Cuerno Verde on his return from a raid on Taos. They killed the chief, his son, 4 of his war chiefs, a medicine man, and 10 warriors. They took back a hundred mules loaded with spoils and reported the death of 104 other Native Americans.

Several years of further harassment by Anza forced the Comanches to terms during 1786 and 1787. Some gave up warfare with the Utes and traded peacefully at Spanish settlements for the first time in a generation. Others requested the help of thirty Spanish settlers to build a permanent village on the Arkansas near the mouth of the San Carlos River. For four months the new pueblo of San Carlos seemed a success, until restlessness and a belief against living where a member of the tribe had died emptied the first adobe town in Colorado.

Anza's work established an equilibrium on the plains for a generation. Having participated in Anza's campaigns, the Utes signed another treaty in 1789 and carried on relatively peaceful commerce. Comanche raiders turned their attention toward Texas and northern Mexico. After the Comanches, however, new tribes appeared in eastern Colorado in the early 1800s, following the established route southward along the mountains. The largest of the new tribes was the Cheyenne, a people whose home in the 1600s had been the Red River country of Minnesota and North Dakota, where the Sheyenne River still bears their name. In their Algonquian tongue they call themselves *T sĭs tsĭs tăs,* or "people alike." In the 1700s, they pushed onto the open plains, learned to ride horseback, and reached the area north of the Black Hills in the half century between 1750 and 1800. As George Bent commented, "They now became a typical plains tribe of buffalo hunters, and securing horses near the hills, then began to wander far afield, waging war on many tribes."[5]

In the Black Hills the Cheyennes also met the Arapahos, another Algonquian tribe who had already adopted the plains culture and who ranged as far west as the Rockies. The two tribes were firm friends from their first encounter, camping together for long periods, intermarrying, and uniting in war. In the first or second decade of the nineteenth century, segments of the Cheyennes began to follow Arapahos south across the Platte in search of wild horses and the great southern buffalo herd. One result of the move was the division of each tribe into Northern and Southern groups with lands north and south of the Platte. A second result was the renewal of warfare in the 1820s and 1830s, as Southern Cheyennes pushed the Utes back into the Rockies and forced the Comanches south of the Arkansas at the decisive battle of Wolf Creek in 1838.

The Southern Cheyennes and Arapahos were in their prime during the years in which they occupied the Colorado plains. Their lifestyle was typical of all of the plains tribes who had cut loose from their woodland and village origins. With horses for transportation and the tepee as a shelter easy to erect and disassemble, they could follow the two great buffalo herds that roamed north and south of the Platte River. Buffalo provided the needs of the Native Americans — meat and fat; horn and bone for tools and utensils; tanned skins for bedding, clothing, and shelter; rawhide for shields, buckets, and bindings. The most important industry of the men was hunting; that of the women was cleaning and curing the skins. The duty of the headman was to decide where to place the camp for the annual hunt and when to organize it.

When the hunts went well, there was more than enough for all. There was leisure time for feasting, gaming, and talking over past exploits in the winter and spring before the buffalo were fat. There was also the opportunity to accumulate wealth through hunting or raiding for horses. The focus of attention was the young man and the status he could acquire — the number of his buffalo robes, his horses, his feats against the enemy. Warfare was less a tribal undertaking than an elaborate ritual played out by individuals and small bands, in which the object was to display bravery and to steal horses. Like other plains tribes, the Cheyennes counted their coups, relating to each other how they had touched this enemy with a bare hand, how they had killed that one, how they had ridden down an armed man on foot, how they had captured a shield and a lance. War was a central institution.

> Success in war brought not only status to the warrior but also wealth. War parties were formed to take vengeance upon hostile tribes — a vengeance expressed by killing an enemy warrior and by capturing his horses. Horses constituted

wealth and war yielded this wealth to the Cheyenne warrior. ... Fast, nimble ponies assured success on the hunt, feasts to publicize the prestige of the family, and the means to start the offspring properly upon military careers. Horses became a basis for property distinctions among the Cheyennes, and this basis was best maintained by military activity. The relationship of war and its fruits was obvious to the young Cheyenne brave, and outstanding military careers led to wealth and preferment within the councils of the tribe.[6]

The band, rather than the whole tribe, was the community unit for most of the year. To find enough grazing for their ponies, the Arapahos split into four distinct groups for the winter, each with its own chief and headmen. Membership in the Long Leg (Antelope) band, the Greasy Face band, the Beaver band, or the Quick-to-Anger band was determined largely by birth, but one could move voluntarily from one to another. By tradition, the head chief of the tribe was the most widely respected of the Antelope leaders. The Cheyennes at the beginning of the nineteenth century counted ten bands, each with four chiefs. When the bands assembled in the spring, their leaders constituted the tribal council with the addition of four elder priest-statesmen. Members of the council made their own choices to fill vacancies, but only after lively debate within the tribe. To carry out its responsibility for the general spiritual and material welfare of the people, the council of forty-four had to sample popular opinion and find acceptable positions before it could announce major decisions.

The long summer days before the annual hunt when the chiefs met together were also the time for rituals of renewal. The Sun Dance ceremony, which was common to almost every plains tribe, originated with the Cheyennes and Arapahos in the eighteenth century. It was an eight-day festival in which every member of the tribe was expected to share. Each band raised its tepees in a meticulously arranged circle, which might spread to a mile in diameter and always had an opening to the east. Held in June or July when the grass was lush and the cottonwoods were in leaf, the Sun Dance offered a chance for shared experiences, an opportunity to fulfill vows, and a time for the reaffirmation of the harmonious relationship with the sun and earth. The center of activity for both tribes was the Sun Dance pole, a tree felled and raised again in the camp circle with a Sun Dance lodge built around it. The priests of the tribe, the warriors, and the "pledger" (who was sponsoring the dance because of a promise made during the previous year) spent many days in preparation. The dancing began when the Sun Dance lodge was complete. There were prescribed songs, patterns of movement, styles for painting the body, offerings, and prayers. Some of the participants in the ceremonies fasted or tortured their bodies as a means of sacrificing to bring good fortune. The ceremony ended with rituals of purification. The Cheyenne name for the Sun Dance indicates its purpose — "new-life-lodge," or "renewing the earth."

Among the Arapahos the term *Bayaawu* ("All the Lodges") referred both to the Sun Dance and to the age societies, another institution that held them together as a tribe. Every Arapaho man who was not an outcast belonged in turn to several age-graded societies that cut across band divisions. Each society drew its members from a different age group, held different ceremonies, and performed different functions within the tribe. The equivalent among the Cheyennes was the warrior societies, military organizations most young men joined in their midteens and in which they remained active until they no longer fought. Each society again drew members from all of the bands, had its own symbols, rituals, and leaders, and felt a strong sense of comradeship. Together the organizations took the lead in warfare and maintained order in the camp. Without the cooperation of the Wolf-Soldiers, the Bull-Soldiers, the Bowstrings, the Fox-Soldiers, or the Dog-Soldiers, the council of forty-four had no way to enforce its decisions. The result was often an uneasy balance between Dog-Soldiers and chiefs, impulse and caution, war and peace.

Tribes such as the Cheyennes and Arapahos managed a remarkable adaptation to the horse, but even so its use amounted to a new technology that had revolutionary effects. "Steam, electricity, and gasoline," wrote historian Walter Prescott Webb, "have wrought no greater changes in our culture than did horses in the culture of the Plains Indians."[7] In a sense, adoption of horses by Native Americans brought a sort of "future shock," initiating a cultural change so rapid that many of the old ways simply disappeared. Tribes on the high plains forgot how to make pottery and how to farm and lost some of the stable ways of their own culture. Anthropologist Ruth Underhill called them "the new rich" and pointed out that a special belligerency existed among them, because each individual had to establish his own worth by feats of bravery or special visions. Many of the troubles

Anglo-Americans later faced in dealing with the Cheyennes and other plains tribes arose from the lack of clear lines of authority, from the need of individual warriors to prove themselves, and from the uncertainty of the Native Americans about their homelands and their history.

The history of the Cheyennes, Arapahos, Comanches, and Utes also shows that Spanish authorities in New Mexico faced an inherently unstable situation to their north and east. The spread of the horse opened the way for huge shifts of population. Historians speak of the Great Plains as being a sea of land across which entire peoples moved like waves. In the region that is now eastern Colorado, currents of migration converged from the north, west, and south. A century of fighting proved only that Native Americans on horseback were the equal of Spanish troops and that Spain lacked the power to take the Great Plains or the depths of the Rockies by force from the Native Americans. Two hundred years after the establishment of the New Mexico colony, the lands of Colorado still belonged to the Utes and Cheyennes.

# CHAPTER 3

# NEW MEXICO'S
# NORTHERN FRONTIER

In the seventeenth and eighteenth centuries, Spain drew no boundaries to New Mexico. The province stretched as far to the north as military expeditions could enforce periodic recognition of Spanish power among the Native Americans of the mountains and plains. To the east it stretched into Apache and Comanche country until it encountered the sphere of influence of the French settlements at New Orleans and St. Louis. Even after 1763, when European diplomats declared that the entire region from the Rocky Mountains to the Mississippi River was Spanish territory, officials made no effort to divide precisely the six hundred miles of open landscape that separated Santa Fe from San Antonio or the nine hundred miles between Santa Fe and St. Louis.

The U.S. purchase of the Louisiana Territory in 1803 forced negotiations over a more exact boundary. In 1819 the Adams-Onis Treaty set the border between Spanish and U.S. territory along the Red River to the 100th meridian, north on that line to the Arkansas River, west again to the river's source, north to the 42nd parallel, and thence to the Pacific. In force until U.S. annexation of Mexican lands in 1848, the boundary left the southern plains, the Rockies, and the plateau country of Colorado in Spanish and (later) Mexican hands; the remainder of the Colorado plains and the Front Range belonged to the United States.

In the years preceding 1870, the sections of Colorado south and west of the international boundary developed as an economic frontier of New Mexico. Traders from the Rio Arriba were making illegal trips into the Colorado mountains as early as 1712. In 1765 Juan de Rivera led a party through the high San Juan Mountains and along the Gunnison River in search of minerals and trade. A decade later the Dominguez-Escalante expedition followed Rivera's path on the first part of its search for a trail to

California. Padre Escalante complained of the number of Spaniards who spent months at a time engaged with the Utes in the "vile commerce in skins." Decrees prohibiting commerce with the tribe and occasional trials of violators in northern towns such as Abiquiu had little impact. After 1803 the New Mexican government shifted its position, encouraging Native American trade as essential for securing the friendship of tribes now open to U.S. influence. By the second decade of the 1800s, not only the Utes but also the Comanches in West Texas, plus the Pawnees, Cheyennes, and Arapahos in Colorado, had come to expect regular visits from New Mexico, with the established rendezvous at the confluence of the Purgatoire and Arkansas where tribal territories came together.

The character of this northern trade changed following Mexican independence from Spain. From 1803 to 1821, Spanish officials had tried to sweep American intruders from the plains. Patrols crisscrossed the lands south of the Arkansas at every rumor of American activity. In 1807 they tracked down Zebulon Pike in his winter quarters in the San Luis Valley and brought him to Santa Fe as a prisoner. St. Louis merchants and trappers during the 1810s were eager to lay out their wares in the Santa Fe plaza. The fortunate among these adventurers lost only their goods to Spanish authorities; several of them spent years in Spanish jails. It was Missourian William Becknell, who had formed a small party "destined to the westward for the purpose of trading for Horses and Mules and catching wild animals of every description," who had the luck to discover the change in policy under the new regime. Departing in September 1821, he was back in Missouri by January 1822 with many sacks of Mexican silver and the news that New Mexico now welcomed U.S. trade.

News of Becknell's enormous profits and safe return encouraged other Missouri traders into the new business market. By 1824 a caravan of twenty-five wagons had replaced Becknell's pack train. Four years later a hundred wagons made the trek across the prairies and high plains, driving Mexican goods from the Santa Fe market with hundreds of thousands of dollars of cheap U.S. merchandise. For caravans that chose the old military and trading route that wound up the Arkansas and south through the foothills of the Rockies, Raton Pass offered a barrier that made the successful passage of every wagon an open question. "The debris of wagons, such as felloes, loose tires, and tongues snapped short off" littered the route like the bones of buffalo. Travelers who took the Cimarron Cutoff across the southeast corner of Colorado could avoid the mountains and shorten their journey only at the expense of "encounters with thirst and the redmen."[1]

From the start, Missouri–New Mexico trade was tied to the commerce in furs. Many of the goods hauled to Santa Fe were bartered directly for beaver pelts gathered by New Mexicans. Other Americans established themselves in the Mexican province specifically to trade for furs or to outfit trappers ranging the southern Rockies. Because it lay near the headwaters of the Arkansas, Rio Grande, South Platte, and San Juan rivers, Taos was their favored location. Most of the trappers they supplied were experienced Americans or Franco-Americans trying a new country after years of work in the northern Rockies. With the market for beaver on the rise in the 1820s, mountain men from Taos trapped the Gila Valley of southern Arizona, the Rockies of central Colorado, and the tributaries of the Colorado River as far as Utah.

The careers of two leading trappers illustrate the mutual support between the Santa Fe commerce and the fur trade, which depended on each other like the poles of a tepee. Ceran St. Vrain came to New Mexico in 1825 as agent for a large St. Louis company. Instead of returning to Missouri at the year's end, the young man remained in Taos, joining trapping parties traveling into Arizona and Colorado and outfitting other mountain men. As he wrote his family in July 1825, he "equipt Sum men to goe trapping, thinking that it will be the most profitable for me. I have Sold the greater part of my goods a verry good profite if I am fortunate cnought to be paid. The men I have Equipt is all the best of hunters, if they make a good hunt, I will doe verey good business."[2] In 1830 St. Vrain cut his last ties with his previous employer to join forces with Charles Bent, an experienced fur trader who had been squeezed out of the Missouri River trade by the American Fur Company monopoly. Their business — the Bent, St. Vrain and Company — was an efficient partnership. Bent, who captained the principal Santa Fe caravans in 1832 and 1833, brought trade goods from St. Louis to New Mexico. St. Vrain used some of the merchandise to stake trappers and to fill his store in Taos. The rest he sold in Santa Fe or shipped south to Saltillo and Chihuahua, taking out Mexican citizenship to facilitate his dealings.

In this round of activities in the early 1830s, Bent, St. Vrain and Company typified the Santa Fe trade. The company also pioneered a new phase in the fur business and almost single-handedly shifted the fur trading headquarters from Taos to the Arkansas River. American trader John Gantt and a party of trappers had spent the winter of 1832–1833 in a log fort on the Arkansas near the mouth of the Purgatoire but had still marketed their furs in Taos like other mountain men. In 1833 Charles Bent's brother William built a rival post at the mouth of Fountain Creek, the present site of Pueblo. The following year Gantt abandoned his first post for an adobe structure called Fort Carr a few miles upstream from Bent's establishment. To cap what was now a direct rivalry for trade with plains Indians, Bent transferred his business to a new adobe fort located on the north bank of the Arkansas between the present towns of Las Animas and La Junta. Yellow Wolf of the Cheyennes suggested the shift eastward because the new site was closer to the buffalo range and therefore more likely to attract Native Americans. Although construction on what has since been known as Bent's Old Fort may have started as early as 1833, it is not certain that it was in use before 1835.[3] Within two days' ride were the sites of the villages visited by Ulibarri and Valverde, the pueblo of San Carlos, and the rendezvous used by New Mexican traders in the 1810s.

Until 1849 the fort was in continual use, the first semipermanent European settlement in Colorado. The central compound covered a rectangle approximately 140 by 120 feet and enclosed an inner plaza. Extra buildings and enclosed corrals extended it 40 feet on the east and south sides. For its construction, Bent brought in workers from Taos, who tested the clay between finger and thumb before mixing it with raw wool to give it strength. Within the fort was usually "a *melange* of traders and employees, government officers and subordinates, Indians, Frenchmen and hunters."[4] Adobe walls 3 feet thick and 14 feet high formed the back walls of a ring of dormitories, workrooms, and storerooms surrounded a large courtyard. Their slightly slanted roofs were made of poles covered with a foot of mud. Round towers at two corners allowed small cannons to sweep the walls. About a hundred employees worked at the fort, ranging from hunter Kit Carson to Mexican laborers who earned $6 a month.

A new commercial system centered on the fort. Two hundred miles closer to the warehouses of Missouri than was Taos, it was soon a preferred outfitting point for independent trappers who still pursued beaver in high valleys and hidden lakes. In the 1830s men from Bent's Fort also met trappers from further north who were trying the park country at the headwaters of the South Platte after exhausting the supplies of beaver in Wyoming, Idaho, and northern Utah. More important by the late 1830s was the barter of buffalo robes that was carried on at the fort and by parties of traders who visited the several tribes of the plains. As Thomas Farnham reported in 1839, the site of the fort was "the common field of several tribes. . . . The Eutais and the Cheyennes . . . and the Pawnees of the great Platte come to the Upper Arkansas to meet the buffalo in their annual migration to the north; and on the trail of these animals follow up the Comanches."[5] In the fort itself, employees pressed into bundles the skins bought from these tribes and from the Kiowas and Arapahos as well. The Southern Cheyennes and Arapahos in particular were special friends and clients of the fort, wintering each year along the Arkansas. Charles Bent retained responsibility for guiding the annual shipment of furs to St. Louis. William married Owl Woman, daughter of the Cheyenne Chief White Thunder, and spent part of each year among his second people.

From the base on the Arkansas River, the company constructed a territorial empire. It established one secondary post at Fort Adobe on the Canadian River in Texas, another at Fort St. Vrain on the South Platte, about six miles north of the present town of Platteville. Managed by Ceran St. Vrain's younger brother Marcellin, the latter establishment was to counter trading posts erected along the same stream by Louis Vasquez and Andrew Sublette in 1835, by Lancaster Lupton in 1836, and by the American Fur Company in 1837. A year later the American Fur Company and Bent, St. Vrain and Company agreed to reduce ruinous competition by dividing the territory approximately along the present Colorado-Wyoming border. In the face of the cartel, both independent dealers lost all but a trickle of business by 1841. During the late 1830s and early 1840s, there was also a short-lived post at Brown's Hole in northwestern Colorado (Fort Misery, the trappers called it) and a fort on the Gunnison run by Antoine Robidoux. None of these independent efforts, however, challenged the Bents and St. Vrains in their commercial mastery of the Colorado plains and the southern Rockies.

What was now a Colorado-based company continued to expand its influence in New Mexico. Ceran St. Vrain became the

William Bent's career as a frontier trader and Indian agent placed him at the intersection of three cultures. Photograph ca. 1846 shows the scars left by smallpox Bent contracted in the early 1830s while he was constructing his fort.

U.S. consul in Santa Fe in 1834, opening a branch of the business there while maintaining his residence and store on the south side of the plaza in Taos. Charles Bent married into the prominent Jaramillo family in 1835 and settled in the same town. The firm gave jobs to scores of New Mexicans, directly or indirectly, in its trading operation, on farms, and on ranches. New Mexico supplied the corn, beans, onions, and chilies and a portion of the trade goods used at Bent's Old Fort — flour, blankets (worth ten buffalo robes among the Native Americans), and, occasionally, whiskey. Simultaneously, the company made money from a hotel and restaurant business. The fort was a way station for merchants bound to and from New Mexico, for explorers and travelers in the southern Rockies, and for detachments of the United States Army watching the borders of the Louisiana Purchase.

Another rival trading post was "the Pueblo," built by George Simpson in 1842 on the site of the present city of Pueblo. As the nearest U.S. point to Taos and the junction of several trails across the mountains, the settlement was intended to supplant the Bents' enterprise. In appearance it was more a New Mexican country house than a fort, with a low wall enclosing a courtyard and buildings. Within a year the original founders moved to start a marginal farming settlement at Hardscrabble, near the present town of Florence. The Pueblo remained in use by a succession of independent Mexican and U.S. traders who bought and sold flour, whiskey, and blankets from New Mexico; coffee, tobacco, and manufactured goods from St. Louis; and hides and furs from the Native Americans. Many of the Americans were trappers who had been forced into trade by the collapse of the beaver market. Almost every facet of their new business involved smuggling whiskey across the border from Mexico or violating the United States Trade and Intercourse Act of 1834, which was intended to protect western Native Americans from the intrusion of Anglo-Americans

With the outbreak of the Mexican-American War in May 1846, the commercial domain of Bent's Old Fort was effectively absorbed within the rising empire of the American republic. Where Spanish columns had probed to the northeast a century before, U.S. troops now marched in the opposite direction. Footsore and parched, elements of the newly formed Army of the West arrived early in July, followed by their commander, Stephen W. Kearny, on July 29. Kearny had visited the fort the year before on a reconnaissance mission and had discussed plans for the attack on New Mexico in June when Ceran St. Vrain and Charles Bent paid a quick visit to Missouri. At the post on the Arkansas, Kearny rested his men, plotted the actual invasion of New Mexico, and followed General Winfield Scott's orders to "add valuable men at Bent's Fort." A party of scouts led by William Bent screened the sixteen-hundred-man force as it moved out on August 2. When the conquest of Santa Fe was complete on August 18, Kearny promulgated a legal code, created new public officials, and named Charles Bent the first U.S. governor of New Mexico.

Along with U.S. annexation of the Southwest, the coincidence of other changes conveyed an unmistakable message that the Bent–St. Vrain enterprise had played out its twenty-year role as the contact point between two cultures. During a short-lived revolt at Taos in January 1847 the new governor was killed in the front room of his own house. Two years later William Bent and Ceran St. Vrain dissolved their partnership, as St. Vrain increasingly turned his attention to local politics and his New Mexican investments. At the same time, increasing friction with the Comanches and Arapahos and a cholera epidemic among the Cheyenne ruined an already declining robe trade. In August 1849 Bent abandoned his fort, perhaps destroying it to prevent its use by Native Americans. With its demise went the importance of the upper Arkansas Valley as a rendezvous for migrating peoples. Bent moved downstream to the Big Timbers country and set up a smaller post, but he never restored his business. The brief prosperity of the Pueblo was also ended by the disruptions caused by the Mexican War, although the settlement remained in sporadic use until December 1854, when the Utes killed or captured its handful of residents.

Increased travel of merchants to Santa Fe and of emigrants up the Platte also disrupted the lives of the Cheyennes and Arapahos and threatened their hold on the Colorado plains. In 1853 Indian agent Thomas Fitzpatrick wrote that the tribes were "in abject want of food half the years. . . . Their women are pinched with want and their children constantly crying out with hunger." No longer self-sufficient hunters but dependent upon the various white merchants, many of the tribespeople lived on odd jobs and handouts. By the end of the decade, in David Lavender's description, William Bent was not so much a trader as a spokesperson and intermediary who struggled to secure equitable treatment from federal officials for the people he had adopted through marriage.[6]

Even as the hide and fur business was collapsing in the decade of U.S. conquest, New Mexicans found another use for southern

Colorado. The Spanish-speaking population along the upper Rio Grande experienced a minor population explosion in the early nineteenth century. Perhaps sixteen thousand or twenty thousand strong in the 1790s, they totaled sixty thousand by 1850. The growing scarcity of irrigable land in the Rio Grande Valley and the struggle to survive on farms subdivided among generations of male heirs forced what geographer Donald Meinig has called a "spontaneous unspectacular folk movement," which "impressed an indelible cultural stamp upon the life and landscape of a broad portion of the Southwest."[7] Beginning in the 1820s and 1830s under Mexican rule, Hispano villagers reoccupied lands abandoned to the Comanche by their grandfathers — the eastern slopes of the Sangre de Cristo and Manzano ranges, which shielded Santa Fe and Albuquerque.

Mexican officials also marked out lands to the north of the Rio Arriba for future settlement. In a series of immense land grants between 1833 and 1843, they parceled out the extreme headwaters of the Rio Grande, the San Luis Valley, and the eastern plains from the Canadian River north to the Arkansas. Four properties lay entirely or largely within the future state of Colorado. The Conejos Grant was issued in 1833 and reconfirmed in 1842 to include the upper Rio Grande and much of the San Juan Mountains. The Sangre de Cristo Grant covering the San Luis Valley was drawn up in 1843, the same year Gervacio Nolan received a smaller tract south of the site of Pueblo. The valleys of the Huerfano, Cucharas, Apishapa, and Purgatoire, which drain the east slope of the Sangre de Cristos, went simultaneously to a partnership including Taos official Cornelis Vigil, Ceran St. Vrain, and Charles Bent. Under the terms of the several grants, the recipients were obligated to settle permanent colonies of loyal citizens in order to hold the territory for Mexico.

The first permanent settlement came west of the mountains. Eighty families who tried to settle the Conejos Grant as early as 1833 returned to Abiquiu with tales of lost stock and Navajo raiders. Utes defeated a similar effort in the early 1840s. Permanent Hispano settlement within the borders of Colorado finally came when families from Taos moved to San Luis in 1851. Colonization along both sides of the San Luis Valley followed at San Pedro, San Acacio, Guadalupe, Conejos, and other villages. More than 2,000 migrants put at least forty irrigation ditches to use along the bottomlands by 1860. The flow of Hispano population from the Chama Valley into the San Luis country continued in

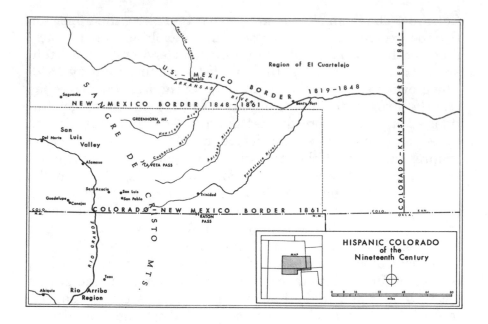

the next decade, as Anglos in New Mexico joined the competition for scarce land. By 1870, when Costilla and Conejos counties held a total of 4,200 people, Hispanic settlement had reached as far north as Saguache and the lands of the Conejos Grant.

The demand for wool uniforms for soldiers in the Civil War induced other settlers to try the lands covered by the Vigil–St. Vrain Grant. A number of American mountain men and New Mexicans had tried to create agricultural settlements along the upper Arkansas in the early 1850s, but had abandoned them by mid-decade in the face of Native American hostility. Many of the new villages that appeared north of Raton Pass in the 1860s and early 1870s were founded by informally organized groups from the same New Mexican village or by members of a single family. One early migrant described the process: "On getting back home, I told my father and brothers of the fine lands and grass around Trinidad. I proposed that we form a colony and move there. This suggestion was adopted and my father's family all came."[8] North from New Mexico came convoy after convoy of fathers, sons, brothers, and cousins, with families and distant kinspeople, armed men on horses, and burros, cattle, hogs, sheep, and goats in separate herds trailing more than a mile long, with creaking wagons filled with household goods struggling to keep pace. Ninety percent of the 6,400 residents of Las Animas and

Huerfano counties in 1870 were either New Mexican natives or the children of New Mexicans.

These Hispano pioneers re-created as closely as possible the culture they had left behind. As with Anglo-Americans who moved west, New Mexico's frontierspeople ventured into a new land to build a more prosperous version of the society they had left behind. In the San Luis Valley, the earliest settlements, such as Costilla, were built for protection in the form of a plaza or enclosed square. Increased population often brought the addition of *corrilleras*, or terraces of houses flanking the road to the plaza. A further extension was the "line village," an arrangement adopted in the Rio Arriba whenever the danger from Native American attack seemed small. Individual farmsteads — a two-room or three-room adobe house, garden, shed, and corral — strung out like beads along a river or irrigation ditch, fifty or a hundred yards apart. Each farm extended in a long, narrow strip from the stream into the hills behind, with fields of grain and gardens of beans and chilies close in and grazing land stretching behind for five or ten miles.

The pattern of settlement tended to promote equality within the villages. Each farm had roughly equal shares of arable land, pasture, and wasteland, and each holding was apportioned in the original grants according to the size of the family and the abilities of the farmer to utilize the acreage. Irrigation facilities were cooperative enterprises, and outlying pastures were used as a commons even though technically under private ownership. Despite its lack of geographic focus, each village maintained an identity centered around its church and local leaders who traded on respect for themselves and their families to supervise cooperative work, dispense justice, and represent the village to the outside world.

East of the Sangre de Cristo Range, where the first settlers were exposed to the Cheyennes and Comanches and where migrants arrived in smaller groups, the dozens of small plazas, or *placitas*, were typical rather than exceptional. Low adobe sheds, workshops, and houses were built with common walls to encircle a hollow square. The backs of the buildings were left without windows or doors, making the complex a small fortress that could shelter livestock as well as people. Many of the plazas of Colorado were originally built for a single extended family, as their names testify — Los Medina, Los Gonzales, Los Madrid. Plaza dwellers in the 1860s and 1870s grazed large herds of

The Hispanic town of Conejos in the San Luis Valley in 1876.

sheep on the mesa tops and used short ditches, or *acequias*, to cultivate farms of ten to a hundred acres in the bottomlands of the Purgatoire. The common plow was an iron prong tied to a simple wood triangle that was pulled by two oxen and was capable of scratching up three inches of soil. To U.S. observers accustomed to a different style of agriculture, Mexican farmers were "shiftless" members of a "degraded" race, their methods of agriculture "slovenly and without signs of thrift."[9]

For most of the plazas, contact with the Anglo world was funneled through a patron. In small settlements the patron might be the family patriarch, in other areas a large landowner who provided jobs for farmhands and tenants. The patron took the responsibility for selling local produce, supplying goods for the community, solving local disputes, acting as political spokesperson, maintaining a limited standard of living, and doing small favors. In return, he gained respect from the community, often as *compadre,* or godfather, to children not related by blood. He could usually depend on acquiescence to his economic schemes and on block voting to help him bargain with Anglo authorities.

The Roman Catholic Church at Guadalupe in 1876.

The religious life of the settlers appeared equally strange to European-Americans. In the 1870s and 1880s, the peculiarly New Mexican religious order of the Penitent Brothers — Los Hermanos Penitentes — flourished in the San Luis Valley, eastward into Las Animas and Huerfano counties, and westward into Archuleta County. Although the origins of the Penitentes are still debated, the order probably emerged in New Mexico around 1800 to fill the vacuum resulting from a lack of trained priests. In many isolated villages the hermano mayor also served as an informal town leader, and the activities of the local society provided a structure for town life. Operating without special secrecy in the early nineteenth century, the Penitentes went underground when Protestant missionaries and French-trained priests brought in by Roman Catholic Archbishop Jean Baptiste Lamy of Santa Fe tried to alter the local customs. To many participants, the preservation of the brotherhood, with its annual re-enactment of the Passion and the custom of physical penance, symbolized the retention of Spanish culture and Spanish Catholicism in the face of outside intrusions. Certainly for travelers who saw piles of crosses waiting for use on distant hillsides and heard lurid stories of self-torture with whips and cactus, the

The contact of Anglo and Hispanic cultures at Francisco Plaza near La Veta, on the Denver and Rio Grande Railroad, 1876.


existence of the order isolated Spanish-speaking Colorado as alien territory.

In practical terms, a single town served as the point of contact between the eastern Hispano settlements and Anglo Coloradans. Members of both groups were simultaneous founders of Trinidad. This "first and only Mexican town to be found north of the Raton Mountains" struck most U.S. visitors as a poor place indeed.[10] In fact, the straggling village along the Purgatoire became the center for U.S. influence as the seat of government for the new Las Animas County after 1866 and as a point on the stage and telegraph lines between Denver and Santa Fe. The dusty streets and mud-floored houses sheltered not only New Mexicans but also U.S. merchants along the main street. Mounting tensions exploded on Christmas Day, 1867, when an Anglo resident shot a Hispano. When a group of Americans attempted to rescue the accused killer from jail on January 1, they found themselves surrounded by scores of Hispanos led by Sheriff Guiterrez of Las Animas County, who tried to prevent a lynching while holding the culprits. Only with the arrival of U.S. troops on January 5 did the Americans feel it was safe to surrender. Not until late spring did feelings subside enough to allow the army's withdrawal.

As the Trinidad incident indicates, Hispano society in southern Colorado quickly came under strong pressure from Anglos moving south from the core area of U.S. settlement. The newcomers had the normal Anglo-Saxon disregard for dissimilar cultures. In their minds their intrusion was part of the "rapid progress of civilization," and they felt no compunction about displacing a population they considered "ignorant and debased to a shameful degree."[11] U.S. control was evident by the mid-1870s not only in Trinidad but also in the "American" towns of Saguache and Alamosa, which grew as a center for Anglo retailers as soon as the arrival of Denver and Rio Grande Railroad tracks symbolized the coming of "a superior race."

For the next decade or so, although Hispanos still provided the bulk of the rural population in Conejos, Costilla, Huerfano, and Las Animas counties, a few people tried to bridge the two cultures of town and country. Some members of this "dual elite," such as John Lawrence of Saguache County, were Anglos who retained the spirit of entrepreneurship while acting as patrons to the dozens of tenant-herders who worked for them. Lawrence handled the Hispanos' personal business, guided them in encounters with U.S. law, loaned money and supplies, settled small disputes, and dictated their votes. At the same time he accumulated capital, boosted his locality, and effected changes in the structure of the local economy. Other transitional figures were plaza patrons who moved to towns such as Trinidad to pursue careers in business and the professions or as local politicians who retained the obligation to provide jobs and political favors for their followers.

The most famous of these politician-patrons was Casimiro Barela. A migrant from New Mexico in 1866, Barela moved immediately into local politics in Las Animas County, winning election to the legislature in 1871 and to the state senate in 1876, where he served continuously until 1912. In his private life Barela was indistinguishable from a U.S. entrepreneur. He invested in land, banking, railroads, ranching, and urban real estate; he built a merchandising and forwarding business; and he joined the Trinidad Chamber of Commerce. At times he seemed to reject the role of political leader, but he arrived in Denver for the biennial session of the legislature with an entourage of retainers, and he tried to guard the interests of Spanish-speaking Coloradans from the strange bureaucracy of the Anglos. In so doing he helped to cushion the village society of Hispano Colorado from the changes being forced upon it.

Barela's position in Trinidad was not unique. The town contained a number of Hispanic storekeepers and professionals who crossed the "culture line" to participate in the Chamber of Commerce, Knights of Columbus, and other civic organizations. As historian Sarah Deutsch has pointed out, the town also offered Hispanic women opportunities for wage labor outside the house. Such women could act as the heads of their own households while retaining ties to their social community.

Despite the cultural accommodation in Trinidad, the general pattern in southern Colorado was for development-minded Anglos to squeeze Hispanos out of positions of significant influence. The problem was at heart a clash between a people accustomed to the eighteenth century and a nation waiting impatiently for the twentieth. As early as 1871, the European purchasers of the Sangre de Cristo Grant refused to recognize the rights to the use of common land claimed by the original settlers brought in by Carlos Beaubien. By the turn of the century, the Spanish-speaking population in the San Luis Valley had abandoned lands north of the Conejos River to the "active American population."[12]

In the Arkansas Valley, the development of coal mining and timber industries and the influx of European immigrants to work for the new companies accelerated a slow displacement of Mexican farmers. New corporate landowners denied personal responsibility for tenants. Corporate purchases and the creation of national forest reserves constricted the free range available for the herds of Hispano villagers. Unlike the understanding patrons, absentee managers had no sympathy for stories of hardship or bad crops. U.S. roads and railroads broke up much of the rich bottomland, and erosion damaged the remainder, as the best timber went for ties and mine bracings. In the early 1900s many of the old plazas were abandoned by inhabitants who moved to coal camps to work as guards, teamsters, and laborers or to Walsenburg and Trinidad to earn wages from the Anglos. Others cut railroad ties from the pine forests of the Sangre de Cristos, worked in railroad repair crews, or found jobs with Anglo-American ranchers. Participation in the cash economy helped to preserve ownership of individual farms and homesteads but ended much of the isolation and self-containment of Hispano Colorado.

In the mid-nineteenth century the boundary between New Mexico and Colorado continued to reflect the balance of cultures on the western frontier. After the U.S. annexation in 1848, the government in Washington trimmed unoccupied territory from what was now the Territory of New Mexico but left all areas of Hispano settlement under the supervision of Santa Fe. Not until after the first gold rush did Congress create a Colorado Territory identical to the present state. The new boundaries, set in 1861, cut the pioneers of the San Luis and Arkansas valleys from their homeland. Recurrent protests from the New Mexico legislature failed to move Congress to undo this fragmentation of a single cultural region.

In an immediate sense, the congressional action reflected the influence of land speculators among Republican politicians. In a much broader sense, however, it signified that after a century and a half of doubt, all of Colorado was part of the Anglo-American West. Since the early 1700s the southern Rockies, the San Luis basin, and the Arkansas Valley had been zones of contact among dissimilar peoples — Utes and Apaches, Comanches and Spaniards, Frenchmen and Spaniards, and, above all, New Mexicans and Americans — competing for control of the same territory. The tiny expeditions, the small battles, the single settlements and forts — many of these events seem, in retrospect, merely preliminary for what was to follow. Yet, as viewed from a different perspective, the lands of Colorado were one of the major frontiers of world history, a zone of interpenetration between the expansive societies of Hispanic and Anglo America.

CHAPTER 4

# THE PIKES PEAK GOLD RUSH

*Here you are, gentlemen; this ace of hearts is the winning card. Watch it closely. Follow it with your eye as I shuffle. Here it is, and now here, now here and now [laying the three on the table with faces down] — where? If you point it out the first time you win, but if you miss you lose. Here it is you see [turning it up] now watch it again [shuffling]. This ace of hearts, gentlemen, is the winning card. I take no bets from paupers, cripples or orphan children. The ace of hearts. It is my regular trade, gentlemen — to move my hands quicker than your eyes. I always have two chances to your one. The ace of hearts. If your sight is quick enough, you beat me and I pay; if not, I beat you and take your money. The ace of hearts; who will go me twenty?*[1]

Every report on Colorado in the year 1859 gave a prominent place to the professional card shark. During the preceding months, the thousand people who had wintered among the cottonwood groves of the South Platte had been amply entertained by experts in monte and faro who came from Santa Fe, Salt Lake, and the western army posts to deal hands to new customers. When Albert Richardson penned his description of three-card monte in June, gamblers in the canvas-roofed hotel known as the Denver House kept six tables busy day and night. The constant cries of "Who'll go me twenty? The ace of hearts is the winning card!" kept Horace Greeley awake past midnight. On the other streets of the new town, saloons and gambling halls "shouldered each other in rows, and . . . night and day, their doors were never closed." Fifteen miles to the west Golden City offered the same array of "gaming tents, restaurants, stores, [and] little doggeries where government whiskey is retailed 'at ten cents a nip.'"[2]

The card player was only the most obvious gambler among Colorado's Fifty-niners. Every Anglo-American who followed the echoes of "Gold!" as the word reverberated through the Mississippi Valley in 1858 and 1859 staked his or her prosperity on a new venture. Miner and merchant, barkeeper and hardware salesperson, editor, land dealer, and politician were all speculators. Each risked his or her future on the wager that the richness of Rocky Mountain ores and the openness of the new society would compress into a few years the career that would have required a lifetime of hard work in the established East. Only people without vision saw the road to Colorado as seven hundred miles of wagon ruts with sterile granite at the end. To most Fifty-niners it was a shortcut to success with a paying business proposition waiting in welcome.

As a new field of enterprise, Colorado had attracted attention at the same time the nationwide commercial depression created panic in the fall of 1857. In that year perennial reports that gold could be found in the central Rockies set off excited rumors. In the spring of 1858, two parties of prospectors — Georgians led by William Green Russell and Cherokees from Indian Territory organized by John Beck — rendezvoused on the Arkansas, passed Bent's Old Fort, and proceeded to the South Platte, where a third group of Missourians joined them. From June 24 to July 4, over a hundred people swirled pans in the cold waters of Cherry Creek, Ralston's Creek, and other small streams without finding "color," the prospector's word for the glint of gold. Not until July 7 or 8, several days after most of the discouraged prospectors started the long trek home, did the thirteen stubborn holdouts pan small pockets of the precious metal from the banks of Little Dry Creek, a few miles up the South Platte from its confluence with Cherry Creek.

News of the find spread immediately. An itinerant trader named John Cantrell visited the party on July 31. When he left five days later, he carried a sack of pay dirt that he panned before a crowd when he reached Kansas City. Other Native American traders and mountain men quickly spread the word north to Fort Laramie, south into New Mexico, and eastward toward the Kansas settlements. Indeed, thirty hopeful miners from Lawrence, Kansas, arrived at Clear Creek early in September. For the past two months, the Lawrence group had been part of a larger party that had spent frustrating weeks separating sand from sand in the streams of South Park and the San Luis Valley. With the

Lawrence party, Russell's people, and other mountain men who drifted in for the winter, the South Platte diggings boasted perhaps eighty inhabitants by the time Missouri Valley newspapers published their first headlines of confirmed discoveries.

The original group of Lawrence prospectors had also included twenty-year-old Julia Archibald Holmes, who had walked rather than ridden from Kansas in order to build up her endurance. For freedom of movement she wore the "American costume" advocated by supporters of women's rights — a calico dress over calico bloomers. On August 5 Julia Holmes became the first American woman to reach the top of Pike's Peak, reading from the poetry of Ralph Waldo Emerson at the summit. After descending in an unexpected snowstorm, she accompanied her husband to New Mexico, where she became a correspondent for the *New York Tribune*.

The news hit first and had the most effect in the towns closest to the new gold fields. The Missouri River Valley from Council Bluffs south to Kansas City had been a scene of wild land speculation and mushrooming hopes in 1856 and 1857. By 1858 it was a land of bankruptcies, where people gathered in front of the post office to talk over what had failed. The first arrival of gold dust on August 26 thus called forth not sober analysis but cries of "The New Eldorado!!! Gold in Kansas Territory!!" Over the next several weeks, citizens of Kansas City, Lawrence, St. Louis, Omaha, and Leavenworth jammed mass meetings to consider the reports. Their newspapers made up for the lack of hard information with headline after headline: "New Gold Discovery," "Gold Excitement on the Increase," "Kansas Gold Fever," "Gold! Gold!! Gold!!! Gold!!!! Hard to Get and Heavy to Hold. Come to Kansas!!" Word that $8, $10, or $15 was a normal day's take circulated, along with stories of four-pound nuggets and gold by the kettleful. Those without jobs or businesses found it easy to take action. "Gone to Pike's Peak" was the story in the Kansas City *Journal of Commerce* on September 14, "Off for the Mines" in the Crescent City *Oracle* three days later, "Ho! for Pike's Peak" in the *Missouri Democrat* the following week, and "Outfits for the Mines" in the Topeka *Kansas Tribune*.[3]

The eight hundred or one thousand citizens who left the Missouri River towns before winter interdicted travel all hoped to make their fortune, but only some expected to use pick and shovel. Dozens among them were practitioners of "the popular Anglo-American art of townmaking." As Henry Villard wrote, these townsite speculators "desired not to pitch into, but on the ground. They cared less for good placers than promising places."[4]

The most successful proved to be William Larimer, a Pennsylvania politician and hotelkeeper who had moved west after the panic of 1854. When three years of strenuous promotion failed to make Larimer City the great metropolis of Nebraska, Larimer moved to Leavenworth, where he was operating a freighting service when he heard the news from Pikes Peak. Seizing the opportunity for another speculation, he recruited his son and about thirty others and set out for Cherry Creek in October. Within twenty-four hours after his arrival on November 16, Larimer sized up the situation and made his move. Along the left bank of Cherry Creek where it entered the South Platte he found the town of Auraria, laid out by members of the Russell party less than two weeks before. Along the right bank were the stakes with which the Lawrence party had marked out the town of St. Charles. Since the St. Charles Town Association had soon thereafter left the plains to obtain a territorial charter and spend a more comfortable winter in the East, Larimer took his chance. According to Denver folklore, he fed liquor to Charles Nichols, who had been left to guard St. Charles, and convinced him to sign over the town. On November 17 Larimer's party occupied the undeveloped townsite and five days later organized the Denver City Company, named for the governor of the Kansas Territory. What Larimer had in mind he later expressed in a letter to his family: "We are bound to have a territory if not a state, and the capital will be Denver City with the state house near Will's and my claims."[5]

Auraria and Denver provided quarters for most of the migrants of 1858. Despite the fierce rivalry between the two companies of speculators, the towns functioned together as a unit from the start. Cooperation was a necessity, for the plains at the base of the Front Range were crisscrossed by the tracks of those in search of advantageous sites for competing cities. Pikes Peak City, Golden Gate, Santa Fe, Nonpareil City, San Francisco, Sacramento, Russelville, Forest City, Junction City, and others whose names have not survived were never more than plans on paper. Mountain City eight miles up the South Platte from Auraria, Highland across the river, Arapahoe City on Clear Creek, El Paso near the site of Colorado Springs, Boulder City, and Fountain City, however, passed the initial test in the winter of 1858–1859 by attracting at least a cluster of cabins. Their promoters devoted long evenings to writing enticing accounts for the newspapers back East. As one miner wrote after weeks of frustration with shovel and sluice, "We were quite surprised a few days since when we read the glowing account in the Missouri river papers, of what the miners are doing out here. I pronounce them a pack of lies, written and reported back by a set of petty one-horse town speculators."[6]

Town boomers were not the only businesspeople who hoped to make their fortunes from miners rather than mining. Messrs. Blake and Williams of Crescent City, Iowa, opened the first general store on October 29, 1858. The first Taos whiskey was sold by "Uncle Dick" Wootton, who arrived from Raton on Christmas Day with a wagon train of goods. While waiting for the mines to open in the spring, various entrepreneurs set up ferry service across the South Platte, wrote home for a supply of hats (sure sale guaranteed), and platted the territory's first official cemetery. Attempting to beat the spring rush, William Byers imported a printing press and associated paraphernalia from Nebraska over roads frozen at night and muddy by day. In the first issue of his *Rocky Mountain News*, published on April 23, 1859, he explained his reasons for establishing a newspaper in terms that spoke to most of the early Anglo Coloradans: "We have done this because we wished to collect and send forth reliable information, because we wished to help mold and organize the new population, and because we thought it would pay."

Those who stayed behind rather than risk the winter in a mud-chinked cabin on the South Platte were equally adept at turning the gold fever to profit. The uppermost thought in each of several dozen Missouri River towns was to channel the expected flood of Colorado emigrants down its own main street and through the doors of its own merchants. On August 27, the day after it announced the new El Dorado, the Kansas City *Journal of Commerce* remarked that the best route to the gold fields lay through Kansas City. Within weeks every town had staked its claim on the expected trade, offering itself as the most favorable point for obtaining a good price on wagons, teams, pans, rockers, boots, flour, coffee, blankets, and the other necessities of life. The citizens of Wyandotte, Kansas City, Leavenworth, and other towns assembled to hear "glorification speeches" that urged local merchants to take full advantage of the superior position for trade so beneficently bestowed upon each city by divine providence.

Several towns employed traveling agents to haunt the railroad depots and steamboats of the western states in search of customers. Seventeen guidebooks to the Pikes Peak Gold Region supplemented their efforts. Luke Tierney, the author of a *History of the Gold Discoveries on the South Platte River*, and William Parsons, who wrote *The New Gold Mines of Western Kansas*, had been among the original prospectors, Tierney with the Russell party and Parsons with the Lawrence people. Most of the other volumes were compiled by journalists, surveyors, and town boomers. With no personal experience at the new mines, they rushed into print to take advantage of the spring onslaught. At worst the authors fabricated information to fill their pages; at best they reprinted without comment uncorroborated reports and letters from the miners. Whether admitted or not, most of the books were written to advertise a particular route and town (the Leavenworth City Council supposedly subscribed to twenty thousand copies of one guide). A prospective emigrant who conscientiously surveyed the lot would have been hard-pressed to choose between Wyandotte, Kansas City, Atchison, St. Joseph, Plattesmouth, and half a dozen other towns as a point of embarkation. Even Tierney's book plugged the nascent town of Auraria in which the author had an interest, noting its "liberal" laws and constitution, its "substantial dwelling houses," and its "other valuable improvements."

In February and March 1859, thousands of argonauts assembled along the Missouri, spurred by bad crops and the pressure of debts. Passing their time until the grass turned green, they could dine at the Pikes Peak Lunch Room on beef cooked "a la mode Pikes Peak" and pudding served with "Pikes Peak sauce." In purchasing their outfits ($600 would buy three yoke of oxen, wagons, tools, tents, flour, bacon, and coffee for four people) they could patronize the Pikes Peak Outfitters for "Pikes Peak hats and Pikes Peak guns, Pikes Peak boots, Pikes Peak shovels, and Pikes Peak goodness-knows-what-all." One disgruntled newspaper suggested the need for "Pikes Peak goggles to keep the gold dust out of the eyes of the fortune hunters." Some idea of the rigors of the trip was given in James Redpath and Richard Henton's *Handbook to Kansas Territory and the Rocky Mountains and Gold Region,* which suggested testing one's trunk by "throwing it from the top of a three-storied house; if you pick it up uninjured, it will do to go to Kansas."[7]

How many people actually set out for the diggings and how many arrived is impossible to determine. For several weeks in April and May, editors in the major Missouri River town crossings reported the passage of forty, seventy-five, or one hundred teams per day, and observers found the roads leading west from the river "white with the wagons of Pikes Peak emigrants." As the migration westward was beginning in earnest, however, editors began to worry that no shipments of gold had yet appeared from those who had wintered on the South Platte. In early May the first reports of the "go-backers" appeared: stories of disappointed prospectors who had reached the Cherry Creek settlements, tried their hand at panning, and pronounced the whole thing "HUMBUG!" Many of the dissatisfied migrants had expected their gamble to pay off immediately.

> A large majority of the emigrants were men who lacked energy and industry, with no means — almost starving — finding no provisions in the country (the Mexican supplies not yet having arrived) — seeing no gold lying upon the ground — discovering Cherry Creek to possess properties similar to other waters, and not one bit yellow — wanting the vim to prospect and prosecute what they had undertaken to do — became dissatisfied, discouraged, furious and raving mad; took down the Platte — some in boats, some on foot, and some with their teams — turning back all who were on the way here that would listen to their tales.[8]

By mid-May the ragged, foot-weary returning migrants had intercepted thousands of wagons halfway to Colorado. Their bitter denunciations of dishonest fabrications and deceptive speculators convinced most of the westbound gold seekers to turn around. The gold mania of April became a "humbug mania" by the first of June, when twenty-five hundred wagons rolled eastward from the diggings, filled with migrants cursing mad and hundreds of dollars poorer. According to Horace Greeley, the total of go-backers may have been as high as forty thousand. Reacting to disaster with as much exaggeration as they had displayed with good news, editors filled their columns with stories of the Great Bamboozle.

Against the nearly universal conviction of humbug, those with a stake in the permanent growth of Denver — such as William Byers of the *Rocky Mountain News* and John Fox of the Leavenworth and Pikes Peak Express Company — made little impression with either ridicule or pleas for common sense. By early May Denver had lost two-thirds of its people, and the entire population of the gold region was perhaps three thousand, a small increase over January and February. Indeed, the Rockies had gone through an entire cycle of boom and bust on false premises. Initial excitement had been based on tiny deposits of placer gold worth at most a few thousand dollars. Just as important, the stampede back to Missouri was, ironically, at its height at a time when the existence of substantial rich gold ores within the Front Range was already known.

As with the false boom of '58, the key to the recovery of enthusiasm for Colorado mining was timely publicity. Although rich placer mines were in operation at Gold Hill above Boulder and along the South Fork of Clear Creek near Denver by the end of April, they were still isolated by snow and distance and made little impression on the skeptical public. George Jackson, for example, had found gold near the future site of Idaho Springs in January but kept the news quiet until the spring could thaw the ground and give him time to organize a mining company. New reports of people making $5 or $10 per day sounded suspiciously like the accounts in circulation eight months earlier.

The break came on May 13. Denverites were astonished by the display of a vial containing $80 worth of gold brought from diggings found a week earlier by John H. Gregory on the North Fork of Clear Creek. Letters written from Denver and Auraria over the next three weeks chronicled a rising excitement as more gold arrived from the Gregory diggings, and prospectors decided to check for themselves whether the new pay dirt was associated with gold-bearing quartz. By the end of May the excitement was so intense that the towns looked "as dull as New England villages on Sabbath day." "Traders locked up their stores," wrote Henry Villard, "bar-keepers disappeared with their bottles of whiskey, the few mechanics that were busy building houses abandoned their work, the county judge and sheriff, lawyers and doctors . . . joined in the general rush."[9]

Convincing those on the scene was the easy step in reversing the reputation of the South Platte diggings. Changing the opinions of citizens back East required the more disinterested testimony of reporter Henry Villard of the *Cincinnati Times*, reporter Albert Richardson of the *Boston Journal*, and editor Horace Greeley of the *New York Tribune*, the most widely read periodical

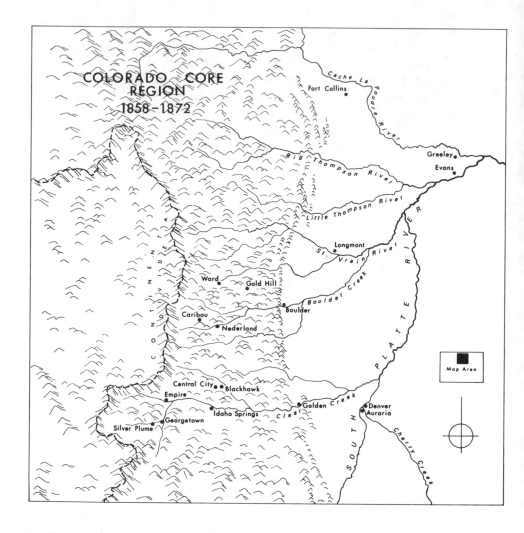

COLORADO CORE REGION 1858–1872

in the nation. Traveling together on the first leg of a transcontinental journey, Greeley and Richardson arrived in Denver on June 6 to see for themselves. Teaming with Villard, who had been in Colorado for several weeks, they mounted mules for the forty-mile trip to Gregory Gulch. Their joint dispatch reported that a single sluice might yield anywhere from $21 to $494 per day. Published as an extra in the *Rocky Mountain News* on June 11, the report was widely copied in eastern papers with Greeley's name giving it the necessary weight. "We regarded the whole thing as a huge humbug," wrote the *Atchison Union* on June 25, "until we read Greeley's statement. . . . We never admired him as a politician, but as a business man, Greeley's opinions are as good as the gold."

Although the last third of the Greeley Report had been an extended admonition against extravagant hopes and an ill-advised rush, the next month saw the recurrence of Pikes Peak mania in the form of "Gregory Fever." At the time of Greeley's visit, the wooded slopes of Gregory Gulch sheltered a population of four thousand or five thousand prospectors who slept in tents or lean-to shelters of pine boughs, eating and cooking in the open air. Over the next month, five hundred newcomers arrived daily. They jammed into an area perhaps four miles square, digging prospecting holes, uprooting the eighty-foot pines, and desolating the landscape in search of "pockets" or "crevices" of pay dirt weathered from the main lodes.

Around July 1 it became apparent that most of the gold was locked firmly with quartz and that there were not enough workable claims to support a population estimated at ten thousand or fifteen thousand. The "second stampede" lasted another month. Thousands made their way back across the plains, satisfied that they had finally "seen the elephant." Others who lacked the capital for hard-rock mining turned to new gulches and new hopes: Left-Hand Creek, Twelve-Mile Diggings, Chicago Creek, Cache la Poudre, and the Jackson Diggings in the Front Range; over Kenosha Pass to South Park and the towns of Montgomery, Buckskin Joe, Fairplay, Tarryall, Hamilton, and Jefferson; and north over Hoosier Pass to American and Humbug gulches across the Continental Divide in the valley of the Blue River. These and other finds date from the summer of 1859 when every report of a new strike had the effect of an electric shock, "instantaneously producing a feverish restlessness and an increased thirst for gold."[10]

As many as one hundred thousand gold seekers may have started for the gold fields over the course of 1859, but observers believed only forty thousand reached Denver. Perhaps twenty-five thousand entered the mountains between April and October. About ten thousand were left in Colorado by early August — two thousand of them in Denver, a few hundred at Golden, and most of the remainder engaged in systematic placer operations with flumes and sluices or in serious attempts to work the quartz ores with blasting and crushing apparatus. As late as September 24, twenty-three hundred were counted at work in the six-square-mile gulch region along the North Fork of Clear Creek. By the time the mining season closed in October, roughly $250,000 had been taken out of streams and hills. Only four thousand or five thousand merchants and miners wintered in the new settlements, the remains of the influx of the previous fall, spring, and summer.

June had been the flush month in the mountains, but Denver's first era of commercial prosperity lasted from August through November. Although the majority of migrants had passed through the twin towns of Denver and Auraria, significant amounts of gold did not reach there until midsummer. At the same time, a number of merchants arriving with extensive stocks of goods bid up real estate in their hurry to open businesses at a favorable location and catch the booming market. During the Greeley-Richardson visit, half of the buildings in Denver had been abandoned and were open to anyone who wanted to take occupancy; ten months later one liquor dealer paid $50 per month for a one-story frame building, eighteen feet by thirty feet, with no floor and only half a ceiling. As the great hotel and storehouse for the gold regions, Denver provided personal services to luxury-starved miners and businesspeople traveling to the diggings, sold boots and shovels to the miners, and furnished vital professional and commercial services. Its location on the South Platte, twenty miles east of the mountains, placed it near the junction of several important routes into the mining regions. By January 1860 the two towns claimed over two dozen stores and a dozen wholesalers, about thirty eating and drinking establishments, and over two dozen doctors and lawyers. Population reached two thousand in 1859 and topped forty-five hundred the following year.

Economic growth called for physical refinement. Newcomers who accepted log and canvas walls, dirt walls, and mud roofs in their haste to set up businesses turned to the improvement of their properties during the fall. Window frames with glass replaced empty holes, sawed lumber supplanted logs, and brick appeared on a few of the finer stores. Settlers poured an estimated $700,000 into building their city, and by November its citizens could claim that "everything here now, in this double capital, looks about as it does in any established city of the Western States." The settlement's success confirmed speculators in Denver land and commerce in their ambitions. "We have," wrote one resident, "as sharp and sagacious merchants, as shrewd real estate speculators, as cunning and ambitious lawyers, as numerous doctors, as fine looking young men, and as handsome and stylish women, almost as can be scared up together in any single corporation this side of St. Louis or Chicago."[11]

A boom in local politics accompanied the commercial success. One Denverite complained in the fall of 1859 that "a weekly election treat bids fair to become one of the permanent institutions of the country. A Monday and an election have become inseparable things." What he viewed as tiresome was, in fact, vital to the prosperity of Colorado. As hopeful businesspeople and prospectors found the uncertainty of mining to be gamble enough without added problems from unchecked disorder, functioning local governments sprang up spontaneously. Their appearance was perhaps proof of Frederick Jackson Turner's dictum that "American democracy . . . gained new strength every time it touched a new frontier," proof also that in new settlements beyond the reach of established institutions, Americans were forced to govern themselves or face social disaster.[12]

The first efforts met the needs of both speculators and settlers. "We have a claim club," reported a new Coloradan in January 1859, "whose business it is to see that all town sites and farming and timber claims are recorded."[13] As on earlier frontiers, farmers and land boomers in the several valleys at the base of the mountains agreed among themselves to respect and defend each others' claims until the extension of the federal land survey made legal purchase possible. The El Paso Claim Club, the Arapahoe Claim Club, the Platte River Claim Club, the Cañon City Claim Club, and others were organized in 1859 or early 1860 to adopt a written constitution; to establish size limits and requirements for holding farm lands, timber claims, and townsites; to take the responsibility for recording claims; and to note changes of ownership. Club members warned off newcomers, and club directors sat as a jury in disputes of ownership to resolve whether lands were "jumpable" or "not jumpable." In new towns such as Golden, the clubs supplemented the work of the town companies in defining and protecting property.

Claim clubs provided civil law for new residents of the South Platte and Arkansas valleys. People's courts filled the need for criminal law and the protection of individuals against violence. Especially in Denver, whose central location and prosperity seemed to attract "hoards of villains of the blackest dye, murderers, thieves and blacklegs of all kinds," ad hoc judicial bodies were a necessity in the absence of legally constituted courts.[14] Over the course of 1859 and 1860, there were fourteen recorded trials for murder. Most trials ran with strict regard for the presentation and cross-examination of testimony, with a twelve-member jury and one to three judges. Only six of the men tried were sentenced to death, a fact that illustrates that Denverites were as interested in reproducing a functioning replica of the U.S. judicial system as they were in mob revenge. Attorney Hiram Bennet later remembered that he had drawn rules of procedure from the fourteen volumes of Iowa statutes he had packed with him to Colorado. Vigilantes figured in the maintenance of order only in September 1860, when they lynched three rustlers and created a furor over their clandestine activities. In the first months of 1860, a short-lived "Provisional Government of Denver, Auraria, and Highland City" also tried to establish a city marshall and a night police. Golden first organized a "citizens' court" in December 1859 and then a people's court in September 1860. The courts were a remarkable effort by citizens with a permanent stake in Colorado to preserve their future against disorder.

Miners showed the same familiarity with the procedures of self-government. The discoverers of Gregory Gulch organized the first mining district on June 8, 1859. A mass meeting adopted ten simple rules that defined the boundaries of the district and the terms under which mining claims could be held. More important, the meeting defined an equitable process for resolving disputes by an impartial board of arbiters. A month later the Gregory Gulch miners elected new officers and on July 16 gave the officers power to summon miners to witness, to hold trials, and to keep records. By September miners in other valleys had also agreed on sets of regulations enforced by voluntary compliance and community pressure. In Boulder County at least eight districts functioned, in Clear Creek twenty-seven, and in Gilpin twenty-seven more. The names of the districts reflect the origins of the miners and the hopes they brought with them: Kansas, Wisconsin, Bay State and Illinois Central, Phoenix, Independent, Enterprise, and Quartz Valley.

The second year of mining saw the refinement of district codes. Despite prohibitions against practicing lawyers, code makers found it necessary to give increasingly legalistic definitions to lode, gulch, placer, tunnel, ditch, water, building, and ranch claims. The districts also took on responsibility for combating crime, with trials and specified penalties for minor cases. Many followed the lead of the Nevada District near Central City in resolving that "there shall be no Bawdy Houses, Grog Shops, or Gamboling Saloons," as such activities were "degrading to the Morals, detrimental to the sway of peace and order, and Disgraceful to the name and character of the District."[15] By the end of 1860, some of the districts were taking the further step of providing positive government. In the Central City region the ad hoc officials called out the inhabitants to work on the roads during slack seasons. Miners of the Central District imitated federal land policies by setting aside one claim in each lode for a school fund. Prospectors usually turned out by the hundreds to vote for the officials of what had become, in effect, functioning county governments.

Simultaneous with the growth of mining districts and claim clubs were efforts to organize state or territorial governments. Citizens involved in local activities were primarily interested in protecting their businesses and property, but many of the movers of areawide agitation were political speculators. Those whose ambitions had been unfulfilled in older, more settled states moved into the new settlements "to acquire a sort of priority title to the many places of both honor and profit that are created in the course of the development of an embryo community."[16] By taking the lead in establishing a regional government they hoped to start at the top — as senator, governor, or at least member of Congress. For them the gold-bearing ores of the new territory were offices of public trust; the sluice and pan were regular elections. As early as November 6, 1858, thirty-five citizens met to choose A. J. Smith as delegate to the Kansas legislature and Hiram Graham to speak for the settlers in Washington. The following spring a caucus of Denverites chaired by William Larimer proposed that representatives of nearby settlements meet on the future of the new community. The call for a constitutional convention for a new state of Jefferson, issued by the gathering, ended with a ringing peroration that "government of some kind we must have, and the question narrows itself down to this point: Shall it be the government of the knife and the revolver, or shall we unite in forming here in our golden country . . . a new and independent State?"[17] The convention that assembled on June 6 found that the Gregory Gulch excitement precluded any action other than the appointment of eight committees. Their reports were accepted on August 1 by a reassembled body in which 167 delegates represented thirty-seven "precincts." A month later the residents of the Pikes Peak territory were offered a choice between a state constitution and a memorial to Congress requesting territorial status. By a margin of 1,468 votes — 2,117 to 649 — the voters rejected statehood out of a fear of taxation, preferring territorial status in which Washington paid the bills.

Political promoters resumed their activity when the coming winter began to shut down the working of the gulches. On October 3 eight thousand voters chose Beverly D. Williams over half a dozen rivals as their delegate to Congress, simultaneously choosing a convention to write a territorial constitution. Three weeks later the hard-worked voters turned out again to voice approval of the Territory of Jefferson by a margin of 6 to 1 and to elect a full slate of provisional officers. R. W. Steele, a member of the Nebraska legislature, was chosen governor. He was aided by a secretary, an auditor, a treasurer, an attorney general, a chief justice and an associate justice, a marshall, a superintendent of public instruction, and a full set of legislators.

In the aftermath of the electoral hustling, a number of Coloradans wondered whether the question asked months before more accurately should have read, Are we to have here, among the ravines and gulches of the Rockies, an office for every ambition and an appointment for every aspirant? Whether it was "started by a few to satisfy the ambitions of a few," the provisional government of Jefferson turned in a creditable performance.[18] Meeting from November 1859 into January 1860, the assembly marked off twelve counties and incorporated the city of Denver, provided for a census, established a three-tier court system, adopted civil and criminal codes, and passed laws relating to mineral, land, and water resources.

Despite the solid start, however, Jefferson Territory ran into problems during the course of 1860. When Congress ignored petitions for the granting of territorial status, the local government found itself operating in limbo. Unable to collect taxes without legal status, its officials had to operate on goodwill and voluntary compliance. Mining districts provided an effective governing agency that made Jefferson Territory superfluous for the mountain settlements. As early as January, prospectors of the Gregory District rejected their provisional county government by a vote of 395 to 95. Miners in other areas took oaths to refuse a proposed poll tax. Although the territory retained more influence in the plains settlements, the second territorial election, which returned Governor Steele to office and chose a new legislature, was an empty gesture.

The decline of Jefferson Territory opened the way for other political entrepreneurs to have their try at government-making. In Golden in October 1860, statehood advocates convened again. Another convention at Central City elected a delegate to Congress. It also renamed the territory "Idaho" and proposed that judges govern the region's several districts until Congress acted. Although a few spoilsports insisted that the area was legally divided between Kansas and Nebraska, miners elsewhere joined in indulging their Anglo-American talent for self-government. The Mount Vernon District declared itself subject only to the federal government and wrote its own constitution; the South Platte District selected its own congressional representative; and the United Mining District at the headwaters of the Arkansas chose its own circuit judge, marshall, legislative committee, and — of course — delegate to Congress.

Perhaps to escape a virtual army of petition-bearing delegates, Congress finally acted to provide the area with a legal government. In the spring of 1860, proposals to organize a territorial government ran afoul of sectional conflict over slavery, positions pro and con on the issue of popular sovereignty, and rivalries over the location of a transcontinental railroad. In February 1861, however, the secession of Texas with the rest of the Deep South brought the threat of rebellion within two hundred and fifty miles of Denver. As well as needing to hold the Rocky Mountain settlers for the Union, Republicans wanted to demonstrate the peaceful intentions of the North. The consequence was the quick passage of acts that established governments for Dakota, Nevada, and Colorado without reference to slavery. Four days before his term ended, President James Buchanan signed the law giving Colorado its recognized place as a territory of the United States.

Creation of a territory coincided with the end of Colorado's first era of Anglo-American settlement. The year 1860 had been one of heavy and hopeful migration. More than five thousand immigrants crowded through Denver in a single week, and the Platte River route again "contained for a full month but a single train, which extended from the mountains to the Missouri River."[19] News of new diggings scattered across the state had caused the population to congregate first in one area and then in another. In 1861, however, the industry began to settle down. The threat of the Civil War, the need for capital to invest in quartz mining, and the news that the best mining districts were already overcrowded dampened enthusiasm for a third year's gold rush. The rich placers of Clear Creek and Boulder counties were already exhausted, although most of the miners remaining in Gilpin County or across the Divide still found it possible to make $3 to $5 per day. The lode miners of Gilpin County supplied perhaps 40 percent of Colorado's total production. Miners used water and steam to operate more than a hundred stamp mills and drove shafts by the hundreds into the hillsides. To reach the working levels of the Bobtail Mine, 260 feet below the surface, visitors had to clamber down long ladders connecting wooden platforms and swing down a rope for the last 10 feet. In all, the mines of Colorado yielded over $3 million annually from 1860 through 1864.

With the stabilization of mining, it was appropriate that formal government should materialize to aid the transition from frontier to organized community. Much of the work the territorial legislature performed in its sixty-day term in the autumn of 1861 repeated that of the provisional assembly in 1859. It laid out seventeen counties, bestowed a charter on Denver, organized courts, and adopted a legal code copied in large part from that of Illinois. In the interests of continuity and unhindered growth, it also validated the actions of the improvised local governments. The findings of the Denver people's courts were ratified except when they contradicted new statutes. The new city charter specifically recognized the acts of the more recent People's Government of the City of Denver, which had operated since October 1860. Rights of occupancy and possession of land as determined by local custom were validated, and the records of claim clubs and mining districts were ordered to be deposited with county clerks. Looking toward the expected sophisticated economy of the future, the same assembly incorporated several private water companies, ordered preparation of an official map, petitioned for a branch mint and assay office, and took the first steps to establish a university.

Another pressing necessity for the new government was the defense of Colorado Territory against Confederate sympathizers and the Confederate army. The newly appointed territorial governor, William Gilpin, raised Union volunteers and issued $375,000 in drafts on the federal treasury to pay the bills. The national government refused to honor the drafts and thereby undercut Gilpin's short political career, but the First Regiment of Colorado Infantry, commanded by John Slough, soon proved its worth. In the early winter of 1862, it marched to New Mexico where it joined other forces at Fort Union. Facing the Union troops was a small army of Texans under Henry H. Sibley, who had taken Santa Fe and Albuquerque and who contemplated striking first at Fort Union and then at the Colorado gold fields. At Glorieta Pass the Union army routed the Confederates in late March and helped to hold the entire Southwest for the federal cause. John Chivington, an ambitious Methodist minister turned major of volunteers, played a key role when he took his troops over steep cliffs to capture the Confederate supply wagons and force their retreat.

Legitimate government meant a stable, legal environment for speculative business proprietors as well as a stable field of operation for ambitious politicians. The two candidates for the position of territorial delegate in August 1861 were both experienced politicians. The "Union" party man, Hiram P. Bennet, had served as speaker of the house in the Nebraska Territory. The People's party candidate, Beverly D. Williams, had been Jefferson Territory's lobbyist in Washington. Bennet's eventual victory rested on a shrewd alliance with *Rocky Mountain News* editor William Byers and on efforts to label Williams a secessionist. The winning margin of 2 to 1 was a rough measure of the balance between settlers from the North and those from the border states and the South. At the same time, as Howard Lamar has noted, "the first and second Colorado assemblies . . . seemed much more professional than most frontier lawmakers."[20] Most of the territory's settlers were deeply familiar with politics, for campaigning was the great public spectacle and popular entertainment of antebellum America. Jerome Chaffee and George M. Chilcott parlayed their election to the first legislature into political careers that carried them to the U.S. Senate. Other members of the first assembly were versatile frontier entrepreneurs with interests in mining, banking, land speculation, ranching, and railroads. That the success of business enterprise was, by midcentury, inextricably linked to government subsidies, contracts, regulation, and law enforcement seemed proof that public service and private duty — politics and business — were one and the same.

Territorial government also meant opportunities for carpetbaggers. The term was usually applied to those outsiders who seized political control in the South after 1865 and worked to further their own interests. It could just as easily be used for the federal appointees who served the West as territorial judges, secretaries, and governors. Most were people without previous residence in the territory whose appointments came as a political reward and whose ambitions centered on their bank accounts. In the West as a whole, the typical territorial governors spent most of their time selling railroad stock for eastern capitalists and tending mining interests or speculating in land; they usually resigned before their terms were out to pursue their own businesses. Colorado's first two governors, although more conscientious than many, showed strong traces of this pattern. William Gilpin, Lincoln's first appointee, arrived in Denver with a decade of experience in Missouri town booming. Along with a sincere desire to promote the "progress, prosperity, and power" of the new settlements, his eye was open from the start for promising land deals. John Evans of Chicago, who replaced Gilpin in 1862, was adept not only at real estate but also at railroad promotion. Already a founder of a segment of the Pennsylvania Railroad system, he arrived in Denver as a member of the circle of entrepreneurs active in organizing the Union Pacific.

What these entrepreneurs hoped to build, of course, was a society in which legal stability furthered economic growth. A population that could buy goods in quantity, ship raw materials by the trainload, build, invest, and consume was the best guarantee of individual prosperity. To a large extent, it seemed they had what they wanted by the mid-1860s. The proprietors of the two plats of Denver and Auraria had sealed their consolidation by exchanging stock in April 1860. The town government incorporated in November 1861 listed enough officials for any one town — a mayor and six aldermen, a police magistrate, city marshall, clerk, surveyor, treasurer, and street commissioner. As early as 1865, Denverites had developed a clear distinction between the ice cream socials and balls that entertained the middle and upper classes and the gambling and drinking of the lower classes. Sophistication was promoted by three newspapers, a Methodist seminary, social clubs, and the frequent visits of distinguished literary figures, artists, and public figures.

The city also began to "assume metropolitan airs" in its physical appearance.[21] Distinct commercial and residential sections emerged, with a central business district around Blake, Larimer, Market, and Fifteenth Streets and a stylish residential area southeast from Fourteenth and Arapahoe, where John Evans's house set the pattern for merchants, promoters, and land speculators. After a serious fire in April 1863, the city rebuilt in an

Black Hawk in 1864, looking up Gregory Gulch toward Central City.

improved style. In the business area two-story and three-story brick structures replaced wooden frame houses after the municipality forbade wood construction downtown. Residential areas blossomed with two-story houses in Victorian styles. The completion of an irrigation ditch in 1865 made possible the planting of trees and lawns and helped the town escape its reputation as "Dustyopolis." The new effect delighted visitors, who found this "square, proud, prompt little place" an oasis of architectural quality in the dreary West.[22]

At Gregory Gulch the towns of Central City and Blackhawk quickly replaced the tents and wagons of the first prospectors. The organization of fraternal societies in 1860 and 1861 ushered in social refinements. Lodges of Masons, Odd Fellows, and Good Templars, public schools, churches, a literary society, and the *Miner's Register* were in existence by 1863, when visitor John Nicolay (on detached duty from his job as Abraham Lincoln's private secretary) saw two "passable" plays. A year later the establishment of two city governments completed the outlines of a typically American institutional life. When Samuel Bowles visited Gregory Gulch in 1865 he was able to write, "here these towns are, thriving, orderly, peaceable, busy, supporting two of them each its daily papers, with churches and schools, and all the best materials of government and society that the East can boast of." Surviving records show that the miners were law-abiding in the extreme. The wearing of guns was a rarity by 1863, and, in the one recorded shoot-out, men standing forty feet apart emptied their revolvers without hitting each other. Only sixteen men were killed in shootings and brawls in the decade from 1862 to 1872, and only two murderers were convicted and hanged. The local judge who complained that "biz in the Police Court is dull" summed up what everyone knew about the entire territory by mid-decade: that it was in large part a settled American community.[23]

"Making governments and building towns are the natural employments of the migratory Yankee," Albert Richardson wrote after his first visit to the Pikes Peak mines. Superficially, his comment could be taken as an unkind dig at the speculation rife on the Colorado frontier. It was more than sarcasm, however. In the process of speculating on the future of the Colorado mines, the settlers found it necessary to reproduce the foundations of the Anglo-American business civilization. Historian Earl Pomeroy has observed that "conservatism" was the central impulse on the western frontier — the conservative re-creation of the cultural milieu of institutions and customs left behind. If the purpose of the migration was, first, to make money, it was also to reconstitute Wisconsin or Ohio in the wilderness. In the process those who would have struggled for prosperity in the East could more easily find room at the top of the social hierarchy. One Fifty-niner summed up the speed of the transition that was both necessary and desired and indicated what Colorado's development meant to its participants. "I run all over town," he wrote in June 1859, "saw more gamblers and gambling than I ever saw before, and went to bed wondering what the Anglo-American race were approaching, and concluded that a universal triumph and conquest was its destiny."[24]

# CHAPTER 5

# THE ERA OF THE BOOSTER, 1863–1876

Speculation was fundamental to Colorado's growth in its first five years of Anglo-American settlement. Boosterism — that uniquely American combination of faith in the future and vociferous promotion — was the key to the next decade. Success on the Colorado frontier came to those with visionary minds. A fluid society offered less reward for the specialist than for the entrepreneur who could edit a newspaper one month, organize a bank the next, and preach a sermon or run for Congress before the year was out. Traits common among successful businesspeople, journalists, and politicians of the day were self-confidence and a willingness to promote the territory. The builders of the new Colorado were those who could not only anticipate new growth but who could also persuade and recruit others to share their expectations and risks.

The frontier entrepreneurs could afford to neglect their individual enterprises to work instead as community builders and leaders, for every settler expected to benefit from regional development. Immigration and investment meant customers for the merchant, lawsuits for the attorney, real estate transactions for the land speculator, and hungry stomachs for the farmer to fill. As residents realized from one end of the Mississippi basin to the other, it was the "self-imposed labors . . . of earnest-souled, iron-willed, active-minded citizens" that accounted for much of the section's growth. Promotion of one's town was a civic duty so deeply felt that some frontier businesspeople identified themselves and their futures with their new home. William Larimer merely articulated the attitude of dozens of early Colorado leaders when he wrote, "I am Denver City."[1]

Public-minded Coloradans faced all they could handle in the mid-1860s. Simple enthusiasm had been enough to bring settlers and investors flocking in during the first years of the gold rush.

The same excitement, however, created problems that quickly multiplied into a severe economic depression. Between 1860 and 1866 the territory's population dropped from 34,277 to 27,931. Another 50,000 or 60,000 may have tried their luck in the territory and abandoned it as hopeless, according to Coloradan Frank Fossett. Visitors to Denver in the second half of the decade described the city as being little more than a quiet village, with listless business, few new buildings under construction, and many old ones advertised "To Let." Denver's population dropped to 3,000 after the Civil War — down by a third from its flush years — and an official of the Union Pacific Railroad remarked that the town was too dead to bury. Here, too, the total figures masked a "vacillating" population, as pioneer historian Junius Wharton complained in 1866.[2] Only 10 percent of the 4,759 persons counted in the town by the 1870 census had lived there as long as five years; the remainder were newcomers who had replaced disappointed earlier residents.

Colorado's obvious problem was declining production from its mines. On a map published in 1867, Ovando Hollister marked a "Developed Gold and Silver Region" that curved from Lake County through the towns of Fairplay and Tarryall to Clear Creek, Gilpin, and Boulder counties. In fact, the tide of population receded as miners abandoned played-out sites deep in the mountains. By mid-decade only a quarter of the territory's stamp mills were still pulverizing ore. The resulting dust was washed on copper plates coated with mercury to collect the gold. The value of gold taken from Colorado hillsides and ravines dropped by almost half in just four years — from $3.3 million in 1864 to $1.7 million in 1867. Most of it came from Gilpin County, the only area in which large-scale mining continued after 1865. Travelers were already fascinated by sights of the first ghost towns deep in the mountains — places like Montgomery or Buckskin Joe — where signboards and sardine tins cluttered the empty streets, aspens grew in abandoned chimneys, and assay apparatus gathered dust in back rooms. Even within the "Little Kingdom of Gilpin" available ores had become difficult to process. Below the depth of about one hundred feet, miners ran out of weathered and oxidized ores, whose gold content could be easily recovered by amalgamation with mercury. The deeper ores were leaner and held their metal locked chemically with sulfides. Use of known processes on the "refractory" or "rebellious" ores could recover, at most, only 40 to 50 percent of the gold content. Frequently, however, as much as 80 or 90 percent of the metal was left in the tailings.

Mismanagement exacerbated the technical difficulties. In October 1863, the promoters of the Ophir Gold Mining Company proved that it was easier to "work" their eastern investors than the western lodes. Local miners were quick to exploit the interest aroused by five years of gold rushes and by the rising premium on gold during the Civil War. They made Colorado mining properties one of the hottest speculations in the East. The sale of established claims, the opening of a mining stock exchange in New York, the overcapitalization and watering of stock, the floating of companies that owned lodes already played out or mines flooded with groundwater — these were the stages of the speculation, as legitimate investors and Wall Street manipulators jumped to join in the mining frontier they had heard so much about. In less than a year the excitement was responsible for the creation of two hundred new corporations, most of whose securities rose like balloons filled with the hot air of their promoters.

Few of the new owners actually knew how to get gold out of Gilpin County's ground. Often a company's claims were too small or scattered to be worked efficiently at any depth below the surface. Many firms sent managers from the East who lacked practical experience and who only repeated each others' mistakes, spending their working capital on everything but digging out the ore. Most were willing to gamble on any new technique that held the slightest promise of extracting a higher percentage of gold. Interested visitors to Gilpin County could see demonstrations of half a dozen new methods guaranteed to "draw gold from a Rocky Mountain turnip."[3] One disgruntled observer commented that everything from superheated steam to tobacco juice was tried on the rock. Many processes required elaborate buildings and machinery that could only be paid for if tests of the process proved successful. Money not wasted on the "process mania" went for managers' salaries and for assistants. Local residents began to view the speculative enthusiasm as making the territory a dumping ground for incompetents such as the cashiered Civil War general Fitz-John Porter, who spent his days galloping up and down Gregory Gulch with his quasi-military staff and reviewing his battalions of workers and miners.

Even when a company raised ore, it was seldom rich enough to pay dividends on the watered stock. Companies went bankrupt or suspended operations, and the market for Colorado mines collapsed in the spring of 1864, leaving investors with empty pockets and the conviction that mining in Colorado was a fraud. In Gilpin County a visitor in 1866 found that "the deserted mills, the idle wheels, the empty shafts and drifts for miles along this and the adjoining ravines — the general decrease of population everywhere in the mountains — indicate a period of doubt and transition." Other travelers in the later 1860s noted the desolate appearance of the towns of Central City and Black Hawk, with rusting machinery, unused mills, and abandoned shafts as "thick as anthills or prairie-dog holes." Clear Creek County looked the same: "everywhere evidence of great expectations and slight results." The blame, wrote mining specialist Rossiter Raymond, lay equally with "the scientific men without practice and the practical men without science, the honest men without capacity and the smart men without honesty."[4]

Along with the depression in the mines, Coloradans in the early 1860s had to cope with the increasing isolation of their territory. Demas Barnes described the discomforts of stage travel: "A through-ticket and fifteen inches of seat, with a fat man on one side, a poor widow on the other, a baby on your lap, a band box over your head . . . makes the picture, as well as your sleeping place, for the trip."[5] Freight wagons drawn by oxen took at least forty days to make the trip from the Missouri River. Even under ideal conditions, the expense of transporting merchandise, food, building materials, and machinery exhausted much of the capital available for land development. The summer of 1863 brought a drought that burned up the grass on the plains; that winter severe storms blocked travel. The following spring torrential rains drowned the fords and turned the roads into impassable muck.

In the first years of gold mining, the Native Americans of the plains had let travelers cross Kansas and Colorado unhindered. In the spring of 1864, however, at the same time investors were showing the first signs of caution about mining stocks, bands from the Cheyenne and Arapaho tribes raided isolated ranches, ran off horses, and clashed with detachments of cavalry who were itching for action after a long winter of boredom in cold, damp barracks. The murder and mutilation of the Hungate family in June on their ranch only thirty miles from Denver turned worry into panic. In August members of the tribes scoured the plains for stray stock and wagon trains and killed several dozen settlers in Colorado, Kansas, and Nebraska. The overland stage suspended service. Mail arrived by way of San Francisco. George Bent, son of William Bent and Owl Woman of the Cheyennes, described the summer as the Native Americans saw it: "War parties were setting out every day, and other parties coming in loaded with plunder and driving captured herds of horses and mules. As I rode past each village I saw war dances going on in each one, and every lodge was full of plunder taken from captured freight wagons and emigrant trains."[6]

The Native Americans, of course, were reacting to the danger the continuing immigration posed to their lands and their way of life. In the 1851 Treaty of Fort Laramie, the United States had negotiated a general settlement with the Cheyenne, Arapaho, Sioux, Shoshone, and Crow tribes. The Native Americans called the three-week meeting of ten thousand tribespeople "the Big Issue" because of the clothing, calico, flour, sugar, and coffee the government disbursed. More important, the treaty confirmed the Southern Cheyennes and Arapahos in joint control of a vast territory lying between the trails to Oregon and Santa Fe. Embracing most of Great Plains Colorado, the southeastern corner of Wyoming, and parts of Nebraska and Kansas, it gave them the unbroken buffalo range between the North Platte and the Arkansas that they had used for two generations.

Ten years later, in the Treaty of Fort Wise, the same tribes surrendered the bulk of their land under pressure from the U.S. government and from white settlers who had appropriated the heart of their hunting ground near the base of the mountains. Most of the leaders of the Arapahos and the peace chiefs of the Cheyennes, led by White Antelope and Black Kettle, supported the new agreement. Many of the younger members of the Cheyennes and of the warrior societies claimed they had never agreed to the giveaway and that the fraction of land north of the Arkansas retained by the tribes did not contain enough game to support their people. The record of the next two years shows occasional episodes of stealing livestock from farms and ranches near the mountains and sporadic negotiations, as Governor John Evans tried to reaffirm and extend the 1861 treaty to make all the Cheyennes and Arapahos dependent on government handouts.

The frustration of Anglo settlers matched that of the Cheyennes. From the point of view of the new Coloradans, the Native Americans of the plains were a hindrance to settlement. Under the best of circumstances there would have been little place for them in the world foreseen by the Anglo-Americans. In the 1860s Native American presence interfered with the confirmation of land titles and interdicted trade. Booster papers such as the *Rocky Mountain News* called for a "few months of active extermination against the red devils." By August 1864 Governor Evans had used the issue of the Anglos' mounting fear to obtain Washington's permission to recruit the Third Regiment of Colorado Volunteer Cavalry for one-hundred-day terms. Command went to Colonel John Chivington, a Methodist preacher and hero of the battle at Glorieta Pass. As a war hero and an active member of the Denver wing of the Republican party, Chivington made no secret of his political ambitions. A few months before his appointment he had proclaimed that "the Cheyenne will have to be soundly whipped before they will be quiet. If any of them are caught in your vicinity kill them, as that is the only way."[7]

Members of the Third Regiment were nearly unanimous in their feelings about the Native Americans. When miners and teamsters were thrown out of work by raids or merchants were unable to replenish their shelves, they blamed the Cheyennes as being "an obstacle to civilization." In the viewpoint of Governor Evans and Colonel Chivington and his troops, it was too late to worry about keeping the peace or enforcing a treaty. The only alternative was extermination. "I am fully satisfied that to kill them is the only way to have peace and quiet," said the colonel.[8] His opportunity came on November 29, 1864, just a few days before the short terms of enlistment of his troops expired. In a shallow valley along the dry bend of Sand Creek in southeastern Colorado was an encampment of Cheyennes and Arapahos led by Left Hand, White Antelope, and Black Kettle. According to later testimony, they believed they were under the protection of U.S. authorities at nearby Fort Lyon. In fact, Governor Evans had issued a series of contradictory orders and instructions to the Native Americans during the summer. Chivington's troops opened fire at dawn from the low ridges on both sides of the stream. George Bent was with the Native Americans and later reported, "I looked toward the chief's lodge and saw that Black Kettle had a large American flag tied to the end of a long lodgepole and was standing in front of his lodge, holding the pole, with the flag fluttering in the grey light of the winter dawn." When the shooting ended around noon, ten of the volunteers were dead. So were an uncounted number of Native Americans, but certainly more than one hundred. Most of the Native American women had been

John Chivington.

raped and mutilated, the children shot for the sport. The "bloody Thirdsters" collected scalps that were later displayed in a Denver theater and draped around the mirrors in saloons.

> White Antelope, when he saw the soldiers shooting into the lodges, made up his mind not to live any longer. He had been telling the Cheyennes for months that the whites were good people and that peace was going to be made. . . . Now he saw the soldiers shooting the people, and he did not wish to live any longer. He stood in front of his lodge with his arms folded across his breast, singing the deathsong: "Nothing lives long, only the earth and the mountains."[9]

Governor Evans and most of the military personnel in Colorado had been convinced for a year or more that full-scale war was the only remedy to end the drain of continual raiding and harassment by the Native Americans. At Sand Creek they tapped the frustration of Colorado settlers to precipitate the conflict with public support. After the massacre other Cheyennes came to Sand Creek and reported what they saw there. The survivors joined with a thousand Arapahos, Cheyennes, and Sioux in two attacks on the freighting station in Julesberg in early 1865, killing forty whites and again blockading Denver. William Bent, still close to the Cheyennes through his marriage and the great trading days of the 1830s and 1840s, helped to negotiate a new treaty at the end of 1865, but sporadic warfare continued into 1867, when the two tribes agreed to move to Oklahoma under the terms of the Treaty of Medicine Lodge.

Even with the new treaty, Colorado endured two more summers of raids and rumors before the last battle was fought between Anglo-Americans and Native Americans on the Colorado plains. In 1868 fifty scouts led by Major George A. Forsyth endured a nine-day siege by Northern Cheyennes and Sioux at Beecher Island in the Arikaree Fork of the Republican River in northeastern Colorado. Black Kettle lived through Sand Creek to fall four years later when Colonel George A. Custer mounted a dawn attack on his camp along the Washita River in Oklahoma. The last battle on the Colorado plains was July 11, 1869, at Summit Springs (near Atwood) where U.S. forces defeated Southern Cheyenne Dog-Soldiers who had left their reservation in Kansas.

Behind the tragedy of the Cheyennes and Arapahos lay the blindness of Colorado's new masters. The decade of war was the result not merely of competition for needed land but also of the friction between two dissimilar cultures. The Treaty of Fort Wise had envisioned a reservation on which the Native Americans would learn American farming; the framers of the treaty did not stop to consider whether a nation of hunters and warriors would voluntarily change their ways. Nor did more than a handful of Americans understand the structure of Cheyenne and Arapaho society. The older chiefs of the Cheyennes, for example, could set policy, but only the members of the warrior societies could carry out the decisions. As long as U.S. soldiers continued their provocations in the 1860s, it was impossible for the peace chiefs to persuade many of the younger tribespeople to test the possibilities

Ute encampment on the plains near Denver. In the 1860s and 1870s, bands of Utes frequently visited for trade.

of accommodation. In turn, their refusal to cooperate with Anglo-American plans and projects threatened the prosperity of the new community. Captain Silas Soule, who testified to the atrocities at Sand Creek before an investigating commission, was shot to death on the streets of Denver. Other Denverites screamed at visiting senators holding hearings on the Native American problem a single phrase: "Exterminate them! Exterminate them!"

To realize the potential of their territory, Coloradans had to reverse its reputation. For a decade in their annual messages every governor stressed the need for the capital that had been frightened off by the collapse of mining stocks and for immigrants who had been turned away by magazine articles published during the Native American crisis with engraved prints of mutilated bodies sprouting war arrows. In a nation whose every region was hungry to join in the post-Civil War boom, the territory had to battle for its share of scarce inputs of capital and labor by broadcasting to the public at large its peculiar virtues and advantages — "its present and prospective capacities" for growth. The community boosters were not merely salespeople for a particular investment; they spoke for the entire commonwealth. Half of the argument was an account of growth accomplished. Figures on everything from population to tax assessments to public schools proved that civilization had indeed vanquished savagery on the slopes of the Rockies. The other half was a detailed and enthusiastic evaluation of waiting resources not already developed by Colorado's energetic and broad-gauged citizens.

The daily responsibility for expounding the idea of local development lay most heavily on newspaper editors, who constituted the infantry among the legions of Colorado boosters. Almost every journal in the 1860s declared its intention to advertise the wealth and prosperity of the Rocky Mountain mines. The Central City *Miner's Register*, the *Cañon City Times*, the *Colorado Chieftain* of Pueblo, and the *Colorado Miner* of Georgetown acted as local boards of trade. Their editors opened their columns to business news, compiled statistics, solicited correspondence and articles on local industry, and urged residents to mail copies back East. Each editor viewed his or her paper as a "mouthpiece and engine of future progress" for his or her town and took credit for the notice and notoriety it gained.[10]

Publicity for the territory came also from a number of citizens who compiled city directories, gazetteers, and even a *History of the City of Denver* before the town was ten years old. Along with lists of residents and businesses and presumably reliable descriptions of the local scene, they offered information on how to travel to Colorado and provided bright forecasts of success for the intelligent immigrant. A few titles indicate the scope of the publications: *Denver City and Auraria: The Commercial Emporium of the Pikes Peak Gold Region* spoke for particular interests, whereas *The Rocky Mountain Gold Regions: Containing Sketches of Its History, Geography, Botany, Geology, Mineralogy and Gold Mines* aimed for comprehensive coverage. The best of the lot for in-depth analysis was Ovando Hollister's *The Mines of Colorado*. This was the work of a Central City editor who believed a new era was soon to dawn in Colorado and that to exaggerate regarding the subject of mineral resources was almost impossible.

Europeans as well as Americans were interested in Colorado as a home for themselves or their money. In 1867 the territory appointed a commissioner to represent its interests at the Paris Exposition and dispatched a sampling of its richest ores. A year later, Robert O. Olds of Georgetown established the British and Colorado Mining Bureau to encourage British investment in

Colorado refining works and to sell Colorado mines. At its headquarters directly behind the Bank of England, visitors could inspect the more than five hundred samples of ore; browse through Colorado newspapers, maps, and reports; or obtain one of the sixteen thousand copies of Olds's pamphlet entitled "Colorado: United States, America." The official Colorado Territorial Board of Immigration, established at the suggestion of Governor Edward McCook in 1871, took an even broader view of its duties. After William Byers of the *Rocky Mountain News* assumed leadership in 1872, the board printed even more pamphlets (seventy-seven thousand altogether); appointed immigration agents in England, Germany, and throughout the United States; and secured reduced railway fares for four thousand settlers.

Within Colorado, the propaganda served a second function. Constant discussion of the territory's future helped the residents define their own ideas about its growth, and Colorado writers moved toward consensus on the primacy of certain accomplishments and possibilities even while addressing outsiders. Debate over goals, and means for reaching them, acted as a journalistic blast furnace in which viable projects were separated from dross and fused into a coherent strategy for economic development. At the same time, popular economic thought built upon an ideology that proclaimed the importance of western growth in the scheme of world history. To many Americans in the nineteenth century, the Great West from the Mississippi Valley to the Pacific promised affirmation of the success of the national experiment in democracy. The center of wealth, power, and national excellence seemed to be shifting from the tradition-fogged coast to the great central valley where the nation stood on "the eve of a great, permanent and propitious social advancement." With nothing to hinder the inventive and moral energies of its people, the new West would be the most American part of America. Its mines and fields would pour forth a golden harvest, and its prosperity would guarantee the political independence of its people. Progress, both spiritual and material, would usher in "the last, the greatest, the most glorious, wealthy and powerful empire in the world."[11]

William Gilpin, among all of the writers who enunciated this grand theme, carried out the most systematic analysis and defined in greatest detail Colorado's role in the unfolding pattern. Gilpin was already an advocate of the territory's future when appointed its first governor in 1861. He had traveled with Fremont in 1843 and visited the Colorado plains on his return trip, joined in Kearny's conquest of New Mexico as a major of volunteers, and toured the southern Rockies on expeditions against the Navajos. By the time of his return to Missouri in 1848, he had fallen in love with the San Luis Valley. In 1858 and 1859 Gilpin found a receptive audience among his neighbors in Kansas City for articles and speeches about the new gold discoveries. A year later he revised and published these and earlier writings as *The Central Gold Region: The Grain, Pastoral and Gold Region of North America.*

Already widely recognized as a specialist on the American West, Gilpin easily resumed his career as writer and promoter at the end of his one-year term as governor. In 1863 he scraped together $41,000 to purchase a five-sixths interest in the Beaubien Grant, the old Mexican landholding that spread over a million acres in the San Luis basin. Profits from the enormous speculation depended on resale to settlers or to capitalists with adequate funds for development. It was an advertising job uniquely suited to Gilpin's talents. Before he completed his major deal in the early 1870s (selling half the property to a Dutch syndicate through the offices of the English speculator William Blackmore), Gilpin sponsored geological reports on the tract, printed innumerable articles, addressed the British Association for the Advancement of Science, and made the major contribution to two or three pamphlets and a book signed by Blackmore. In a different setting and culture his energy might have made him another Lawrence of Arabia; in the United States he became a booster.

Gilpin's writing about Colorado drew on a multilayered theory of western growth. The first premise was a favorable evaluation of his adopted territory. He viewed the mountains as natural vaults of precious metals and the great parks lying between as lands that lacked no "element of sublimity." He pictured the new Vale of Kashmir in the San Luis Valley, where lands of "luxuriant fertility" shimmered beneath the high walls of the Sangre de Cristo Mountains. Blessed enough with its soil and air, Colorado multiplied its advantages from its position within North America. Europe, Asia, and South America, Gilpin proclaimed, were fragmented continents. Massive mountains rising in their centers cut populations into small maritime pockets and blocked invigorating commerce. Convexity, isolation, stagnation, and disharmony went together in the older world. Not so in North America, whose interior presented toward heaven "an expanded bowl, to receive and fuse into harmony whatsoever enters within its rim."[12]

Within this "amphitheatre of the world" Colorado occupied a position "pre-eminently cosmopolitan." The global "axis of intensity" snaked its way around the Northern Hemisphere. In this belt of temperate climate had risen the great world civilizations from East to West — China, India, Persia, Greece, Rome, Spain, Britain, and now the republican empire of North America. Echoing the old dreams of Thomas Jefferson and Senator Thomas Hart Benton of Missouri, Gilpin foresaw that trade in the coming age would flow from Europe to Asia across the United States. Located on the 40th parallel on the western edge of the great valley, Colorado was the point where the "vast arena of the Pacific" met the Atlantic world, the place where "the zodiac of nations closes its circle." With the help of the railroad, Denver and Colorado could be the crossroads of the world, "the focal point of impregnable power in the topographical configuration of the continent."[13]

Gilpin's vision and that of other boosters required practical measures for realization. As long as Colorado remained an outpost separated from the rest of the nation by six days of racking stage travel, grand strategies were no more than evening boasts and pastimes. From the first months of settlement most newcomers assumed that the slow-moving wagon trains that crept up the valleys of the Platte and Arkansas were but a temporary means of transportation. Even in the first winter, William Larimer told a local assembly that Denver City should demand a place on the route of the projected Pacific Railroad. The *Rocky Mountain News* took up the theme a year later, asserting that "the road must pass through the South Platte gold fields, and this, our consolidated city at the eastern foot of the Rocky Mountains, will be a point which cannot be dodged." Gilpin soon argued that Denver's location in "the trunk line of intense and intelligent energy" would make it a vital link in the continent-spanning cosmopolitan railroad of the future.[14]

The Union Pacific, in fact, had no plans to build through Denver and climb the highest point in the Rockies. Because the federal subsidy that made its construction possible was based on mileage completed, it headed directly for southern Wyoming, where reasonable grades made track-laying easier. An October snowstorm in 1866 ended Colorado's slight chance for the railroad when it caught chief engineer Grenville Dodge in the

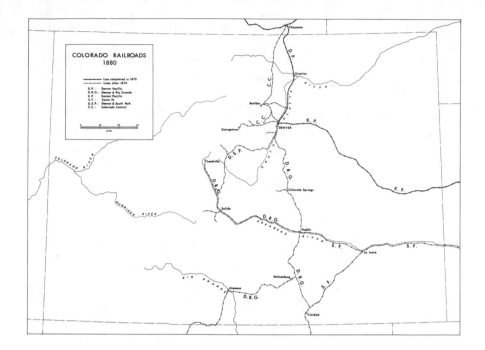

mountains while inspecting Berthoud Pass and barely allowed him to escape with his life. The Union Pacific's decision, announced later that year, threatened to make Cheyenne the major supply center for the central Rockies and left the future of the depressed territory in the hands of its own squabbling businesspeople. W.A.H. Loveland and E. L. Berthoud of Golden and Henry M. Teller of Central City promoted the Colorado Central Railroad as the answer to the territory's problems, proposing to build from Golden to Cheyenne to link up with the Union Pacific. The company signed an agreement for joint construction with the Union Pacific in 1867 and began grading early in January 1868. After rejecting an opportunity to participate in financing the Colorado Central, Denver businesspeople organized their own railroad — the Denver Pacific — with the same intention of building north to tap business on the Union Pacific. With $800,000 in its treasury from local stock subscriptions and Arapahoe County bonds voted as a subsidy, the Denver Pacific, too, reached an agreement for joint construction and integration with the Union Pacific system.

The competition between the two rail companies was part of a larger rivalry between two of Colorado's biggest towns. Neither city was willing to scale down ambitions fixed during the peak of the gold rush, and each fought fiercely for the limited openings for growth available in the territory in the late 1860s. Denver represented itself as the spokesperson for the entire region; Golden countered with claims to stand with the mountain settlements against the selfishness and exclusiveness of its plains opponent.

The urban rivalry extended from commerce to politics. The dominant Republican party was split into rival cliques known as the Golden Crowd and the Denver Crowd. The former group centered about Loveland and Teller, along with Alexander C. Hunt and territorial Chief Justice Moses Hallett; the latter around Denver banker Jerome Chaffee, John Evans, John Chivington, and George Chilcott. Because the Democrats were in the minority during Colorado's early years, the important political contests in the 1860s were really fights within the Republican party over the spoils of potential office. Which — the Denver Crowd or the Golden Crowd — would name the first U.S. senators? The Golden group successfully battled statehood movements during the mid-1860s in part to keep their rivals out of high office. Would Denver investors aid the Colorado Central in the interests of territorial growth? Only if the Central moved its shops and headquarters to the city on the South Platte. Was Denver or Golden to enjoy increased business from being the territorial capital? Golden held the honor from 1864 to 1867 before losing to its rival.

With the leading directors of the two local railroads as political enemies, it is not surprising that neither was willing to yield to the other. When the Union Pacific backed off from its promise of aid to the Denver Pacific with the line only partly graded, former Governor Evans took on the job of financing and finishing the road for the good of his city in 1869. He discharged his responsibility by negotiating a deal with the Kansas Pacific, formerly the Union Pacific Eastern Division but now an independent railroad building west from Kansas City to Denver. The Kansas Pacific received a half interest and a traffic-sharing agreement; Evans received the right to manage the line for five years and the funds to finish it. The 106-mile Denver Pacific opened between Denver and Cheyenne in June 1870. In August the Kansas Pacific also reached Denver, giving the city a choice of outlets. A month later the slower-moving Colorado Central extended a 15-mile branch to the Denver Pacific and two years later penetrated the mountains as far as Black Hawk. Not until

1877 did the Colorado Central connect with the Union Pacific line by way of Boulder, Longmont, and Fort Collins. Two years later the Union Pacific emerged from a contentious legal battle with W.A.H. Loveland and other Golden investors with full control of the Colorado Central.

The effects of Colorado's new railroad connections appeared spectacular to most contemporaries. New towns sprang up along the lines. At the age of three weeks, the town of Evans, the halfway point between Cheyenne and Denver, consisted of forty or fifty houses of raw boards and half-shingled roofs. "The earth was cut up in every direction by the ruts of wagon wheels, and piles of newly sawn lumber lay about. In the middle of all snorted the locomotive." The first railroads also marked "the proudest year in the whole history of Denver," confirming its commercial supremacy and giving it a fresh start in its race to greatness.[15] Both population and mercantile business tripled in three or four years as the city shed its pioneer brashness for urban sophistication.

Much of the impact of railroads came from savings on freight bills, which, for the entire territory, may have totaled as much as $3.5 million annually in the mid-1860s. As early as 1867 the approach of the Union Pacific had lowered costs of labor and supplies by 30 to 50 percent from 1864 levels. At the end of the decade, conditions were ripe for a new boom. The abandonment of Gregory Gulch by eastern corporations had opened the way for more practical experimentation. Local miners aided by skilled immigrants from Cornwall in Britain consolidated inefficient claims by lease and purchase and used scrapped machinery for new stamp mills suited to native ores. Refractory ores received a longer and finer crushing and a longer exposure to mercury. The new mills could process only half the tonnage of older establishments and still lost from one-third to two-thirds of the potential gold, but Gilpin County citizens swore the mills were the only possible expedient. James Lyon made the first experiment with smelting in 1865, shipping ore to be processed in New York, but his prototype smelter in Black Hawk was too small and too poorly conceived to pay. Professor Nathaniel Hill of Brown University devoted the years 1865, 1866, and 1867 to studying the possibilities of smelting, traveling from New England to Colorado to Germany and Wales and back again, consulting European experts and shipping seventy tons of mineral from the Bobtail Lode across the Atlantic to Swansea for experimental processing. With funds from New England capitalists, he put the Boston and

Colorado smelter into operation at Black Hawk in 1868. It was a technical success from the start, but its operating costs were so high at first that it processed only the richest ore and left the rest to stamp mills.

The process Hill used took advantage of the copper and iron sulfides that made the deeper ores yield so poorly to stamp milling and amalgamation. First, the new ores or old mill tailings were roasted to drive off most of the sulfur in great noxious clouds of sulfur dioxide that clogged the narrow valley. Then the mineral was smelted in a reverberatory furnace, whose curvature distributed and focused heat to 1400° centigrade. Gold, silver, and copper sank to the bottom along with iron and copper sulfides, while the slag floated on the surface. The slag was skimmed and discarded; the rich copper "matte" was tapped, cooled, and shipped to Swansea for additional refining into its constituent metals. From the start, Hill's operation depended on superintendents with European expertise — first Herman Beeger from the Royal Saxon Bergakademie at Freiberg, then Cornish engineer Richard Pearce from the Royal School of Mines. As would be true ten years later at Leadville, it was Colorado prospectors, eastern investors, and European technologists in combination who brought prosperity to the Rockies.

The arrival of the first locomotives in Denver in 1870 and in Black Hawk two years later changed the terms of trade in the mining business. The value of precious metals remained the same, but the cost of every factor in their production went down. The expense of machinery plunged, the prevailing wage rates dropped with the price of food and clothing, and the cost of fuels fell sharply. Both mills and smelters could now operate more cheaply, allowing profits from poorer ores. At the same time, the Black Hawk branch of the Colorado Central brought the extremely rich silver lodes of the Georgetown area within twenty miles of a railhead, setting off a new boom in Clear Creek County, where only two years before travelers had seen abandoned shafts and rusting hopes. For the first time, local mills could be run economically and high-grade ores shipped out for special processing. Hill's smelter was a prime beneficiary of the expanded market and added its own refinery in 1873. From 1870 to 1875 the Gilpin mines produced close to $1.5 million in gold each year, and the annual product of silver along the other branch of Clear Creek climbed from $.5 million to $2.0 million. Together these two counties served by the Denver Pacific and Colorado Central railroads yielded nearly two-thirds of Colorado's mineral wealth prior to 1875.

Boosterism, promotion, and entrepreneurship rescued Colorado from economic disaster by 1870. Even so, the transformation was far from complete. The vast territory still held only a small pocket of Anglo-American settlement. A semicircle radiating sixty or seventy-five miles westward from Denver held about three-fifths of the total population. Its railroads were local lines with less than two hundred miles of track between them; its mines were far behind those of California or Nevada. Only 2,200 Coloradans worked in the mines, 12 percent of the territory's total employment. The final establishment of Colorado as the keystone of the Rocky Mountain region required the further effort of William Jackson Palmer, a man who combined all of the impulses vital to the development of the territory. The drive of John Evans, the talent for publicity of William Byers, and the vision of William Gilpin blended within this single remarkable figure who built a thousand-mile railroad — the Denver and Rio Grande — and opened a new route south and west of the Clear Creek nucleus.

Palmer's vision, like Gilpin's, came almost as a religious conversion from his experience in the plains and mountains. A cavalry general in the Civil War, Palmer came west in 1865 to work for the Union Pacific Eastern Division. During 1867 and 1868 he led the survey of a railroad route from Kansas across the southwest to California. His report spoke enthusiastically of the mild climate, the opportunity for agriculture, and the "vast, uninterrupted belt of uniformly superior pasturage."[16] Separated from the rest of the United States by distance and by a semiarid zone, the Rocky Mountain West could develop a semiautonomous economy, growing its own food, mining its own coal, building its own factories. To integrate its different parts into a self-sufficient unit, Palmer reasoned, the Rockies needed a regional rail system, a line running north and south where the mountains met the plains, with spurs up every valley and canyon. Palmer planned the Denver to Santa Fe route as the first segment, with possible further extension to Mexico City. That the projected line cut across the grain of the U.S. railroad system was no cause for worry. The transcontinental lines would detour north and south of the great Colorado mountains, leaving Palmer an inland empire with piedmont cities such as Denver and Pueblo as its hubs.

Palmer's railroad was as much a social vision as a business proposition. William Gilpin had told a hundred audiences that by settling the West, Americans would forward their mission "to stir the sleep of a hundred centuries — to teach old nations a new civilization . . . to shed a new and resplendent glory upon mankind — to unite the world in one social family." Palmer spoke of the chance to realize within the space of years the progress of centuries, to create new commonwealths, and to redeem a third of a continent from barrenness. "I thought how fine it would be to have a little railroad a few hundred miles in length," he wrote in 1870, "all under one's own control with one's friends, to have no jealousies and contests and differences, but be able to carry out harmoniously one's view about what ought and ought not to be done."[17]

In 1870, just after he guided the Kansas Pacific into Denver as the line's chief engineer, Palmer organized the Denver and Rio Grande Railroad. His intention was to occupy territory for his railroad in advance of settlement with an eye to future traffic rather than current dividends. Building south from Denver, he pushed the tracks to Colorado Springs at the end of 1871 and to Pueblo by June 1872. A national depression in 1873 forced a four-year delay before Palmer could find the money to continue construction to El Moro near Trinidad and to the foot of La Veta Pass. The delay cost the Rio Grande its monopoly in southern Colorado, for the Atchison, Topeka and Santa Fe also ran a line up the Arkansas River to Pueblo in 1876.

The next four years witnessed a complicated war between the two companies. With its greater resources and more profitable traffic, the Santa Fe had the capacity to challenge Palmer's railroad in its plans for both the Rockies and New Mexico. The first success went to the Santa Fe in February 1878. When its construction crews reached Raton Pass a day ahead of the Rio Grande engineers, it effectively blocked the easiest route south. Two months later the rival corporations fought to a standoff in the Royal Gorge of the Arkansas, the only feasible route from Pueblo toward the new boomtown of Leadville. Employees of each firm occupied opposite ends of the canyon while the dispute went through the courts; the Rio Grande crew went so far as to build two small forts to hold their claims. From October 1878 to June 1879, bondholders fearful of suspended interest payments forced Palmer to lease the Rio Grande trackage to the Santa Fe, but a decision by the U.S. Supreme Court, which gave Palmer priority in the gorge, furnished him the chance to recover control. Claiming violations in the terms of the lease, Palmer and his subordinates plotted an armed coup and seized control of the line on June 11, ousting Santa Fe employees from the property at gunpoint in a well-planned, coordinated maneuver. The final peace treaty came in 1880, when the two companies partitioned the Southwest much as European diplomats parceling out colonies. To the Rio Grande went the territory north of the 36th parallel and west of its present tracks, to the Santa Fe the region east and south. The decision turned the Rio Grande into a pre-eminently Colorado railroad. Between 1878 and 1883 it cast over the Rockies a net of tracks totaling close to 1,500 miles. One trunk line ran from La Veta to Durango with spurs to Silverton, South Fork, and Espanola, and another ran from Pueblo to Salt Lake City and Ogden, with branches to Crested Butte and Leadville.

As much as any other railroad builder of his day, Palmer realized that tracks were laid to serve people, not landscape. Before incorporating the Denver and Rio Grande, he and his associates purchased much of the real estate along the right of way at cut rates. Throughout the 1870s he worked to develop the land with subsidiary companies. The Central Colorado Improvement Company, for example, concentrated on the land and minerals of the Nolan Grant. Palmer and his friends had bought this fifty-thousand-acre tract along the Arkansas River in June 1870. Broadsides, bird's-eye views, and articles planted in the U.S. and British press spread information about its advantages as a farming area; as a site for smelting works, rolling mills, and foundries; and as the location for the new city of South Pueblo, established on railroad land within sight of the older town. Immigrants could expect a new life with "better health . . . better climate . . . large crops . . . the absence of imported competition either in the products of the soil or of industry."[18]

The arrival of the railroad in southern Colorado indeed triggered industrial growth of surprising strength. Pueblo became the great iron and steel city of the New West. Its factories employed 1,071 persons in 1890 and 5,448 by 1900. In the latter year its manufacturing output of $30.8 million rivaled Denver's $41.4 million. Farther south, the town of Trinidad competed with larger cities for attention. Convinced of its advantages for the manufacture of iron, leather, and woolen goods, Dr. Michael Beshoar doubled as a booster. According to his 1882 pamphlet "All

A narrow-gauge railroad about 1880, showing the topography that made the narrow gauge economically practical.

About Trinidad," the town was "a beacon which directs many of our citizens to the fount of wealth and the goal of happiness."[19]

Closer to Palmer's heart and the public's attention were the efforts of the Colorado Springs Company. The general viewed his railroad not only as a "mode of making money, but [as] a large-scale model way of conjoining that with usefulness on a large scale solving a good many vexed social problems." All of its workers would share in the ownership and prosperity of the company, use the schools and libraries it built there, and live without class strife. He came closest to his dream in the "Fountain Colony," his original name for Colorado Springs. As advertised throughout the United States and Britain, the new settlement was for the well-to-do. Membership was open to anyone of good moral character and teetotaling habits who could afford a hundred-dollar land certificate plus the additional purchase price for a lot and permanent buildings. Revenues from two-thirds of the land were set aside for operating expenses and public improvements, for Palmer intended that the town should be "the most attractive place for homes in the West," a place for schools, colleges, literature, science, and first-class newspapers. "I would not lower the standard under the pressure of temporary poverty," he vowed in the town's first months.[20]

The results of Palmer's efforts were impressive. As historian Herbert Brayer wrote, "It was essentially the railroad, and in an equal measure the land companies it founded, that gave substance" to the development of south and west Colorado.[21] The railroad's builders were single-handedly responsible for the creation of such towns as Alamosa, Garland City, and La Veta and for tripling the population of Pueblo in a year's time. Colorado Springs lived up to its mission as a utopia of refinement for the upper class. There were eight hundred residents within six months of the groundbreaking in July 1871, fifteen hundred by the end of 1872, and three thousand by 1874. Its residents were pleased with the high quality of the shops and restaurants, the wide streets, and the parks and cottonwood trees along the irrigation canals that were cared for by professional gardeners. Heavy immigration from abroad gave Colorado Springs a decided British tone and earned the nickname "Little London" for the half-finished town.

In a larger sense, the decade in which Palmer built the Rio Grande was the decade in which Colorado proved itself a success. Population in the counties within the Rio Grande's sphere of influence rose from about 10,000 to 40,000 during the 1870s and in the entire territory from 39,864 to 194,327 during the same period. The Colorado Central, finished to Georgetown in 1877, and the Denver, South Park, and Pacific, opened from Denver to Buena Vista in 1879, supplemented the mileage of the Rio Grande and helped to lower the costs of mining in the state. The railroads allowed new discoveries at Lake City, Silverton, Ouray, Silver Cliff, and Leadville to be exploited more rapidly and extensively than even the most energetic booster could have dreamed fifteen years before. The booming economy of the territory and state was organized around Denver, Golden, Pueblo, and Colorado Springs as the points of contact between investors and miners. Investment capital came largely from New York, Chicago, and St. Louis. Although Denver was Colorado's clear economic leader, the other cities at the base of the Rockies had their own mountain hinterlands and their own links to the eastern business world.

Skilled laborers, metallurgists and mineralogists, judicious capitalists, and intelligent managers flocked to Colorado. Their efforts, combined with the silver bonanza at Leadville, pushed mineral production to over $23 million in 1880, a sixfold increase in a decade. New towns, new schools, new public institutions — booster Frank Fossett grew weary of describing them all. "A trip to Colorado would be far more effective," he wrote in 1878, "and the only way to obtain a true appreciation of her wealth, enterprise, and general attractions. The reader can then see for himself how new regions are explored, the wilderness settled up, and towns and cities built."[22]

# COLORADANS IN 1876

Visitors to the U.S. Department of the Interior's building at the Philadelphia Centennial Exposition in 1876 usually paused for a second look at the exhibit of the Hayden Survey. Here were the results of eight years of systematic exploration of the Rockies. For the amateur scientist there were cases of minerals and geological maps. To satisfy the curiosity of the general public there were breathtaking photographs of Yellowstone and the Colorado Rockies as well as clay and plaster models of the newly discovered Native American ruins along the Mancos River near Mesa Verde.

As interesting as the exhibits themselves was the man on hand to answer questions. Tall and straight at age thirty-three, William H. Jackson had been the official photographer for the Hayden Survey since 1870, accompanying it first through Wyoming and then through Colorado in 1873, 1874, and 1875. The exhibit was his personal creation. For six months preceding the Exposition Jackson had worked in Washington preparing the models and displays. In prior summers he had discovered and photographed the ancient ruins, photographed the Mount of the Holy Cross, and made pictures of the Yellowstone country that helped to generate enthusiasm for the establishment of the nation's first national park.

One of the visitors to Jackson's exhibit surely must have been Sue Hall of Central City. When she returned to Colorado in mid-July, her husband would have listened with fascination to her description of all the sights of Philadelphia, from the Jackson pictures to the great Corliss engine whose 2,500-horsepower capacity symbolized the progress of an advancing age. From the window of their apartment in the Teller House hotel, Frank Hall could look across the street at the offices where he edited and published the *Daily Central City Register*. He may have wished that the pressure of debt and the wearisome business of filling the columns of a small-town daily had not kept him in the West.

Frank Hall.

During the previous winter he had campaigned vigorously for Colorado participation in the Exposition as "the most rational proposition for the prosperity of the whole commonwealth."[1] He had criticized the legislature for appropriating only $6,000, had applauded the efforts of Colorado's centennial commissioners to gather exhibits, and had reminded readers that Colorado would have to compete for attention with the well-financed representatives of Nevada's Comstock region. From May through October he published a regular newsletter about the centennial and enthusiastically reported that the state's official display of minerals was attracting attention.

Hall's support for the Centennial Exposition was not his first venture into boosterism. In his fifteen years in Colorado, Hall had frequently searched for original vehicles of publicity. He had successfully pushed the idea that Colorado Territory be represented at the Paris Exposition in 1867. That same year he sent to the East as many copies as he could afford of A. E. Mathews's *Pencil Sketches of Colorado,* a book of lithographic views of Denver and the mines. The volume, he told his mother, was "designed to convey an illustrated view of our Country."[2] In a decade as editor he also worked to make the press and the public partners in the great enterprise of territorial improvement and to spark local residents into the "full blaze of enthusiastic power."[3] Less grandiloquently he described for his family the practical mission of a newspaper in a developing region:

> We are expected to chronicle each morning all the incidents of the previous day, note the number of mills at work, tell what each is doing, where the ore is obtained, how much is consumed, and what it produces. If any new discoveries are made, we must tell the public about it. . . . This is not done so much for the gratification of our own people as for those who read our papers in the outside world. Our circulation extends to almost every state in the Union, and to many parts of Europe. Those people are to be favorably impressed with the country and induced to emigrate hither, bringing capital, science, labor, and all the elements that are essential in building up a new state.[4]

Although he frequently complained about the burden of frontier journalism, Hall was deeply excited about the growth of Colorado. Denver, he said, was a wonder among cities, and its newspapers were better than those of Syracuse or Rochester back home. The completion of a railroad to the East would be "a stupendous monument erected to perpetuate the glory of American Civilization."[5] His politics expressed the same faith. He was a Republican and proud of it, an ally of Jerome Chaffee and other entrepreneur-politicians. From 1866 to 1874, while still in his thirties, Hall served as territorial secretary, a post that made him acting governor when the chief executive was absent from Colorado and that allowed him to become acquainted with national figures — Ulysses S. Grant, William Seward, William Tecumseh Sherman, and especially his friend Vice President Schuyler Colfax. Hall viewed his task as a political leader in the same terms as his journalism, working whenever he could to advance the commercial interests of Colorado and bring its mineral resources to the notice of outsiders.

Hall's conviction that Republicanism was a synonym for progress was common in the late nineteenth century. Certainly it was shared by another of Chaffee's allies in the largely Democratic realm of Huerfano County. German-born Fred Walsen had served the Union during the Civil War and had tried his hand as merchant at Fort Garland from 1864 to 1870. He then struck off on his own, recrossing the Sangre de Cristo Range to open a store at Plaza de los Leones, a tiny settlement of adobe buildings that lined a single street running up from the Cucharas River. Six years later the free-thinking Walsen had built a thriving business among the Catholic Hispanos, had platted and incorporated an Anglo-American town to supplant the old plaza, and had spread the gospel of Republicanism. In 1872 he had worked for the election of Chaffee as territorial delegate, aided by the location of the local polling place in his warehouse. His reward came two years later when Chaffee secured not only a post office but also the name Walsenburg for his new town.

By 1876 Walsen could have felt well satisfied as he relaxed in his new house of proper American brick with bay window, scrollwork porch, and picket fence. He had helped to bring in the first Republican majorities in southern Colorado, he had guided his own town as mayor and trustee, and he had even founded a local chapter of the Benevolent and Protective Order of Elks. His work had not been easy. Everyone was familiar with the potential of northern Colorado, but persistence was needed to gain a hearing for the south. Too many people agreed with Frank Hall that the area was hopelessly backward, with a Hispanic population "always opposed to any change that bears the appearance of improvement."[6] Walsen had worked hard to persuade local residents to approve the new town government and to accept public schools. It had taken both his business reputation and political influence to obtain the county seat for Walsenburg and to convince General Palmer and Governor Hunt to route the Denver and Rio Grande Railroad through the young town.

Hall and Walsen promoted Colorado because they believed in the mission of growth. Others of their generation made the state the great romance of their lives. Helen Hunt, for example, had arrived in Colorado Springs in November 1873. She was a forty-three-year-old widow who was forced to write for a living and who had come to Colorado in search of a cure for her bronchitis. Later to become famous as the author of *A Century of Dishonor*, a scathing attack on U.S. policies toward Native Americans, in

Helen Hunt Jackson striking the pose of an author
deep in thought.

1873 Hunt brought a reputation as one of the nation's best-paid
essayists and poets. For the next half dozen years, both before
and after her marriage to a local civic leader named W. S. Jackson (no relation to the photographer), she spent her time enrap-
tured by the valleys and waterfalls that encircled Pikes Peak.
For the *Atlantic Monthly* and *Scribner's Magazine* she wrote ver-
bal sketches of Colorado in language suited to so lofty a subject.

On first appearance, she confessed, Colorado Springs had
seemed gray and forbidding. Behind her, as she arrived in late
autumn, had stretched "bleak, bare, unrelieved, desolate
plains," and in front of her was the "dark range of mountains,

snow-topped, rocky-walled, stern, cruel, relentless." Years of acquaintance with the region, however, gave her a new opinion: it was the "fairest spot on earth." In one essay after another, she reiterated descriptions of the shape and color of the sweeping landscape as "a symphony in yellow and red."[7] She loved to describe her jaunts into the sheltered valleys and glens along the slopes of Pikes Peak or into canyons whose high-walled heads reminded her of cathedrals. Here in the Rockies, she told her readers, was the ideal combination of grandeur and gentleness — high rocks, majestic pines, and meadows bright with wildflowers.

Jackson the photographer shared the same admiration for the landscape. If Hunt sat at the edge of the mountains and let herself react to their beauty, Jackson took himself into their heart. For three consecutive years — 1873, 1874, and 1875 — he had packed his equipment into Colorado's interior as head of the Hayden Survey's photographic division. There was Jackson himself, two packers and a cook, two or three other scientists and assistants, four mules to carry grub and tents, and two others to carry Jackson's photographic plates, chemicals, cameras, and portable darkroom. On days when bright weather promised good exposures on the slow-acting glass plates, Jackson would choose a camera — 5 × 8, 11 × 14, or stereoscopic — pack the equipment on his mule, Dolly, and head for a good vantage point. Each exposure usually required half an hour or more. Each plate had to be coated with collodion and silver in the dark tent, backed with wet blotting paper, carried to the camera for exposure, and returned to the tent for immediate development. In pursuit of scenic views in the Front Range, Sawatch, Elk, and San Juan mountains, Jackson was single-minded to the point of fanaticism, shrugging off dangers such as electric storms or climbing accidents and scaling every peak that promised a good photographic view.

His results were spectacular. In 1878 Jackson settled down for a twenty-year stay in Denver and opened a photographic studio, but nothing in his later work would ever equal the excitement of his earlier photographs. They fixed the image of Colorado in the American mind just as cyanide solution fixed the exposures on his plates. In 1874, it was Jackson's pictures of Native American ruins that people remembered, not reports in the *New York Tribune* by Ernest Ingersoll, the highly competent reporter who accompanied the party. A century later, whereas

William H. Jackson (left) loading his photographic equipment on his mule.

Hunt's writings may seem quaint and Hall's and Walsen's boosterism may seem like flamboyant relics, the eloquent photographs of W. H. Jackson remain as one of the best views into Colorado's past landscape.

CHAPTER 6

# THE BONANZA YEARS

*There has never been a time or locality more favorable for individual or company investments and organizations than this year of 1879, among the mines of Colorado. With a reasonable amount of ready capital to open and push mining development a harvest is very sure to follow that cannot be blighted by floods, frost, nor insects, nor increased or diminished in value, but one that is sure, substantial and enduring — the pure metal itself.[1]*

As many residents argued at the time, the bonanza at Leadville in 1877–1878 was a new beginning for Colorado. In retrospect it was the climax of the booster era in which promoters and visionaries tried to infuse Colorado into the consciousness of every American. To contemporaries, however, it was the first chapter in a new book of progress. The capitalists and workers who thronged to Leadville were expected to seek out new opportunities that would bring miner and mill, lawyer and locomotive into every park and ravine. The actual results of the decade — doubling of Colorado's population, tripling of its property values, sextupling of investment in factories — seemed to Coloradans the logical outcome of their hopes.

As late as 1876 the Leadville region was like an empty beach, washed by two tides of mining activity and littered with abandoned sluices, empty tin cans, and rotting buildings. The prosperity of the long valley of California Gulch, which had attracted thousands of prospectors in 1860 and 1861, died with the exhaustion of the placers. The development of the Printer Boy lode in 1868 promised renewed riches, but by the 1870s the area once again faced the "placid existence of a declining mining district." In its metropolis of Oro City, general-store owner Horace A.W. Tabor and two other businesspeople struggled to make a living out of trade insufficient "to keep a cat alive."[2] Neither 250 people in Oro nor 800 in all of Lake County were enough to fill the dilapidated cabins or to mine more than $200,000 of gold each year.

The future of California Gulch lay not with gold but with the silver locked in the carbonate ores that choked the cradles and sluices. As early as 1872 local residents discussed the need for smelting and transportation facilities before it would pay to work the dark-colored lead carbonates. During the next three years several miners purchased claims they thought were rich in silver and, in some instances, began work in anticipation of future development. Ore samples furnished by William Stevens and Alvinus Wood convinced officials of the St. Louis Smelting and Refining Company to buy into the important claims and to start work on a smelter in the spring of 1877. By the time their company, the Harrison Reduction Works, opened in October, a boom was in full progress. Miners from all over the Rockies sank prospecting shafts and piled up ore for local processing or shipment to the lowlands. The new town of Leadville, near the Harrison Works at the foot of Carbonate Hill, had an initial population of nearly one thousand — among them merchants such as Horace Tabor, who had abandoned Oro City for the new metropolis.

The year 1877 had brought the gulch to the attention of Colorado. The following year brought the United States to the streets of Leadville. Hundreds of newcomers swelled the town each week. They jammed its stores, sidewalks, and saloons, creating the atmosphere of a perpetual Fourth of July. After a season of immigration, Leadville spread for three miles up and down the valley, "over-running the plateau, exploring the gulches, and swarming up the flanks of half-cleared foothills."[3] A count of businesses found 51 groceries, 17 hardware stores, 12 shoe stores, and 9 book and stationery shops, along with 4 banks to supply credit for purchases. Teams of six mules or horses hauled in hay at $200 per ton and butter from the San Luis Valley at $1 per pound. For the personal needs of the miners, most of whom worked on hills within a mile or two of town, there were 31 restaurants, 35 brothels, 115 gambling houses, and 120 saloons. The two-story business buildings on Chestnut Street and Harrison Avenue stood out from among the two thousand shacks and shanties. Neither the flies and filth that choked the city nor the rickety housing bothered the residents, for it was obvious to everyone that a log cabin in the land of silver was superior to the finest mansion in a land of mortgages and debt.

A land of silver it was. Production in Lake County climbed from $26,000 in 1876 to $500,000 in 1877 to $2 million in 1878 to $9.4 million in 1879 to $11.5 million in 1880. When the richest claims might yield $1 million a year, a spiral of speculation in mining property was inevitable. "Men who had made fortunes from working or selling their mines," wrote Frank Fossett, "turned around and bought up prospects, or newly developed properties, at what would have seemed fabulous prices in former times."[4] A spectacular example was the Little Pittsburgh mine, owned in part by Horace Tabor, who had secured his interest by grubstaking the original prospectors. The mine was discovered in May 1878; in September Denver entrepreneurs Jerome Chaffee and David Moffat bought a one-half interest for $265,000. In 1879 the owners incorporated the property and offered 200,000 shares at $20 each. Eastern investors snapped up the offering and bid the price to $34 by December. Tabor, the last of the original owners, sold his one-third interest for $1 million to devote his time to the equally promising Chrysolite mine.

Successful mining depended on the efficiency of Leadville's new smelters as much as it did on the luck of prospectors. The carbonate or silver-lead ores needed to be processed in blast furnaces, where charcoal or coke helped reduce the carbonate ores and a flux agent such as iron ore displaced sulfur impurities to leave a residue of lead and silver. The Harrison Works soon developed the pattern of processing low-grade ores on the spot and hauling the high-grade ores over the mountains to be processed in St. Louis. The expansion of the smelting industry matched the growth of mining. By 1880 Leadville was the largest silver-lead smelting center in North America. It counted fifteen smelters with thirty-seven blast furnaces, most only a year old. As smaller firms folded under the intense competition, four companies came to dominate Leadville smelting — the Harrison Reduction Works, the Grant Smelter, the La Plata Smelter, and the Utah Smelter. These successful companies used the most current technology and employed engineers and operators trained in Europe.

The great bonanza of 1879–1880 attracted extraordinary interest and returned Colorado to the national notoriety it had enjoyed in 1859. After several years of severe depression and deflation in the mid-1870s, Americans were hungry for reports about new chances for miraculous wealth. At the same time, the decline of production from Nevada's Comstock Lode shifted attention to other parts of the West. The Tombstone silver strikes had come in 1877, but Arizona was far from eastern population centers. Leadville, however, was ready-made as a media event, only a hundred miles from the civilized city of Denver. Writers from *Scribner's, The Atlantic, Harper's, Frank Leslie's Illustrated Weekly,* and the other mass-circulation magazines crowded into the new town to inventory the growth of the "Magic City" or the "Cloud City." Local publicists rushed into print with half a dozen guidebooks to *The Silver Fields* or *The Carbonate Camps* or *Leadville and Its Silver Mines* or *Leadville: The City, Mines, and Bullion Product.*

The completion of Denver and Rio Grande tracks to Leadville in 1880 made the Cloud City a standard stop for touring celebrities. Former President Ulysses Grant rode the first train into Leadville for a five-day visit that started with a welcome by five bands and the volunteer fire companies. President Benjamin Harrison visited several years later. Oscar Wilde, the British poet and playwright, lectured to an audience of merchants and miners in the spring of 1882. His talk was followed by an underground banquet in one of the galleries of Horace Tabor's Matchless mine. Had Wilde visited a year later, he could have seen Doc Holliday try to forget his deadly tuberculosis by dealing faro at the Monarch saloon.

Leadville was also special to the mining experts. The *Engineering and Mining Journal* of New York and the *Mining Scientific Press* of San Francisco offered dozens of reports and articles about Leadville and its mines. The latter marveled over the entire bonanza, and the former worried that articles on Leadville could scarcely be kept within the bounds of reason. Rossiter Raymond, whose experiences as troubleshooter, journalist, and U.S. commissioner of mining statistics made him the best-known mining engineer of his day, was also carried away by the Leadville boom. His overly favorable evaluation of the Little Pittsburgh and Chrysolite mines at the height of the excitement helped to deflate the bubble and his own reputation. Also in 1879, Clarence King and his colleagues in the United States Geological Survey chose Leadville (along with Eureka and Virginia City in Nevada) as one of three western mining districts for systematic study. The decision brought Samuel F. Emmons and a cadre of chemists, metallurgists, and petrographers to roam the carbonate hills in 1880 and 1881, probe the geology, analyze the ores, and interview the miners and smelter workers. The resulting report on the *Geology and Mining Industry of Leadville,*

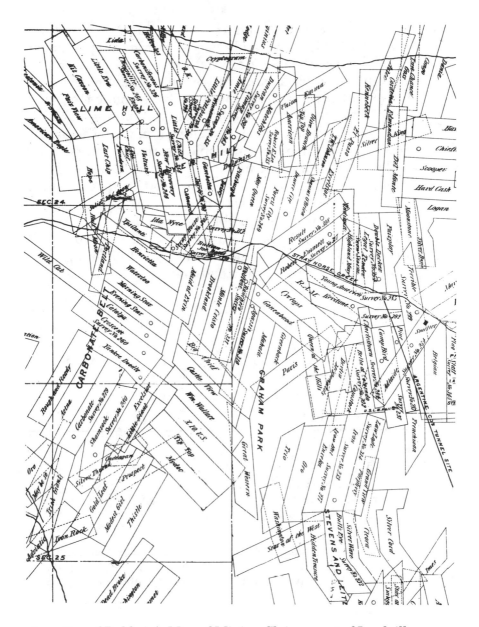

A portion of Baldwin's Map of Mining Claims, east of Leadville, California Mining District, Lake County, Colorado, January 1879. The Little Pittsburgh and Chrysolite mines are in the upper left corner. (1 inch = 1,275 feet).

*Colorado* in 1886 was an instant classic, a "miners' bible" that confirmed the prominence of the Leadville region.

A figure who tied the strands together was Mary Hallock Foote, who followed her husband's career as a mining engineer to Leadville in 1879. She had a reputation as an illustrator who provided sketches for books and articles in national magazines. Living in a one-room cabin in the instant city, she pulled together a sort of informal intellectual circle of casual and regular visitors. Helen Hunt Jackson was one such visitor, who was uncertain whether civilization was possible at ten thousand feet. Rossiter Raymond, Samuel Emmons, Clarence King, and the other leaders of U.S. mining and geology brought talk of public policy and the future of the West. In her long spare hours, Foote turned to writing as well as drawing and produced stories and novels about Leadville. Books such as *The Last Assembly Ball* and *The Led-Horse Claim* combined conventional Victorian plots with accurate descriptions of the Leadville scene.

The bonanza spirit was the key to every aspect of life in early Leadville. Fortunes in real estate matched fortunes in silver. Lots quadrupled in value in a week; they rose from $25 to $5,000 in six months. The town seemed to be the vanishing point of refinement, a city of swearing, whoring, and drinking, where murder was a common occurrence and no one suspected the gamblers of dealing a square game. From the perspective of a century later, however, Leadville's disorder appears to have been more the uproar of excitement than of lawlessness. Activity and animation were the common denominators of contemporary descriptions — "roaring," "wild," "fast," "restless, eager, fierce." Marvel enough by day, Leadville at night glowed with action:

> The miners then drift into town in swarms: a dozen bands are drumming up audiences for the theatres and variety shows, scores of saloons and numerous gambling-houses are in full blast, and the entire scene gives the town and place the appearance of one grand holiday. . . . Those who come on business or pleasure, or to stay, are all bent on seeing what there is to see, regardless of expense, and with as little delay as possible. Such a condition of affairs helps to distribute money among all classes and callings.[5]

The town council of Leadville struggled to provide the framework of government in the first boom year. Under the leadership of Mayor Horace A.W. Tabor, who was already a Lake County commissioner, the town trustees raised funds by licensing the saloons. They defined misdemeanors, tried to enforce the ordinances, and fought to keep city officials from packing off to the carbonate hills. With the proper authorities often immobilized by lack of funds or personnel, Leadville turned to volunteer government. Merchants supplemented the city police with their own "protective patrol," and churches and fraternal societies built needed hospitals. Leading citizens, including Mayor Tabor, raised money to equip volunteer fire companies and to build a water works when the town found its treasury empty.

In the midst of the extraordinary growth, it was not just Mary Hallock Foote who managed to improvise a social order. The town's uprooted residents banded together in Texas, Michigan, New England, and Pacific Coast societies. They joined clubs and fraternal societies. Voluntarily or not, they grouped together by ethnic origins. The Irish lived on East Sixth Street, up Stray Horse Gulch, and on Chicken Hill beyond the Harrison Works, where they mingled with Scandinavians. Most of the saloon-keepers east of Harrison Avenue had Irish names to match the district. The Germans, and their saloons, concentrated on the west side of town. African-Americans were isolated near the vice district on State Street. Immigrants from Cornwall in western England lived in "Jacktown" at the southwest end of town.

The investors who had rushed to capitalize on Leadville mining in 1878 and 1879 based their hopes on extrapolations from the best yields of the richest claims. The Little Pittsburgh mine, in particular, which paid $100,000 in dividends for each month from June through December 1879, seemed to guarantee the success of other investments. However, the crash finally came in 1880. The most famous mine was the first to belie the overblown estimates of its reserves. Gutted to provide payments to its inflated list of stockholders, the Little Pittsburgh ran out of rich ore early in the spring. Its stock plunged from $34 to $7.50 in March and to $1.95 by year's end. Despite uneasiness on the New York Stock Exchange, the Chrysolite mine briefly helped to sustain confidence, producing ore valued at $242,641 in March alone. Between mid-April and September, however, the value of shares in this equally mismanaged property fell from $40 to $3.75. After eighteen months as the hottest investment in New York and Chicago, the Leadville mines were blighted in reputation — "notorious" rather than famous.

The miners' strike that split Leadville in the late spring of 1880 was directly related to speculation in Chrysolite stock. The Knights of Labor had organized the Miners' Cooperative Union in Leadville during the previous winter under the charismatic leadership of Michael Mooney, a labor activist from the coal fields of Pennsylvania. The trigger for the strike was the sudden imposition at the Chrysolite of new work rules that forbade talking on the job. The next day — May 27 — Mooney helped to lead six thousand workers off the job with a demand for a pay raise from $3 to $4 a day and a uniform eight-hour day. Some observers of the strike and some historians since have argued that the Chrysolite owners and managers deliberately provoked and prolonged the strike to conceal the fact that their mine had run out of ore. At the least, the strike allowed them time to unload their Chrysolite stock before the public learned the truth.

Whatever its origins, the strike gained a life of its own from the demands of the workers. A Miners', Mechanics', and Laborers' Protection Association replaced the miners' Cooperative Union as the chief spokesperson. The mine owners posted guards, built barricades, and hired a few strikebreakers. In the third week a group of mine owners and merchants, including Horace Tabor, organized a Citizens' Executive Committee of One Hundred as comic-opera vigilantes and persuaded Governor Pitkin to declare martial law on June 13. The Pinkerton detective who was appointed military commander for Lake County helped the vigilantes force the strike leaders out of town. Most strikers were back on the job at their old wages within another week. The confrontation was temperate in comparison with bitter Colorado strikes after 1890, but it set the precedent for broadening an economic conflict into a confrontation between miners and the state government.

After the crash and strike, Leadville entered a decade of more sober growth. In the surrounding areas of South Park and the Upper Arkansas Valley, the five thousand residents of 1870 had grown to sixty thousand by 1880. Mine owners consolidated adjoining properties to achieve more efficient operation and to avoid expensive legal contests over wandering veins. Production peaked in 1882 and 1883, but miners found fewer carbonates and more "dry ores" that lacked the lead necessary for efficient smelting. The smelters fought constant battles to remodel, improve technology, and expand their capacity. The most successful smelter entrepreneur was James B. Grant, who had arrived in

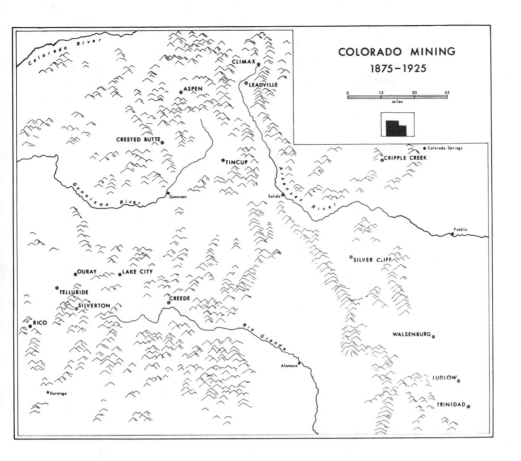

Leadville after service in the Confederate army, education at Cornell and at the mining institute in Freiburg, Germany, and experience in the mines of Gilpin County.

Leadville was the state's second-largest city in the early 1880s. With a population of around fifteen thousand it slowly adopted a kind of middle-western decorum. The railroad certainly helped, making it possible to import conveniences and luxuries that put Leadville on a level with eastern cities of the same size. Merchants wore coats and ties as they awaited their customers. Newly paved streets eliminated the need to shovel the oozing sludge out of their stores on spring mornings. The town's upper crust of merchants, mine managers, and bachelor engineers self-consciously emulated the customs of proper society with spring dances and summer picnics. The police made most of their arrests not for murder and mayhem but for disorderly conduct and vagrancy; the City Council officially closed the gambling halls in 1888.

Even the Leadville saloon business showed the change in the tone of life. In 1880 a Leadville newspaper reported that 249 saloons did an annual business of $4 million, making them the number three business after mining and banking. Most of the establishments, however, were little more than tents or log cabins with a few chairs, a scant assortment of whiskey, and a bar across one end. As the number of saloons slowly declined, their size increased. The grand drinking palaces of Harrison Avenue represented investments of $5,000 or $10,000 — five or ten years' wages for a miner. Saloons such as the Board of Trade, Texas House, and Wyman's Place sported gilt mirrors, billiard tables, elegant bars, and regular entertainment. Several dozen middle-sized saloons represented the steady work of small entrepreneurs who left jobs as barkeepers, hotel clerks, or government employees to build up their own businesses.

A new wave of travelers and journalists took as much pleasure in correcting the image of a wild and wooly town as their predecessors had in creating it. To the British tourist Phil Robinson, Leadville looked disappointingly like "some thriving provincial town," whose every step toward thrift and prosperity reduced its peculiarity. A reporter for *Harper's Weekly* found that the modern Leadville was "as steady going as Salem or Plymouth Rock." He quoted the complaint of one old resident that "this ain't Leadville. It's only some infernal Sunday-school town that ain't been named yet." Ernest Ingersoll summed up the rapid change in 1883: "The rough old camp has crystallized into the city she resolved to become."[6]

Stabilization and the slow decline of the silver yield at Leadville were balanced by the continued development of mining regions on the Western Slope. In the mountains above Gunnison there were mineral strikes at Tin Cup, Gothic, and Pitkin in the same years as the Leadville boom. The first rush to Aspen came in the early spring of 1880, with steady growth for the next decade. Arrival of the Denver and Rio Grande and the Colorado Midland railroads more than made up for the town's isolation. Peak production came in 1889, when the mines of the Roaring Fork country produced $10 million in bullion. Aspen's eleven thousand citizens (and six newspapers) constituted the largest Colorado town west of the Continental Divide in 1890.

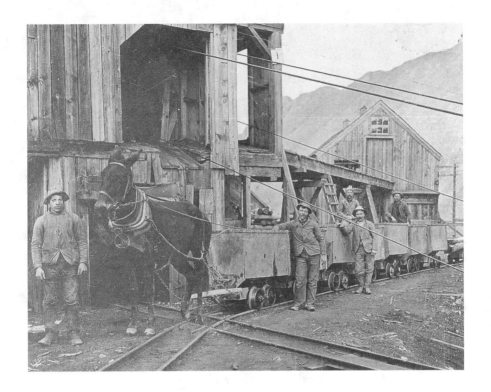

Miners in San Juan County.

Transportation facilities were even more crucial for the development of mining in the isolated San Juan Mountains of southwestern Colorado. Rich mineral deposits were well-known in the 1870s but were not substantially developed until the 1880s. Rico, Telluride, and Creede were mining camps built in the midst of the mines, whereas Lake City, Silverton, and Ouray were supply centers for mines miles deeper and thousands of feet higher into the range. Most of the San Juan camps were tied together and were linked to the larger world by toll roads built by Otto Mears. Between 1881 and 1884, he pushed roads from the Uncompahgre Valley to Placerville and Telluride, from Silverton to Las Animas and Red Mountain, from Ouray to Red Mountain and Mt. Sneffels. Fred Walsen helped to finance the construction with $86,000. Loaded ore wagons creaked cautiously down the roads to meet Denver and Rio Grande spurs in Ouray and Silverton. At the end of the decade, Mears turned to railroading and built the Rio Grande Southern to connect Telluride, Ophir, and Rico to the new town of Durango.

Burro train preparing to haul supplies at Georgetown.

The "Silver San Juans" made Durango a model success story of western town promotion. It was laid out by William Bell and Alexander G. Hunt, associates of William Jackson Palmer, in anticipation of the Denver and Rio Grande tracks whose arrival they helped to control. A company organized by Bell and Palmer also bought the Silverton Smelting Works and moved the operation to a new plant at Durango. The "Denver of southern Colorado" started with high ambitions and came closer to realizing them than most new towns. It had two thousand residents by 1881. The townsite company gave away free lots to churches, encouraged businesses, and helped to secure the county seat. Nearby farms and ranches used Durango as a market center for food to supply the San Juan mines. There was a shootout on the streets between rival cattle gangs from Durango and Farmington in 1881 and a red light district that catered to the miners, but those who made the decisions were energetic businesspeople who valued the town's "in" with the railroad.

Early Durango enjoyed a succession of newspapers that mixed local gossip, loud boosterism, and louder politics. Caroline Romney arrived in 1881 to start the *Durango Record* after hauling

The Elkton Mine at Cripple Creek. The bare hillside pitted and strewn with debris is typical of the landscape of the Cripple Creek district.

her printing press by wagon from Leadville. She was a "very pretty" lady who devoted her paper to women's rights, law and order, the future of "the new wonder of the Southwest," and a one-sided feud with a disdainful Denver. Dave Day added to the roster of colorful editors when he settled in Durango in the 1890s. He ran the *Durango Democrat* in the same style as the earlier *Solid Muldoon* he had edited in Ouray. He idolized William Jennings Bryan, defended the Democratic party, took up causes, fought with neighbors, argued with friends, and punctured hypocrisy. In the description of historian Duane Smith, the egotistical Day was "controversy looking for a cause."[7]

The final mining bonanza of nineteenth-century Colorado came at Cripple Creek in the shadow of Pikes Peak. Cattleman

Robert Womack had prospected the unpromising region for several years and made a small find of gold ore in the winter of 1890–1891. The next spring and summer brought a small gold rush and the production of about $200,000 worth of gold. One of the participants was Winfield Scott Stratton, a Colorado Springs carpenter who staked what became the fabulous Independence mine. Small success in 1891 brought more development in 1892, when $500,000 worth of gold was mined. Laid out on the site of a cattle ranch, Cripple Creek emerged as the metropolis of the new gold region. Production of $2 million in 1893 and 1894 was just a taste of wealth that brought heavy investment in smelters and mines and frenzied trading on two Colorado Springs stock exchanges later in the decade. Annual output on the high plateau southwest of Colorado Springs climbed to $19.5 million in 1899 and held above $15 million for the first decade of the new century.

Boomtown though it might have been, Cripple Creek was more an industrial city than a roaring prospectors' camp. Only a day's journey from Denver and four hours from Colorado Springs, it lacked many of the problems of isolation endured by other mining towns. Even in its first years, residents enjoyed electric lights and telephones along with the customary bars and brothels. After a devastating fire in 1896, the city of twelve thousand residents was rebuilt in brick instead of wood and with paved streets rather than mud. Electric interurban cars tied Cripple Creek to the adjacent towns of Victor and Independence, and many miners rode to work like urban commuters. If one were to blank out the mountains in old photographs, Cripple Creek would resemble any lively turn-of-the-century city. Jobs were still to be had and money was to be made, but the boom was almost routine.

Whether in Cripple Creek, Leadville, or Telluride, the entrance to the mine shaft was the gateway between two different worlds. The larger and deeper the mine, the greater the ordinary dangers. Miners worked in air fouled by waste gases from blasting and by accumulations of carbon dioxide from candles, rotting timbers, and their own breath. They paused from their work in the deep shafts to gulp fresh air from blower tubes. Temperatures in the tunnels quickly climbed to 80° or 90° or 100°, and miners often worked up to their ankles in water. At the end of their long shift, they ascended in a few minutes into

Deep mining by the 1880s and 1890s required an extensive investment in supportive timbering.

the frigid air of the Colorado highlands. Rheumatism and pneu-
monia were leading causes of death in Leadville in 1880. Drill-
ing holes for explosive charges with hammer and steel raised
dust enough; power drills run by compressed air shot out clouds
of abrasive rock dust. Miner's consumption — silicosis — was a
contributing factor to 30 percent of the deaths among Colorado
miners by the end of the nineteenth century. Miners who
worked the common silver-lead carbonate ores faced the additional danger of lead poisoning.

Mining disasters were included with occupational diseases in
the life-and-death equation for Colorado miners. There was constant danger from cave-ins and falling rocks, even when the
supportive timbering seemed adequate. Explosive gases could
build up at the unventilated heading of a tunnel or drift. Missed
holes were undetonated explosive charges that might be set off

accidentally by a later shift. Snowslides or fires in the shaft house could trap miners below. The lifts that lowered miners from the surface to the working level were a special danger. It was easy for a miner to pitch out of the buckets used in smaller mines or to fall from the cage used in larger operations. Inattentive lift operators could spill an entire crew or catch a worker between the speeding cage and the shaft wall. One of the most notorious accidents in Colorado came at the Independence mine in Cripple Creek in 1904, when fifteen men were tossed out of a lift cage that was pulled over the sheave wheel at the top of the shaft and fell fifteen hundred feet to the bottom of the shaft.

By the 1880s hard-rock miners from every part of the state demanded mine safety inspection. Although an inspection bill passed in 1889, the legislature rendered it ineffective by refusing appropriations. The complaints from miners that were compiled by the Colorado Bureau of Labor Statistics were confirmed by death rates among the state's miners. In 1896, for example, twenty-six of the three thousand miners in the Cripple Creek district lost their lives in industrial accidents. In the last years of the century, five or six of every thousand underground workers throughout the state died on the job each year. Significant improvements in mine safety and a decline in the death rate did not come until the twentieth century.

What modern tourists in the Colorado Rockies see of the past is not the working world beneath the surface but the skeletons of mining towns that survive in their old buildings. Everyday architecture in Ouray, Aspen, and Leadville and in the slightly older towns of the Clear Creek region went through the same evolution. Within the first few years, log cabins gave way to the standard style of working-class cottages. One-story frame houses set with the gable toward the street climbed the narrow valley on the north side of Telluride, lined the streets west of Harrison Avenue in Leadville, and scattered over half-empty blocks as Silverton sprawled across the high basin of Baker's Park along the Animas River. The more settled households boasted modest gingerbread trim around the front window and the small porch at the front corner. The assistant managers, senior bank tellers, and prosperous merchants built larger two-story versions that members of the high-style elite now buy and sell for the price of a silver mine in fashionable towns such as Aspen.

Public buildings were even more clear in their testimony to the optimism and self-satisfaction of the silver-mining generation.

Imposing hotels such as the Beaumont in Ouray represented the ambitions of new mining towns.

The instant main streets started with one- and two-story buildings that sported square false fronts, life imitating the art of the western movie set. The second stage was the construction of new brick business buildings that jutted above the roof line of wooden sheds and gave the town center a gap-toothed grin. The Newman Block in Durango was a good example, an Italian palazzo built with money from the mines of Rico. A new hotel was both a symbol of civic success and a necessary facility to impress visitors. Telluride claimed the Sheridan Hotel and Central City the Teller House. Ouray enjoyed the Beaumont Hotel, built in 1886 with mansard roof and corner tower. The Strater Hotel opened a block and a half from the Durango depot in 1888. Four stories high with its own tower, it was "strictly first class in all appointments."[8] The Tabor Grand Hotel in Leadville commanded a strategic corner on Harrison Avenue and dominated the surrounding buildings. It replaced the Clarendon, which occupied an ordinary frame building, as Leadville's high-class hotel. Throughout the mountains historic districts recognized by the National Register

The San Juan County Courthouse in Silverton.

of Historic Places preserve something of the main-street environment of Central City, Crested Butte, Georgetown, Leadville, Silverton, and Telluride.

Local governments also built for permanence. School buildings were solid brick cubes, with the corners perhaps picked out
by sandstone trim. The newly created counties on the Western
Slope required new courthouses, perhaps on a smaller scale but
in the styles remembered from Ohio and Wisconsin. The Lake
County courthouse opened in Leadville in 1882, the La Plata
County courthouse in Durango in 1892, and the Dolores County
courthouse in Rico in 1893. The San Juan County courthouse
rose in Silverton in 1907. Its clock tower and cupola stand over a
blunted two-story cross with Doric columns at its four entrances,
outlined against the blue sky as if to ignore the dwindling mines
and to remember those who worked them.

# CHAPTER 7

# THE BUSINESSMAN'S STATE

The publication of a spate of panoramic maps of Colorado towns and cities in the first years of statehood symbolized the adulthood of the commonwealth. Denver, Georgetown, and Central City had already attracted itinerant artists who walked the streets, sketched the buildings and landscape, and fitted the details into a composite view taken from an imaginary vantage point two or three thousand feet over the town. Between 1879 and 1882 another dozen bird's-eye views were published for major cities such as Colorado Springs and Leadville and aspiring communities from Greeley to Salida. Each panorama served notice that here, too, along the Purgatoire or the Gunnison or the upper reaches of the Arkansas River, was a town worth noticing. They all carried the message that Colorado was ready to launch into its great era of growth.

The great bonanza at Leadville keyed a decade of enthusiasm about the future of Colorado that fully matched the national temper of the 1880s. There was a continued belief that publicity was the key to progress. At the Fourth of July celebration in 1876, Judge Hiram P. Bennet had offered the final toast to Colorado: "Like the star of Bethlehem, it is rising and the wise men of the east are beholding it and coming to it."[1] Denver merchants and new settlers on the Western Slope might argue over prices and freight rates, but they agreed on the need to sell Colorado's advantages to immigrants and investors. Every newspaper placed boosterism at the top of its responsibilities. Under the editorship of Stanley Wood, former publicist for the Denver and Rio Grande Railroad, the *Great Divide* blended boosterism and literature. Between 1889 and 1894 it used fiction and poetry to celebrate Colorado's natural beauty, its pioneer spirit, and the growth of its towns and cities.

As the Denver and Rio Grande Railroad pushed westward, it triggered the normal flurry of guides and descriptions of the Western Slope mining districts and promotional pamphlets for

Nineteenth-century bird's-eye view of Fort Collins.

new towns. The energetic Durango Board of Trade published "Durango As It Is" in 1892 to booster the economic growth of the San Juan basin and set a goal of one hundred thousand residents. Durangoans simultaneously complained about the greedy ambitions of Cortez, the self-proclaimed metropolis of the Great Montezuma Valley. Another regional response was the West Slope Congress, organized to develop common positions on mutual problems. It held meetings in Grand Junction, Ouray, Durango, and Aspen in the early 1890s and published booster pamphlets on "Western Colorado and Her Resources." Politicians and newspapers shared the concern that only unified action would allow this "empire in itself" to realize its potential.

The National Mining and Industrial Exposition in the summer of 1882 was another example of the promotional enthusiasm of the bonanza era. Impetus and energy for its organization came from members of the entrepreneurial elite, particularly Horace Tabor and William Loveland, the builder of the Colorado Central Railroad who had moved to Denver to publish the *Rocky Mountain News.* One purpose was to advertise Colorado's resources; another was to focus attention on Denver as the natural center of the Rocky Mountain mining region. On May 2 Governor Fred Pitkin and former governors John Evans and John Routt joined the promoters at the forty-acre site on South Broadway to lay the

Grand Junction, Fifth and Main, in ca. 1890, when the city was scarcely a decade old.

cornerstone of the Exposition building. The central hall stretched five hundred feet, with towers at its corners, and there were four long exhibition wings, each guarded by its own set of towers. With long rows of arched windows to light the exhibits from Colorado counties and other western states and with a score of fluttering flags, the building was an impressive exercise in practical architecture. The Mining Exposition opened again in 1883 and 1884, before thinning crowds and mounting debts closed its doors. In 1891, however, a new Mineral Palace in Pueblo took over its function. A giant building with columns topped by spheres and pilasters crowned with elephants, it displayed a collection of Colorado ores and geological specimens until it closed in 1935.

Part of the booster vision was the conviction that social and cultural order would emerge spontaneously from economic growth, with government needing only to set the preconditions for prosperity. Everyone appeared to have a chance at success as long as there was new wealth to share and property waiting to be developed. Historian Gunther Barth's observation that participation in the growth of Denver gave a "vicarious victory" even to

The National Mining and Industrial Exposition Hall at Denver in 1882.

the financial losers can be reasonably extended to the English-speaking population of the entire state.[2] The physical embellishment of cities was a direct expression of the value placed on growth. Public works and public laws, private architecture, and new corporations were servants of economic expansion and symbols of the success of the new commonwealth.

Pride in growth concealed the potential for internal conflict. Despite the rhetoric, all Coloradans did not benefit equally from the bonanza years. The rapid development of California Gulch, for example, was possible in part because it lay on lands already ceded by the Utes. In the first years after the U.S. conquest of New Mexico, the tribe had negotiated a treaty that established a Native American agency at Taos to serve the southern bands. Continued movement of Hispanic settlers into the San Luis Valley, however, set off a brief war. On Christmas Day 1854, the Utes killed fifteen men at the Fort Pueblo settlement and followed with raids along the Arkansas and in the San Luis Valley. By autumn of 1855 campaigns by U.S. troops ended the outbreaks. For several years thereafter, the old mountain man Kit Carson distributed government subsidies and tried to smooth over problems.

During the 1860s the Utes maintained an uneasy balance with white Coloradans. With initial mining development only on the fringe of their homeland, the Utes could hunt in the parks and mountains in their old ways and supplement increasingly scarce game with rations from the government. In 1868, however, Kit Carson and Governor A. C. Hunt persuaded the Utes to abandon central Colorado from North Park to the San Luis Valley — the area in which expanding settlement threatened open hostilities. The treaty reserved most of western Colorado for the Native Americans — 16 million acres south of the 40th parallel and west of the 107th meridian (the line roughly through Pagosa Springs, Gunnison, and Steamboat Springs). Five years later a series of mineral discoveries in the San Juan Mountains precipitated the Brunot Agreement. The new agreement cut a rectangular chunk out of the reservation, leaving Native American lands along the southern and western borders of the territory. Over the next two decades prospectors made the ceded land the scene of one mining rush after another — to Ouray, Telluride, Rico, Ophir, Red Mountain, Silverton, Lake City, and, finally, to Creede during 1890 and 1891.

Successful encroachment on Ute lands encouraged Coloradans to assume that further reductions of Ute territory were inevitable. White residents chafed that a third of Colorado remained unproductive in the hands of the Native Americans but consoled themselves with the thought that "these savage tribes are all waning, and must finally become extinct, leaving their rich possessions to be occupied and developed by a more appreciative race." To hasten the process, in 1876 the legislative assembly petitioned Congress to remove the Utes to Oklahoma. In 1879 Governor Pitkin argued that "if this reservation could be extinguished, and the land thrown open to settlers, it will furnish homes to thousands of the people of the State who desire homes." The governor's secretary, W. H. Vickers, wrote at the same time that the "degeneration" of the tribe had made them "exceedingly disagreeable neighbors. . . . Even those who do not fear the Utes dislike them and would be glad to see them banished to some more appropriate retreat than the garden of our growing state."[3]

The excuse came in September 1879. The Brunot Agreement had established a Native American agency on the Gunnison River to distribute government flour and bacon to the Uncompahgre and Southern Ute bands and an agency on the White River for the northern bands. For more than a year, Nathan Meeker had been the agent at White River. A professional reformer who had founded the town of Greeley in the early 1870s, Meeker dreamed of building another agricultural utopia peopled with Native Americans civilized by his personal efforts. To the Utes, however, Meeker's farm machinery and Sunday school philosophy represented not civilization but confinement. When many of the Utes at the agency ceased to heed his orders or slipped away to the hills, Meeker called for aid from the army. The approach of Major Thomas Thornburg with a relief column triggered a clash that led to the death of Thornburg and thirteen of his troops. At the agency angry Native Americans killed Meeker and eleven other white men and took five women and children captive. Chief Ouray and other Ute leaders soon secured the release of the prisoners, but the Colorado public demanded punitive action. As their senators and members of Congress lobbied for the complete removal of the tribe from Colorado, local citizens read *The Ute War: A History of the White River Massacre and the Privations and Hardships of the Captive White Women Among the Hostiles on Grand River,* a volume issued by two *Denver Tribune* editors within weeks of the tragedy.

A new treaty signed by Ouray and other leading Utes in Washington in 1880 provided the answer to the nearly unanimous cries of Colorado editors and officials that "the Utes must go!" The document provided new lands in Utah for the White River bands and offered a Utah reservation for the Uncompahgre Utes if no suitable location could be found in Colorado. Given the tone of public opinion, it was almost inevitable that this largely peaceful band should suffer deportation from its land. Land developers and settlers gathered in Gunnison in the summer of 1881 to wait for the Utes to vacate the western edge of the state. Even before the last of the Uncompahgres left Colorado in September 1881, Anglo-American settlers were laying out new towns such as Delta and Montrose on old Ute lands.

The confluence of the Grand (Colorado) and Gunnison rivers looked like an especially likely site for a new community. George Crawford, an experienced townsite developer from Kansas, and James Bucklin, a young attorney from Michigan, put together the Grand Junction Town Company in October 1881 and laid out the new city the following March. Before the year was over, the town had a mayor, aldermen, and the *Grand Junction News*. Promoters of the town struck a deal with the Denver and Rio

Grande Railroad, trading a half interest in unsold Grand Junction real estate for a promise to locate shops and make Grand Junction the railroad division headquarters. Four years later the town had several hundred residents, five churches, and a dozen voluntary associations. The social profile of Grand Junction in 1885 was like that of Denver in the early 1860s, with far more men than women and a population overwhelmingly in their twenties and thirties.

Removal of the Utes was also good for the mining business. Prospectors and miners enjoyed a new feeling of safety as they explored the Elk Mountains and scattered new mining camps around the year-old silver city of Aspen. "From a narrow strip of settlement, extending along the immediate base of the Rocky Mountains," reported the 1880 census, "the belt has increased so that it comprises the whole mountain region. . . . Miners have spread over the whole mountain region, till every range and every ridge swarms with them."[4]

The 1880 treaty left about eight hundred Mouache, Capote, and Weeminuche Utes on a reservation 15 miles wide and 110 miles long in the southwestern corner of Colorado. As the population of Durango passed two thousand in the mid-1880s, Coloradans again placed pressure on the federal government for further removal of the Native Americans. They revived the old canards that the Utes were a threat to life, that they ran off stock, and that they blocked the orderly development of resources. As much as anything, however, white Colorado simply wanted to be rid of the bother of the presence of the Native Americans. It was the Indian Rights Association, an organization of eastern philanthropists who wanted to see stronger efforts to Americanize the Indians, who prevented another Native American deportation. A law in 1895 parceled out a portion of the reservation to individual tribespeople as private property but retained several hundred thousand acres in two segments as common property for the Weeminuche (now the Ute Mountain Tribe and Reservation) and for the Capote and Mouache bands (the modern Southern Ute Tribe and Reservation).

With the removal of the Utes as a backdrop, politics in Colorado during these boom years was an elaborate show with businesspeople in the leading and supporting roles. John Routt, the last appointed governor of the territory and the first elected governor of the state, exemplified the leadership. Before his term expired he had left Denver to join the Leadville crowds, digging in overalls in his Morning Star mine and begrudging the time needed for state affairs. Other politicians also flourished among the carbonates. James Grant owned and operated a major smelter in addition to serving as governor. Horace Tabor built a career as lieutenant governor and senator on the strength of his mining properties. Senator Jerome Chaffee invested heavily at Leadville, and Alva Adams of Pueblo banked a fortune from Leadville mines prior to becoming governor. Other mining areas produced their share of entrepreneur-politicians in the first fifteen years of statehood. Senator Thomas Bowen of Del Norte and Governor Frederick Pitkin of Ouray both made their fortunes from the San Juans, and Nathaniel Hill's wealth allowed him to move from the offices of the Boston and Colorado Smelter to Washington.

Many of the mining kings bought their offices, although not so blatantly as the phrase implies. An eleven-day contest in 1883, when the general assembly took ninety-six ballots to choose Thomas Bowen over Horace Tabor to serve a full term in the United States Senate, is often considered the prime example of the prostitution of politics. Despite accusations of bribery during the contest, the decision depended much more on political bargaining than on the direct corruption of legislators. Tabor and Bowen used their fortunes to buy the *opportunity* to run for office, not the office itself. The complaint that ability and brains had been subordinated to bonanzas as political qualifications was recognition of the fact that political parties rewarded those who aided them. For five years Tabor had used his money and energy to benefit the state and to stoke the engines of Republicanism. As a public figure he devoted his fortune and efforts to booster events, such as the National Mining and Industrial Exposition, and to booster organizations, such as the Denver Chamber of Commerce. Simultaneously, Tabor was a party stalwart. Speeches, campaign contributions, subsidizing a party newspaper, hard work in party committees — if these could not earn one an occasional political nomination, what could?

Colorado politics in the late 1870s and the 1880s was a battleground for cliques and factions not because of the special venality of the age but because of the lack of divisive issues. Between 1876 and 1893 the Republicans ran the state. They controlled the legislature without interruption, they elected all seven senators and five of seven governors, and they delivered the electoral vote in every presidential contest. The brief interruptions by Democrats in the state house made little real difference. Both parties agreed that the overriding mandate of government was to promote economic growth. Through subsidies, contracts, and the enactment of laws favorable to business, they believed, the purpose of the state was to help people make money. With no important issues splitting the voters, the result was a politics centered on personalities. Whether the occasion for conflict was Leadville versus Denver, northern counties versus southern, or old guard versus insurgents (Windmills versus Argonauts, in local terminology), the real cause was the struggle for individual advantage and advancement in office.

The substantive actions of Colorado's officeholders followed the guidelines laid out in the state constitution. When the constitutional convention had assembled in December 1875, the antirailroad and anticorporation Granger movement was at the height of its power in the Middle West. In Colorado the core of "Granger" sentiment was in the South Platte Valley counties of Weld, Boulder, Jefferson, and Arapahoe, where settlement was well advanced and railroads were already in operation. Proposals to control railroad rates, however, aroused the condemnation of leading entrepreneurs who feared anything that might discourage outside investment. Within the convention itself, five members who doubled as railroad executives led a successful opposition by southern and western delegates whose regions still lacked rail facilities. The final document declared that railroads were common carriers, but it failed to establish a public utilities commission to supervise them. To encourage the mining industry, it granted a ten-year tax exemption and offered aid for scientific investigation. It also furnished favorable procedures for incorporation without troublesome controls on stock issue, annual meetings, and reports.

In their attempt to "take a middle ground," the convention delegates tried to balance provisions favorable to business with clauses instructing the legislature to provide regulatory services. Over the next two decades, however, the legislators consistently refused to implement the relevant policies from fear of hampering Colorado's economic growth. An 1877 law prohibiting the labor of children under fourteen in mines, establishing safety regulations, and creating the position of a commissioner of mines to enforce the rules lasted only four years before its repeal as an "unjust burden upon the mine owners."[5] In 1883 the assembly authorized the office of coal mine inspector yet ignored other types of mining despite its constitutional charge. The Bureau of Labor Statistics, created in 1887, was purposefully made dependent upon the voluntary cooperation of employers. The pattern with the railroads was similar. In 1885 complaints about pooling, rebates, and discrimination against local manufacturers aroused interest in railroad rate regulation among groups as conservative as the Denver Chamber of Commerce. Of twenty-four such bills introduced in the legislature, the only one to pass set up a railroad commission that had only advisory duties. The general assembly cut off all appropriations after one year of funding and abolished the office of commissioner in 1893.

Reactions to the concept of forest conservation were similarly shaped by the desire for economic growth. Although the state constitution provided that the legislature should act to prevent the wholesale destruction of forests on state and federal lands, the lawmakers delayed for a decade before creating the office of forest commissioner. To put the office on equal footing with the mining and railroad commissions, the legislature withheld funds for operation and passed no laws for it to enforce. In the late 1880s, when the idea of forest reserves on the Western Slope was first seriously discussed, Coloradans were split in their opinions. Some saw the need for government protection against exhaustion of resources, but others feared reserves would freeze out local residents in favor of easterners.

Federally mandated conservation, in fact, came to Colorado in several stages. After Congress passed the Forest Reserves Act, President Benjamin Harrison in 1891–1892 set aside 3.1 million acres in the White River, Pikes Peak, Plum Creek, South Platte, and Battlement Mesa reserves. Around the turn of the century, the federal government suggested procedures for limiting the free use of public lands for grazing by requiring permits and fees in the forest reserves and leasing other tracts of the public domain. The proposals split the Colorado ranching industry down the middle, with many large ranchers in favor and smaller ranchers in fierce opposition. Massive new forest reserves were created in 1905–1906, when Theodore Roosevelt set aside more than 9 million acres, or 14 percent of the entire state.

A number of Colorado politicians around the turn of the century built their careers around the anticonservation sentiments of many citizens. John Shafroth and Edward Taylor reached the U.S. House of Representatives on a platform of opposition to conservation, and Elias Ammons and Shafroth attained the governor's chair after 1900. The "locking up" of valuable resources, said many of the state's leaders, impeded state growth. A policy of husbanding resources was said to strike a blow at every rancher, lumberman, miner, and homesteader, depriving the state of the "benefits that would arise from the use of its lands." U.S. Senator Henry Teller, the first political leader of national stature to emerge from Colorado politics, viewed the question with an attitude common in his state: "I cannot rid myself of the idea that a home on a piece of land is infinitely better than a piece of unbroken timber."[6] Other members of Congress such as Franklin Brooks and Robert Bonynge, who had less direct interest in the issue, also found it convenient to follow the lead of the vocal anticonservationists.

Public opinion in Colorado was, in fact, more complex than might first appear. The issue did not simply pit reformers against businesspeople, or Denver against the Western Slope, but also divided the Western Slope against itself. Although not as vocal as the opposition, the Colorado Horticultural Society and the Colorado State Forestry Association kept up the scientific advocacy of conservation and began to articulate the values of preserving a wilderness. At the other end of the argument, smaller ranchers led the opposition out of fear of losing access to public lands for their cattle and sheep. They were the most vocal in the northwest quadrant of the state and spoke through newspapers in Rifle, Meeker, and Steamboat Springs and through groups such as the Roaring Fork and Eagle River Stockgrowers Association. Farming communities, in contrast, saw great benefits in the preservation of forests on the headwaters of Colorado rivers, to hold snow and rainwater and to maintain steady stream flow without erosion. Towns such as Fort Collins, Pueblo, Grand Junction, Delta, Montrose, and Mancos were centers of support for forest reserves.

The anticlimax of the debate was the Denver Public Land Convention in 1907. Called by the Colorado legislature, it brought together representatives from all the western states. Its sponsors hoped to present a unified western front against Roosevelt's conservation policy, but the result was a fizzle rather than a confrontation. Governor Henry Buchtel was careful to appoint a balanced Colorado delegation that represented the actual spectrum of opinion in the state. Accusations by each side that the other had packed the meeting diverted attention from the deliberations, the speeches failed to strike sparks, and the mild resolutions were a disappointment to the diehards.

Education developed within the same context, serving both the impulse to economic growth and the aspiration to reproduce the features of a stable eastern society To demonstrate the growth of educational facilities on the plains and in the mountains, the Colorado exhibit at the Centennial Exposition in Philadelphia included photographs of twenty new school buildings. In 1870 the territorial legislature appropriated funds for instruction in mining and geology, the one discipline residents found unexcelled in "utility of purpose" and "magnificence of results, both scientific and politico-economical."[7] Four years later the territory officially opened the Colorado School of Mines, whose importance was recognized in a special clause in the state constitution. The University of Colorado offered its first classes in 1877 and Colorado Agricultural and Mechanical Arts College in 1879. The University of Denver reopened permanently in 1880 after an earlier trial run, and the State Normal School at Greeley followed in 1890 (becoming the State Teachers College in 1911). Massive new college buildings symbolized the desire to build a cultured commonwealth and affirmed Coloradans' faith in the practical application of learning to railroads, mining, irrigation, and industry.

The new institutions made important contributions in the final decades of the century. From its first years the agricultural college at Fort Collins offered "farmers' institutes" as well as classes on campus. These predecessors of the cooperative extension program offered an early version of 4-H programs, classes on homemaking, and instruction in scientific farming. During the 1905–1906 academic year, more than one hundred fifty institutes were held in rural communities around the state. In the nearby town of Greeley, Teachers College president Zachariah Snyder built a nationally recognized teacher training program between 1891 and 1915.

Coloradans expected colleges to bring benefits to their towns as well as to their graduates. Although the University of Colorado was a tiny institution in its early years, it loomed large in the ambitions of Boulder. The territorial legislature had designated Boulder as the site of a future university as early as 1861. In 1870 the town mobilized to fight off an unexpected move to shift the designation to Burlington (now part of Longmont). Actual construction of the first building waited until

The construction of "Old Main" at the University of Colorado in 1876 symbolized the early commitment of Coloradans to higher education.

Boulder residents could raise $15,000 to match a legislative appropriation in 1874. The *Boulder County News* summarized the mixed motivations behind the organization of a university. Not only would it draw to Boulder the most upstanding of the participants in the westward tide, argued the editor, but "as soon as the first of the University buildings is completed, there will not be an acre of land or a town lot in sight from its cupola but will bear enhanced value by reason of its erection."[8]

The expectations and rivalries were similar among a dozen other settlements that viewed a college as any other state institution that might help to secure growth. Golden fought off Denver's claim to the School of Mines with the complaint that Denverites had already captured the territorial capital. By tradition, the Agricultural College went to Fort Collins after Cañon City chose the penitentiary. Gunnison obtained designation as a site for a Western Slope normal school in 1901 but found appropriations for buildings blocked for eight years by the jealousy of Delta, Glenwood Springs, Montrose, Grand

Junction, and Durango. A headline in the *Gunnison News-Champion,* when the legislature decided for Gunnison, epitomized and parodied the booster attitude toward higher education. Under the announcement of the basic decision, it continued, "It Will Bring Other Good Things. It Will Win Broad-gauging of the Colorado and Southern and Extension to Delta. It Will Win a Smelter. It Will Win Manufactures. This Is the Turn of the Tide. Things Are Moving Around Us. Now Is the Time to Push Gunnison."[9]

If this public fixation on growth offered a dangerous environment for the survival of the forests or the flowering of the arts, it did provide fertile soil for big business in mining. The last decades of the nineteenth century were an era of industrial consolidation all over the United States. The Civil War had been a huge practice exercise in logistics, and the expansion of railroads had already forced experimentation in new forms of corporate management. The extension of rail mileage in the 1870s and 1880s opened up distant sources of supply and merged local into regional or even national markets, forcing industry to reorganize for operation on a matching scale. The economic advantages of large-scale operation outweighed any drawbacks in the minds of U.S. manufacturing magnates and financial bosses.

In Colorado hard-rock metals mining had been dependent on outside capital for tunneling, equipment, and processing since the 1860s. By the time of the Leadville discoveries, Coloradans were like successful storekeepers who had learned the techniques for attracting customers. Probably the most successful and wide-ranging business was conducted by the partnership of Eben Smith, Jerome Chaffee, and David Moffat, men who made their fortunes by the constant buying and selling of mine properties. In 1879 Chaffee hired a private railroad car; loaded it with food, liquor, and cigars; and gave over two dozen engineers, investors, and journalists a free visit to Leadville and the Little Pittsburgh mine. The partners sold eighty thousand shares to the excursionists and thousands more with the help of the publicity. Easterners who lacked the wealth to merit such special treatment could still join in the game through special mining stock exchanges in New York, Boston, Philadelphia, St. Louis, and Chicago.

The mid-1880s saw a lag in investment, but Cripple Creek revived the great days in which those with properties to sell could sit back and wait for customers to browse through an assortment of mines and mining securities. One source has counted over three thousand corporations organized in the United States during the 1890s to engage in Colorado mining; Great Britain issued over one hundred charters for the same purpose. The shares of many of these companies were traded not in the East but on four Colorado Springs exchanges through the offices of 275 local brokers crowded along Tejon Street. Philadelphians or Londoners with money to invest sent it to friends and relatives in the exclusive resort town where first-hand information and hot tips were presumably to be had at every tea and piano recital. By 1898 one expert estimated that three-fourths of the Cripple Creek mines were locally owned or controlled.

A trend toward the consolidation of smelters occurred in the same decades. Dozens of small plants that opened in new silver regions — at Tin Cup, Gothic, Kokomo, Silver Cliff, Breckenridge, St. Elmo, Summit, Ten Mile, Aspen — operated for only a few years before shutting down or merging into more efficient units. Several larger companies that accumulated working capital from successful boomtown businesses moved from the mountains to Denver or Pueblo. The cities offered a larger and cheaper labor force, access to coking coal, and railroad systems that allowed the firms to process ore from every Rocky Mountain mining district. Nathaniel Hill's Boston and Colorado Smelter was the first, moving from Black Hawk to Denver in 1879. Architect Robert Roeschlaub designed the new complex and the associated company town of Argo. After a disastrous fire at its Leadville works, the Grant Smelter moved to Denver in 1882. Every day the five hundred employees at the new plant fed four hundred tons of ore to its thirty-five furnaces. Denver's third giant smelter was the Globe, erected in 1886 with company housing that formed the nucleus of Globeville.

Pueblo was the other logical location for smelters. It boasted good railroads, proximity to the Trinidad coal fields, an easy route down the Arkansas Valley from Leadville and Aspen, and a core of ardent boosters. Pueblo Smelting and Refining was started in 1878 and the Colorado Smelting Company of Anton Eilers in 1883. The most important Pueblo smelter arrived in 1888, when the Guggenheim family used profits from Leadville mining to build the million-dollar Philadelphia Smelting and Refining Company. The eager townspeople offered free land, tax abatements, and $25,000 cash to seal the Guggenheim decision and keep the plant from Denver.

The piedmont smelters were obvious candidates for merger into national corporations. Most of the firms had long-standing connections with middle western or eastern refineries to which they shipped partially processed matte. Their managers juggled shipments of ore from Idaho, Montana, Arizona, Mexico, and Colorado as they searched for the perfect balance of silver, lead, and copper content. Capital from the investment markets of Boston and New York could be used to finance consolidations that formalized the informal business relations. The Grant smelter led the way in 1883, merging with the Omaha Smelting and Refining Company to form an integrated firm with several sampling agencies, two smelters, a refinery, and a marketing arm. It added the Durango smelter in 1896. August R. Meyer took the initiative in creating Consolidated Kansas City Smelting and Refining in 1887, with mines in Mexico and smelters at Leadville, Kansas City, and El Paso. United Smelting and Refining added Pueblo's Colorado smelter to plants in Chicago, Helena, and Great Falls in 1890, and the Guggenheims expanded operations with new facilities in Mexico and New Jersey.

The next major step came in 1899. Henry Rogers and William Rockefeller of Standard Oil wanted to control copper matte from western smelters in order to realize an imposing plan to fix the international price of copper. They agreed to help finance consolidation of the large companies and independent smelters in return for the contract to sell the copper for the new smelter giant. The American Smelting and Refining Company (ASARCO), formed in 1899 and capitalized at $65 million, absorbed Consolidated Kansas City, Omaha and Grant, United, Globe, Pueblo Smelting, and several other firms. The "Smelter Trust" controlled two-thirds of the U.S. smelting and refining capacity, with six plants in Colorado and nearly a dozen in other states. It retained a strong Colorado character. The key operating positions went to August Meyer and James Grant, who continued to supervise daily decisions from his old Denver office.

The final move came in 1901, when the Guggenheims acquired a one-third interest in American Smelting and Refining. During the summer of 1899 they had fended off a strike by granting substantial wage increases, while James Grant had shut down the ASARCO plants in bitter opposition to the union. The Guggenheims made immense profits as ASARCO began to choke in red ink. With the ASARCO plants in need of capital for modernization, the cash-rich Guggenheims wrote their own merger terms to create what Coloradans soon called the "smelter monopoly." Daniel Guggenheim was elected chair of American Smelting and Refining, and Simon, Morris, Isaac, and Solomon Guggenheim took seats on the board. In the same year the United States Reduction and Refining Company brought together five cyanide and chlorination plants for gold ore in the Colorado Springs–Cripple Creek area. Mining people viewed the Smelter Trust as an offspring grown so large and oppressive as virtually to strangle the industry that had created it.

The growth of coal mining involved corporate enterprise from the start. The fuel demands of western railroads largely accounted for the transformation of coal mining from one-person or two-person operations that hauled their product to market one wagonload at a time into a big business. Annual coal production rose from one hundred thousand to 3 million tons between the mid-1870s and the late 1880s. Mines operated directly by railroads or through subordinate firms such as the Union Coal Company (Union Pacific) or Cañon City and Trinidad Coal and Coking (Santa Fe) supplied over 80 percent of the state's output. Except for a few mines west of the mountains, Colorado coal came from the northern fields of Boulder, Jefferson, and Weld counties, a middle field around Cañon City, and the southern field from Walsenburg through Trinidad. By 1906, according to the *Engineering and Mining Journal*, coal mining employed a tenth of all Colorado workers.

The largest of the railroad coal companies was, in fact, the seed for Colorado's most important corporation. Put together in 1880 from three smaller firms, Colorado Coal and Iron was a part of William Jackson Palmer's Rio Grande empire. It was intended to sell town lots and agricultural lands, to mine and market coal, to manufacture coke, and to produce iron and steel at Pueblo. The steel plant — complete with blast furnace, Bessemer converter, blooming and rail mills, foundry, and machine shops — was built in 1880 and 1881 on two square miles of open mesa beyond the railroad's town of South Pueblo. The first pig iron was run through the Bessemer process in April 1882, and for the next decade Colorado Coal and Iron sold pig iron, pipes, spikes, and steel rails to a smattering of customers. The growing Denver and Rio Grande provided the principal market for its rails, with the Union Pacific and Colorado Midland as occasional customers. As most western railroads continued to rely on eastern suppliers, a shift of control from Palmer to Henry Sprague in 1884 did little to improve the prospects of the $2 million steel works. In fact, it was the sale of domestic and railroad coal and the production of coke for Colorado smelters that kept the company alive.

Despite the size of Colorado Coal and Iron, entrepreneur John C. Osgood mounted a successful challenge in the late 1880s. Osgood organized his Colorado Fuel Company in 1884 to supply coal to the Chicago, Burlington, and Quincy Railroad, wisely involving many successful Denver businesspeople in the corporation. The new competitor aggressively acquired coal lands in the Las Animas–Huerfano region and around Glenwood Springs and Crested Butte. Between 1888 and 1892 Osgood's corporation emerged as the largest coal producer in the Rocky Mountain West, capturing most Denver business and signing contracts with the Union Pacific and Missouri Pacific railroads.

The result was a merger — on Osgood's terms — in 1892. The new Colorado Fuel and Iron Company (CF&I) owned sixty-nine thousand acres of coal lands that provided twelve tons of coal a day, or 45 percent of the state's output. It ran two iron mines, four coking plants, and the only integrated steel plant in the West. Its operations stretched through a dozen Colorado counties, with the heaviest activity in Las Animas, Huerfano, Pueblo, Fremont, Gunnison, Pitkin, and Garfield counties. Over the next decade CF&I absorbed smaller coal mines to raise its share of Colorado coal production to 75 percent. It modernized the Bessemer works at Pueblo at a cost of $20 million between 1899 and 1903 and tripled the output with the help of a national pooling agreement. Charles Schwab of Carnegie Steel and Elbert Gary of Federal Steel recognized the importance of Osgood's company by allocating it 7 percent of the national market for steel rails. From Wyoming to New Mexico, CF&I employed an army — fifteen thousand workers, from clerks to coal weighers.

The six thousand employees in Pueblo had the resources of a city available, but the nine thousand workers at the company's thirty coal mines, iron mines, limestone mines, and coking plants were dependent on CF&I for their daily lives as well as their livelihoods. Under the direction of Dr. Richard Corwin, the company maintained a physician in each of its mining camps and a hospital in Pueblo. Corwin also launched a Sociological Department in 1901 as a corporate response to criticisms raised during that year's coal strike. It promoted self-improvement through kindergartens, home economics training, night classes for immigrant workers, reading rooms, and recreation centers. The company also learned to build more acceptable housing in its twentieth-century towns than it had in the 1880s and 1890s. Most of the houses in Primero, Segundo, Tercio, and Cuarto, west of Trinidad, were frame boxes with three or four rooms. Houses at Morley were built from concrete blocks molded to imitate stone and sported porches and hip roofs. Redstone along the Crystal River, where Osgood built a forty-two-room mansion, was a showplace, with a Tudor-style boarding house and shingled cottages with simple scrollwork and painted trim.

The issuance of new stock and convertible bonds to finance modernization opened CF&I to takeover. During 1901 and 1902 John W. Gates of Chicago attempted to buy control, with the expectation of selling the company to the new U.S. Steel Corporation. A plunger in business and at the gambling table, "Bet-a-Million" Gates had angered such sober tycoons as Andrew Carnegie and J. P. Morgan. Although defeated in a dramatic series of court battles, the Gates takeover scheme forced John Osgood into alliance with railroad mogul George Jay Gould and with John D. Rockefeller. When failure to complete renovation and disruption from the financial war brought the firm near bankruptcy in the following year, Rockefeller quietly took control. Colorado's largest business had been annexed to the nation's largest business empire.

In its first half century Colorado was run by its entrepreneurs. It was first a speculator's frontier, then a booster's territory, and then a businessperson's state. The key to personal success and public influence alike was the ability to assemble the capital, labor, and expertise necessary to exploit the land's natural resources. The state recognized demigods of development as its leaders, people like John Evans, whom contemporaries described as a "seer and statesman," as "one of the great Captains in civil life, a projector, an organizer, a man with the ability to conceive and execute great undertakings among the people."[10] Was a man such as Evans a politician or a booster, a business leader or a speculator? The question is not relevant, for Evans moved freely and smoothly from one role to another, from one venture to the next, pyramiding profits from one investment to finance another and feeding his new funds into yet another scheme.

With this pattern in mind, historians have sought to identify the typical Coloradan among these entrepreneurs. William Byers, John Evans, Jerome Chaffee, and David Moffat have all been nominated: booster-capitalist and businessman-politician in varying combinations. The twentieth-century historian could just as well name Horace Tabor as the embodiment of the state's growth. Today he is seen as a figure of ridicule, an antihero of folklore posed between the granite face of his first wife, Augusta, and the pink smiles of his second wife, Elizabeth McCourt Doe (Baby Doe). Tabor had wealth, fame, and position and lost it all through business mistakes and reverses and the notoriety of his divorce from Augusta and remarriage to Baby Doe. His life story was the stuff of which legends are made; it has been a favorite Colorado tradition that adds a touch of human drama, pathos, and buffoonery to the saga of western growth. To his contemporaries, however, H.A.W. Tabor was a different man than the person whose personal tragedy eroded all of his successes. He was, more than anyone else, the symbol of fabulous Leadville. Tabor's career, from mining camp merchant to mine owner to wealthy capitalist, parallels the evolution of Colorado mining. The Tabor Opera House, which he built in Leadville, his Tabor Block of offices, and the Tabor Grand Opera House in Denver were focal points for civic pride, monuments of social and economic achievement that marked new eras for their cities. Those actions Tabor took in building his own career duplicated in miniature the steps by which Coloradans fashioned their state into a successful commonwealth.

CHAPTER 8

# THE OTHER SIDE OF THE COIN: A GENERATION OF INDUSTRIAL WARFARE

From midnight until dawn on the cold night of September 30, 1903, Emma Langdon worked to get out the Victor *Record*. As members of the National Guard were hammering on the door of the *Record* office demanding entrance in the name of the governor of Colorado, she was composing the morning issue on the cumbersome linotype machine. When householders in the mining town stepped out into the crisp morning air for their daily paper, they saw a headline that read "SOMEWHAT DISFIGURED, BUT STILL IN THE RING!" The story on page 1 reported that at 11:05 the previous evening, a squad of armed soldiers led by Major Thomas McClelland had arrested Emma Langdon's husband and other members of the newspaper's staff as "prisoners of war." The alleged offense that precipitated the raid and kept the *Record* staff in the military lockup for more than twenty-four hours was an article detailing the criminal records of several guardsmen on active duty in the Cripple Creek mining district.

In the minds of guard officers, the real misdeed was the *Record*'s consistent support of the Western Federation of Miners (WFM) in its two-month-old strike against Cripple Creek mine owners. Since February the WFM had been battling to obtain an eight-hour workday for smelter workers in Colorado City, an industrial suburb of Colorado Springs. Unable to force the largest smelter companies to recognize their union, the federation leadership had resorted to a sympathy strike. On August 8, Cripple Creek miners had walked out on the local mines that shipped ore to nonunion mills and smelters in Colorado City. When a mine fire and several beatings marred the peacefulness of the new strike, Colorado Governor James Peabody had answered the petition of local businesspeople with units of the Colorado National Guard. His order of September 4, 1903, sent nearly one thousand troops into Teller County "to prevent . . . threatened insurrection," "to protect all persons and property . . . from unlawful interference," and to see that "public peace and good order be preserved upon all occasions, to the end that the authority and dignity of this state be maintained and her power to suppress lawlessness within her borders be asserted."[1]

A similar order on March 3 had dispatched three hundred soldiers to protect the ore reduction works and smelters in Colorado City. November 20 brought a third proclamation and two troops of cavalry — four hundred men in all — to help the sheriff of strike-torn San Miguel County enforce the laws and constitution in the town of Telluride in the San Juans. On March 23, 1904, Governor Peabody called out the militia yet again, sending three hundred soldiers into Las Animas County to suppress a presumed state of rebellion among coal miners.

Colorado City, Cripple Creek, Telluride, and Trinidad were only a few of the towns in which labor disturbances divided Coloradans in 1903 and 1904. During 1903 coal miners in the northern fields conducted a successful strike for an eight-hour workday. The Idaho Springs Miners' Union, WFM, shut down several companies in Clear Creek County from May through July, and the Denver Mill and Smeltermen's Union, WFM, struck the Globe and Grant mills of the American Smelting and Refining Company on July 3. Both unions walked out in support of demands for shorter hours. In Denver strikebreakers protected by city police nullified the efforts of the mill workers by keeping the plants in operation. At Idaho Springs a dynamite blast at the Sun and Moon mine on July 28 provided the excuse for the owners and businesspeople of the Citizens' Protective League to run twenty-two union leaders out of town and to end the strike through systematic harassment.

At the root of each strike was the defiance of state law by the corporate community in Colorado. As early as 1899, the Colorado General Assembly had passed an eight-hour workday law for mine, mill, and smelter workers. Colorado Fuel and Iron and the Smelter Trust had responded by cutting wages in proportion to the reduction in hours. A month after the assembly's law went into effect the Colorado Supreme Court had declared that it violated the right of workers to sell their labor as they saw fit. Three years later Coloradans countered the court's objections by voting — 72,980 to 26,266 — for a constitutional amendment permitting adoption of an eight-hour workday law. Under heavy pressure from corporate lobbyists, however, the general assembly in its 1903 session squandered weeks in debate and adjourned without taking the action clearly mandated by the electorate.

Observers all over the state echoed journalist Ray Stannard Baker. The legislature's failure to act was labeled a "brazen, conscienceless defeat of the will of the people," an example of "lawlessness by finesse." Even a conservative newspaper like the *Denver Post* called on organized labor to establish its own eight-hour day. In response the WFM formally launched a campaign for the eight-hour workday, and union president Charles Moyer blamed the legislators for the labor troubles. Coming after the spontaneous strikes in Idaho Springs and Denver and building on WFM efforts earlier in the year to organize the mill workers in Colorado City, the drive led directly to the Cripple Creek strike in August and to a walkout by mill workers and miners at Telluride on September 1. A member of the Cloud City Miners' Union in Leadville expressed the mood of most working miners: "If the eight hour law don't suit the s —— s of b —— s it suits us and they will have to give us eight hours whether they want to or not."[2]

In the southern coal fields under the shadow of the Spanish Peaks, miners faced not only the failure of the eight-hour movement but also the systematic violation of special protective statutes. In September 1903, after fruitless negotiations, members of the United Mine Workers shut down the mines with demands that scarcely went beyond the requirements of state law: semimonthly paydays, definition of a ton as two thousand rather than twenty-four hundred pounds, and payment of wages in U.S. currency rather than in company scrip. Coal miners knew they faced danger every day from collapsing shafts. The companies pretended that workers were independent contractors and paid by weight of coal produced. The temptation was strong to cut corners on the "deadwork" of timbering and shoring up the tunnels. Miners also demanded enforcement of the law requiring adequate ventilation, as the coal dust stirred up within the shafts could form a combination with methane, or "fire damp," that was as dangerous as nitroglycerine. Accidental ignition could send tongues of flame racing through the mines consuming all of the oxygen and leaving the miners to suffocate. Time and again the foothills and mountains echoed with the rumble of underground explosions, which added to the toll from accidents with mining machinery. In 1901 and 1902 Colorado coal mines killed or crippled three hundred workers; most of the casualties were among the nine thousand workers in Las Animas and Huerfano counties. During the longer period from 1884 to 1912, the rate of accidental deaths in Colorado coal mines was twice the national rate.

The strikes of 1903 and 1904 climaxed two decades of union activity among Colorado's industrial workers. A strike in 1880 in Leadville had not been an auspicious start for Colorado workers. From 1881 through 1886, however, there were at least thirty-five successful strikes in the mining industry. A statewide coal strike in 1883, led by the Knights of Labor, and a victory by the Knights in an action against the Union Pacific Railroad a year later were especially important in attracting new members to the union. By 1892 the Colorado Bureau of Labor Statistics counted nearly 16,000 unionists in 206 organizations.

The expansion of the 1880s brought growing strength to the Denver labor movement. The Knights of Labor tried to fight the saloon and organize working-class households around positive institutions such as reading rooms. With the onset of economic depression in 1893, the Trades and Labor Assembly organized soup kitchens for the unemployed. Despite the problems, Labor Day 1894 brought out two thousand marchers representing one hundred unions, with a picnic at Manhattan Beach following the parade. "It seemed that every laboring man, his son, dog, and cat, were out keeping step with the band. . . . All the fire companies were out, and I think I never saw so many pretty horses," wrote Josie Guggenheim to her friend Charles Wolcott.[3]

The spread of unions in the 1880s was the response of workers to the increasing constriction of opportunity within Colorado industry. A survey of attitudes of Colorado workers in 1888 showed widespread dissatisfaction with what increasing numbers of people were coming to think of as "the slavery of the laboring classes." Union leaders of the 1880s decried the concentration of capital among a few large corporations and the disappearance of independent prospectors and skilled crafts workers. "The man who can rise from the wage condition in these days," complained the *Labor Enquirer* of Denver, "must catch a windfall from his uncle or [a] bank unlocked."[4]

In the early 1890s these same complaints became the basis of a new political party. On September 9, 1891, representatives from seventeen counties met in Denver to organize the People's party of Colorado. Many of its founders were members of the Farmer's Alliance or of the short-lived Independent party of 1890 — native-born Protestants from the farming counties who were more concerned about the problems of small entrepreneurs than about the plight of wage laborers. When the Populists developed their platform for the 1892 election, however, they adopted strong stands for an eight-hour workday, employers' liability legislation, a child labor law, and state operation of coal mines. Gubernatorial nominee Davis Waite, a long-time reformer who founded the Aspen *Union Era* in 1891, feared the corruption of politics by big business and stood ready to battle the monopolists wherever they appeared. As the campaign progressed, Populists in search of the largest pool of votes put increasing emphasis on the needs of industrial workers laid off from their jobs because of the falling price of silver and did battle against the large corporations in their speeches.

The election was a remarkable victory for the new party. Populist presidential candidate James Weaver received 57 percent of the Colorado vote. Davis Waite led the entire state ticket to victory with 48 percent against two opponents. Voters elected twenty-seven Populists to the state house and twelve to the state senate. Unlike the Populists of the Great Plains states, who represented dissatisfied farmers, the Colorado party drew the bulk of its supporters from the economically depressed mining counties. According to studies by historian James Wright, old Farmer's Alliance members were increasingly dissatisfied with the party's radical turn. It was the miners and the foreign-born workers who responded to the party's changing appeal with votes for Waite and Weaver. One supporter reported to Waite the excitement in Silverton, high in the San Juans, when the results were known: "We will run all night — Barrells of Beer and 'Galons of Whiskey' — Free to drink but no forceing — Temperance mens weakness Respected."[5]

In spite of the enthusiasm of workers in Leadville, Aspen, and the San Juans, Waite had no chance to implement the party's program of "paternalism for the common people." The nationwide financial panic in May 1893 threw as many as forty-five thousand Coloradans out of work by July. Unemployment ran at more than 50 percent in some of the mining towns. With Populists in the minority in both houses of the Colorado General Assembly, Governor Waite found that a special session of the legislature in the first months of 1894 was unwilling to enact the bulk of a thirty-three-point program for aiding debtors, protecting laborers, and reforming the political structure of the state. The lawmakers did accept mine inspection laws, antiscrip laws requiring payment of wages in cash, and anti-Pinkerton laws against private mine police, all of which were passed but not enforced. The proposal for an eight-hour day was steadily watered down until it applied only to state employees.

When the governor ran for re-election in 1894, he could cite only this small list of achievements and call for further change to rescue Colorado from industrial slavery. His Republican opponent, Albert McIntire, argued that the Populists had disgraced Colorado in the eyes of the nation, frightened off capital, and fostered a spirit of anarchy. He pointed with special emphasis to Waite's use of the militia to support striking mine workers at Cripple Creek in 1894. Putting the state on the side of unions for the first time, Waite had neutralized the El Paso County posse and helped striking miners gain an eight-hour day. On election day Waite's appeal to economic-class interests brought him 75,000 votes and continued support from miners and immigrants, but the law-and-order Republicans won with 93,500 votes from native-born Americans on the farms and in the large cities.

The rejection of the Populist program for comprehensive reform did not end the political involvement of Colorado labor unionists. As former Populists, Democrats, and maverick "Silver Republicans" scrambled to unite behind the presidential banner of William Jennings Bryan and the unlimited coinage of silver in 1896, Colorado labor leaders organized the State Federation of Labor. Representing the full range of trade unionism, the federation worked for the package of laws whose enforcement was at issue during 1903 and 1904: the eight-hour workday, abolition of company scrip, liability of employers. It also maintained advocacy of the broader reforms of the Populist party in demands for municipal ownership of utilities, the nationalization of railroads and mines, a graduated income tax, and direct legislation through the initiative and referendum.

Much of the political strength of organized labor came from the growth of two new unions among miners dissatisfied with the often ineffectual Knights of Labor. In 1889 and 1890 Colorado coal miners participated in the formation of the United Mine Workers (UMW), a new national organization intended to meet the great coal corporations with equal strength all across the country. Hard-rock miners from Aspen, Creede, Ouray, and Rico similarly helped to organize the WFM in 1893. In 1901 the WFM moved its headquarters from Butte to Denver. William D. "Big Bill" Haywood ran the office as secretary-treasurer. Emma Langdon joined the team in 1904 after being kicked out of Cripple Creek. By 1903 the WFM's forty-two Colorado locals provided nearly eight thousand of its twenty-seven thousand members among western metal miners and smelter workers.

Fighting its first strikes to prevent the reduction of wages during the depression of the 1890s, the WFM took the offensive at the end of the decade. It climaxed a series of labor disputes with a strike in May 1901 against the Smuggler-Union Company of Telluride. Two months later the WFM emerged from the bloody confrontation with a clear victory — the maintenance of the eight-hour workday at prevailing wage rates and recognition of the union in a three-year contract. To federation leaders the victory proved the effectiveness of the policy of militancy. When the strike was still in progress, the ninth annual convention of the federation heard WFM President Edward Boyce denounce the subservience of existing parties to corporate influence and call for "a complete revolution of present social and economic conditions to the end that justice may be meted out to all people of the earth."[6] On June 3 the delegates demanded radical alternatives to the capitalist-dominated political parties and their policies of status quo. A year later the tenth convention took the additional step of recommending that local unions adopt the platform of the Socialist Party of America.

It is nearly impossible to determine how many of the rank and file of the WFM accepted socialism, but Boyce, his successor Charles Moyer, and William Haywood were deeply committed. They argued that a united stand against big money by the working classes was the only defense for individual rights. As Big Bill Haywood put the issue to an audience of striking miners, the organization was "the only friend you have against corporate oppression." In the face of the concentrated economic power represented by Colorado Fuel and Iron, by the Smelter Trust, and by other examples of "solidified commercialism," the workers' only hope was counterorganization. Circumstances of life and labor in the Rockies, not theories borrowed from Europe, caused Haywood to compare the tyrannous corporations to George III and Boyce to assert that

Members of the Colorado State Militia guarding the Emmett Mine at Leadville in the fall of 1896. The intervention of the militia after the violence against the Emmett and other mines helped to break a strike by the Western Federation of Miners.

> There are two classes of people in the world; one is composed of the men and women who produce all; the other is composed of men and women who produce nothing but live in luxury upon the wealth produced by others. Realizing this to be a fact, the time has arrived when this organization should array itself upon the side of the producers and advise its members to take political action and work for the adoption of those principles that are destined to free the people from the grasp of privileged classes.[7]

A logical next step was the participation of Haywood, Langdon, and five other Denverites in the 1905 convention that founded the Industrial Workers of the World — the "one big union" that was supposed to redress that balance between capital and labor.

The socialism of the WFM helped to drive Colorado businesspeople into aggressive reaction. At stake, many thought, was employers' control of their own businesses. In the eyes of someone like coal tycoon John Osgood, the leaders of the WFM and the UMW were despots who extracted more "blind obedience" and "absolute surrender of independence" than the czar of Russia.[8] Behind the immediate issues of wages and hours in every major strike from 1890 to 1915 was the question of recognition of unions as agents for collective bargaining. Like Charles MacNeil of U.S. Reduction and Refining in Colorado City in 1903, many managers acted as if the unionists on strike had simply resigned their positions and severed all ties with their jobs. Franklin Guiterman, general manager for the Smelter Trust in Colorado, stated the basic stand of the employers during the Denver strike of 1903: "The issue is whether the corporations which are an integral part of the industrial community . . . shall be subject to the domination and dictation of an irresponsible body which assumes to represent the working classes."[9]

Equally galling to the captains of the mining industry was the political influence of unions in areas with large populations of hard-rock miners. Antilabor politicians could seldom secure a majority in Teller or Lake counties or in the San Juans. Teller County's sheriff in 1903, for example, was a member of Miners' Union No. 40. Town councils in Victor, Altman, and Goldfield were also sympathetic to the WFM, although Cripple Creek remained a business-dominated town. As events were to show, an unstated goal of the business interests during the strikes of 1903 and 1904 was to break not only the miners' unions but also their influence on local governments.

Events in Telluride confirmed the worst fears about industrial unionism. The WFM won the 1901 strike by violence. Unionists laid siege to strikebreakers working the Smuggler-Union mine and killed three men before the mine owners capitulated. A year later, on the evening of November 19, 1902, an unseen assassin fired a load of buckshot into Smuggler-Union manager Arthur Collins as he sat at home with his back to an open window. The death of Collins convinced other mine operators that they were fighting literally for their lives against the "Western Federation of Murderers." Destruction of mine property at Idaho Springs and Cripple Creek in 1903 provided additional evidence that unions were criminal conspiracies of bandits and terrorists. The diary of Robert Livermore, a recent graduate of the MIT engineering program and a new arrival in Telluride, shows the inability of the managers to understand the real grievances of their workers. The rank and file of the WFM, he was convinced, were held in line by intimidation orchestrated by an "inner circle" in which Bill Haywood was the "arch conspirator." The complaints of the miners struck him as "vague and various. Though there was no particular objection to wages and hours, numerous excuses were found for a strike."[10]

Colorado business owners met unions with counterorganizations. Mine owners' associations appeared in such towns as Telluride and Cripple Creek in 1901 and 1902, representing management in a united front against labor's demands. During the spring of 1903, many Coloradans also found a new secular religion in the citizens' alliance movement. Recently suggested by the president of the National Association of Manufacturers, the citizens' alliances were intended to combat labor unions in the name of industrial freedom. The Denver alliance had three thousand members by the end of April and played an important part in crushing the city's smelter strike in July. Throughout the summer excited businesspeople in towns across the state held meetings to form their own alliances. The logical follow-up was the formation, in October, of a State Citizens' Alliance of Colorado, claiming twenty thousand members.

By 1903, then, rhetoric anticipated reality. Having heard time and again that society was irreconcilably divided, the citizens of Colorado chose to side either with the capitalists or with the workers; there was no middle ground. "On the one hand," wrote one analyst, "we see united the mine owners and others whose economic interests coincide . . . with those of large properties and business in general; a considerable part of the bench and bar; most of the higher state officials and members of the legislature; ministers of religion, to a great extent, and practically all of the important newspapers." In opposition were laborers, "standing practically as a unit where organized and supported to a certain extent by workingmen outside of the unions, some small businessmen dependent on the miners' trade, and scattered reinforcements from other parts of the population."[11]

In every strike in these pivotal years, the most powerful third force in Colorado was thrown directly on the side of the business community. With the backing of state courts, Governor Peabody used the National Guard to break the influence of the United Mine Workers in the coal fields and of the Western Federation of Miners in the San Juan Mountains and in Teller County. He bent the law to condone illegal actions by mine owners' associations

(MOA) and citizens' alliances, while at the same time he punished union members for exercising their civil rights. As Peabody interpreted his duty, his task was "to preserve the commercial and industrial enterprises of Colorado from assault and annihilation."[12] Telluride and Cripple Creek, to Peabody's mind, raised the question of the survival of public order against rebellion.

Officials on the scene were even more blunt. To anyone who would listen, Adjutant General Sherman Bell bragged that he had taken command at Cripple Creek "to do up this anarchistic federation."[13] With the arrival of state troops, according to Bell, the strike had become a criminal conspiracy, a "secret rebellion." In September and October his soldiers arrested dozens of men without warrants (among them the Victor *Record* staff) and held them without formal charges in a military stockade. General Bell answered a writ of habeus corpus from the District Court by surrounding the courthouse with armed officers, placing snipers on the rooftops of nearby buildings, stationing a Gatling gun in the street outside, and marching the prisoners into the courtroom escorted by three dozen armed guards. "Habeus Corpus, hell!" he roared. "We'll give 'em post mortems." In the uproar over this demonstration, the governor instructed Bell to obey the orders of the court. Nevertheless, his officers continued to arrest and rearrest union members without formal charges.

On December 4, 1903, Governor Peabody formalized the premise under which the National Guard had acted for three months, declaring Teller County to be in a "state of insurrection and rebellion." The declaration came months after Bell had already defied the courts. In the opinion of Bell and his field commander, Colonel Edward Verdeckberg, the proclamation imposed martial law on Cripple Creek. Verdeckberg prohibited large gatherings, mounted raids to gather hidden firearms, and declared criticism of the guard to be illegal. Verdeckberg told complainers that "we are under orders only from God and Governor Peabody." In an extraordinary edict he stated that "no publication either by newspaper, pamphlet or handbill reflecting in any way upon the United States and the State of Colorado, or its officers, or tending in any way to influence the public mind against the government of the United States and the State of Colorado, will be permitted."[14] Behind the screen provided by the National Guard, the Mine Owners' Association and the Cripple Creek District Citizens' Alliance whipped local businesspeople into line and supervised the reopening of the mines with strikebreakers. By spring it took a "recommendation card" issued by the Mine Owners' Association to secure a job at Cripple Creek.

The withdrawal of state troops in April set up the last battle in the long struggle. Early in the morning of June 6, a massive explosion ripped the Independence railroad station, killing thirteen nonunion mine workers. That afternoon a mob of nonunion workers led by MOA members wrecked the WFM hall. Other alliance and MOA workers had already forced the resignation of the Teller County sheriff. Over the next several days militant business owners carried out a small revolution, securing the replacement of thirty officials sympathetic to the union and deporting dozens of union members. Troops sent back to Cripple Creek on June 7 questioned 1,569 members and shipped 238 of them out of the district. After a second withdrawal of the National Guard on July 27, MOA mobs continued what the *New York Times* called a reign of terror, destroying union property and banishing still more "agitators." In November the voters of Teller County had no alternative but to endorse the Republican ticket, which included the members of the mine owners' association and the citizens' alliance who had led the attack on the union. Court action eventually freed the vast majority of the strikers charged by Bell, and the state paid $60,000 to strikers forced across the border by the militia.

The same techniques for union-busting that proved successful at Idaho Springs and Cripple Creek were also used in San Miguel and Las Animas counties in the winter and spring of 1904. Mass deportations of dozens of workers, first by the National Guard and then by the Telluride Citizens' Alliance, effectively cleared that town of WFM activists and allowed reopening of the mines with scab labor. Official records show that guardsmen in the coal fields hauled fifty-two workers to the state line and warned them never to return. The "inconvenience" to those torn from families and homes was excused by military officers and Governor Peabody as "nothing by comparison to the suffering brought upon innocent members of the community by their acts."[15]

The 1904 state election was a showdown between two disparate visions of Colorado's future. Labor's slogan was "Anybody but Peabody." Major corporations supported the incumbent governor as a true friend who fought the unions and cleared his judicial appointments with big business. For the 1904 election, the Colorado Supreme Court appointed poll watchers from lists furnished by the Republican party to oversee Denver Democratic precincts while turning down Democratic requests for watchers in Huerfano, Las Animas, and Costillo counties. Although initial returns showed Democrat Alva Adams victorious by ten thousand votes, the Supreme Court began systematically to reject the returns in areas in which frauds were reported. Because the hearings were confined to heavily Democratic precincts in Denver, Boulder, and Las Animas counties, the court reversed Democratic control of the state senate. In its turn, the newly created Republican majority in the general assembly declared Adams's victory void because of voting irregularities and installed Peabody for another term as governor. In a face-saving gesture forced by moderate Republicans, Peabody resigned immediately, passing the office to Republican Lieutenant Governor Jesse McDonald.

By 1905 and 1906 it was clear that organized business had won an important war against Colorado's workers. In scarcely a single mining camp from the southern piedmont to the Utah border did a strong miners' union remain in a position to fight the large companies. Indeed, another wave of industrial violence in the 1910s was little more than a measure of the failure of radical unionism in the previous decade. The troubles came, ironically, after some halting steps had been made toward the improvement of working conditions. Disasters in 1910 at CF&I's Primero and Starkville mines brought calls for reform even from Denver newspapers. A 1913 mine safety bill was a compromise that the big companies could live with but that put cash-starved competitors in a bind. It required better ventilation, frequent inspections, and efforts to keep coal dust down by techniques such as spraying pulverized rock.

Nevertheless, on September 16, 1913, nearly ten years after the start of the last coal strike, members of the United Mine Workers presented a list of demands to coal mine operators in Las Animas and Huerfano counties. A week later at least eight thousand miners walked off their jobs, struggling through driving snow and sleet to move their families and belongings from company housing in the foothill canyons to tent colonies on the open plains. Many of the strikers were recent immigrants. They were people like Louis Tikas who had immigrated from the Greek island of Crete to Denver in 1906, moved to the coal fields in 1912, and become the leader of the tent colony at Ludlow in 1913. The months of struggle helped to break down ethnic barriers among the workers such as the historic antipathy between

Greeks and Bulgarians. The roles of immigrant women also grew. Many provided leadership in the tent colonies and helped to preserve a sense of community solidarity in trying times.

The course of the new strike paralleled that of the 1903–1904 strike. Governor Elias Ammons — "a second Peabody" in the words of reformer Edward Costigan — dispatched the National Guard on October 28 in response to skirmishes between mine guards and armed strikers.[16] Command went to General John Chase, who had served under Sherman Bell at Cripple Creek and who used his two regiments of infantry and three troops of cavalry to harass unionists. From November through March his troops detained nearly two hundred UMW leaders without charges and periodically raided the strikers' camps.

At question in 1913 and 1914 was the control mine owners wielded over their employees. Critics agreed that the motto of the large corporations in the coal counties could be expressed in two words: "We Rule." To support county political machines, the larger firms such as Colorado Fuel and Iron "voted every man and woman in the employ, without any regard to their being naturalized or not, and even their mules . . . were registered, if they were fortunate enough to possess names."[17] County officials, in turn, placed the local machinery of law-making and law enforcement at the command of the companies. Colorado had a mine death rate twice as high as that of any other state; yet, in only one example, coroner's juries in Huerfano County in the early 1900s blamed eighty-nine of ninety fatal accidents on the carelessness of coal miners themselves. CF&I in particular also controlled the personal lives of its workers, forcing them to use company houses and company stores, as well as picking their teachers, doctors, preachers, movies, magazines, and books. Its policy was "to assert ownership throughout southern Colorado, the ownership of courts, executive and legislative officials, of coroners and other juries, of the churches, of the saloons, of the schools, of the lands, of the houses upon the lands, and eventually a certain ownership over the men who toil upon the lands."[18]

The coal strike was a desperate effort to challenge this influence. As they had in 1903, the strikers asked that the state of Colorado reassert its authority in the southern counties. Pointing to existing statutes, they demanded an eight-hour day, the abolition of company scrip, the enforcement of safety regulations, the removal of armed guards, the right to choose their own checkweigh clerks, and the right to live and trade where they pleased. In addition, the union requested a 10 percent wage increase and company recognition of the United Mine Workers. More than any other, the corporations resisted this final demand. Coal executives preferred a strike to even an informal conference that might be taken as recognition of the union. Along with claims that the UMW broke contracts in other mining districts and violated the freedom of its members, the mine owners stated their essential objection that collective bargaining interfered with their right to manage their properties as they saw fit.

The attitudes of public officials also showed how little the Colorado establishment had changed over the decade. In his initial orders Governor Ammons instructed the National Guard to confine itself to the protection of property. Under pressure from Colorado business interests, however, he ended the guard's neutrality in November by extending state protection to imported strikebreakers. General Chase, along with many of his officers, believed the union preached a rival loyalty that subverted the state. He reported to the governor that he had found a "thirst for blood" and a "long-continued disregard and contempt for all civil government" among union members. Even a peaceful demonstration by strikers against a court order appeared to him as "an intimidation to the civil authority."[19]

The six-month standoff in the coal fields ended April 20, 1914, when a detachment of the National Guard opened an attack on the tent colony at Ludlow. Located eighteen miles north of Trinidad at a railroad intersection near two large mines, the camp was considered such a trouble spot that the National Guard had raided it four times previously. The battle on April 20 lasted the entire day before National Guardsmen, with two machine guns, routed the defenders from protected positions behind the camp. Five strikers and one militiaman fell in the fighting, one boy died from a stray bullet, and two women and eleven children choked to death on thick smoke in the cellar underneath one of the tents when the National Guard set fire to the colony.

In the coal fields the result was ten days of civil war. More than one thousand armed miners swarmed over the hills to fight pitched battles with company guards and state troops. In Trinidad the miners displaced the elected authorities and effectively constituted a provisional government. Over a twenty-mile stretch between Trinidad and Walsenburg, they burned mine property and laid siege to the better-protected mines.

With 650 men, General Chase hovered along the railroad to the north but hesitated to challenge the rebellion. Not until President Wilson assigned 1,600 federal troops to southern Colorado with orders to disarm everyone in the strike zone — militia, company guards, and miners — did the warfare cease.

The initial reaction among the public at large was horror at what the press quickly termed the "Ludlow Massacre." In Denver ten thousand citizens stood in driving rain to cheer speakers who called Elias Ammons and the CF&I management "traitors to the people." Newspapers all over the country struggled to express their disgust with the coal barons. Over the next several months attention increasingly centered on John D. Rockefeller, Jr., the absentee owner of the Colorado Fuel and Iron Company. Union propagandist Walter Fink, for example, described in detail the "oilfed fire started by Rockefeller's murderers" with cans of Standard Oil kerosene.[20] The U.S. Commission on Industrial Relations (popularly known as "the Walsh Commission"), an independent investigating committee created by Congress in 1912, called Rockefeller to testify in January and May 1915. Although Rockefeller disclaimed any personal knowledge of the management of the company at the first session, in May commission chair Frank Walsh produced extensive correspondence that showed Rockefeller had approved every antiunion step taken by his people in Colorado. His power in the state had been such that he had even helped to ghostwrite an account of the strike for Governor Ammons to forward to President Wilson.

It was more as an investor cutting his losses than as a Christian gentleman that Rockefeller developed his highly publicized "Colorado Industrial Plan." In September 1914, with federal troops still in Colorado, President Wilson had proposed a scheme for settling the strike that would have recognized most union demands. At the same time that the owners rejected the idea, Rockefeller acknowledged to his Colorado agents that "public opinion will demand the acceptance of the President's proposition or some constructive suggestions from the operators."[21] A year later, after the publicity from the Commission on Industrial Relations, Rockefeller visited Colorado and announced that Colorado Fuel and Iron employees would receive a workable grievance procedure and would be allowed to elect representatives to joint worker-management committees on working conditions, sanitation, and safety. Underneath the rhetoric about industrial democracy and an "industrial constitution," the

Members of the Colorado National Guard riding the trains during the coal strike of 1913–1914.

company retained all authority over hiring and firing. In place of the United Mine Workers, which had withdrawn from southern Colorado in defeat, the employees of Colorado Fuel and Iron now had a "company union" without the right to collective bargaining. Although the CF&I program did make improvements in working conditions during the 1920s, the company's workers opted out of the company union in 1933, as soon as New Deal legislation gave them the option.

The voters of Colorado had already chosen sides in the dispute. In a three-way race for governor in the fall of 1914, Republican George Carlson used a "law-and-order" campaign to pile up

Evidence of the burning of the Ludlow tent colony under guard.

118,000 votes against a combined total of 115,000 for his Democratic and Progressive opponents. CF&I officials admitted before the Walsh Commission that they had sent out people to campaign for Carlson. CF&I President Jesse Welborn also wrote Rockefeller expressing pleasure over the re-election of Colorado Attorney General Fred Farrar, a man who had been "actively engaged for several months in connection with the work of grand juries in various coal counties, where indictments have been brought against those who participated in the rioting."[22] With the help of a sympathetic judge appointed by the new governor, a prosecuting attorney who had worked for CF&I, and a jury handpicked by the company, in the spring of 1915 Farrar secured the conviction of union official John Lawson on the charge of murdering a mine guard. Even though no direct evidence of guilt was ever presented, the Colorado Supreme Court did not overturn Lawson's conviction until 1917.

The year after the Ludlow incident also saw the creation of the Colorado Industrial Commission. The general assembly gave the new agency the power of compulsory investigation in all disputes over wages, hours, and working conditions that involved four or more employees. Either party to a dispute was required to file a thirty-day notice of any change in labor conditions and was forbidden to engage in a strike or lockout until the commission

Colorado Fuel and Iron emerged as one of the state's most powerful corporations in the early twentieth century.

finished an investigation and suggested a nonbinding solution. The legislation was entitled the "Colorado Industrial Peace Act," but it aroused the bitter opposition of all Colorado unions, as the cooling-off period allowed a company to make preparations that deadened the effect of a strike. Over the next decade the Colorado Industrial Commission proved useful in minor disputes but was ineffectual in major confrontations in which either side had something of value to lose. Violence during a steel strike in 1919, a tramway strike in 1920, and coal strikes in 1921 and 1926 showed how far Colorado remained from true industrial peace.

Over the span of two decades, from 1900 to 1920, Colorado business operators out-organized the state's industrial workers. In 1903 and 1904 corporate interests used the mine owners' associations, the citizens' alliances, and the Republican party to appropriate the state government and to freeze union members out of jobs. Indeed, the interested companies in each case directly financed the use of the National Guard by cashing certificates of indebtedness issued by the state. A decade later their hold was still as strong, as they used political influence to neutralize labor organizations and to establish a framework for labor negotiations favorable to business. With their tight hold on the important political resources of money, influence, and organizational expertise, corporate leaders had been able to bend the state to their will. "Solidarity Forever" was a rallying song for Colorado's industrial workers, but Colorado's businesspeople had just as much justification to join in a rousing chorus, singing that "union makes us strong."

# CHAPTER 9

# FARMING AND RANCHING IN THE AMERICAN DESERT

The first agricultural fair in Colorado opened September 21, 1866, a mile and a half northwest of Denver. An early snowstorm had delayed the fair's start by a day and turned the forty acres of fairgrounds to cold mud, but the visitors were delighted with the new facilities. The exhibition hall was an octagon three hundred feet in circumference, with a display shelf running along the wall and another counter in the middle for chunks of ore and prize quilts. According to Yankee traveler Silas Seymour, the mammoth vegetables captured everyone's attention — fifteen-pound turnips and thirty-five-pound cabbages from the South Platte Valley. Outside were stalls for prize livestock and a half-mile racetrack. The highlight came at the end of the four-day fair, when three thousand people watched nine women match their equestrian skills. Miss Carrie E. Barker of Boulder took the silver saddle with an exhibition of bareback riding after the judges were unable to decide on a first-place winner.

The fair was organized by city people. The Colorado Agricultural Society, which sponsored territorial fairs in 1866, 1867, and 1868, had first been advocated by the editors of the *Denver Republican* and the *Rocky Mountain News*. Only three of nine directors and officers at its formation in March 1863 were farmers. The others were urban businesspeople — an editor, a lawyer, a manufacturer, and merchants. During the next several years the organization continued to fill its executive posts with politicians, real estate speculators, and even a billiard hall owner.

The slow start of the society was typical of early farming in the new territory. During the same initial years in which Colorado advocates proclaimed unbounded mineral treasures, guidebooks had to admit that its possibilities for agriculture were as yet untried. The first year with even a fair showing was 1866, when perhaps fifty thousand acres were planted along the South

Platte River and its tributaries. Three years later local proponents estimated production at 1.8 million bushels of grain, but the ninth census in 1870 found only seventeen hundred farms (most in southern Colorado) and fewer than one hundred thousand acres of improved farmland.

As the history of the Colorado Agricultural Society also shows, urban promoters took some of the important first steps in the development of local farming. During the lean years of the mid-1860s, Robert Strahorn published the *Colorado Agricultural and Stock Journal* at the same time he supervised circulation for the *Denver Tribune.* Ned Farrell's *Colorado: The Rocky Mountain Gem* and Ovando Hollister's *Mines of Colorado* devoted chapters to the delights of piedmont farming, and William Byers was always prepared with an editorial on the theme. Their optimistic predictions failed to conceal serious worries about the effect of retarded agriculture on Colorado's future. To political philosophers the absence of a large farming population implied that Colorado might miss the purifying influence of that "conservative element of all national and political and social growth." In more practical terms, urban businesspeople thought the lack of well-developed farms deprived the mining industry of a vital component. Agriculture, said the *Rocky Mountain News,* was "the only means by which our mines can be developed, for unless we can become self-sustaining, we may not hope that the necessities of life can be furnished here at rates that will warrant extensive mining operations."[1]

The boosters of Colorado farming of necessity advocated an innovation in U.S. farming techniques. Potential settlers were aware that the burden laid on Colorado agriculture by sun and cloudless skies could only be lifted by irrigation, a procedure unfamiliar and forbidding to farmers accustomed to the steamy summer nights and towering thunderstorms along the Tennessee or the Wabash. An immigrant to Colorado would have to learn how to measure flowing water, how to prepare and maintain headgates, when to turn the water onto the fields and how much to apply, and which crops to favor and which to shun. In *Colorado as an Agricultural State,* William Pabor summed up the basic constraint: "As compared with Illinois, Minnesota, Nebraska, or Kansas, Colorado is not a farming country. . . . There is a 'water line' to go beyond, which means disappointment and destruction to the stalwart sons of the soil who seek to gain a livelihood from the bosom of Mother Earth. Inside the line, certain conditions being complied with, success is certain."[2]

In response to eastern uncertainties, Coloradans argued that irrigation was not a burden but a pleasure. A steady and assured water supply, they said, was obviously superior to reliance upon sporadic cloudbursts. At the same time, advocates claimed that irrigation water from the mountains continually replenished the soil with nutrients carried in suspension. It was an established fact, said the *Colorado Tribune,* that irrigation allowed crops 50 percent greater than those on bottomlands farmed in the eastern manner. Stories of two-foot-long beets and yields of seventy or eighty bushels of wheat per acre seemed sufficient proof. The costs of irrigation were also less than the expense of draining Midwest prairies, and the Colorado farmer never needed to worry about grubbing out the rank weeds that exhausted the soil in humid climates. Crops could cure in the field without fear of mildew, mold, or rot. Because irrigation allowed high productivity, the average farm could also be forty acres or smaller, making possible the dense settlement required to support schools and civilized society.

Success in the pictured paradise required a modification of behavior customary in the East. "One man alone cannot build an irrigation canal many miles in length and so redeem broad prairie land from the curse of sterility," wrote Pabor. "It takes combined energy, skill, and capital to construct them."[3] Following the analogy of railroad land grants, the *Rocky Mountain News* as early as 1864 appealed to Congress to authorize grants from the public domain to corporations that would undertake irrigation canals in the arid West. A more practicable scheme for spreading the costs of ditch building and maintenance, however, waited for another voice from the city. In the *New York Tribune* of December 4, 1869, agricultural editor Nathan C. Meeker announced a public meeting for the purpose of forming a colony for settlement in Colorado. Later in the month, an enthusiastic gathering organized the Union Colony Association with Meeker as president, Robert A. Cameron as vice president, and Horace Greeley as treasurer. Membership fees of $155 were to be pooled for the purchase of land, with each member entitled to receive a farming plot and to purchase a town lot. Surplus funds were to be applied by the trustees to "improvements for the common good" — schools, a town hall, and the top priority, irrigation canals. Farm and town property was to be owned privately by members of the colony; public improvements and irrigation facilities would be held collectively through the association.

On April 12 the *New York Tribune* announced the purchase of twelve thousand acres of Denver Pacific land along the Cache la Poudre River in northern Colorado and the filing of a preliminary claim on sixty thousand additional acres in the public domain. Within a month colonists began to arrive in the new settlement, the first of three thousand men and women to arrive before the end of June. A frame hotel hauled in from a nearby town housed the vanguard. The Union Colonists settled in a central village rather than scattering among separate farmsteads. Not only could capital be pooled for the experiment but skills, knowledge, energy, and companionship could be shared as well. The venture was described not as a utopian society on a new model but rather as an effort to reproduce the best of the American experience in the most efficient manner. Within a year the new town of Greeley was a "fixed fact." Over four hundred houses, a Colony Hall, two brick business blocks, a library, a lyceum, schools, and churches accommodated the town's fifteen hundred inhabitants. The absence of liquor stores, saloons, and billiard halls, said the temperance advocates who founded and peopled the colony, accounted for its "sobriety, good order, peace, harmony, and prosperity."[4]

Greeley was eloquent testimony to the potential of irrigated agriculture. As an enterprise backed and publicized by the *New York Tribune,* the most widely read periodical in the nineteenth-century United States, success or failure could determine the character of territorial development for years to come. The first ten-mile irrigation ditch, put into operation at the end of the first summer, followed the bottomlands of the Cache la Poudre River and flowed through the Greeley townsite. Those who had committed their fortunes to transforming a patch of gravel and browned grass into a garden thought the first water "came dancing through the flumes like a ministering angel." A second canal finished early in 1871 was the first irrigation facility in Colorado long enough to lift water out of the immediate floodplain of a river onto higher benchlands distant from the stream. Twenty-seven miles long, thirty feet wide, and four and a half feet deep, it watered twenty-five thousand acres on the north side of the river through an elaborate system of laterals. "Colonization introduces a new era," stated one contemporary. "It overcomes all the

A GOOD HOME IN A GOODLY LAND.

# PLATTE RIVER COLONY,

Located Thirty-five Miles from Denver, in the Center of
the Arable Lands of Weld County, Colorado.

MEMBERSHIPS FROM $50 TO $250.

CHOICE LOCATIONS FOR RESIDENCES.

GOOD BUSINESS OPPORTUNITIES.

EXCELLENT AND CHEAP FARMING LANDS.

LOW RATES OF FARE FROM THE EAST
FOR ACTUAL MEMBERS.

GOOD GOVERNMENT AND RAILWAY LANDS

IN THE IMMEDIATE VICINITY.

LOCATED ON THE
DENVER PACIFIC RAILWAY,
With Direct Communication EAST and WEST.

Address for more complete information,

WM. E. PABOR,
Superintendent,
PLATTEVILLE, COL.

Advertisement from the
*Colorado Business
Directory,* 1876, after
the proven success of
the Greeley and
Longmont colonies.

obstacles attending single efforts, and aids materially in the quick development of every industrial pursuit."[5]

The example of Greeley inspired a number of Chicago's leading businesspeople and journalists to organize the Chicago-Colorado Colony in the fall of 1870. In practical arrangements the new enterprise followed the advice of Byers, Cameron, and Meeker, all of whom addressed the members during the winter of 1870–1871. Early in the new year the locating committee bought fifty-five thousand acres irrigable by St. Vrain, Left Hand, and Boulder creeks. Purchase of membership carried terms similar to those offered at Greeley. Hundreds of colonists arrived during the spring to construct canals, plant crops, and build the thriving town of Longmont. The colony trustees confined their activities to purchasing and distributing land, providing water, laying out the town, and governing it until it was incorporated in 1873.

Other colony efforts were less perfect in reproducing the Union Colony model of private enterprise within a cooperative framework. The St. Louis–Western Colony attempted to imitate Greeley in the railroad town of Evans, only four miles from Meeker's settlement. Members received farm plots in return for $150 in fees that were used to cover the original cost of the land and the expense of community irrigation works. Evans attracted several hundred residents during 1871, but mismanagement, proximity to Greeley, and perhaps the abundance of saloons combined to hinder its permanent success. Other piedmont settlements of the early 1870s that advertised themselves as "colonies" were, in fact, real estate speculations. Platteville, New Memphis, and Monument were among those that failed; Fort Collins was prominent among the successful settlements. Its promoters bought the site of an abandoned military post, subdivided the land, and sold "memberships" entitling purchasers to town and farming lots. As an inducement to migration, however, the company built the necessary canals for the entire settlement.

The early 1870s constituted a distinct era, a trial period for Colorado farming under advantageous circumstances. By mid-decade success had begun to attract city slickers by the score with schemes for usurping local resources. Some ideas were as ridiculous as the proposal for a crescent lake formed by a dam two hundred miles long between the Arkansas and South Platte rivers. Most were more predictable attempts to monopolize water for private profit. The result was boom-and-bust agriculture in the first twenty years of Colorado statehood. Outside intervention, speculative excitement, and collapse that damaged both investors and residents was a pattern that repeated itself on the piedmont, the cattle ranges, and the wheat lands of the high plains.

An undertaking such as Fort Collins, for example, had represented a transitional stage in the provision of irrigation facilities in Colorado. By the end of the 1870s, the necessary pooling of resources was accomplished through corporations. Investors were attracted by the increasing demand for water rights and by the claim that the diversion of water into a company ditch gave ownership of the water to the firm and, with it, control of nearby land values. Especially active in canal building during the 1880s were the English investors who financed the Colorado Mortgage and

Investment Company, organized to help in the development of lands owned or served by the Kansas Pacific Railroad. Through subsidiary firms it built the fifty-mile-long Larimer and Weld Canal in the Cache la Poudre watershed, the Loveland and Greeley Canal out of the Big Thompson, and the High Line Canal, which eventually wandered seventy-one miles from the mouth of South Platte Canyon to the plains northeast of Denver. The High Line Canal cost $650,000 between 1879 and 1883, with a fourteen-foot diversion dam in South Platte Canyon and an average width of forty feet. The company expected to make its money by selling land and leasing water to farmers for annual fees that bought the right to water when it was available. The actual acreage the High Line irrigated varied from eight thousand acres in dry years to twenty-five thousand acres in wet years.

These projects of "the English Company" and hundreds of other ditches made the South Platte basin a vast network of canals and spread farming downstream toward Fort Morgan and Sterling. To assure an even flow, the larger companies also constructed reservoirs to hold water from spring thaws through the growing season. The canal boom also opened large tracts in the southern half of the state. An early leader was George Swink of Rocky Ford, who experimented with new crops such as cantaloupes and sugar beets in the 1870s and created the Rocky Ford Ditch Company in the 1880s. Also downriver from Pueblo were the 105-mile Fort Lyon Canal, the 48-mile Catlin Ditch, and dozens of other corporate and community projects that watered the lands around Rocky Ford, La Junta, and Lamar. Across the mountains, canals financed by the Travelers Insurance Company brought water to thousands of acres near Del Norte and Monte Vista. Publicity spoke of "profitable investments, permanent homes, abundant crops, magnificent soil, steady reliable markets, wonderful climate, health, wealth, and comfort for the landless."[6]

One of the last of the state's semiutopian farming colonies was created by the Salvation Army. William Booth, the Salvation Army's founder, dreamed of moving the urban poor of England and the United States to agricultural settlements on English-speaking frontiers. The most successful in the United States was Fort Amity, started near Holly in 1897. The first families were drawn from the "worthy poor" of Chicago. In return for signing an agreement to live an upright life, each family received ten acres and the chance to use a full set of community facilities built by the Salvation Army command. Fort Amity at its peak housed several dozen families among three square miles of melon, grain, alfalfa, and beet fields, but salt buildup in the soil forced the Salvation Army to sell out after ten years.

The irrigation boom lasted for a decade. Many of the companies discovered that settlement was not dense enough to support their investment; others found that farmers resisted paying annual royalties in addition to purchasing water rights at $5 to $8 per acre, paying assessments for upkeep, and perhaps buying the land at a hefty markup. In 1888 the Colorado Supreme Court decided in a case brought against "the English Company" that ditch companies were common carriers; they could charge small annual service fees but not royalties on water they did not own. Many of the corporate irrigation systems were reorganized as cooperative companies in which farmers owned stock in proportion to their water rights. In 1901 the state recognized the new situation with a law authorizing landowners to form irrigation districts, to purchase and construct irrigation facilities, to issue revenue bonds, and to levy land taxes for debt service. Even a single decade of profit-oriented ditchdigging, however, had nearly quadrupled the number of farms in the state and sketched out the basic canal system of Colorado's Eastern Slope. Irrigated land totaling about 1 million acres in 1890 — over half of the state's improved farm land — reached eastward from the Front Range in fingers along the South Platte and Arkansas rivers and southeast from the San Juan Mountains along the Rio Grande.

Colony associations, canal corporations, and cooperatively owned ditch companies were all developed to build irrigation facilities on a large scale. It took only a few of their canals tapping a single stream to reach the limits of available flow. The first open conflict over the appropriation of water came in the dry summer of 1874, when the diversion of the Cache la Poudre River through the Fort Collins ditch dried up the Greeley canals downstream. It was obvious to both sides in the dispute that the doctrine of riparian rights that had evolved in English common law was inapplicable in the arid American West. The traditional law had two central principles — that the right to use water lay only with the owners of land along a water course, and that a user could not appreciably alter the flow of a stream. Either principle would have made western irrigation impossible, as the entire purpose of canal building was to bring water to properties away from the stream and allow it to soak into the fields.

The main street of Rocky Ford in 1886. As the sign for an agricultural implement store indicates, the town developed as a market center for the irrigated farms along the Arkansas River.

When the Colorado Constitutional Convention met a year and a half later, delegates were aware of the need to resolve existing and potential disputes. The new document laid the foundations for state control by declaring that "the water of every natural stream, not heretofore appropriated, within the state of Colorado, is hereby declared to be the property of the public." Drawing on customs recently evolved in farming communities and in the mining districts, where water was diverted for placer operations, the constitution also stated a new doctrine of prior appropriation:

> The right to divert the unappropriated waters of any natural stream to beneficial uses shall never be denied. Priority of appropriation shall give the better right as between those using water for the same purpose . . . those using the water for domestic purposes shall have preference over those claiming for any other purpose, and those using the water for agricultural purposes shall have preference over those using the same for manufacturing purposes.[7]

The first sentence contravened the basic principles of riparian rights, the second established a new basis for the diversion of water, and the third confirmed the primacy of agriculture in the vision of Colorado's future growth.

To put the new principles into operation, the state created new agencies of local government. Prodded into action by plans for the Larimer and Weld Canal, farmers met in 1878 to suggest a system of water regulation to the General Assembly. The response was legislation in 1879 and 1881 that created the legal machinery for administering Colorado's rivers and deciding questions of priority. The new laws parceled the state into three water divisions and ten districts conforming to natural drainage basins. A state engineer headed the organization, and water commissioners in each district determined prior rights, measured available flow, and supervised equitable distribution. Contests over available water were to be settled through suits and hearings in state courts. The entire "Colorado system" for the public control of water on the basis of prior appropriation proved to be one of the most successful innovations made by migrants facing the problems of agriculture in new circumstances. It not only provided a legal framework that prevented chaos during the canal boom of the next decade but also offered a model for similar systems in most of the other western states.

The best legal framework, however, could not prevent environmental damage. The larger and more elaborate the irrigation system, the more vulnerable its complex of dams and headgates to flood damage and silting. Irrigated crops along the Arkansas River consumed about 40 percent of the water that reached them; other water was lost through seepage and evaporation from canals. Each reuse of water increased its salinity, which attracted the salt cedar, an alien "weed tree" that appeared in the 1910s and sucked up huge amounts of water. By evening out seasonal flows and reducing spring floods, irrigation also created an inviting environment for cottonwoods at the expense of cash crops. As early as 1900 the Arkansas River was "overdecreed," with recorded water rights that exceeded the normal flow. Environmental changes simply compounded the mismatch between available water and economic ambitions.

From the beginning, Americans had assumed that Colorado could support oasis agriculture at the base of the mountains. Adaptations of accustomed techniques were necessary, but the example of the Mormons in Utah and the Hispanos in New Mexico proved that experimentation could be successful. The high plains of Colorado had a different reputation. In 1822 a map of the West drawn under the supervision of explorer Stephen Long had lettered the words "Great Desert" from the Texas panhandle across western Kansas and eastern Colorado. Long's map, along with his official report, fixed U.S. opinion for more than two decades, as journalists, atlas makers, and politicians extended the idea of a vast and unbroken desert to cover the entire area between the 98th meridian and the Rocky Mountains.

Not until the mid-1840s did a new attitude emerge. Writers such as Josiah Gregg, chronicler of the Santa Fe trade, and John C. Fremont argued that the abundance of natural grasses made the area not an American desert but the Great Western Prairie. Building on their argument, William Gilpin in the 1850s lent his talents for publicity to convincing the American people that lands beyond the 98th meridian were in fact the "PASTORAL GARDEN of the world." In speeches and articles Gilpin popularized the term "Great Plains" for that vast region where "delicate grasses grow, seed in the root, and are cured into hay upon the ground by the gradually returning drought." The first Anglo-American settlers in Colorado tended to see sandy wastes glaring hot in the sun between the green strips along the river beds, exactly as their geography books had told them. By the mid-1860s, however, the potential of Gilpin's interpretation was evident to almost every resident, who could now see in the Great Plains the foundation of a "novel and immense order of industrial production." The same boosters who argued the pleasures of irrigation emphasized the joys of feeding cattle on the rich grasses that provided food in summer and winter. They virtually wore out the story of the bullwhacker who had worked his oxen "till in single file they hardly cast a shadow," turned them loose to fend for themselves in the fall, and found them six months later sleek and fat. The *Daily Colorado Tribune* proclaimed the common belief when it wrote that "our land area sustains its grazing stock with a like spontaneous bounty, as the ocean breeds and feeds its . . . fish."[8]

Following the pioneering effort of Charles Goodnight in 1864, Texas cattle raisers began to drive large herds north to Colorado where local dealers bought and fattened them for city families, miners, or crews working on the transcontinental railroad. The trail blazed by Goodnight and by Oliver Loving slanted westward to Las Vegas, New Mexico, where it turned north to cross

Raton Pass or Trinchera Pass and skirted the base of the mountains to Denver and Cheyenne. With access to eastern markets opened by the Union Pacific and Kansas Pacific Railroads, the territory's stock raisers built their herds from 147,000 in 1867 to 271,000 in 1870 and 488,000 in 1875. An early Colorado cattle baron such as John Wesley Iliff, who purchased 10,000 to 15,000 head of cattle per year in the 1870s, could figure an average yearly cost of only $2 for steers that sold for as much as $25. The grass on the unsettled plains, after all, was free; the only expenses were herding, shipping, recordkeeping, and occasional feedings of hay during the winter. Operations on an enormous scale were possible with a small investment, for the control of land along scattered water courses gave a monopoly on the adjacent range. One Coloradan described the situation in 1879: "Wherever there is water there is a ranch. On my own ranch (320 acres) I have two miles of running water. . . . The next ranch from me in one direction is 23 miles; now, no man can have a ranch between these two places. I have control of the grass the same as though I owned it." John Iliff, in a spectacular example, invested less than $10,000 in 105 parcels of land totaling 15,558 acres. He gained a monopoly on water in a stretch of range sixty by one hundred miles along the South Platte River. Probably 90 percent of Colorado cattle grazed on public property, and most ranchers would have agreed with rancher Luke Cahill that "land did not interest me, for all the earth was mine."[9]

The open-range cattle industry required as much cooperation among individual entrepreneurs as did irrigated agriculture. Bent County stockmen formed the first countywide cattlemen's association in 1870. A year later ranchers organized the Colorado Stock Growers Association. Other local societies and regional groups such as the Southern Colorado Cattle Growers Association appeared in following years. Whatever their scope of operation, these voluntary organizations performed similar services for their members. To protect the owners of livestock they published brand books, posted rewards, hired legal advisers and detectives, and dispatched brand and health inspectors to major shipping points. For the general encouragement of the business they circulated favorable publicity and lobbied for state and federal legislation.

The cattlemen's associations cooperated with the legislature in erecting the legal framework for a style of stock raising unknown in the East. In 1872 the territorial assembly provided for the registration of brands on a countywide basis. Seven years later the assembly set up a state inspection service as a defense against rustling and losses from strays. In 1885 it established a veterinary board to enforce the quarantine against cattle suffering from "Texas fever" and required brand registration on a statewide basis. The state also provided for spring roundups. After 1879 it divided Colorado into roundup districts with district commissioners who set dates and assured the observance of well-defined rules on branding, the disposition of strays, and similar problems. In practice the governor appointed people suggested by local stockmen's groups. In late April or May, ranchers in each district assembled to drive scattered bunches of cattle into great herds from which the cows and calves belonging to each owner could be cut into separate herds. Each rancher tried to hold the herd on a particular section of range through branding time in July and August on into the fall, when the surplus was culled for sale and the remainder were turned on their own for the winter.

The establishment of procedures for protecting property in open-range stock raising had an effect similar to the codification of the Colorado water rights law, opening a new field for European investors and fast talkers from Kansas City eager to profit from the growth of the West. In the second half of the 1870s, the number of cattle in Colorado jumped to eight hundred thousand. Coloradans publicized the profits to be made, citing the experience of pioneers such as John Iliff. In 1875, in an imaginative publicity stunt, Denver merchants and the Colorado Stock Growers Association cooperated to sponsor an excursion that brought six hundred potential investors to spend a day and a night under open skies on a ranch in Elbert County. Articles in magazines such as *Harper's* and books such as James Brisbin's *The Beef Bonanza, or How to Get Rich on the Plains* agreed that free grass, low overhead, and natural increase of herds assured profits ranging upward from 25 percent annually. Cattle that fed on Colorado bunch grass, enthusiasts argued, were too fat even to stray. By the time the transplanted German nobleman Walter von Richthofen of Denver published his book *Cattle-Raising on the Plains of North America* in 1885, the public was already convinced that there was "not the slightest element of uncertainty" in the business.

The early 1880s were extraordinary years. A continuing rise in prices meant that prime beef cattle might bring as much as $35 to $40 between 1882 and 1884. The number of cattle in the state increased by more than half, as outside money poured in. Investors seemed to agree with the *Colorado Live Stock Record* that "cattle is one of those investments that men cannot pay too much for, since if left alone, they will multiply, replenish, and grow out of a bad bargain." Four corporations were organized in Colorado for the purpose of stock raising in 1881, twenty-three in 1882, twenty-nine in 1883, fifty-eight in 1884, and forty-three in 1885. The lists of stockholders read like the membership lists of the Harvard Club of Boston and the Union League Clubs of New York and Chicago. After the death of John Iliff in 1878, the largest single operator in Colorado was the Prairie Cattle Company, which ran nearly sixty thousand head on 2 million acres of range. Its reports of 26 percent earnings in 1881 and dividend payments ranging from 10 to 20 percent were key factors feeding the boom. "Cattle were never so high before," wrote the *Boulder County News* in 1883. "There never was a time before when capital was so crazy for investment in cattle growing."[10]

The boom in Colorado was part of a cattle mania that extended from New Mexico to Montana and the Dakotas. Ignorance of grazing conditions and mismanagement by outside investors soon resulted in serious overstocking on the western ranges. Between 1884 and 1887 a series of droughts alternating with severe winters left the plains littered with scrawny carcasses. The price of beef cattle simultaneously began a ten-year decline that cut the average value by about 40 percent. Investors who tried to cut their losses by abandoning the business simply accelerated the fall. Those cattle ranchers who remained turned away from open-range operations in favor of sedentary ranching designed to produce stock of high quality. Fencing, wells and windmills, crops of alfalfa along the bottomlands, and controlled breeding programs were all part of the new style. By the turn of the century many Colorado cattle ranchers had made a complete transition, with the bulk of their investment now in land, fencing, and farm machinery rather than in free-roaming herds. A rancher in the new century spent more time typing letters to railroad agents and feed dealers than breathing the dust of the trail.

The boom-and-bust patterns in Colorado irrigation and grazing were the unforeseen results of successful adaptations to the state's natural conditions. Because cattle growers in the 1870s developed an open herding system that made efficient use of the grass nourished by spring rains, outside investors in the next decade rushed to share in the profits and, thus, ruined the ranges. The success of Greeley and Longmont similarly set the stage for overexpansion by corporate canal companies. The third major use of the Colorado plains, in contrast, was an effort to ignore the physical conditions rather than to adjust to them. The story of cash grain farming without irrigation was a serialized adventure in which the same disaster occurred at the end of each episode. A warning from the 1880s might have been repeated each decade: "Those who reach Colorado with certain ideas of society, soil, climate and country, based upon what they have left behind them, are likely to be disappointed, as they would if they were to go to Alaska."[11]

Everyone who settled in or visited the state knew that the Colorado plains were dry, with fifteen to twenty inches of rain in normal years. For farmers moving westward from the rain zone of twenty to twenty-five inches annually along the Missouri River, however, there was no obvious stopping place. Each new valley was only slightly browner than the one before; if traditional farming had been successful twenty miles to the east, why not here or in the next county? Equally important for understanding American reactions is the fact that periods of abundant rainfall and drought have occurred in regular cycles on the plains. The years from 1865 to 1872 were dry; those from 1873 to 1885 were wet. Droughts then came in cycles of twenty-one years, with the driest years occurring in 1892, 1912, 1934, and 1953. Total rainfall in the bad years dropped 15 to 25 percent below normal, with most of the reduction during the July and August growing season. Armed with national optimism and faith in growth, plains farmers for the past century have assumed that the wet years are normal and the dry years abnormal, not that both are parts of a regular cyclical pattern.

The wet years of the early 1880s, for example, furnished perfect copy for railroad land departments eager to attract farmers to unsold lands along their tracks. The Northern Pacific Railroad discovered a "Tropical Belt" and a "Continental Wheat Garden" on the plains of Montana; the Union Pacific described the Platte Valley as a "flowery meadow of great fertility"; and the Chicago, Burlington, and Quincy said, "follow the prairie dogs . . . and you will find good land." The Colorado Farmer remained skeptical, but Denver's Field and Farm, the revived State Board of Immigration, and private land joined the Burlington companies in 1886–1887 in glowing praise of the Colorado "Rain Belt" that

Dawn on a ranch in eastern Colorado. Photo by Myron Wood.

had moved to within eighty miles of Denver and made the prairies too soggy for grazing.[12] Experts asserted that the years of increasing rainfall were evidence that the Great Plains were being permanently transformed from desert to garden. The specific cause might be electricity discharged by telegraph wires, the concussion in the atmosphere caused by passing trains, the planting of trees, or the increase in groundwater and evaporation through irrigation and cultivation, they speculated, but the general process was simple enough for the slogan "Rain follows the plow."

When corporations and scientists told them what they wanted to hear, small wonder that American farmers moved by the thousands from Nebraska and Kansas onto the high, sweeping plains of Colorado. In the previous decade settlement had reached only fifty miles east from the base of the mountains. From 1886 to 1889, however, towns mushroomed along the new tracks of the Rock Island and Missouri Pacific and the slightly older lines of the Santa Fe, Burlington, and Union Pacific. In the same years thirteen new counties were formed in response to the migration: Washington, Phillips, Yuma, Sedgwick, Logan, Prowers, Morgan,

Otero, Lincoln, Kit Carson, Cheyenne, Kiowa, and Baca. A well-to-do ranch wife scornfully described the influx:

> We began to notice forlorn little shacks built here and there on the open range by the poor home-seekers who, attracted by the prospect of free land, had begun "homesteading." They built flimsy little houses, scratched up the surface of the prairie form a few inches, and raised pitiful, straggling crops. The settlers were coming in! The opening wedge of that great onrush had thrust deep into the heart of the prairie.[13]

Sowing grain with the tools, seeds, and techniques brought from the humid East, new settlers were surprised by the drought of 1889–1890. Those who stuck it out with the help of food, coal, and seed grain sent by both the state legislature and relief committees in Denver and Colorado Springs found that 1891 and 1892 lived up to expectations. By 1894, however, the weather was drier than anyone remembered. Only ten inches of rain fell at Yuma, eight at Burlington, and seven at Holyoke. Three years of searing drought forced many farmers to abandon the lands so eagerly taken up. Others turned for survival to stock raising on a small scale with herds of three hundred head or less. Total population of the twelve eastern counties dropped between the years 1890 and 1900, in some by as much as 40 percent.

In the same years of adjustment, Colorado farmers showed their first interest in the techniques of dry farming — the use of drought-resistant crops and moisture-conserving tillage. The state established a dry-land Agricultural Experiment Station, and the Burlington Railroad operated a model farm to show the possibilities of frequent cultivation and subsoiling. Along with renewed migration into Colorado after the turn of the century came lively attention to new seeds and crops and new planting and cultivation practices. The peak of the second wave, which revived dead towns and created twenty thousand new farms during the decade, was in 1906. The first meeting of the International Dry Farming Congress in Denver the following year was a token of interest in innovative techniques. The organization was a hybrid of scientist and booster, fervently devoted to settling the plains on the most correct and progressive basis.

Promising starts at dry farming since 1907 have twice crashed against American overoptimism triggered by booming markets and wet summers. The surging price of wheat during World War

Sand blowing near Granada, Prowers County, April 15, 1936.

I coincided with several seasons of heavy rainfall. As the price climbed from $0.80 to $2.00 per bushel, new, inexperienced settlers plowed up land that had been returned to pasture or opened new fields and planted them for grain. Tiny plains towns such as Flagler, along the Rock Island Railroad, found new prosperity with two banks, two lumberyards, two car dealers, and two hotels along its two-block main street. Wheat acreage in the state rose by a factor of three during the decade 1909 to 1919. The results were predictable. Agricultural depression in the early 1920s drove some farmers from Colorado and others out of the grain business. Those who hung on sowed greater acreage to maintain a stable income.

In the Yampa Valley of northwest Colorado, where completion of the Denver and Salt Lake Railroad to Craig in 1913 brought a boom decade, the land went through an entire cycle of use and abandonment within fifteen years. The new homesteaders fought their first battle with sagebrush. "First thing you did," Hilda Shelton Rawlinson remembered about her childhood, "you got your ax and you chopped the sagebrush. . . . We lived in a tent from March until January, and it was very cold. . . . You know what our wood was? Sagebrush! . . . You were busy clearing the

Dust storm, 1935.

sagebrush to plant a little garden so you'd have something to eat."[14] Moffat County recorded 5,000 dry crop acres in 1914, 131,000 by 1925, and just 35,000 five years later. There were nine hundred farms in 1920, twenty-four hundred in 1924, and only seven hundred by 1928, as homesteaders turned the land back to grazing or abandoned it to tax sales.

Drought years from 1933 to 1938 completed the virtual destruction of the Great Plains. As C. F. Kraenzel has written, "The chief measure of the non-adaptability of the humid-area culture to Plains conditions is the movement of dust. Dust indicates an overextension of farming into areas best used for other purposes. It also indicates an overemphasis upon intensity of farm operations."[15] Indeed, the great Dust Bowl of the 1930s occupied the region that Stephen Long had marked as the Great American Desert. Although its center shifted from year to year, for five consecutive years Coloradans in the eastern counties found that towering dust storms ravaged their land. An exodus of farmers cut both the population of the plains counties and the number of farms by 15 percent. With the abandonment of cultivation for grazing, renewed interest in drought-resistant crops, and desperate soil conservation measures by remaining farmers, the scene on the plains was a replay of the late 1890s, although with the federal government now taking an active role through crop insurance and price-parity programs, the Soil Conservation Service, and the Rural Resettlement Administration.

In the 1940s and 1950s Colorado farmers went through the cycle one more time, as yet another wave of landowners learned the same lessons. Good rains and booming prices after 1939 brought the tractors out of storage like great beasts emerging from hibernation. Speculators who had purchased plains acreage at rock-bottom prices in the 1930s outvoted experienced settlers in soil conservation districts. By 1945 and 1946 land reclaimed and sown to grass a decade earlier was being plowed up along with virgin soil in the zones receiving fourteen to seventeen inches of rainfall. When a new drought hit in 1953 and 1954, the harvest of dust was ready again. The total cash value of Colorado farm products dependent on irrigation — sugar beets, potatoes, fruits — remained steady during the 1950s, but the average cash income from grain fell from $150 million between 1950 and 1952 to $40 million between 1953 and 1957 before it recovered with the advent of a new wet cycle.

In the mid-1940s one soil conservationist voiced a bitter complaint about the repetition of errors. "For half a century this margin zone has been the scene of repeated cycles of frontier crashing, bankruptcy, and abandonment," he wrote. "Greenhorn settlers have pushed out into the arid plains beyond the established frontier zone. They have messed up the place, gone broke, and vacated it to lie idle again until a new crop of suckers is ripe."[16] In fact, the effects of drought in the 1950s were less severe than those in the 1890s or the 1930s, partly because of the slow adoption of suitable farming practices advocated by agricultural experts at Colorado State University. In place of deep plowing, which experience had shown to be a disastrous mistake, farmers now worked the soil with disk cultivators and Graham-Hoeme plows, incorporated crop residues in the upper soil, and took other measures to hold the land against the wind.

Grain farmers in the twentieth century have shared their increasing dependence on the federal government with stockmen and ditch farmers. The end of open-range operations turned the interest of cattle ranchers toward the legally sanctioned use of public lands. Since 1899 the U.S. Department of Agriculture has issued grazing permits for the use of the state's 13 million acres of national forest. Some of the state's agricultural journals and many ranchers greeted the introduction of a fee system in 1906 with bitter denunciation, but by the 1920s stockmen pastured three hundred thousand to four hundred thousand cattle and twice as many sheep for at least part of the year on Forest Service lands. In the same years the majority of Colorado cattlemen also favored systematic procedures for the use of public lands remaining outside park and forest reservations, either through a leasing provision or through cession to the state. The Taylor Grazing Act of 1934 answered the basic demand, setting aside the remaining public domain for use by stockmen on ten-year permits issued at low fees by the Bureau of Land Management. In combination with the use of privately owned ranch lands along streams for hay and forage crops, the grazing permit system has formed the basis for the cattle industry for the past generation, making possible long-range planning and conservation of available grass. The same system, it should be noted, has made Rocky Mountain and Western Slope counties attractive for an industry increasingly displaced by grain farmers on the plains.

If ranchers accepted federal involvement with occasional reluctance, irrigators greeted it with rousing celebrations. Indeed, government aid in the provision of irrigation works grew into a regional crusade around the turn of the century. Western politicians considered federal participation a necessary subsidy on the model of railroad land grants, an expression of the national duty to promote economic growth. For reformers such as John Wesley Powell or William E. Smythe, founder of the National Irrigation Congress in 1891 and author of *The Conquest of Arid America,* it was a moral cause whose end was the expansion of cooperative rural settlements on the model of Mormon Utah or the Greeley Colony. Let the nation reach into the desert, Smythe wrote, and "that which lay beyond the grasp of the Individual yields to the hand of Associated Man." To Colorado farmers the vision was more mundane but equally compelling: "fenced farms, pasture and wheat lands, substantial farm houses and barns . . . thrifty communities, civilized societies."[17]

The Newlands Act came in 1902. Proceeds from the sale of public lands in sixteen western states were set aside as a reclamation fund for water diversion, storage, and distribution facilities; user fees to repay initial costs would provide a fund for future projects. During its first decade the Bureau of Reclamation undertook two major projects in the Colorado drainage system, where settlers since the mid-1880s had attempted to construct adequate irrigation systems with meager resources. In the Uncompahgre Project the bureau bored a five-mile tunnel to

Triumphal Arch at Montrose celebrating the completion of the
Gunnison River Tunnel and Uncompahgre Reclamation Project.
President Taft spoke at the ceremonies in 1909.

bring water from the narrow gorge of the Gunnison River to irrigable lands along the Uncompahgre. President Taft opened the
project five years after bureau engineers unpacked their tapes
and theodolites in 1904. In the Grand Valley beyond the junction
of the Gunnison, the federal authority took over a second project
from private interests in 1912, completing a sixty-two-mile canal
and delivering water by 1917. The immediate result of these efforts was the doubling of irrigated land on the Western Slope
from three hundred thousand to six hundred thousand acres.
Mesa, Montrose, Delta, and Garfield counties became the centers of agriculture in western Colorado, with six thousand farms
by the 1910s. The indirect result of irrigation was to build market towns such as Paonia, Fruita, Delta, and Montrose into substantial communities in the early twentieth century. Grand
Junction emerged as the regional focus for the Western Slope —
the major city between Denver and Salt Lake.

Coloradans used their expanding acreage for new products.
The first settlers of the Grand Valley had enthusiastically planted fruit trees and began to harvest apples and peaches in the

Putting up hay with the farm machinery of 1929.

1890s. An apple boom hit west-central Colorado about 1895 and carried through the first decade of the new century. The boom times ended around 1915 because of overirrigation and oversalination of orchards, infestation by the coddling moth, and competition from new orchards in the Pacific Northwest. Nevertheless, a million fruit trees remain in production eighty years later.

More important for both sides of the state were sugar beets. Ever since the late 1860s, boosters and agricultural experts had canvassed the prospects of a sugar beet industry, and farmers had experimented successfully with the crop. The practical realization of these ambitions was a Western Slope "first." After a decade of discussion, Mesa County promoters persuaded Denver investors to erect the state's first sugar beet factory in Grand Junction in 1899. The backers of the Colorado Sugar Manufacturing Company included Charles Boettcher, John F. Campion, Eben Smith, and J. J. Brown — all of whom had made their fortunes in Leadville before the crash of 1893. Built on a fifteen-hundred-acre site donated by the Grand Junction Town Company, the factory was hailed by Grand Junction newspapers as the most important event in the town's history and the "opening wedge for an influx of capital . . . such an era of prosperity will

Celery pickers near Littleton, 1918.

never have been witnessed, as will come with its erection."[18] Slow growth of beet farming on the Western Slope cut expected profits and turned the original investors to the South Platte Valley, but the plant continued to operate under new ownership until the Great Depression.

The focus of the sugar industry shifted to the Colorado plains in the first decade of the new century. In 1900 the American Beet Sugar Company opened a processing plant at Rocky Ford, and the National Beet Sugar Company built not only a processing plant but also the entire town of Sugar City fifteen miles to the north. Like a mining boom town, in its first year Sugar City housed a mixture of two thousand executives, engineers, construction workers, merchants, farmers, and German-Russian immigrants. Factories followed in most of the towns of the South Platte between 1901 and 1903, with Boettcher and his associates taking the lead. Helped by the American Sugar and Refining Company Trust, the Platte Valley plants consolidated as the Great Western Sugar Company. Several other factories merged into the Holly Sugar Company in the same year. With processing facilities available and marketing supervised by powerful corporations, farmers raised 108,000 acres of beets in 1909 and 166,000 acres in 1919. Beet sugar in the twentieth century has served as a reliable cash export, and processed beet pulp has provided feed for livestock.

By the 1920s and 1930s the irrigation of more than 3 million acres strained the available supply of water. Lands east of the Front Range, where farmers continued to shift from grain to water-intensive vegetable crops, received less than half the needed water during the years 1925 to 1933. The Great Western Sugar Company, the South Platte Valley railroads, Colorado Agricultural College, local newspapers, and chambers of commerce organized the Northern Colorado Water Users Association in 1934 to lobby for the diversion of water across the Continental Divide. Against the resistance of conservationists and of Western Slope Congressman Edward Taylor, who changed to a backer after obtaining several Eastern Slope concessions, Congress approved the Colorado–Big Thompson Project in 1937 as a means of providing supplemental water for 615,000 acres east of the mountains. The Bureau of Reclamation started work the following year on Granby Reservoir and Shadow Mountain Lake and on a thirteen-mile tunnel under Rocky Mountain National Park from Grand Lake to Estes Park, where the diverted water would be used for hydroelectric power before distribution to nine plains counties. Although the first water flowed through the Alva B. Adams tunnel in 1947, the project was not finished until 1954, in time to save the valley from the worst effects of the new drought years. The Fryingpan-Arkansas Project, begun in 1964 and completed at the start of the 1980s, was a similar effort to supplement the water supply of Arkansas Valley farmers and Pueblo and Colorado Springs townspeople with a massive transmountain diversion costing over $200 million. As of 1980 the diversion of four hundred thousand acre-feet of Western Slope water to the Mississippi River drainage was roughly equal to the natural flow of the South Platte River, with about one-third of the diversions to the Arkansas Valley and two-thirds to the Platte Valley.

Colorado's water projects in the mid-twentieth century were built within a legal framework of interstate treaties, or "compacts," that allocated the water of major rivers that flowed across state lines. In 1922 Secretary of Commerce Herbert Hoover facilitated an agreement among the seven states that share the Colorado River. Hoover and the state delegates met half a dozen times in Washington, Phoenix, Denver, and, finally, Santa Fe, where they hammered out an agreement giving roughly half of the river's flow to the upper basin states of Wyoming, Colorado, Utah, and New Mexico and the rest to the downstream states of Nevada, Arizona, and California; in turn, Colorado received 51.75 percent of the upper basin share. The agreement was flawed because it overestimated the average flow of the river, but the federally approved mandate for dividing the waters has remained in effect for more than seventy years.

The problem along the Arkansas River was the fact that Pueblo, Colorado Springs, CF&I, and thousands of farms used up nearly all of the water before it could reach Kansas. The first step toward a solution was bistate support for the U.S. Army Corps of Engineers to build the John Martin Dam near Las Animas. Built between 1938 and 1946, the dam was designed to store winter flow and make it available to Colorado and Kansas farmers in the spring and summer. Three years after its completion, the two states and the federal government signed an Arkansas River Compact that formalized the sharing of the water resource.

As with every other U.S. community in the nineteenth century, Colorado liked to call itself the "Garden Spot" of the nation, for it was considered axiomatic that "every interest traces its life and dependence to that single great source, the production of the soil."[19] In fact, mining was the first engine of economic growth in Colorado, and gold and silver were the products that brought money into the state during its first two generations. Agriculture was little more than a service industry, the oil that kept the machinery moving. Agriculturalists found their first and best markets in the mining towns and the commercial cities that served them. Even though a significant percentage of the cattle raised after 1870 was sold outside the state, farmers through the century did not harvest enough crops to feed the home population.

The relationship changed around the turn of the century. All branches of Colorado agriculture emerged from the frenzy of the 1880s and the depression of the 1890s on sounder footing. At the same time that employment in mining fell from 20 percent of the state total to less than 5 percent, continuing expansion of irrigation and grain farming brought new areas under the plow. By 1920 wheat and sugar beets had made Colorado a net exporter of foodstuffs. Agriculture provided 13 percent of Colorado jobs in the 1880s, 21 percent by 1900, and 27 percent by 1920. Most of

Farm couple near Kersey, 1939. Photo by Arthur Rothstein for the
Farm Security Administration.

the industrial growth in the state in the early twentieth century
also involved the processing of agricultural products. The complex of stockyards, flour mills, Armour and Swift packing plants,
and sugar refineries in the vicinity of Denver is just one example

of the growth that raised the share of value-added in manufacturing attributable to food products from 18 percent in the 1910s to 29 percent by 1939. Not until the years from 1900 to 1940, then, did the Great Plains and plateau areas of Colorado take their places beside the Rocky Mountain backbone and fulfill the prediction of an early Colorado booster that "the valley lands of Colorado are as valuable . . . as are its hills. . . . In the hills, the pick; in the valleys, the plow."[20]

# CHAPTER 10

# THE PEOPLE OF COLORADO, 1876–1916

Colorado's admission to the Union seemed so certain by early July 1876 that the people of Denver decided to celebrate simultaneously the nation's centennial and the birth of the centennial state. Although the southern portion of the territory — its Hispanic residents leery of northern Colorado's dominance — refused to sanction statehood, superior numbers north of Pikes Peak and east of the Continental Divide guaranteed that the measure would be approved. Pueblo and South Pueblo barely approved federal ties, and Colorado Springs rejected them by more than 2 to 1, but large pluralities in such communities as Georgetown and Boulder were sufficient to overcome the protest. In Pueblo the *Chieftain* graciously admitted that statehood would help Colorado attract capital while removing "spavined shysters" from territorial jobs.[1] In Denver the victory was savored on the banks of the South Platte, where hundreds gathered for Fourth of July festivities.

The marchers and merrymakers that day included Scandinavian and German athletes, the Odd Fellows astride their milk-white horses, temperance-minded Red Cross Champions, the Knights of Pythias, the Governor's Guard, and thirty-eight women, each representing a state in the Union. If they expected the principal orators of the day, Owen J. Goldrick and Reverend Ellis, to be brief, they were disappointed. Goldrick, a pioneer newspaperman and a pedant of equally long standing, spent nearly an hour reviewing eighteen years of Denver's history, and Ellis spoke almost as long recounting the glories of Greece, Rome, and the American Revolution. Enmeshed in a turbulent era, the speakers preferred to dwell on memories of long-lost times. For the Civil War, with its six hundred thousand dead still haunting families North and South, Goldrick and Ellis spared a few paragraphs. For former slaves, even then being reduced to peonage, the speakers found a few lines. For Colorado's thousands of foreign-born, whose brethren would soon transform the United States into a nation of nations, the orators had but a few patriotic words. And for women, their struggle to secure suffrage rebuffed by state constitution makers, there was the twelfth of thirteen toasts: "Woman — the last and best gift of God to man. . . . May there yet be had a fuller recognition of her social influence, her legal identity and her political rights."[2]

The gratuitous twelfth toast hardly appeased those Coloradans who had urged full enfranchisement of women in the new constitution. Judge Henry P. Bromwell of Denver and Agipeto Vigil representing Huerfano and Las Animas counties favored equal suffrage, but most of their colleagues preferred to defuse the issue by granting women the right to vote in school elections and referring the question of fuller suffrage to a referendum set for 1877. Susan B. Anthony and Lucy Stone, national suffrage leaders, tirelessly stumped the state that year, only to see their efforts frustrated by sermons from the pulpit and cannonades from the press. Dismissed as "bawling, ranting women, bristling for their rights" by the Reverend Thomas Bliss, a Presbyterian divine, and as "battalions of old maids disappointed in love" by Roman Catholic leader Joseph P. Machebeuf, the women found that frontier Colorado held fast to the past.[3] Despite Vigil's leanings, most of his fellow Hispanos in southern Colorado strongly opposed suffrage. In northern and central sections males bred in the United States or northwestern Europe also generally followed tradition; Boulder County alone approved of equal suffrage.

Seventeen years later a handful of women, organized as the Colorado Non-Partisan Equal Suffrage Association, sensed that the time was right for another campaign, although national suffrage leaders doubted that Colorado was ready. "Have you converted all those Mexicans?" Susan B. Anthony skeptically asked. "Why did you introduce a bill now?" queried Lucy Stone, the movement's grandmother.[4] "I have talked with no one who feels there is the slightest hope of success in Colorado," wrote Carrie Chapman Catt. "Are you sure you have talked with anyone who understands the situation here?" replied Denver newspaperwoman Ellis Meredith.[5] Women in southern Colorado, she reported, were threatening to run their antisuffrage state senator out of the county; Populist governor Davis Waite endorsed suffrage, as did Republican ex-governor John Routt. The opposition saloonkeepers and brewers were asleep. Thirty-three newspapers surveyed approved of suffrage; only eleven were opposed. Thomas Patterson, publisher of the *Rocky Mountain News,* did not care for equal suffrage, and his paper was officially neutral, but Ellis Meredith, whose father was managing editor, labored "to get some good work under my own signature." She admitted that "we may fail, but there is a very strong chance our enemies may let it go by default."[6]

Underpinning the temporary alliances formed by Meredith and her co-workers were larger forces working in the women's favor. The 1890 census revealed that Hispanos were no longer as politically significant as they once had been and that the state's male voters substantially outnumbered the potential female electorate, with the male-female imbalance exceeding 2 to 1 in some mining towns and among the foreign-born. Over 70 percent of Colorado's females over age nineteen were married; less than 20 percent were single or divorced. Given this stable, domestic contingent which, if enfranchised, would constitute less than 30 percent of the electorate, men were not risking political suicide by approving equal suffrage. Indeed, native-born Americans, fearing the loss of their economic and political power to naturalized citizens, may well have recognized that abandoning one tradition might help preserve others, for by enfranchising women, natives gained more ballots than did foreigners.

Comforting though such statistics may have been to Meredith and friends, their hopes were tempered by financial realities. "We might just as well talk of raising mountains as money," Meredith told Carrie Chapman Catt.[7] Lucy Stone sent $300, a welcome addition to a war chest that contained only $25 at the campaign's outset. Anthony gave freely of her advice. Warning against linking suffrage to prohibition, she insisted that advocates "know nothing, push nothing but suffrage pure and simple."[8] Fearful that the Colorado effort would fail, Anthony stayed away, but Catt agreed to lecture. "I have a voice like a fog horn and can be heard in out of door meetings," she assured organizers, advising them that some men shunned gatherings in churches. She was, however, well prepared for the pious: "I have a Sunday school speech — The Bible and Woman Suffrage — which will not offend the most orthodox and has done some good among conservatives." National leaders suggested that Coloradans import fiery Mary Lease to snare Populists, but Meredith rejected the Kansas hellraiser as "too ultra," preferring instead the services of Emma DeVoe, whom Catt recommended. "If she isn't a Populist . . . she can talk that way when necessity arises."[9] To the voices of out-of-staters were added the journalistic talents of *News* society columnist Minnie J. Reynolds and novelist Patience Stapleton. Grand Junction's Dr. Ethel Strasser, Colorado Springs's Dr. Anna Chamberlain, and Dr. Jessie Hartwell of Salida joined such teachers as Denver's Martha A. Pease, president of the Equal Suffrage Association, to convince men that women were intellectually capable. Socialites including Denver's Mrs. Nathaniel P. Hill, wife of the smelter magnate, lent their names; social outcast Baby Doe Tabor, wife of the erstwhile silver king, lent office space.

In the end, careful planning and a low-key campaign yielded a six-thousand-vote margin for equal suffrage. Men moved more by "impulse than conviction," reporter William McLeod Raine observed, voiced their "dissatisfaction with existing conditions" by broadening the franchise.[10] Reflecting on the nearly thirty thousand "no" votes, Meredith concluded that "the illiterate, the vicious and the lower classes of foreigners are always opposed on general principles."[11] Anthony, pessimistic throughout the battle ("my dear girls, don't be discouraged or crestfallen if defeat comes"), tardily sent congratulations: "Oh how glad I am that at last we have knocked down our first state by popular vote."[12]

Nearly a decade later, after women had chiseled their victory into the state constitution, Anthony wrote to Mary Coninc, one of Colorado's first female legislators: "Maybe . . . if you promise to elect me senator of the United States I will come to Colorado, maybe I will take on a new lease on life."[13] If the eighty-two-year-old suffragist was serious, she was also poorly informed. Between 1894, when three women were elected to the general assembly, and 1913, when the legislature lost the power to select U.S. senators, only a handful of women sat in the assembly.

Yet, women's influence was known. In 1907 Colorado granted localities authority to prohibit liquor sales and was a full three years ahead of the rest of the nation in going completely dry. Edward Taylor told his colleagues in Congress in 1912 that Colorado's women had helped enact over 150 statutes, ranging from an 1899 law making the white and lavender-blue columbine the state flower to a 1908 measure prohibiting the display of anarchistic flags. Much of the legislation Taylor cited protected women and children. Pimps were prohibited from pocketing prostitutes' profits; a model juvenile court law was passed; wives were permitted to homestead property so it could not be sold without their consent, and they were accorded rights as household heads if they provided the family's chief support.

United on some issues by bonds of self-interest, women were divided on others by chasms of class, nationality, race, and religion. Governor Waite, expecting gratitude for endorsing equal suffrage, found in 1894 that many women preferred his Republican rival, Albert McIntire. Twenty years later, as old Mother Jones, Mary Harris, fought for miners' rights and as the national conscience recoiled at the news from Ludlow, Denver clubwomen argued that miners had rejected adequate company housing. Instead, said the women, the workers lived in "wretched little shelters of loose boards, tar paper and old tin cans" because they choose to squander their money on drink or to use it for return passage to their homelands. "Many of the mines," lamented the Women's Law and Order League, "are owned by Denver citizens whose whole means of livelihood has been suddenly swept away by the burning of their property."[14]

Women's suffrage did not provoke social or economic revolution. By 1900 women were well represented in some professions: there were more than one thousand female teachers and more than one hundred women doctors in Colorado. But they were vastly outnumbered by legions of servants, dressmakers, and waitresses. For most women, daily life after 1893 was much the same as it had been before. Rural women bore and raised children, kept house, and often toiled on the land. They usually worked with their husbands, but single women also farmed. Women, for example, constituted 18 percent of the homestead entries in Lamar in 1907. And married women, such as Dorothea Wall, a German-Russian living near Burlington, were sometimes forced to run farms alone while their husbands took winter work in Denver or Pueblo or in one of the coal-mining towns.[15] Many women quickly adapted to the treeless, rattlesnake-infested, sod-house world of prairie fires and flash floods, dust storms and blizzards that engulfed them in eastern Colorado. Nearly fifty years after she and her husband homesteaded near Holyoke in 1886, Mrs. S. S. Worley recalled one of her first nights in Colorado when she slept in a "hole in the ground twelve by twelve feet, four feet deep, board roof, no doors or windows, gables not closed and no floor but the ground." Mrs. Hans Christensen, a Yuma County pioneer, enjoyed slightly better accommodations

— a frame house "so small that a good wind would blow it off its foundations." Mrs. W. H. Clatworthy's shanty was so small that she hung the chairs on the wall to make room to let the bed down at night. Somehow she managed to crowd in an oil stove and a melodeon, a musical touch of civilization in the rude world of Morgan County in the 1880s.[16]

Although in time conditions improved for some women, for many others privations persisted. At first Annie Green, a member of the Union Colony, lived in a tent in Greeley; later she moved into a small cottage. Still she found life hard. Once she seized her broom, "the woman's weapon," to drive off fifty head of cattle eating sprouting oats on the Greens' farm. She failed in her attempt. Kneeling in the field, she "wept and prayed to God for a change in my wretched life, winding up with a wish that Horace Greeley and N. C. Meeker, the founders of Union Colony, were in the bottom of the sea." Reflecting on life in northeastern Colorado, one woman asked at a prayer meeting "whether God would look after them the same as any place else, since they'd shown so little sense in coming into such a country, where they had gotten into such a state they couldn't leave and had to make the best of it?"[17]

Other women faced similar difficulties in central and western sections of the state. Maggie Brown, whose feckless physician husband Charles failed to collect his debts and sank his money into worthless mines, bemoaned her lot at Villa Grove: "I feel if I do stay here two years longer I will be lost body and soul. . . . I would give five years of my life if I had never seen this state." As Nellie C. Robinson traveled on the Denver and Rio Grande Railroad, she told the conductor that she was going to teach school in the Disappointment Creek Valley in Dolores County. "I tho't so," he replied, "and I am sorry for you. The country where you are going is a land of cheeko, sagebrush, and lonely cowboys. I've taken many a teacher down there and never yet have I got one back."[18]

Despite hardships, some women achieved a degree of equality with men simply because women's labor was vital to economic survival. Historian Katherine Harris demonstrates in her study of Logan and Washington counties that women's butter, egg, and garden earnings often provided much of a farm family's cash income. Harris shuns sweeping generalizations but does conclude that the families she studied "strongly suggest women's considerable status within the family. Men and women generally had different roles to play, but the mutuality between the sexes, enforced by the needs of homesteading, expanded women's power to negotiate and win."[19]

Besides economically buttressing their families, women did much to build their communities. In *Those Strenuous Dames of the Colorado Prairie,* Nell Brown Probst tells of dozens of hard-working women. Carrie Ayers, at age fifteen, set up Sterling's first school, teaching twenty students in a fourteen-by-sixteen sod schoolhouse. Mary Pratt opened Yuma's first school in 1885, accepting students as old as twenty-four. Education-minded parents around Julesburg had to send their children to school in Sidney, Nebraska, more than thirty miles distant, until Amelia Guy established a local school in 1885.[20]

Hispanic women, against great odds, maintained their beleaguered communities and traditions. First came the 1848 U.S. political conquest of the Mexican Southwest. Then, as historian Sarah Deutsch explains, Anglo-Americans sought, often through economic means, to "perfect the incomplete conquest" while Hispanos tried "to prevent it." As Hispanic men left their villages to take seasonal work, women kept the communities alive. Deutsch writes: "Through their visiting, their sharing of food, plastering, childbearing, and, most important, their stability, production, and earnings as non-migrants, women provided for increasingly mobile villagers not only subsistence, but continuity and networks for community, health and child care, for old age and emotional support."[21]

In mining communities women fought to transform towns from chaotic camps to proper places. Successes often turned to dust as booms turned to bust. Sometimes, at least for a few decades, the women succeeded. Georgetown, although founded in 1859, did not graduate its first high school class until 1879. In 1880 it hired one of its own alumnae, eighteen-year-old Lizzie Rattek, to teach at the school. That same year Roman Catholics opened an elementary school conducted by the Sisters of Saint Joseph, one of many women's religious congregations that established orphanages, schools, and hospitals throughout the state. By 1900 the Georgetown area could boast that 95 percent of local children between ages eight and sixteen were in school. After studying community life in the upper Clear Creek region between the 1870s and 1900, historian Leanne Sander concluded: "Rocky Mountain mining town society was not 'male dominated.' . . . Women and men created Western mining society together."[22]

In creating western society women sometimes assumed non-traditional roles. Visitors to the 1876 Centennial Exposition in Philadelphia flocked to the Colorado exhibit to see hundreds of stuffed animals and birds, shot and mounted by the "Colorado huntress" Martha Maxwell, whose taxidermy fooled the emperor of Brazil into whistling at a stuffed terrier. Staying more within the bounds of "ladylike" pursuits, Alice Eastwood spent much of the last quarter of the nineteenth century collecting plants in Colorado, an avocation that eventually made her one of the nation's top botanists. Recognizing that pot hunters and curio seekers might destroy Mesa Verde's cliff dwellings, Virginia Donaghe McClurg and Lucy Peabody, both ladies of leisure, left their parlors to lobby for protection of the ruins. Nor did working-class women in the Cripple Creek mining district allow notions of proper feminine behavior to keep them from militantly supporting their husbands as they unionized and fought mine owners and state troopers. Historian Elizabeth Jameson learned of one such woman, Hannah Welch, who "had two great big butcher knives, and she kept those knives razor sharp. And she always said if one of those militia men ever come in her house in the middle of the night, they'd leave with less than they brought in!"[23]

Journalism offered a few women scope for their talents and an opportunity to question the male-dominated status quo. Emma Langdon, who published the Victor *Record* after its pro-labor staff had been jailed, won an honorary membership in the Western Federation of Miners for her courage. During the 1880s and the early 1890s Caroline Nichols Churchill trumpeted women's causes in her Denver-based weekly newspaper *The Queen Bee*. "Society," she insisted, "will never construct a government worthy of the respect [of its citizens] . . . until women form part of its councils." Learning that a woman had beaten a man in a prize fight, she exulted: "Some of these men have to have the conceit taken out of them even if it is done on a physical plane." With similar verve Albina Washburn, who began publishing a women's column in Denver's *Labor Enquirer* in late 1887, argued that city and farm women should join laboring men to fight the "mob of rich men — rich only in stolen wealth — crying for our blood." Women such as Churchill and Washburn, as well as those studied by Harris, Deutsch, Probst, Sander, and Jameson, clearly belie the stereotypical notion of powerless women serving merely as men's "helpmates" in building Colorado.[24]

In 1910 more than a third of Colorado's 368,327 women lived in the state's three largest cities: Denver, Pueblo, and Colorado Springs. Each city offered leisured and professional women educational opportunities, clubs, and social activities. Denver's exclusive Wolcott School, along with the Roman Catholic St. Mary's Academy and the Episcopal Wolfe Hall, prepared young ladies for finishing at eastern colleges or at local institutions such as Loretto Heights College or Colorado Woman's College. Club women, of whom there were more than three thousand associated with the state federation by 1898, fought against the demon rum and for civil service reform and supported numerous eleemosynary enterprises including Denver's National Jewish Hospital, which benefited greatly from Frances Wisebart Jacobs's fund-raising talents. Some women also found time for weekly lectures ranging from "Realism in French Art" at the You and I Club to "Causes of the Civil War" at the Twenty-Second Avenue Club. Reflecting the social parallelism born of a segregated society, African-American women led by former Howard University professor Elizabeth Ensley formed the State Federation of Colored Women's Clubs, which by 1911 counted thirty-three affiliates from Grand Junction to La Junta.

Most urban working women — trapped in an economy that afforded male laborers scant surplus and females even less — found the benefits of suffrage and the joys of club life elusive. Fortunate was the single woman bookkeeper in Colorado Springs who, because she lived at home for free, pocketed most of her $8 weekly salary. More typical at the turn of the twentieth century were the many female laundry, factory, and mercantile workers whose wages, some as low as $3 a week, were quickly absorbed by room and board charges. Asked by a state investigator if she could save any money, one stenographer replied: "about the cost of a funeral or a short spell of sickness."[25]

Economic and social pressures caused most women to marry young and to stay married. In 1910 more than 70 percent of women between ages twenty-five and forty-five in Denver and Pueblo were married; scarcely more than 1 percent were divorced. One divorcée, Emily French, whose husband left her after thirty-one years of marriage, kept a diary. It chronicles a stressful life, one typical of other women without husbands: "November, Sunday 9, 1890 — I never combed my hair or sat down all day. . . . I come unwell last night. I am very bad of late, my age, must be. I am so glad no more babies for me."[26]

Thousands of widows found themselves in similar difficult circumstances. Often their husbands had been able to save little money. The breadwinner's death left his distraught wife to seek employment in a society that paid women poorly and offered them few "respectable" jobs. Some took in laundry, some did sewing, some set up boardinghouses. Many found it impossible to support their children. Joyce Goodfriend, in her study of Denver widows, tells of "half-orphans," the institutionalized children of impoverished women who could not keep them at home. Widows of Civil War veterans who fought for the North drew a government pension; others relied on private charity or begged the county for relief. Not until 1912 did Colorado enact a Mother's Compensation Act to help women keep their children at home. Even that progressive measure, Goodfriend discovered, ill served women because it was poorly funded and administered.[27]

A few women, probably 1 percent or less, made vice of economic necessity by turning to prostitution. As early as 1871 respectable Denver women suggested placing "fallen" women in private homes where they could be rehabilitated, but the *Rocky Mountain News* opposed the idea, fearing that the scheme would corrupt other women. Largely unchecked in the late nineteenth century, ladies of the night frequented Denver's Market Street, Pueblo's Precinct Eight, and smaller tenderloin districts of towns throughout the state. The head of Denver's Home of the Good Shepherd, a Roman Catholic refuge for some two hundred "wayward girls," reported in the late 1880s that some Denver prostitutes were as young as ten. By 1912 tolerance of sex for sale had declined sufficiently in Denver that Police Commissioner George Creel judged the time right to launch a holy war. Assisted by Josephine Roche, a Vassar graduate turned social worker, he reduced the number of Market Street prostitutes from 700 to 250. Political infighting, however, checked Creel's crusade. When Philip Van Cise became Denver's district attorney in 1921 he found that the "row," although less brazen in its operation than it had been before 1912, still flourished: "some sixty houses were operating, in addition to the girls in the small downtown hotels."[28]

The specter of prostitution dogged women anxious to retain and expand their political rights. "Only the dregs of womankind vote in Colorado," declared former Governor Henry Buchtel. "Mothers," he said, "have to be practically driven to the polls." Muckrakers charged that in Pueblo fallen women were driven to

These Colorado Hungarians of the early twentieth century were
typical of many immigrant groups who combined allegiance to their
adopted homeland with perpetuating the heritage of the old country.

the polls, where they were pressured into casting pro-police ballots. In the steel city, wrote Lawrence Lewis, even the wives of
"the lowest and most ignorant class of Italian laborers" voted.
Despite such warnings about prostitutes and foreign women being manipulated by police, priests, and corporation chiefs, the
nativist-tinged pro-suffrage arguments remained strong. Protesting a 1910 proposal to repeal equal suffrage, the Salida
*Record* argued that denying women votes would place them "on
a lower plane of intelligence than the negro or foreigner for no
one disputes their right to vote."[29]

Although most Coloradans admitted that African-Americans
and naturalized citizens had the right to vote, this begrudging
concession to the Constitution scarcely meant that native U.S.
whites felt fully comfortable with a society that grew increasingly heterogeneous as the nineteenth century wore on. In 1870
there were over 6,000 foreign-born immigrants in Colorado,
comprising nearly 17 percent of the population. Forty years
later the percentage, although still above the national norm,

had dipped slightly, but the absolute numbers of foreign-born had grown to nearly 130,000. Not only had the size of this contingent increased dramatically; its composition, mirroring the national experience, had also changed. In 1870 over 95 percent of Colorado's foreigners were from the German states, the British Isles, Scandinavia, France, Switzerland, and Canada. Many spoke English as their native language, and most of the rest had learned it before venturing to the Mountain West.

In 1910 the old groups were still numerically important. There were over ten thousand Germans, Irish, English, and Scandinavians and nearly ten thousand Canadians, many of whom were English or Irish, but the percentage of northern Europeans in the total immigrant population had fallen to less than 70 percent. Slovenians, Czechs, Slovaks, Croatians, Serbians, Russians, Poles, Greeks, Mexicans, Hungarians, Japanese, Chinese, Dutch and Finns — groups represented sparingly, if at all, in 1870 — counted their adherents by the hundreds or thousands by 1910. Italians and German-Russians, statistically insignificant in 1870, each claimed over ten thousand representatives in 1910. Unlike the earlier arrivals, these latecomers often did not initially speak English, and many were not long removed from the hills and meadows of the Volga, the villages of Italy, the farms of Poland, or the ports of Japan.

Each of these immigrants could testify to the forces that uprooted tradition-bound people from their homelands. Economic factors moved most groups. The wealthy discovered that interest rates were higher in Colorado than in Europe, and shrewd westerners often promised and sometimes delivered profitable investment opportunities. Britons James Duff in Denver and William Bell in Colorado Springs channeled foreign funds into railroads, irrigation projects, mines, ranches, and real estate ventures. Mining engineers such as Philip Argall, Thomas Rickard, and Richard Pearce — many of them from Cornwall and Wales — unlocked the processing secrets that eventually assured the profitability of Colorado's precious-metals industry. Managers such as cattleman Murdo MacKenzie, a Scot, found great challenges and rewards in supervising vast western enterprises.

Although experts and investors were important to the state's development, they constituted only a small fraction of Colorado's immigrants. Far more numerous were the desperate thousands who fled continual deprivation in their homelands. For the Irish the potato famine of the late 1840s triggered a mass exodus that saved Erin from ruin and its children from starvation. "Dear Patrick come! A dollar a day for ditching, no hanging for stealing, Irish petaties a dollar a bushel and Whisky the same! Dear Patrick come: if you can't come in one vessel, come in two!"[30] The letter was apocryphal, the economic inducement typical and persuasive. Endemic poverty in southern Italy and Slavic Austria, annual starvation in China, land hunger in the Netherlands, wages of ten cents a day in Mexican quarries, chronic unemployment in many countries — all of these factors made Colorado attractive.

Often economic factors were coupled with political considerations. Germans who had settled in Russia during the eighteenth and early nineteenth centuries were distressed both by drought and by Czar Alexander II's campaign to press their sons into his army and their children into his schools. Peace and prosperity, their agents told them, could be found in Nebraska. Employment in sugar beet fields, dreams of their own farms, and work in Denver and Pueblo industries drew them to Colorado from Nebraska and states east; later, as remittance money increased, some came directly from Russia. Jews also fled from Russian autocracy. Hyman Siegel, a twenty-one-year-old Lithuanian, escaped the Russian draft in 1904. He landed in New York City and quickly found work on an upstate ice farm, which he left after a year to join relatives in Cleveland. In 1908, hoping for a homestead, he and his brother journeyed to Colorado, where they worked for the Colorado and Southern Railroad and tried to make fruitful a barren patch near Cotopaxi. Defeated by winter, the brothers abandoned their cave dwelling and walked over one hundred miles to Denver's Eastern European Jewish ghetto, where Siegel scrounged junk, laid bricks, and sold groceries. For the Reverend Jens Madsen, a Danish-born Lutheran, Colorado offered both the hope of recovery from tuberculosis and the opportunity to do the Lord's work at Eben-Ezer Sanitorium, which Jensen founded at Brush in 1903. In the Denver area consumptive Swedes found rest at the National Swedish Sanitorium; German Lutherans were welcomed at Lutheran Hospital; German Jews had National Jewish Hospital; Eastern European Jews, initially thrust upon the strained resources of their impoverished brethren, were eventually rescued by Dr. Charles D. Spivak and the Jewish Consumptive Relief Society. Bethesda Hospital drew Dutch from throughout the country to create an enclave of Hollanders in South Denver.

As powerful as were the promises of health, wealth, and freedom, there were other factors that forced uprooted people to leave their homelands. British lords exiled ne'r-do-well second sons to the Wet Mountain Valley, where, if they disgraced the family, they did so at a distance. John Orth, a shepherd living near La Junta, reputedly forfeited his royal Austrian patrimony because he married a commoner. Baron Eugene Von Winckler, a Denver real estate developer, supposedly left Germany in disgrace after having fallen off his horse in the kaiser's presence. Others simply thought their lives would be improved by a sojourn, at first thought temporary, in the United States. An Italian woman, unable to find a husband in a village depopulated by emigration, sought the local priest's help. Soon she had a picture of, and an engagement to, Giano in Colorado. Fearing that she could not buy wedding rings in a place "where Indians lived," she purchased her bands in Italy. On arriving in Colorado she found Giano living in a house with a stove but no pans, a table but no chairs. "I tell Giano I no marry him without chairs in the house, so Giano say, 'I get them.'" Satisfied, she married him. "So I work, work and have babies — one every year."[31] John Rougas, a Greek college student yearning for a better life, abandoned his education, defied his father, and permanently left Greece. Running out of money in Kansas City, Rougas took railroad work, ten hours a day at fifteen cents an hour. That brought him to Colorado, where he lived in a boxcar a mile from Fort Morgan. Contemplating his prodigal state, blistered hands, and sore back, he asked: "What am I doing here?" Eventually attracted to Pueblo by better wages, seventeen and a half cents an hour, he labored in the steel mill hefting 165-pound bundles. By 1908 he was making $70 a month — "Good money and I liked it."[32]

For Rougas the journey west was relatively easy; an eighty-dollar fare had taken him from his native Patras as far west as Kansas City. Others faced greater obstacles. Jane Edelstein of Pueblo recalled that her Jewish-Russian mother hid her children in hay wagons to get them across borders. Family treasures were sold to buy food. "When they got into Hamburg, my mother had a few things left. She said: 'Well, it's a choice between the candlesticks and my sons' eating,' so she sold the candlesticks."[33] Late arrivals spent about two weeks at sea. Earlier voyagers, subject to the vagaries of the wind, often took longer. Charles Yrden, a Swede, passed five weeks helping bail a leaky sailing ship bound from Scotland to New York City. Following a pattern typical of

Colorado's foreign-born, he moved west by stages. First he went to Rockford, Illinois; then to Burlington, Iowa; then to Topeka, Kansas; then, in 1871, to Denver; then to Del Norte; then to Summitville; and finally back to the Del Norte area, where by the early 1880s a small Swedish community was forming. The paths trod by Yrden, Rougas, Siegel, and the Edelsteins were typical of those followed by countless others. Most landed in New York City, although some disembarked at such ports as Boston, Baltimore, Philadelphia, Quebec, Montreal, Galveston, and New Orleans.

Reporting that "an immense tide of immigration is about to set in from the Old World to the New World," the *Rocky Mountain News* advised in 1865 that "Colorado should take such steps as will secure her share of these immigrants." Surveying the labor demands of the territory, Governor McCook argued that Colorado "needs muscle, as much as, or more than, capital."[34] To secure a share of the muscle Colorado's entrepreneurs tried various schemes. A short-lived territorial board of immigration scattered literature in the eastern United States and England. Englishman Thomas Tonge, a minion of the Denver Chamber of Commerce, flooded his homeland with booster material. The Gould railroad system warned Italians away from crowded eastern cities, advising them to seek Pueblo, the "Pittsburgh of the West," a city served by two Gould roads.[35] Some were lured by the Colorado Fuel and Iron Company, by coal concerns, and by labor contractors who sometimes received saloon concessions in company towns. Barman John Aiello brought Italians from Grimaldi to work Berwind's mines; in Engleville the Tarabino brothers enjoyed a similar arrangement; in Gray Creek John Corich supplied Slavs; and in Central City mine owners looked to the Gilpin County Cheap Labor Bureau for help. Ethnically homogeneous agricultural towns attracted a few immigrants. Ryssby, a Swedish settlement northeast of Boulder, temporarily prospered, but in the Wet Mountain Valley colonizing Germans grew disillusioned. In Cotopaxi Eastern European Jews soon learned that the paradise promised them was a waterless waste, and in the San Luis Valley Dutch colonists, bedeviled by mismanagement, saw their dreams turn to nightmares as their children died of diphtheria.

Although usually lacking the protection promised by the organized colonies, most foreigners softened potentially traumatic transitions with cushions of community and companionship, thereby fostering population concentrations that were further focused by heavy demands for cheap labor in mining towns, in the major industrial centers of Denver and Pueblo, in sugar beet producing areas, and, to a lesser degree, in Colorado Springs and smaller regional hubs. Some, especially Germans, Scandinavians, English, and Scots diffused themselves throughout rural Colorado, but their regiments were easily matched by the battalions of immigrants in cities and towns. Of Otero County's 11,522 residents in 1900, only 9 percent were foreign-born. Mesa and Routt reported similar percentages, whereas in Conejos County foreigners comprised less than 5 percent of the population. In total these places mustered fewer than 3,000 immigrants, falling, as did most rural counties, far below the state norm of 17 percent foreign-born. In contrast Pueblo tallied nearly 5,000 foreigners, a figure that almost doubled by 1910. Colorado Springs had over 2,200 foreign-born whites in 1900, and Denver, clearly and consistently the state's ethnic capital, held about one-fourth of the state's ethnic population with 25,000 immigrants.

Mining towns also recorded high ethnic concentrations. Over 40 percent of San Juan County's small population was foreign-born; over one-third of the people in Lake and Gilpin counties were immigrants; in populous Teller and Las Animas counties, there were more than 8,000 non-natives. The ethnic composition of towns within mining counties varied widely. Starkville, Aguilar, Berwind, and Engleville were, in 1900, like most other coal camps in Las Animas County — heavily immigrant. Martinez and Varros, among many other towns, however, insulated their original Hispanic settlers from newcomers. In Boulder County, Lafayette and Erie attracted a broad range of foreigners; Louisville harbored many Italians; Lyons drew Swedes to its quarries; and Longmont proved popular with both Germans and Swedes.

Nearly half of Colorado's German-Russians and over half of its Irish lived in Denver at the turn of the century. A few southern and eastern Europeans farmed, as shown by the Slovak-dominated settlements of Calhan and Ramah in El Paso County; in the Italian truckgardens in Avondale, Blende, and Vineland east of Pueblo; and in Welby north of Denver. Many latecomers lacking both savings and dryland agricultural experience turned to mining, industrial, and service jobs. Concentration among some groups — first the Chinese, then Italians, later Mexicans, Greeks, Japanese, and Koreans — was further strengthened by the banding of unattached males into work gangs, a system that helped workers find employment and assured employers a reliable labor supply. Unfortunately, bosses sometimes mercilessly abused their workers. Denver's Italian vice consul, Giuseppe Cuneo, denounced these padrones as "a class of creatures my people are sold to every day — a curse to their own people, a disgrace to their country and a stain upon any country that gives them hospitality."[36] When disgruntled laborers hacked a "tyrant boss" to death as one of the conspirators strummed a harp, the *Rocky Mountain News* understood the provocation and saluted the musician: "He reminds us of the artistic grace the Italian throws even into his crime."[37]

Within cities and towns ethnic neighborhoods enhanced group cohesiveness and temporarily preserved Old World ways that were vital to all but were particularly important to non-northern Europeans and non-Protestants, who faced hostilities spawned by linguistic, religious, and racial differences. In Denver German-Russians, Poles, Slovenians, Croatians, Czechs, Slovaks, Serbians, Greeks, and Russians packed Globeville, a noisome northern industrial suburb the city annexed in 1902. Within Globeville there was a further refinement of neighborhoods, with the major groups congregating near their particular national churches. Chinese factions gathered in several distinct lower downtown enclaves. Eastern European Jews, divided along national lines, settled along West Colfax; German Jews lived more comfortably in East Denver. Italians, initially relegated to the squalid Platte River bottoms, eventually moved to higher ground in northwest Denver. English, Irish, and Scandinavians were more widely scattered, although the latter two groups were concentrated somewhat in the city's older neighborhoods near downtown.

In Pueblo, as in Denver, northern Europeans distributed themselves more widely than did Hispanos and later arrivals. On bluffs west of the Fountain River, about a mile from its present junction with the Arkansas, Hispanos established the adobe hamlet of "Mexico" in the 1870s. Evicted in the 1890s, they settled in Salt Creek a few miles southeast of the city and in enclaves such as "El Marrano," dubbed "the hog" because of its filth, and "El Tecolote" called "the owl" because of its darkness. "Mexico," in the meantime, became predominantly Italian. Close to the American Smelting and Refining Company that hired its men, this unincorporated twelve-acre slum of caves and shacks was so jammed with people (five hundred were counted in 1903) that it spared no room for animals save chickens and pigeons. An elaborate, uncharted maze of tunnels offered escape routes for criminals who counted on the Italians' antipathy toward the police. North of "Mexico" was another Italian settlement, the predominantly Sicilian "Goat Hill." "The Grove," home to most of Pueblo's Slovenians and Slovaks and to some of its Croatians, Czechs, Russians, and Serbians, was located dangerously close to the Arkansas. To its southwest, other eastern and southern Europeans settled in Bessemer and Minnequa Heights near the Colorado Fuel and Iron plant and the Eilers and Philadelphia smelters.

Ethnic neighborhoods also emerged in a few of the smaller towns. Many foreigners clustered on Telluride's seamy south side. Durango concentrated its non-northern Europeans near the smelter. In Louisville Slovaks resided in the northwest, Italians in the east, and French in the south. In Fort Collins German-Russians and Hispanos located in Buckingham Place, and even Sterling boasted an "Irish Row."

Whatever protection ethnic neighborhoods may have afforded their residents, such blessings were often mixed with problems born of overcrowding, poor sanitation, and inadequate city services. Denver's South Platte River bottomlands provided immigrants river-borne driftwood and coal pilfered from rail yards and gave their children watercress, which they sold uptown, but this poorly drained area also bred disease. "Children be dyin' down 'ere all the time," testified one resident. "It all comes from these piles of dirt."[38] Chinese quarters along Market Street were convenient to the laundries and restaurants where the Asians worked, but sanitary facilities there were poor even by nineteenth-century standards. Outhouses "crowded together near the sleeping and eating apartments" with "their contents . . . overflowing into the yards, filled with piles of ashes, decayed vegetables, chicken feathers and other refuse" produced, said the *Rocky Mountain News,* "a combination of smells the most horrible."[39] Globeville, perhaps less malodorous because it was spread out, subjected its citizens to noxious smelter fumes mixed with stockyard smells and demonstrated with its unpaved streets and nonexistent sidewalks that city services came late to poor neighborhoods. In Leadville, where only 25 percent of the homes enjoyed sewer connections, immigrants reaped the deadly cost of second-class citizenship during a 1903 typhoid outbreak whose five hundred cases were concentrated in ethnic enclaves on the south and east sides of town.

Several company towns offered almost heavenly accommodations by comparison. Redstone on the Crystal River in Pitkin County provided workers individually designed houses, each painted a different color, and offered recreation in a lavishly decorated clubhouse. At Cokedale, the American Smelting and Refining Company's model town west of Trinidad, workers paid $2 a month for neat houses and were not required to shop at a company store. Most other camps were less idyllic. A miner's wife complained, "I had to live in a pig sty as we called them in Wales."[40] The British socialist J. Kier Hardy toured southern Colorado and reported, "Had I not seen them with my own eyes I should not have believed such conditions should have existed. The men not only receive starvation wages, but they live in company houses, buy what they want from company stores and are completely under the domination of the coal companies. It is terrible."[41]

Boardinghouses, saloons, fraternal organizations, holidays and holy days, newspapers, churches, and schools gave newcomers a sense of continuity and belonging. A census of "Sloveno-Croatians" taken in Globeville in 1902 revealed 586 "souls," including 261 boarders. Rare was the family without a paying guest; many had 8 or more. By 1907 many of Denver's Japanese were living in boardinghouses near Nineteenth and Blake. In Pueblo's Bessemer district Japanese slept in rotation in order to cram over 150 people into 6 small houses. Brioco's boardinghouse in Engleville tallied 28 people in 1900, of whom 21 were Italian boarders; Maria Tabarilla's in the same town counted 12 guests, all Austrians. By 1910 almost every ethnic thirst in Pueblo could be quenched in one or another of that city's 121 bars. Cornish and Tyrolese miners in Gilpin County preferred the drinking company of their fellow countrymen, and Leadville's Irish, Germans, Swedes, and Slovenians imbibed in their own neighborhood taverns. Teutons and Celts were well represented among Denver's bar owners, who often catered to specific groups and to the wider community. "Buck beer day is usually considered a German institution," said the *Rocky Mountain News,* but in Denver "all nationalities took part in its observance."[42]

The ethnic tavern, as historian Tom Noel has shown, served many roles. On West Colfax, Adolph Goldhammer let local organizations meet in his saloon. In Globeville, where housing was scarce, bar operators rented out upstairs sleeping rooms. The elite did not meet at these poor people's clubs, but such dens were centers of political power, serving as springboards for the

An Italian funeral at Mt. Carmel Church in Pueblo in the early
twentieth century.

public careers of many, including the Slav Max Malich and Coun-
cilman Eugene Madden, a second-generation Irishman. Immigrants whose conviviality extended beyond the barroom honed
their political skills, purchased insurance, sang, and celebrated
as members of scores of ethnic associations. A recurring round of
holidays gave these groups ample excuses to march and picnic,
and a healthy foreign-language press kept foreigners aware of
community activities. Pueblo alone produced Italian, German,
Slovenian, and Serbian papers, and Denver boasted dozens of
immigrant sheets.

Saloons and societies mushroomed easily, but churches and
schools dependent on community stability and size emerged
more slowly. Well over a decade passed between the arrival of
Denver's first Germans and the organization of the town's first
German church, a Methodist establishment, and German Catholics were without a parish until St. Elizabeth's was founded in
1878. Territorial Colorado claimed a few Poles, and more came in
the 1880s and 1890s, but not until the new century were they

able to worship together in Globeville's St. Joseph's Polish church. Italians lacked a national parish in Denver until 1894 when Mount Carmel opened, and the city's Irish were condemned to pray in St. Elizabeth's basement until rescued by the wealthy miller J. K. Mullen, whose dislike of German sermons supposedly prompted him to construct St. Leo's. Pueblo's Slovenians congregated in an abandoned broom factory until 1895 when they built St. Mary's, which they shared with Germans and Slovaks until the former split off to form St. Boniface's and the latter to form St. Anthony's.

Because people of piety were not necessarily people of plenty, the vision of impressive structures nurtured by many preachers sometimes lingered long in the realm of fantasy. The Reverend Nicholas Sergelly, a Slovak, struggled to establish his Greek Catholic church in Globeville, only to see part of his flock scatter when Polish Roman Catholics withdrew. Hilko de Beers, a German missionary, accomplished even less. Writing to his wife in 1908, he reported that because only a fraction of Denver's Germans were churchgoers, he was considering earning a living tuning pianos but had been told that the town was "overrun with piano tuners." To save money he spent only five cents a meal "for breakfast, dinner and supper everytime nothing but coffee and rolls. . . . I am so constipated."[43] Perhaps de Beers and Sergelly were exceptions, for by 1916 ethnic churches flourished throughout Colorado. Lutherans — most of them Germans, Scandinavians, or German-Russians — reported members in over half of the state's counties. Jews, principally from Germany and Eastern Europe, tallied nearly twenty-five hundred worshipers, with over 80 percent in Denver. Russian Orthodox churches counted nearly one thousand communicants in Denver, Pueblo, and El Paso counties; Roman Catholics — composed largely of immigrant Irish, Germans, Italians, and native-born Hispanos — claimed over one hundred thousand adherents, or some 40 percent of all of the state's church members.

First-generation immigrants faced two directions: toward Old World pasts filled with tradition, and to New World futures, fraught with uncertainty, filled with hope, demanding of change. Postal employees in Pueblo smiled when a Japanese customer showed them a large stone to signify that a letter should be sent to Boulder. Denverites chuckled when they read of a local lawyer's failure to make his clients understand ancient Greek, but to non-English-speakers knowing some English, altering some customs, and often learning a new occupation were serious matters. Most historians now doubt that immigrants were fused in a giant melting pot, but few scholars would deny that foreigners were transformed by both necessity and accident. Often contradictory pressures nurtured curious ambivalences. Germans fought to have German taught in public schools, but their children learned English. When the Hagus family moved from their Brighton farm to Denver, the parents ceased speaking German at home because they thought it would be bad for the children. Bishop Nicholas Matz advised students at Mount Carmel School to learn both Italian and English. Jews on West Colfax sent their youngsters to public school, insisting that they learn Hebrew in the afternoons and on weekends.

Even had newcomers wanted to isolate themselves completely, the task would have been impossible. Large companies sought ethnically mixed workforces, hoping thereby to prevent unionization, and corporations often broke strikes by importing new groups to supplant old. Unrest in 1884 led the Colorado Coal and Iron Company to replace northern Europeans with Italians, Austrians, and African-Americans. During the 1903–1904 coal strike Italians in southern Colorado were replaced by Mexicans and Japanese. By 1900 towns such as Walsenburg reflected the ethnic diversity promoted by CF&I, which by 1903 boasted employees of thirty-two different nationalities.

Intragroup differences etched by centuries of strife further weakened the immigrants and limited their power. All Chinese may have looked alike to native U.S. citizens, but within Denver's Chinese community there were gang rivalries so deep that they sometimes led to mayhem and murder. Lutheran German-Russians scoffed at the "corrupt" German spoken by Catholics; Lithuanian Jews questioned the purity of Rumanians' Hebrew. Factionalism in Denver's Little Italy sparked the burning of Mount Carmel Church and the establishment of a rival parish. German-Russian congregationalists, prodded by powerful laypeople, spiritedly debated whether ministers should wear ties. Inflamed by a potent brew of religion and politics, Irish Orangemen annually battled Irish Catholics in Leadville, and in Pueblo rival Japanese work gangs fought. Northern Europeans sometimes joined native U.S. residents to secure union recognition and improved conditions. Latecomers were usually less fortunate. Historian Philip Notarianni has demonstrated that the

1903–1904 coal strike in Colorado's southern fields failed partly because Italians could not overcome their internal differences.

The political arena also saw earlier arrivals doing better than newcomers. Germans, Irish, and English garnered some power on the local level and occasionally made their influence more widely felt. Peter Breene, the darling of Leadville's Irish, served as lieutenant governor and later as state treasurer; William Meyer, one of several Germans who rose to prominence in southern Colorado, also gained the lieutenant governorship; and Protestant Irishman Robert Morris satisfied warring factions long enough to become Denver's mayor in 1881. Often only ward-level crumbs remained for later arrivals and African-Americans, and Asians were totally excluded from politics. Some immigrants did not even become citizens, perhaps because they intended to return home, because they feared officials, or because they did not see the use. A number found it difficult or impossible to qualify. Between 1908 and 1918 over 30 percent of all naturalization applications filed in Colorado were denied, making the state the seventh most stringent in the nation. Foreign-born Chinese had virtually no hope of citizenship after the Chinese Exclusion Act of 1882 denied them naturalization.

For a few the trappings of political office and the protection of labor unions were of little importance. Luck, skill, and perseverance sometimes rewarded foreigners as well as natives. Irishman Tom Walsh prospected for years before discovering Ouray's Camp Bird mine. In Leadville another Camp Bird mine made the Irish-born Gallagher brothers wealthy, and in Cripple Creek three Irish — John Harnan, James Burns, and James Doyle — reveled in gold from Battle Mountain. Germans such as George Tritch and William Barth found more mundane pay dirt by investing in Denver real estate. Charles Boettcher, a profit-seeking Prussian, parlayed his hardware business into a financial empire built of cement, sugar, banks, and investment houses, and another German, brewer Adolph Coors, put his hope in hops.

Yet for every Boettcher, Burns, or Barth there were thousands of less fortunate immigrants occupying the bottom rungs of the economic ladder and suffering from poor pay and difficult working conditions. In Denver in 1900, 1 of every 7 Italians was a huckster or a peddler, whereas fewer than 1 in 400 natives hawked goods. There were over 350 native white physicians and surgeons, but there was only one Polish doctor. Nearly 20 percent of all Swedes and over 25 percent of all Italians were enumerated as unspecified laborers, a category that embraced only 7 percent of U.S. natives, 6 percent of the British, and 15 percent of the Irish. Such common laborers were usually poorly rewarded, although until the early 1890s Colorado's workers were better paid than their counterparts in most midwestern and eastern cities. Before 1893 Denver's smelter furnace workers got $3.00 for a twelve-hour day; from 1893 to mid-1899 they settled for $2.75. Yardmen during those difficult years considered themselves lucky to have jobs at $1.60 a day. Wages and conditions were also poor outside the cities. Sam Vidano mined coal for twenty-one of the twenty-four working days of February 1899. Loading more than five tons on some days, he produced eighty-five tons during the month, for which he received $85.00 minus $14.50 in deductions for food, coal, blacksmith services, and hospital insurance.

Poor pay was not the only problem with coal mining. Writing to her sisters in Rome, Italian nun Frances Xavier Cabrini told of Colorado's hellish coal pits, of "dark tunnels where breathing is difficult [and] where the only available light is that of a few tallow candles."[44] Poor ventilation and unsafe mining practices led to frequent accidents and sometimes brought on major disasters. Fatality lists from the larger calamities tell not only the grim realities of the immigrant struggle but also indicate the variety and constantly changing composition of the workforce. The state's first major coal disaster, an 1884 gas explosion at Crested Butte's Jokerville mine, killed fifty-nine workers, most of them U.S. natives and northern Europeans. Twelve years later an explosion at the Vulcan mine in Garfield County blasted forty-nine lives, including natives, Germans, Austrians, Italians, Welsh, and Scots. At Primero in 1910 Koreans, Slavs, Italians, Germans, and Welsh died; at Cokedale a year later eleven Poles and four Italians were killed in a single accident. The year 1913 saw over one hundred deaths, including thirty-seven at the Vulcan mine where Bulgarians and Mexicans were among the casualties. Mine inspectors' reports painted a stark picture. Albino Munis, a sixteen-year-old Mexican, was fatally injured coupling cars near Primero in 1901. Wrote the inspector: "The deceased was crushed sideways in this small space and died from his injuries twenty-six hours later."[45] John Lewis, a twenty-eight-year-old Greek, lingered longer; he was crushed on December 6 and died on December 9, 1916. Wrote the inspector: "The mining foreman had been asked three times . . . to place safety blocks in all rooms having a grade. Had this recommendation been complied with the accident would have been avoided." Another Greek, Gregory Anastassopulas, instantly killed by a falling rock, left a wife and two children. Wrote the inspector: "Had another crossbar been set up, as provided for in the timber agreement . . . the accident might have been avoided."[46] Courageous officials sometimes suggested improvements, because Colorado's safety record lagged woefully behind other coal-producing states such as Missouri and Illinois. But in most cases investigators and coroners' juries found corporations blameless. Chiding dead miners for bringing "a stigma upon their employers," one inspector perhaps sarcastically contended that "miners unless restrained will often commit suicide and endanger their fellow workmen."[47]

Before the immigrant stream was slowed by World War I, corporations could more or less readily replace dissident workers; hence many foreigners, particularly late arrivals, usually remained trapped in dangerous, low-paying jobs. But on occasion they successfully resisted importation of cheap labor. One of Leadville's first Chinese residents was bombed out of his cabin; Gregory Gulch miners exiled celestials after having snipped off their queues; discovery of an opium den in Durango left local Chinese fearing for their lives; the threat of being hanged caused Silverton's Asian restauranters to flee; and in Cripple Creek Chinese cooks and waiters also left under duress. Lecturer J.P.C. Poulton's geography may have been suspect, but his sentiments were widely shared when he argued that "capital and labor is bitter enough already without filling the country with lousy opium eaters who live on ten cents a day and send the remainder of their wages across the Mediterranean."[48]

By 1890, scarcely twenty years after the first Asians arrived in Colorado, there were no Chinese in Aspen or Leadville, and Colorado Springs, Durango, Ouray, Trinidad, and Salida all had fewer than 30 each. Only Denver tallied more than 100 Chinese, its 1890 contingent of 974 representing nearly 90 percent of the state's total and nearly 4 percent of the capital city's foreigners. But numbers did not necessarily guarantee safety. In 1880 rioters wrecked the Chinese laundries and restaurants and hanged an inoffensive old man whose principal crime was his failure to outrun the mob. Few were willing to defend the Chinese either during or after the riot. Labor leader Joseph Buchanan often proclaimed his belief in the "Brotherhood of Man"; when reminded of the Chinese he spoke of the "Brotherhood of Man Limited."

Even the Reverend Myron Reed — champion of the downtrodden, spokesperson for the Native Americans, friend of the African-Americans, and local archdruid of the social gospel movement — charged the Chinese with "exploiting us for all we are worth" and declared that his Congregational Church would never have any dealings with Asians, "not if I can help it." Suffragist Mary Lathrop responded: "It was my impression that the Chinaman was imported . . . and that the American who brought him made a liberal percentage out of the speculation." Mary F. Leonard, a child at the time, also thought kindly of the Chinese: "My father was a teamster and he knew many Chinese. They gave me candy."[49]

As the Chinese population in Colorado dwindled to 291 by 1920, the "problem" abated. But the polemics fueled by the first surge of the so-called "yellow peril" were still smoldering when a second wave, this one from Japan, rekindled the fears of native U.S. and European workers. Corporate motives for importing Japanese laborers were, as always, the same — the availability of cheap, reliable labor. Displaced employees also reacted predictably. At the Chandler mine in Fremont County, a mob attacked Japanese in 1902. That same year the legislature asked Congress to bar Japanese laborers from the United States. Local unions, the United Mine Workers, and the Western Federation of Miners, unwilling to wait for national action, excluded most Japanese from northern coal fields and from mountain mining towns. "In the camps," the *Daily Mining Record* reported, "the presence of the yellow peril might mean an American lynching bee with the yellow-eyed son hanging on the dangerous end of the rope."[50]

On the other hand, the state's southern coal regions — which were in the grip of a few powerful corporations and, therefore, lacked effective unions — temporarily absorbed many Japanese, as did Colorado Fuel and Iron's mills and railroad companies, including the Denver and Rio Grande, the Denver and Northwestern, and the large Union Pacific system. Sugar beet growers, rapidly expanding their acreage in the early twentieth century, recruited Japanese stoop laborers or purchased land of their own.

For some the sojourn in Colorado was brief. Some returned home at the call of their government during the Russo-Japanese War of 1904–1905. Some found the prejudice of natives insurmountable. Angry farmers drove Japanese peach pickers from

Paonia in 1906, and in general they were unwelcome in other Western Slope towns. "There must be bloodshed. It is beginning to seem that bloodshed alone will bring the Chinese and Japanese question to the attention of Congress," proclaimed R. E. Crosby at a mass meeting in Denver.[51] Japanese organizations advised members to avoid trouble by being quiet after 11:00 P.M., by talking softly when walking on the street, and by keeping their clothes clean. Following the pattern set by the Chinese Exclusion Act, the United States and Japan agreed in 1907–1908 to stop the flow of laborers. Between 1900 and 1910 the number of Colorado's Japanese increased from a mere forty-eight to over twenty thousand; but from 1910 to 1920 growth leveled off, and only a few hundred more were added.

Asians suffered more than any other immigrant group from the hostilities of economically insecure Caucasians, but Asiatics did not bear the brunt of bigotry alone. Dreading competition from Southern Slavs, Gilpin County's Cornish and Welsh miners temporarily drove the interlopers away. Cripple Creek's "American and Americanized" workers used "the arm and the gun" to bar "not only the Chinaman" but also "the Italian, Austrian, and other Old World labor recruits."[52] Although friction was often based on job competition, other bones of contention were easily dug up and fought over. A game of "finger-pull" led to a row between Finns and Swedes in Leadville that left one dead and another injured. Americans winced when they saw Chinese eating from one rice bowl, snatching "a piece of pork here and there, with heroic indifference to dyspepsia and disregard for table etiquette."[53] Nor did natives appreciate Greeks who lingered at public bath houses for two hours or more, "albeit the corridors are filled with fuming, fretting persons."[54] Temperance advocates, bemoaning the influence of Denver's "boozy Teutons," charged "the offal of foreign immigration is attempting to dictate to the moral element."[55] Linking religious prejudices with economic and political rivalries, U.S. and foreign-born Protestants flocked to the American Protective Association (APA), which in the early 1890s backed candidates pledged to removing Roman Catholics from government jobs. The APA's tool, Republican Governor Albert McIntire, carried out the mandate. As one Irishman was being fired, he predicted that the governor would end his days picking weeds in Conejos County — a curse that apparently worked, because McIntire died in poverty. The demise of both the governor and the APA coincided with the state's economic recovery in the mid-1890s, demonstrating that the organization fed as much on economic fear as it did on religious hatred.

Bigotry aimed at Catholics, Jews, and Southern and Eastern Europeans was also directed against African-Americans, whose American roots usually reached deeper than those of their antagonists. Having spent part of their lives in slavery and the rest in peonage, many of Colorado's pioneer African-Americans escaped the burden of the South by moving West. Nash Walker fled from Alabama in 1863 to join the Union army. At war's end he journeyed to Kansas and from there went on to Denver in 1877, where he eventually organized an unsuccessful Back-to-Africa movement. Kate Little remembered a cruel Georgia master who kept his slaves ignorant of their freedom until spring planting was completed, and Moses Hanner, a Denver barber, looked back on an exciting life as the slave of a pirate.

Not all African-Americans in Colorado had been slaves, however. Lewis Douglass and Frederick Douglass, Jr., sons of the famed abolitionist, were born free, as was William Hardin, who migrated to Colorado in the early 1860s. Nor were all African-Americans of one mind. Frank Loper, loyal to the remnants of the Jefferson Davis family living in Colorado Springs, fondly recalled that when Davis left his Mississippi plantation to assume the Confederate presidency, he asked his slaves to protect his family. "We all cheered him, and promised that we would because Mr. Davis was a kind master, and never would allow us to be whipped."[56]

Yet, the mark of slavery was so deep and newly won protections so fragile that many Colorado African-Americans clung tenaciously to their rights. Led by articulate leaders including William Hardin, Henry Wagoner, Ed Sanderlin, Barney Ford, and Frederick Douglass's sons, African-Americans adroitly played local and national politics to gain power out of proportion to their numbers. Denied the franchise to vote in 1865, they retaliated with a direct appeal to Congress that temporarily crippled the territory's chances of becoming a state. Assured of the vote by federal legislation in 1867, they supported the unsuccessful statehood effort of 1868. In the meantime they had established a night school in Denver and had launched a campaign for integrated education that bore fruit in 1873 when the Denver School Board approved integration, a principle incorporated into

Frederick Douglass, Jr., son of the famed abolitionist, was a prominent black leader in Denver following the Civil War.

the state constitution two years later. In the 1870s African-American police bossed Irish convicts working on Denver's streets, African-Americans sat on juries, and a few African-American children attended school with whites.

Unfortunately, the advances made during the territorial period were not secure. As the African-American population grew from fewer than 500 in 1870 to over 11,500 in 1910, friction and demands for race separation increased. Local African-Americans encouraged their brethren to migrate from Kansas in the late 1870s. "What immigration has done for the white man it can also do for the Black man," argued Henry Wagoner. Ex-governor John Evans thought that "quite a number could be accommodated here in Denver as house servants and stock trainers and the like." But Thomas Patterson cautioned: "Thousands who now denounce southern people on account of alleged persecutions of negroes would become their persecutors in turn because their wages and comforts of their families would be curtailed."[57] Patterson was correct. When the Colorado Coal and Iron Company replaced some white coal miners at Walsenburg and Engleville with African-Americans, the intruders were threatened with death. When F. N. Davis displaced white workers at his Denver brickyard with African-Americans, a fight ensued that left two whites dead.

Rooted in long-held racial attitudes, black-white friction went far deeper than job competition. Most native-born Coloradans came from northern states, and the majority usually voted Republican, but such credentials did not necessarily signify sympathy toward African-Americans. A few had championed African-American rights even before the Civil War. Colonel John Chivington of Sand Creek infamy reputedly "stood by John Brown when he carried his last cargo of slaves into freedom," and Horace Tabor, by his own account, gave "his only pistol to a colored man who was fleeing from the South and slavery."[58] Tabor wanted African-Americans to stay in the Republican party, but employees of the Tabor Opera House in Denver did not want James Hawkins, an African-American man, sitting in the theater's dress circle or parquette sections. White soldiers besieged by Utes north of the White River Agency in 1879 gratefully accepted relief from African-American troops: "We let 'em sleep with us, and they took their knives and cut off slips of bacon from the same sides of bacon as we did." But in Denver in the mid-1880s, militia leaders maneuvered African-Americans

Bicyclists along the South Platte, Denver, ca. 1908.

out of their regiment "because the white officers . . . do not wish to associate with colored men even on a war footing."[59]

Getting a table in a white restaurant, a room in a white hotel, or a prime seat in a white theater was difficult for African-Americans, but going to jail was relatively easy. Denver's police, African-Americans charged, routinely rounded up all African-Americans in a neighborhood when a crime was committed. Sometimes African-Americans welcomed the safety of a cell and the ordered working of the law. Pete Burns, for one, might have appreciated a day in court, but he was denied the opportunity. When his performing bear killed a wrestler, both the animal and Burns were summarily lynched. Calvin Kimblern, accused of molesting and murdering two Pueblo children, was grabbed from the police by a mob of six thousand, dragged and kicked through the streets of Pueblo, and tortuously executed. In La Junta a crowd of "men, women, and little children" watched as schoolboys helped their elders hang Washington Wallace, suspected of assaulting a local woman. And in Limon farmers angered by the murder of an eleven-year-old jettisoned all semblance of due process when they burned an African-American youth, John Porter, at the stake.

African-Americans responded to assaults and insults as best they could given their small numbers; between 1870 and 1920 they never constituted more than 2 percent of the state's population. Allied with sympathetic whites, they secured antidiscrimination statutes in 1885, 1895, and 1917, which at most paid legal lip service to equal rights. In Denver, home of 70 percent of the state's African-Americans, community leaders won minor patronage positions in return for African-American votes. They also protested when rights went unrespected. In 1898 they demanded removal of the Denver police chief after he suggested that the city needed "a regular old Kentucky lynching."[60] In 1902 religious leaders pressured organizers of a national Sunday school convention into allowing African-American preachers to sit with their white brethren under certain circumstances. Perhaps the pinnacle of early twentieth-century African-American power came thirteen years later when the city council forbade the showing of films or plays that cast racial aspersions — an ordinance that quickly proved to be a frail reed when a judge ruled that *The Birth of a Nation,* a film that clearly demeaned African-Americans, did not violate the statute.

As bad as conditions sometimes were for Colorado's African-Americans, they were not as severe as the privations suffered by ex-slaves in many other states. Sunday school convention delegates were so favorably impressed with their treatment that local African-Americans believed some of the visiting preachers could be induced to move to Colorado. Nash Walker urged Denver's African-Americans to migrate to Liberia, but few, if any, went. Nor were they attracted in significant numbers to African-American agricultural communities such as Dearfield Colony in Weld County or the less widely known Manzanola Colony in the Arkansas Valley. Concentrated in Denver, Pueblo, and Colorado Springs, many African-Americans found employment as servants, porters, and common laborers. A few broke through economic and professional barriers. Barney Ford's fortune put him among Denver's wealthiest residents in territorial days, and Lewis Price prospered during the city's real estate boom of the 1880s. Dr. V. B. Spratlin graduated from the University of Denver's medical college in 1892 and went on to become the city's chief medical inspector. Dr. Justina Ford found patients among

African-Americans and other ethnic groups who respected her ability to deliver babies. Willis Hood helped patrol Pueblo, and in Denver William Barker enjoyed a long police career: "There would be frowns when I was forced to beat whites, but I always tended only to duty."[61]

Statistical indicators also show that Colorado's African-Americans were well-off compared to their counterparts elsewhere. Denver's death rate in 1900 was 20 percent higher for African-Americans than for whites, but both rates were considerably lower than in most southern cities, and the differential between the races was far less in Denver than in many other cities. In 1910 over 85 percent of all African-Americans between ages six and fourteen attended school in Colorado, a percentage almost comparable to that for whites and 20 percent higher than African-American enrollment in southern states.

"Girls in Paris Kiss U.S. Soldiers Marching in Fourth of July Parade," proclaimed the headlines in Denver papers on July 5, 1917. Denver celebrated a quiet Independence Day that year, without parades. The Ancient Order of Hibernians, an Irish group, met at Elitch's. At Washington Park fireworks were dispensed with; the crowd listened to patriotic songs instead. In Pueblo a "motley" throng "of all ages, nations, sizes and garb" gathered at City Park. "The faces of some of the foreign-born Pueblans sparkled with the pure joy of the occasion," said the *Chieftain*.[62] Perhaps a few failed to smile because they were wondering how long it would be until the ideals of 1776 would be fully realized. Certainly African-Americans, as they read of race riots in East Saint Louis in early July 1917, had reason to pause. But others, although not fully satisfied, had reason for at least some degree of contentment. Colorado's women, after all, passed their twentieth year of suffrage before that right was nationally mandated. Most Chinese had been pressured into leaving, and the Japanese knew they were unwelcome, but most other foreigners maintained large contingents in Colorado. By 1917 Hyman Siegel's two sons were learning English in public school and his grocery trade was expanding, thanks in part to the acquisition of a horse and a telephone. In Pueblo John Rougas, by then married to a woman from his hometown in Greece, was also doing well in the grocery business. These representatives of the older and first generation of immigrants were destined to see their communities gradually eroded. "Marry within

A turn-of-the-century picnic, by Denver photographer Charles Lillybridge.

the language," Emil Horwart's Croatian mother told him, and many other children got similar advice that grew increasingly meaningless as the language became English for everyone.[63] Moreover, because the immigrant flow slowed after 1914, most groups, except for Mexicans, could not count on large yearly additions to their ranks. Yet in 1917 these impending changes were only small clouds on the horizon. With U.S. natives, many of them their own progeny, immigrants celebrated proudly that year, for they knew they had helped transform a wilderness into one of the Rocky Mountain West's most important states in little more than half a century.

# CHAPTER 11

# THE DISCOVERY OF SCENERY: THE GROWTH OF TOURISM

For more than a century, Colorado has been something special for the American tourist. Since 1870 it has been easily accessible from the East by railroad or automobile. It has made a determined effort to provide the facilities needed to attract vacationers and has accompanied this effort with a barrage of publicity that has made the word "Rockies" mean Colorado to much of the nation. Easy to get to, comfortable to see, and filled with famous sights worthy of a visit, the state has fully exploited the American propensity for traveling. In the process, publicists and promoters once again took a central role in directing its growth.

Today, many of the eastern tourists who visit Colorado think of themselves as explorers. The same routes Coloradans have long traveled without hazard are adventures with unknown dangers and strange peoples around the corner. Each pass surmounted is a triumph to be photographed, each postcard like an official report on the findings of the expedition. Vacationers try gold panning and pronounce Colorado a humbug or an El Dorado, according to their luck. Many return home with souvenirs — a cowboy hat, a lump of ore — and become instant boosters of the wonders of the Great West.

Colorado's first tourists were explorers in fact as well as in fancy. Participants in the first gold rush spared little time for serious consideration of a future tourist trade. In the mid-1860s, however, journalists began to thoroughly explore the territory. Just as visitors scanned the hills for outcroppings of ore and crumbled the soil of its bottomlands between their fingers, the journalist-explorers inspected the scenery with a view to its potential for exploitation. Indeed, the boosters explicitly considered "the climate, mineral waters and scenic attractions of Colorado . . . as resources in themselves." Like the fertile ground, flowing streams, and mines of silver and gold, they argued, the air and mountains were assets that would "bring people and money into this section."[1]

The most peripatetic of these journalist-explorers was William Byers. He regularly entrusted the *Rocky Mountain News* to his assistants and joined John Wesley Powell's and Ferdinand Hayden's survey parties — climbing the same peaks, viewing the same scenery, and reporting his experiences in enthusiastic articles for the *News*. In August 1868 he accompanied Powell in the first recorded ascent of Longs Peak; a few years later he joined the Hayden party on the summit of Mount Lincoln. Byers put his knowledge of the central Rockies to work as an unofficial tour guide, leading important visitors through a circuit that included Berthoud Pass, Middle Park, Hot Sulphur Springs, the valley of the Blue River, South Park, and the canyons of the South Platte. In 1867 he guided professional travel writer Bayard Taylor over the entire route. A year later he helped to introduce to Middle Park and South Park a camping party that included Vice President Schuyler Colfax, Lieutenant Governor William Bross of Illinois, and Massachusetts newspaperman Samuel Bowles.

The result of Byers's tour-guiding efforts was a pair of immensely influential books: Taylor's *Colorado: A Summer Trip* (1867) and Bowles's *The Switzerland of America* (1869). Both of these writers agreed that Colorado offered vast potential for tourism despite the hardships of travel. Americans would soon flock to the nation's interior "for rest and recreation, for new and exhilarating scenes, for pure and bracing airs, for pleasure and for health." The two writers could do little to hurry the railroads, but they did their best to convince a public accustomed to the scenery of Europe that Colorado was indeed another Switzerland. Pikes Peak was "something like" the Jungfrau, the Twin Lakes like Lake Lucerne or Lake Como, and other sights like the Alps of Savoy or the Upper Valley of the Rhine. Local booster Ovando Hollister echoed that evaluation when he wrote that "the Rocky Mountains offer the most delightful Summer resort of the New if not the Old World. . . . The annexation of the Rocky Mountains to the Union by railroads will open a new world to science, a new field of adventure to money and muscle, and new and pleasant places of Summer resort to people of leisure."[2]

In these predictions, publicists such as Hollister and Byers were trying to capitalize on a well-established U.S. propensity for summer vacations. Since the early 1850s outdoor recreation had become increasingly fashionable among the mercantile and professional families of the East, and gazetteers had begun to include lists of "mineral springs, waterfalls, caves, beaches and other fashionable resorts." Newport, Rhode Island, and Saratoga, New York, led everyone's list of places where a proper family of leisure could comfortably spend July and August in a gala round of social events. Next were dozens of other resorts in the cool mountains or on the shore, each with its imposing hotels and less expensive boardinghouses. The range of development by 1872 was indicated by the subtitle of *Appleton's Handbook of American Travels:* "Being a Guide to Niagara, The White Mountains, The Alleghanies, The Catskills, The Adirondacks, The Berkshire Hills, The St. Lawrence, Lake Champlain, Lake George, Lake Memphremagog, Saratoga, Newport, Cape May, The Hudson and Other Famous Localities." Even so, the more exclusive resorts were finding it harder to maintain their preferred tone in the face of an influx of newly prosperous middle-class visitors. To families unable to support a mansion-sized "cottage" at Newport and unwilling to rub elbows at Saratoga with the vulgar crowds who usurped the better hotels, books such as those of Bowles and Taylor offered an answer to their frustrated query of "where to next?"

Another publicist was Anna Dickinson, well-known through the United States as a lecturer on women's rights. In 1873 the thirty-year-old Dickinson made her third visit to Colorado and spent three weeks riding to the summits of Colorado's more accessible "fourteeners" (fourteen-thousand-foot mountains), with interspersed lectures on the progress of women. Early in September she joined with the Hayden survey and William Byers and on the 13th climbed to the top of Longs Peak; the Hayden people thought it worth their while to enlist the support of a well-known writer and speaker. Although Dickinson usually gets credit as the first women to climb Longs Peak, it is more accurate to view her as the first *well-publicized* woman to do so, for both Addie Alexander and a Miss Bartlett had reportedly preceded her by two years.

Along with California, it was Colorado that benefited most from the new opportunity for travel offered by transcontinental railroad lines after 1868. More than in other territories, Colorado boosters promoted tourism with an advertising campaign based on the favorable evaluation of early travelers. Even the state's railroads issued guidebooks. Local writers reminded well-

This overdecorated dining car on the Union Pacific line is typical of the plush accommodations on early transcontinental railroads.

to-do folk that a visit to Colorado required less time and money than did a trip to Europe, and they assured them that "in going to Colorado, one does not necessarily bid farewell to civilization." Colorado was also a chief exhibit in the accounts of western travels that flooded the bookstores of the United States and Great Britain in the 1870s and 1880s. As early as 1880, occasional critics complained that the state was "over-praised and too much written up." Other observers, however, recognized that no other locality had been "as fortunate in the energy and intelligence bestowed upon the work of making this phase of its attractions widely and favorably known."[3]

Tourists to Colorado quickly found a routine that was to remain fixed for a generation. The suggestion of most writers and the habit of most travelers was to use one of the piedmont cities as a base for excursions into the mountains. By the mid-1870s many of the scenic canyons and lakes, the best-known mining towns, and several mountain spas were accessible by railroad. Ranchers in the foothills had begun to build small cabins with the idea of renting to tourists. More extensive travel required greater energy, for conscientious tourism was still a difficult job.

Camp at Mandall's on the Roaring Fork, Bear River, 1899. Campers in the nineteenth century took as much equipment as those in the twentieth.

To hunt, fish, and see the higher mountains and the hidden parks, travelers had to become adventurers on horseback or stagecoach passengers. After a day's pounding from roads that were scarcely more than clearings through the forest, sleeping accommodations might be a spare room in an isolated ranch house or in a raucous saloon. Beds in one mining town hotel might be divided from each other by canvas sheets, and rooms in another might have gaping holes in the walls. Dedicated tourists could also rent a tent, utensils, food, and pack animals when they got off the train. One party in 1873 camped out in the deserted mining village of Dayton near Twin Lakes; one member noted that the town's empty cabins served a constant stream of tourists. There were also unpleasant by-products, for as early as 1880 a writer in *Harper's* was complaining about the debris of tin cans left by careless campers.

Denver's importance as a rail center made it the base of operations for the largest number of summer tourists. Only two days from St. Louis and Chicago and three and a half days from the Atlantic seaboard, Denver attracted perhaps one hundred thousand visitors annually by 1878 and two hundred thousand by the mid-1880s. Half of them stayed in its four largest hotels, which one Englishman described as "capital"; the other half stayed in Denver's smaller inns and boardinghouses. Half a dozen railroads led to the obligatory tourist attractions of northern Colorado: the canyons of Clear Creek, Boulder Creek, and the South Platte; the towns of Central City, Georgetown, and Idaho Springs. Idaho Springs in particular was promoted as a resort unsurpassed in attractions for seekers of health and pleasure. A first-class hotel, bathhouses for users of its warm soda springs, the Chicago Lakes, Chief Mountain, and a bracing high-altitude climate were among its inviting attractions. Fourteen miles farther west was Georgetown, which offered luxurious accommodations in the Hotel de Paris and impressive views from Grays Peak, in addition to the spectacular "Georgetown Loop" on the narrow-gauge line of the Colorado Central.

Middle Park and Estes Park, also reached from Denver, required exhausting rides by stage or on horseback. Although William Byers tried to promote Hot Sulphur Springs as a resort spa, Middle Park into the 1880s remained a region frequented primarily by those who camped, hunted, and fished, many of whom were Colorado residents. By 1890, however, Grand Lake was a well-developed resort village. In the smaller valley of Estes Park, nestled near the base of Longs Peak, Griff Evans operated Colorado's first dude ranch in the early 1870s, renting cabins and providing horses and guide service. Increasing throngs of campers, sightseers, and mountain climbers defeated the efforts of the wealthy Earl of Dunraven to establish a private hunting preserve in the valley. Instead of fulfilling his aristocratic ambitions, Dunraven settled for opening the "first-class" English Hotel in 1877 — to cater to the tourist trade.

Although Denver was a tourist center, it was much more besides — a complex metropolis with many activities to command the attention of visitors. Colorado Springs, in contrast, was a resort center first and foremost. The early growth of William Jackson Palmer's town was based almost entirely on people who wanted to visit or live in Colorado because of its amenities. As Richard Harding Davis wrote, "Denver and Colorado Springs pretend to be jealous of each other; why, it is impossible to understand. One is a city, and the other a summer or health resort;

and we might as properly compare Boston and Newport, or New York and Tuxedo."[4] Within a few years after Colorado Springs was laid out in 1871, it had a full range of restaurants, hotels, boardinghouses, and houses and rooms to rent. By 1878 it accommodated about twenty-five thousand tourists. The completion of the Antlers Hotel five years later gave the town one of the best hotels in the nation. Five miles to the west was the sister resort of Manitou Springs. For generations before, this area had been ground where the Utes and Comanches met in peace; now, in 1872, Denver and Rio Grande interests established the town as a first-class Colorado watering place and spa. This "Saratoga of the West" boasted eight mineral springs with ornamental pavilions, winding pathways, and large hotels, boardinghouses, and private villas to shelter thousands of fashionable tourists.

Much of Colorado Springs's prominence as a resort center was based on its having "a greater number of wonders and attractions easily accessible and within a short distance than any other single locality." Above Manitou Springs is Ute Pass, with its abundance of romantic scenery. Just a few miles north of the Springs is the Garden of the Gods, a set of massive, irregular sandstone formations that became one of the most famous sights in the West. Monument Park offers similar scenery a few miles more distant. South of town the "sparkling brooklets, streams and beautiful waterfalls" of Cheyenne Canyon were only an hour's drive for picnickers or sightseers. And towering over everything is Pikes Peak. By the 1880s a tourist on horseback or in a carriage could ascend the mountain and return in a day, stopping for lunch at the "Halfway House" perched along the trail. A magnificent view could be had with little inconvenience or exertion. After 1891 a cog railroad with small, open cars reduced the journey to the summit to a mere ninety minutes. Those willing to undertake a longer excursion could visit the Royal Gorge of the Arkansas River to gaze at "the appalling view from the main walls" and return "overcome by awe at the magnitude of nature's handiwork."[5]

If Colorado Springs was "a capital center of innumerable attractive drives and excursions," it was also one of the West's most fashionable resorts. Through the 1880s and 1890s its cost of living was high enough to exclude the average American. In the early 1880s an ordinary furnished room rented for $20 or $25 per month. A decade later a magazine writer acknowledged that normal house rentals of $250 to $350 a month were likely to strike a newcomer as exorbitant. A number of English immigrants helped to elevate the town's social tone in an Anglophilic age. Wealthy residents and well-to-do visitors could easily live an "Eastern life in a Western environment."[6] In the mid-1890s one could dine and dance at the Broadmoor Casino; try golf, polo, or pigeon shooting at the Cheyenne Mountain Country Club; shop at stores well stocked with eastern goods; or pass the time in a ceaseless round of parties, dances, social calls, and flirtations. Fifth Avenue and Oyster Bay never seemed far away.

Americans who fell in love with the scenery of the Rockies in the nineteenth century approached the mountains with the expectations of their own generation. Travelers who had been conditioned by European travel looked for the picturesque, for extraordinary landscapes arranged by nature for striking pictorial effects. Other tourists in the age of P. T. Barnum looked for natural curiosities such as geysers, giant trees, and petrified forests. Still others approached the West with eyes trained by the paintings of the Hudson River school. The Rocky Mountain landscapes of Albert Bierstadt exemplified their vision, with misty atmosphere and towering peaks that seemed to represent the most stirring emotions.

Travelers who wanted to record their experience relied on the terminology in common usage. One result was the overworking of abstract adjectives. As one writer noted, "Celebrated travelers, learned tourists, versatile newspaper correspondents, poets, authors and editors have exhausted the vocabulary of laudatory phraseology in attempting to describe the grandeur, beauty and sublimity of the mountain and valley scenery." All through the Rockies were scenes visitors found "enchanting," "thrilling," and "full of infinite suggestion." The mountains called up deep emotions and quickened the currents of the mind. "Such majestic sweeps of distance, such sublime combinations of height and breadth and uplifting into the presence of God; such dwarfing of the mortal sense, such welcome to the immortal thought. It was not beauty, it was sublimity, it was not power, nor order, nor color, it was majesty."[7]

At the same time, visitors tried to anchor their descriptions for those who had never seen Colorado by emphasizing similarities in appearance to familiar objects. The Garden of the Gods near Colorado Springs provided the ideal opportunity for exercising the imagination. Guides were quick to point out that this rock resembled a camel, that one a frog, another an "eagle with pinions spread," and yet another an "angry dolphin." Some tourists compiled their own catalogs, stressing similarities to human figures, to animals, or to the ruins of ancient structures with "bastions, battlements, half-buried marbles, towers, and castles."[8]

Nineteenth-century reaction to Colorado was epitomized in the attention paid to the Mount of the Holy Cross, a peak in the Sawatch Mountains on which snow-filled ravines formed the approximation of a cross that was fifteen hundred feet high. Photographs by W. H. Jackson in 1873 had caused a sensation in the East. Painter Thomas Moran was moved to visit the mountain and later to produce a picture that became a favorite in thousands of homes. Crude engravings that idealized the cross beyond any resemblance to reality became normal illustrations for travel articles and books. Hundreds of tourists detoured to see the cross "rising up at the westward, and saying to a fanciful imagination . . . *in hoc signo vinces.*"[9]

Thousands of sojourners in Colorado in those same years cared little about the details of scenery. They came not to uplift their spirits through the sublime and the curious but to cure their bodies by exposure to Colorado's climate. The first settlers had noticed the "Italian" warmth of many Colorado winters, and observers agreed that the extremes of heat and cold were relatively small. In the sheltered valleys and canyons of the foothills, easterners were advised, picnics could be held in December and trails walked in January. Even stronger praise went to the quality of the atmosphere. The air was pure, exhilarating, stimulating, bracing, and elastic. Colorado's dryness, said several physicians, reduced the capacity of the air to conduct heat and electricity and, therefore, helped to cure diseases of the lungs. Its height above the sea, wrote another, meant the reduction of oxygen content and its replacement by purifying and antiseptic ozone and stimulating electricity. In addition, the altitude was thought to quicken one's life processes. By exciting respiration and increasing capillary circulation it brought decision fast — sudden death to the weak, quick health to those with reserves of strength.

Favorable evaluation of Colorado's climate triggered interest in the state's advantages as a health resort. The journalists who helped to publicize its scenery did the same for its climate. As Samuel Bowles wrote of the entire central Rockies region, "Here would seem to be the fountain of health; and among these hills and plains is surely to be many a summer resort for the invalid." Bayard Taylor, Fitz Hugh Ludlow, Ovando Hollister, and other writers echoed the refrain in the later 1860s, and the Colorado Territorial Board of Immigration and other booster organizations took it up in the 1870s. By the 1880s outside journalists could agree that, despite some overselling, the now familiar advantages of Colorado had proved the state a "great and beneficial sanatorium" for sufferers from pulmonary diseases.[10]

A change of residence was, in fact, the only treatment available for tuberculosis victims. During the first years of the health pilgrimages to Colorado, the only advice to sufferers was to cross the plains slowly, halting for a week or two at various points in western Kansas to allow weakened lungs to adjust to the thin air. In 1884, however, Denver physician Charles Denison joined in organizing the American Climatological Association. Over the next two decades its *Transactions* encouraged scientific discussion of Colorado's climate by Denison, his Colorado colleagues Samuel E. Solly and Samuel A. Fisk, and other writers. Solly was already on record about the amazing benefits of Manitou spring waters for the blood and digestive system, as well as the mountain climate for victims of tuberculosis. The new scientific articles repeated the early evaluation that the state — especially the lands at the foot of the Front Range — benefited consumptives through the abundance of sunshine and the aseptic atmosphere free of moisture and grit. It was a truism among enthusiasts that Colorado provided better conditions for invalids year-round than did even the famous health meccas of Switzerland.

Colorado was also a tonic for ailments less specific than tuberculosis. A weak constitution, nervous exhaustion, dyspepsia, or a "general debility" — whatever the name, the trouble could be cured in the Centennial State. Residence at high altitude, said Dr. F. J. Bancroft, caused "the narrow in chest to become broad, the relaxed in muscle to grow strong, the thin in flesh to gain weight, and thoroughly regenerates those suffering from the bilious diseases caused by prolonged residence in malarial districts." Good food, fresh air, life in the outdoors, and cool nights combined to assure restful sleep. The result was "cheerfulness and a contented frame of mind" — the true requisites of good health. More specifically, Dr. Denison argued that lessened atmospheric pressure relieved the congested blood vessels of the head and had a "salutary influence on the class of overworked brains, which, in the intensity of political, professional and business life, is quite numerous nowadays." Governor Fred Pitkin's claim that "we can almost bring a dead man to life" may be dismissed as boosterism, but many experts of the day agreed that residence in the state quickened and strengthened the functioning of any basically healthy organism. "There is a wealth of life stored up in the dry, sunny climate of this State," wrote Dr. Fisk, "more precious than the hidden treasures which the mountains contain."[11]

Thus, it is no surprise that Americans flocked to test these promises. The custom of traveling for reasons of health was already well established. Colorado, after its connection to the national rail system, offered an attractive destination only $40 away from the population centers of the Midwest. Every November a wave of asthmatics and consumptives fled the cold, dark winters of the East. Thumbing their copies of Denison's *Rocky Mountain Health Resort,* Mrs. Simeon Dunbar's *Health Resorts of Colorado Springs and Manitou,* or the anonymous *Health Wealth and Pleasure,* hopeful people filled Denver hotels and Colorado Springs boardinghouses recently emptied of summer tourists. Poorer invalids sometimes made do with makeshift accommodations. Visitors often reported hundreds of persons living in tent encampments that formed special suburbs of Colorado Springs. In the 1870s and 1880s the common estimate was that one-third of the state's population was composed of recovered invalids. Although that estimate was passed from writer to writer and was quoted by later historians, its validity is impossible to verify. Certainly in Colorado Springs there were enough resident invalids living on outside incomes to buffer the shock of the 1893 depression and to help the town through the hard times without a bank failure. It is also easy to make long lists of distinguished citizens who first visited Colorado as a medical measure, but, again, it is impossible to verify claims that the "one-lung army" of Denver totaled thirty thousand in 1890 and included most of the social and cultural elite of the city. Health statistics for the first decade of the twentieth century, however, record that nearly one quarter of all deaths in Denver were attributable to tuberculosis.

The large-scale migration of tuberculars was already ending when these statistics were gathered. Physicians began to advise institutionalization near the victim's home rather than travel across an ocean or a continent. At the same time, the proof that tuberculosis was a contagious disease incited fears in residents throughout the West. By 1901 and 1902 Coloradans

Tourists waiting for a train in the Idaho Springs area, ca. 1900.

were discussing the possibility of quarantining dangerous cases and blaming the flow of health-migrants on exaggerations broadcast by "selfish interests engaged in transportation and inn-keeping."[12] Dread replaced sympathy for the consumptives. Landlords rejected their applications for a room or house, and employers slammed their doors in their faces. The best substitutes were the new sanatoriums that offered professional care. Colorado Spring had the Glockner and Cragmoor sanatoriums. Denver had the Agnes Sanatorium, built in 1904, to be supported by fees for service, and several charity institutions associated with ethnic groups — the National Jewish Hospital (1899), the Jewish Consumptives' Relief Society (1904), the Swedish National Sanatorium (1905), and the Evangelical Lutheran Sanatarium (1905). By 1911 Colorado ranked first in the West and fifth in the United States in the number of sanatorium beds, with 1,695 in twenty-one institutions.

The transformation of tuberculosis treatment from a tourist industry to a specialized medical problem was one of several changes in Colorado's tourism in the first decades of the twentieth century. Perhaps most important were provisions for serving an enlarged volume and variety of travelers. Central to the effort were facilities to meet the needs of automobile travelers and their strange new machines. By the 1920s Colorado's travel industry scarcely resembled the genteel business of the past generation.

The depression of the 1890s triggered the first alterations. In their scramble for dwindling traffic, western railroads began to offer special convention and excursion rates, which they regularized as low summer tourist fares in the first years of the new century. Glenwood Springs, opened in 1893 as the state's first major resort on the Western Slope, was designed for a new sort of tourist. Most of the visitors enjoyed the Hotel Colorado. With its five stories of luxury "in the Italian style" and its huge swimming basin that was 640 by 110 feet, it attracted travelers on their way to or from California who could afford a few days in the mountains but not an entire summer. Its proprietor also organized planned excursions for middle-aged women. The Denver and Rio Grande Railroad in the same years was particularly active in seeking the patronage of middle-class tourists who could now afford a quick trip through the West. An advertising budget of $60,000 per year was used to attract such people as junketeering schoolteachers to its "Around the Circle Tour," on which $28 would purchase a four-day one-thousand-mile loop through the best scenery in the Rockies. The railroad's publicity office kept busy turning out pamphlets like "Rhymes of the Rockies; or What the Poets Have Found to Say of the Beautiful Scenery on the Denver & Rio Grande Railroad" (1887) and "A Honeymoon Letter From a Bride to Her Chum Describing the Beauties of Colorado" (1899).

Economic crisis in the same years also drove Coloradans to provide artificial attractions that might appeal to people unmoved by sunsets and mountain lakes. Elitch's Gardens on West 38th Street in Denver provided a small zoo and summer theater for visitors, Manhattan Beach on Sloan Lake competed with its own summer theater, and Chutes Park on Cherry Creek offered roller coasters and other amusements. Balloon ascensions, parachute jumps, and flights by powered airships were common methods of attracting paying customers. With little effort on their part, travelers could take a guided tour of the local sights on the open-air observation cars operated by the tramway company. In 1896 Leadville countered with its Ice Palace and Ice Carnival. Over two hundred workers labored for two months to build a Norman castle out of blocks of ice a yard thick set over an ordinary frame building. The ice palace covered three acres and furnished space for skating, dining, dancing, and exhibits. Thousands visited the structure from January through March.

Conventions and festivals also became increasingly popular throughout the West around the turn of the century. In the 1890s Colorado Springs had its Flower Parade, Leadville its Ice Carnival, Rocky Ford its Watermelon Day. After 1898 Boulder sponsored a "chautauqua" — a series of lectures, concerts, and classes on art, music, and current events that brought visitors and publicity to the town every summer. When William Jennings Bryan spoke on "Pending Problems" in July 1899, eight thousand people crowded the lecture hall.

Denver, meanwhile, was matching itself against California resort cities such as Pasadena, host to the Tournament of Roses since 1890, Santa Barbara, home of the Floral Festival since 1891, and Los Angeles, home of La Fiesta de Los Angeles since 1894. Denver's own entry was the Festival of the Mountain and Plain. The idea for the festival originated with the general passenger agent of the Denver and Rio Grande and was quickly taken up by business and political leaders such as ex-mayor Platt Rogers, William Byers, and Robert Speer. The purpose of the first celebration in the fall of 1895 was to note officially the abundant harvest and return of prosperity. It was also to speed that revival by attracting visitors and blazoning forth "the characteristic broad-gauge nature of the people and the wonderful resources and possibilities of the State."[13] Parades of citizens, military personnel, and cyclists took up much of the three-day affair along with band contests, rock-drilling contests, Native American dances, and a grand ball. Festivals from 1896 through 1899 followed the same pattern, with the parades attracting an estimated fifty thousand Denverites and fifty thousand others. The Masquerade Pageant in 1898 offended the proper Frances Peck because "the YMCA was put to open ridicule and the dress was both ungodly and immodest," but she admitted that the Parade of the Silver Serpent was pretty, with its floats representing the countries of Europe.[14]

The festival was revived in 1901 and 1912, but in the new century Denver turned its attention to more dignified attractions. With the help of a $100,000 guarantee, Denver businesspeople persuaded the Democratic party to inaugurate the new city auditorium with its 1908 national convention. The *Post* and *News* led in the effort to squeeze every drop of favorable comment from the event. Thousands of Denverites wore badges reading "I Live in Denver — Ask Me," and a band was kept in constant service, escorting arriving delegations to their hotels. Delegates not adequately entertained by alcohol could watch war dances performed by imported Apaches or make snowballs from carloads of mountain snow. From Denver's point of view, the purpose of the convention was accomplished when delegates had emptied their pockets and eastern correspondents had written glowing dispatches. It was the entrepreneur's dream: boosterism that paid for itself.

The development of Colorado Springs around the turn of the century illustrates the same live-wire business attitude and go-aheadism. More and cheaper hotels were built in the city and up Ute Pass along the Colorado Midland line. "Little London" lost its genteel affectation and showed a new attitude toward tourists, who were now to be welcomed no matter what their manners. "We are glad to see him," wrote the *Gazette*. "For long weary months we have awaited him. . . . He can't travel the world over and get more for his money than he gets right here. . . . Here is to the tourist. He is a part of our system. We like him. . . . We take all we can get out of him, and we get all we can take. He expects it." Hotel runners boarded trains in neighboring states to recruit customers, and the Ashenhurst Amusement Company combed the Southwest for ancient cliff dwellings, then dismantled and reassembled them at Manitou Springs as "authentic" ruins.

With this new attitude it was not surprising that Colorado Springs could embrace Bathhouse John Coughlin, Chicago alderman and front for the machine that ran that city's First Ward. In 1902 "the Bath" arrived at the Antlers Hotel with $88,560 in a tin box, a fraction of his payoff from the crooks, gamblers, confidence men, and whores who made up most of the First Ward's constituents. Despite his associates, Coughlin himself was open, affectionate, honest in his personal life, and eager as a child for fun and play. He opened the tin box long enough to buy a ranch south of town. His love for animals soon transformed the property into a homemade zoo and amusement park that began with abandoned burros and eventually included a roller coaster, Chute the Chutes, Giant Circle Swing, bowling alley, shooting gallery, and an inebriated elephant that downed a pint of Jim Beam daily.

Bathhouse John was colorful enough, but, as Marshall Sprague has pointed out, it was the difference between William Jackson Palmer and Spencer Penrose that epitomized the change from one generation to another. A member of an established Philadelphia family, Penrose had lived in Colorado Springs since 1892 while he made a small fortune at Cripple Creek and a larger one in Utah copper. In 1915 he decided to revitalize the town's sagging economy by sinking $250,000 into construction of an auto road to the top of Pikes Peak. The next year he staged the first of the annual Pikes Peak Hill Climbs to publicize his new highway. At the same time Penrose purchased the old Broadmoor Hotel and Casino, which had been fighting a losing battle against bankruptcy for more than two decades. Three years and $3 million later, Penrose opened his new Broadmoor Hotel, with 350 rooms and all the luxuries and conveniences anyone could possibly think of. Over the next few years he added the Cog Train, the Cheyenne Mountain Highway, the Cheyenne Mountain Zoo, a polo field, an indoor arena, and facilities for almost every other kind of activity. In tune with the 1920s, Penrose publicized his holdings in a style that would have made the retiring Palmer wince. The average American, thanks to Penrose, soon knew Colorado Springs not as a temperance colony but as the home of "the Highest Zoo in the World" and as "the Golf, Tennis, and Polo Capital of the World," where the heavyweight champion of the world or the vice president of the United States allowed himself to be photographed for the wire services.

Another Front Range town, Estes Park, made the same sort of changes in a less flamboyant style after 1910. New inns including the magnificent Stanley Hotel, which opened in 1910, a new road up Big Thompson Canyon, and an "auto-stage line" from Loveland beckoned more tourists. The Estes Park Protective and Improvement Association responded with projects such as a High Line Drive and a fish hatchery. Local business leaders also backed a crusade to make the nearby mountains into a national park. Initiated by naturalist and innkeeper Enos Mills, the campaign gained the support of the *Denver Post,* the Colorado Chamber of Commerce, the state Democratic party, and, finally, the general assembly and the state delegation in Washington. Doubtful members of Congress were sold on the idea by the argument that such a park was more accessible to the people of the Middle West than any other. The bill creating Rocky Mountain National Park passed Congress in January 1915. The park was used intensively from the start. As early as 1920, the year in which Colorado completed construction of the winding Fall River Road to the top of the Continental Divide, 116,000 auto passengers entered the park, 28,000 from out of state.

Colorado's other national park at Mesa Verde was considerably more isolated. William H. Jackson and other explorers had recorded a number of Anasazi ruins in the southwest corner of Colorado as early as the 1870s. However, Balcony House, Cliff Palace, Spruce Tree House, and other great ruins high on the mesa's sides were not explored until 1887 and 1888 by rancher Richard Wetherill, his brothers, and his brother-in-law Charlie Mason. The Wetherills exhibited Mesa Verde artifacts in Durango and Denver and sold the collection to the Colorado Historical Society. They also guided visitors including author Frederick Chapin and Swedish tourist Gustaf Nordenskiold. Their two books, published in 1892 and 1893, respectively, called world attention to the ruins and helped to generate a steady flow of tourists. So did a one-tenth-size model exhibited at the World's Columbian Exposition in Chicago in 1893 by the H. Jay Smith Exploring Company.

The need to protect the ruins from souvenir hunters brought Virginia McClurg of Colorado Springs into the fray. She lectured and lobbied tirelessly on behalf of protection and recruited the Colorado Federation of Women's Clubs to the cause. Lucy Peabody, sister-in-law of future Governor James Peabody, used her family connections for lobbying efforts in Washington. Together, the women organized the Colorado Cliff Dwellings Association in 1900. Their work included numerous meetings with the Utes, on whose lands the ruins were located. Designation as a national park came in 1906 (although not before Virginia McClurg had withdrawn her support in favor of state park status). Senator Thomas Patterson's efforts to prevent the ravaging of Mesa Verde also helped in passage of the Antiquities Act of 1906, which outlawed the disturbance of historic and prehistoric sites on federal lands and marked the beginning of the historic preservation movement in the United States. Mesa Verde remained isolated in its first decades as a park. Although railroads advertised the "homes of the cliff dwellers," only one thousand visitors reached Mesa Verde in 1916 and three thousand in 1921. Residents of Mancos found it less of a bonanza than they had hoped.

Whereas Colorado Springs and Estes Park adapted themselves to the automobile after 1900, Denver fell in love with it. The first speeding ticket in the state and the organization of the Colorado Automobile Club were both accomplishments of Denverites in 1902. In 1905 and 1906 the Automobile Club and the Denver Chamber of Commerce cooperated in sponsoring "Good Roads" conferences and organizing a Colorado Good Roads Association. Their lobbying persuaded the legislature to establish a State Highway Commission in 1909.

In 1911 and 1912 eccentric entrepreneur John Brisben Walker persuaded the Denver Real Estate Board, Denver Motor Club, and Chamber of Commerce to back a city charter amendment allowing Denver to acquire parkland outside the city limits. The same organizations simultaneously campaigned for a bond issue that would enable Denver to begin development of its mountain park system (with the promised results of healthier citizens and empty jails). Within five years the city had kept up with San Diego and Chicago by acquiring ten tracts of land and building seventy-five miles of roadway, including the obligatory skyline drive — this one to the top of Lookout Mountain. Construction had also begun on a motor road to the top of Mount Evans, which local interests, working through the Denver Mountain Parks Commission, hoped to add to Rocky Mountain National Park. Other business leaders had already launched the idea of a 3,500-mile park-to-park highway that would connect the western national parks and be centered in Denver; the route had been explored as far as Yellowstone National Park, six hundred miles from Denver. The Denver Mountain Park system would eventually total 13,500 acres in four counties. Many of its improvements, such as Red Rocks Amphitheater, would be constructed by the Civilian Conservation Corps during the 1930s.

Despite these initial efforts centering in Denver, auto touring in Colorado as late as 1915 was still a strenuous undertaking, safely attempted only in summer. One expert advised motorists driving east and north of Colorado Springs to equip themselves with crowbar, hatchet, shovel, pulleys, and 100 feet of rope; heading south and west they should add cans of oil, gas, and water, and 150 feet of chicken wire to lay over mud holes. In 1917 a trip from Denver to Mesa Verde took more than a week. The first

Auto camping, 1918.

cars had to struggle to the top of the mesa in 1914. The first Colorado property tax for highway improvement was levied in 1914 and the first gasoline tax in 1919. With the help of federal highway aid after 1916, the state's expenditures on road construction and maintenance rose from an average of roughly $3 million annually in the war years to an average of over $10 million per year in the 1920s. Over the same time span the number of motor vehicles in the state increased from fifteen thousand to three hundred thousand.

These improvements and others throughout the nation motorized the United States by the mid-1920s. In 1917 a national park official made headlines in Denver by predicting that one hundred thousand autos would visit the parks within five years. But in fact, by the end of the 1920s Colorado's national parks and national forests were receiving over 2 million visitors, as the family car made both Coloradans and outsiders more mobile. Probably two-thirds of the estimated 1.4 million visitors to the state arrived by car. Many were people who could never have afforded a

The hazards of automobile tourism in the 1910s.

vacation in the railroad age but who now found it possible to pack a tent, cooking equipment, and family into the Model T or farm truck and head for the Rockies. In 1915 Denver opened Overland Park along the South Platte, one of the nation's first municipal campgrounds. It offered water and sanitary facilities, a three-story clubhouse with grocery store and soda fountain, a laundry, and one thousand camp sites. By 1923 nearly 250 auto camps under private and public ownership were used by some 643,000 campers in Colorado. In a number of Western Slope cities such as Durango, the rise of automobile tourism provided new opportunity for boosterism and helped to buffer the decline of mining.

The new access the automobile provided to all parts of Colorado helped to confirm a changing attitude toward the outdoors at the same time it democratized travel. With a car tourists no longer had to go only where the railroads wanted to take them and stop only where the railroad publicity department had decided they would like the view. If they desired, tourists in their cars could avoid the usual sights for views of unspoiled landscapes that could be enjoyed on their own terms.

This changing attitude can be traced in the essays of Enos Mills, Colorado's own nature writer. "The Rocky Mountain John Muir," as he delighted in being called, Mills had moved to Colorado at age fourteen in search of good health. Supporting himself through summer work at mountain hotels and winter jobs on ranches or in mining, he claimed a homestead at the foot of Longs Peak in the 1890s and became a professional guide. In 1902 he established the Longs Peak Inn, where guests could enjoy his services as a guide and his theories on strict diet along with mountain air. At the same time, he embarked on a career as a professional journalist. From 1904 until his death in 1922, scores of his articles were published in general-circulation periodicals such as *Harper's,* the *Atlantic, Worlds Work, McClures,* the *Saturday Evening Post,* and *Outlook,* as well as in popular nature magazines such as *Country Life, Suburban Life,* and *Sunset.* Over the same span Mills published more than a dozen books. At his death, contemporaries mourned him as a member of the small elite of uniquely American writers who helped the nation "to appreciate the gorges, the trees, and the flowers of the West."[15]

Mills's earliest essays, dating from the first years of the century, read like those of other writers whose work fed the country's insatiable appetite for nature lore. Where a romantic such as John Muir could claim that in the wilds "nature's peace will flow into you as the sunshine into the trees," Mills found that "a climb in the Rockies will develop a love for nature, strengthen one's appreciation of the beautiful world, and put one in tune with the Infinite."[16] Where other writers wrote the fictionalized "biographies" of robins, deer, or chipmunks, Mills translated the "autobiography" of a thousand-year-old Colorado pine from its growth rings. In his articles trees were people with different characters, from the queenly silver spruce in her "fluffy silver-tipped robes" to the childlike aspens who liked to play together and stick their toes in the water.

By the late 1910s Mills had made the transition from writer to naturalist. His essays contained less affectation and cuteness, fewer elaborate metaphors, more data on natural processes, and greater facility in scientific, neutral description. His later writings introduced the idea of the nature guide. Every

As these skiers photographed near Estes Park in 1926 indicate, the 1920s and 1930s saw the beginnings of skiing as a tourist industry.

party hiking in the wilderness or visiting a national park, he believed, should be accompanied by an escort who could explain the sights in terms of general principles of geology, botany, and zoology. The nature guide should try to demonstrate the interrelations of ecological systems, "the determining influences of their environments and their respondent tendencies." The development of interpretive nature lectures and field trips as a regular educational service in the national parks was in part a result of Mills's advocacy of his idea, and the modern ranger-naturalist confirms his prediction that "nature guiding will become a nationwide and distinct profession."[17]

The growth of Enos Mills's ideas helped to define an important change in the American approach to nature. The visitors who came to Colorado in the 1870s tried to understand the scenery in terms formulated elsewhere. By the time their grandchildren visited the state, they were beginning to look for wilderness as well as tourist attractions. Indeed, the origins of today's wilderness preservation policy in the Forest Service can be traced to a report on the Trapper's Lake section of Colorado's White River National Forest made by Arthur Carhart in 1919. Over the next two decades people such as Carhart and Aldo Leopold and organizations such as the Wilderness Society and the Sierra Club developed and advocated nationwide the ecological point of view in which wild nature is valued for itself and should be approached on its own terms. In Colorado one of the first results was the creation in 1932 of the Flat Tops Primitive Area within White River National Forest. Today the lands preserved within primitive areas and wilderness areas in Colorado's national parks and national forests are among the most treasured possessions of its citizens.

# CHAPTER 12

# DENVER: THE ROCKY MOUNTAIN METROPOLIS

Most modern visitors to Colorado arrive by way of Denver. They fly into the new Denver International Airport and transfer to feeder airlines or a rented car. They converge on Interstate 70 and Interstate 75 and fan out again to the piedmont cities and mountain passes. The experience of the contemporary tourist is far from unique. Denver has been the gateway to Colorado for over a century. In 1858 and 1859 victims of gold fever could choose among the Platte, the Arkansas, and the Smoky Hill routes. Whichever they traveled, however, prospectors arrived at the same place — the new town on Cherry Creek where roads fanned out again to the northwest up Boulder Creek, to the west toward Central City, Idaho Springs, and Empire, and to the southwest toward Fairplay and Breckenridge. Twenty and thirty years later, Denver was still the "port of entry" to Colorado, receiving thousands of immigrants and tens of thousands of tourists each year by way of the Union Pacific, Rock Island, Burlington, Santa Fe, or Missouri Pacific railroads. Investors, journalists, settlers, sightseers, and weary travelers of all sorts found the city a natural resting place where they could sample the local hotels and saloons or stock up on beans and bacon before boarding the narrow-gauge railroads for the mountains.

Burger Kings, gasoline stations, and their nineteenth-century equivalents have accounted for only a fraction of Denver's services. For nearly a century Denver has been Colorado's metropolis in the full sense of the word: the focus of every activity. Located at the intersection of the plains and the mountains, its people and institutions have tied together the sections of the state at the same time that they have filtered contacts with the outside world. As the political capital and largest city, Denver has been the natural center for decisionmaking. Its clubs, saloons, and hotels have been the places for investors, entrepreneurs, lawyers, lobbyists, and legislators to sound each other's opinions over cigars and whiskey. Its banks and state capitol have been the places where the deals are confirmed. New programs and ideas have normally spread outward through state agencies and private organizations that have Denver headquarters. On the ranches of Wyoming, in the small towns of Colorado, in the western counties of Kansas and Nebraska and South Dakota, Denver has stood out as the center of opportunity. In 1900 as much as in 1990 it was the city one read about in the papers, the city where friends or relatives found jobs, the city that offered a refuge from the loneliness of cold winds and the big sky.

Commerce in goods has also centered in Denver. Because the extension of railroads in the late 1870s and the 1880s gave Denver access to all parts of the West, the city and its hinterland have formed an interdependent economic unit. The dissimilarities that have produced conflict within the state and the nation have created flows of minerals, foodstuffs, and merchandise that are handled most efficiently through a central depot. From a retailing town, Denver grew into the primary supply center for a large portion of the Rocky Mountain West. As the eastern terminus of the Denver and Rio Grande and other narrow-gauge lines, Denver was the necessary break of bulk point for goods shipped in from Chicago or New York. Carloads of freight could be stored until needed, split into individual consignments, and shipped out again to fill the bins and shelves of Leadville stores and the beer taps in its saloons. Simultaneously, at least five factories began to build mining equipment for the Rocky Mountain market. By the early 1890s Denver warehouses and foundries supplied mining towns throughout Colorado, Wyoming, northern New Mexico, and parts of Utah and did occasional business as far away as Arizona, Montana, and Idaho.

The city was equally important as an outlet for the state. The Boston and Colorado Company built the town's first smelter in 1878. The erection of the Omaha and Grant Smelter and the Globe Smelter, the construction of flour mills and stockyards, the establishment of branch packing plants by Armour, Swift, and Cudahy, and the first National Stock Growers Convention in 1898 were all steps that enlarged the city's capacity to process the primary products of Colorado and neighboring states. We can see the pride Denverites took in their industrial growth from the old illustrations of early factories, which show thick black smoke billowing from every chimney in a frenzy of production.

The smoking chimneys of the Boston and Colorado Smelter
symbolized industrial progress to Coloradans in the 1880s.

The growth of trade with the "Rocky Mountain Empire" required new financial facilities. Branch agencies of national insurance firms served customers in Colorado and adjacent states. Banks not only channeled outside investment into Colorado mines, irrigation ditches, real estate, and cattle but also furnished the credit that kept goods flowing throughout the Rockies. Denver banks organized a private clearinghouse in 1885. The federal government designated them as the official depositories for reserve funds of smaller banks in Colorado, New Mexico, and Wyoming in 1900. Fourteen years later the city was chosen for a branch of the Kansas City Federal Reserve Bank, with a territory embracing Colorado and northern New Mexico.

By the beginning of the twentieth century exchange between Denver and its hinterland had produced a single economic community, a "metropolitan region" that included most of the southern Rockies. The trade areas of most U.S. cities are elongated east and west, along railroad trunk lines. Denver's runs north and south, along the base of the mountains. To the east, the competition from Kansas City and Omaha has confined business to Colorado and a fringe of Nebraska and South Dakota, but north and south there is no city of comparable importance between El

Paso and Calgary. In the twentieth century Denver has been the commercial and financial capital of the interior empire foreseen by William Jackson Palmer and William Gilpin.

Boom conditions in late-nineteenth-century Denver did more than put money in bank accounts and fatten railroad treasuries. Prosperity also ignited a population explosion that transformed the pattern of life in the city within a single decade. The initial impulse was felt in 1878 and 1879, with "unexampled activity" in real estate and a gain of several thousand inhabitants. The city added 20,000 citizens in the first half of the 1880s, 50,000 more in the second half of the decade, and an additional 30,000 between 1890 and 1893, for a total of more than 130,000 residents. Increasing business activity and a quadrupled population inflated rents and triggered a land and construction boom. The volume of real estate transactions in Arapahoe County rose from $5 million in 1880 to $29 million in 1887 to $65 million by 1890. The market softened in 1891 and 1892, but the bubble broke only with the coming of a national depression a year later.

Explosive growth meant scarce housing for working-class families. In 1879 J. Guy and Amanda Smith found that a teamster's earnings allowed them to rent two rooms on the second floor of a house on Arapahoe Street. Because the rooms were separated at the front and back ends, the only way to get from the kitchen to the bedroom was down one flight of stairs, through the yard, and up another flight. A decade later a broken marriage forced Emily French to move into Denver and support her children by sewing, cooking, and cleaning house for middle-class families. She also went into debt to build her own house on what is now West 13th. Even an unfinished wooden box with four rooms was better than the tents and shacks that were springing up nearby on the banks of the South Platte. Emily French's neighbors were a cross section of working Denver: carpenter, plasterer, railroad switchman, postal worker, teamster, brick manufacturer. Farms and dairies were scattered through the partly developed neighborhood.

Emily French's sketchy diary records the troubles of a family living on the financial margin. It was still possible to take time off on the Fourth of July, 1890: "Up and dressed all & started for the parade . . . a grand thing. We stood on our horse & buggy on Broadway and 18th 1 hour and watched the parade go by . . . then to athletic park in the even to the fireworks." On other days, however, she roused the family early so they could work on finishing the interior or scrounge old lumber from neighbors in the hope of getting a stable up before winter. "I tried again to get the stable built, no use," she wrote on December 16. "I must build it or twill not be done." When money was available she hired a carpenter or a plasterer for a few hours' work. It is likely, says historian Janet LeCompte, that she lost her house to foreclosure the following spring.[1]

Middle-class Denverites, meanwhile, were building Italianate houses with flat roofs or miniature mansards that mirrored the styles of commercial buildings. They were distinguished by detailed cornices and iron cresting along the roof lines. Dormers, bay windows, balconies, porches, and mass-produced iron fences completed the effect of elegant buildings on a small scale. The Curtis Park Historic District preserves some of this cityscape. As tastes shifted, newer residents added Queen Anne houses with elaborately detailed gables and fish-scale shingles.

By the mid-1880s the upper crust had staked out its own territory in the new Brown's Bluff subdivision surrounding the site of the future Capitol. Tudor, Moorish, Medieval, and Romanesque "palaces" indicated the emergence of the new rich. The professional people and smaller entrepreneurs who supplied support services for the big businesses filled nearby lots with rambling brick piles and eclectic Queen Anne houses. The variety of building styles reflected the influence of the Philadelphia Centennial Exposition of 1876 and the increasing prominence of professional architects eager to experiment with new styles. Rusticated stone symbolized the stability of the new business elite. Expensive building materials and elaborate details — gargoyles, hybrid columns, bays, towers, and tall chimneys — testified to the owners' disposable wealth.

The bonanza era arrived in downtown Denver when Leadville silver magnate Horace Tabor began to invest his profits in commercial real estate. Tabor invited Chicago architect William Edbrooke to design and build his Tabor Block of offices at 16th and Larimer in 1879 and the Tabor Grand Opera House three blocks away on Curtis Street in 1881. The two structures changed the scale of commercial building in Denver and set new standards for design. Each was five stories high and covered a quarter of a block. Their pilasters, cornices, arched doorways, and towers were exotic sights among the small two-story and three-story buildings that had previously lined Larimer Street. A reporter for the *Rocky Mountain News* described the business block as "massive, yet elegant in design, containing the most modern

Historic Denver preserved 1015 Ninth Street as part of Auraria's Ninth Street Historic Park so that late twentieth-century Coloradans could appreciate the architectural heritage of late nineteenth-century Denver.

conveniences that safety permits and experience approves."[2] Opening night at the $850,000 opera house was one of the great social events of the decade and represented equally the triumph of architecture and of theater.

By the late 1880s and early 1890s the Denver business district had begun a slow migration from Larimer Street up 16th and 17th toward Broadway. New commercial buildings towered six or eight stories in order to provide adequate floor space for retailing and office space for wholesaling and finance. Among the dozens of new buildings, the McPhee Block at 17th and Glenarm was especially impressive. The corner of 16th and California boasted both the stately California Building and the new retail palace for the Denver Dry Goods Company. In the opinion of turn-of-the-century historian Jerome Smiley, Denver got its first "modern" buildings in the years around 1890. Architectural historian Richard Brettell more recently agreed that "Denver was built almost exclusively in the six years between 1888 and 1893. Its buildings from this period are its most confident, its most attractive, and its most important."[3]

Hotels were one more example of private buildings that symbolized Denver's maturity. In the 1880s and 1890s Denver served its two hundred thousand business travelers and tourists with the Albany Hotel, the Windsor, the Metropole, the Markham, and a dozen others. The climax of commercial architecture was the H. C. Brown Hotel, built between 1890 and 1892. Designed by architect Frank Edbrooke, William's elder brother, in the style of Louis Sullivan's Auditorium Building in Chicago, it rose nine stories high at the intersection of 17th and Broadway. Its high, arched facade and careful balance of detail made the "Brown Palace" in some opinions "one of the greatest nineteenth century commercial structures in America."[4]

The years between the depression of the 1890s and World War I provided less spectacular but steady growth. After marking time in the late 1890s, the city grew by eighty thousand people in the 1900s — an increase of 60 percent — and added another forty thousand in the 1910s. Many of the new residents settled in suburban developments that had spread south and eastward as early as the 1880s. The construction of middle-class subdivisions in the Montclair, Cherry Creek, Country Club, and University Heights districts pushed the boundaries of the city outward. When the city tripled in area by annexing forty-two square miles between 1893 and 1902, it was catching up with the previous decade as much as providing for further expansion.

The growth of these early suburbs helped to deepen social divisions within Denver, for their new housing was inaccessible to the city's increasing numbers of European immigrants. Where Denver had counted nine hundred natives of Scandinavia, Italy, and Eastern Europe in 1880, new manufacturing jobs had attracted nearly seven thousand by 1900 and sixteen thousand by 1910. Because they needed homes near the stockyards, foundries, railroad shops, packing plants, and smelters running north along the South Platte, the Italians moved into northwest Denver, Slavic immigrants filled Globeville, and many German and Celtic migrants congregated in Elyria. The result was a set of ethnic enclaves isolated from daily contact with the rest of the city. Literally on the wrong side of the tracks north and west of the business district, the communities in many ways were independent villages within an urban framework. For many proper Denverites the only contact with the working-class city was answering the back door to men on the bum during the worst years of the depression.

The African-American community in Denver was equally isolated. From fewer than one thousand at the start of the Leadville boom, the city's African-American population climbed to over six thousand in the 1910s. African-American settlers were welcomed for their economic contributions in a labor-poor state, applauded for their good citizenship, and courted for their votes. They were also walled off within the city. Employers offered a limited set of jobs as waiters, Pullman porters, or domestic servants. Doors seldom opened at white hotels, restaurants, labor halls, and schools, despite state legislation forbidding segregation in public accommodations. The African-American population had lived scattered through the city in the 1870s and 1880s. By the twentieth century it had begun to concentrate in the Five Points area east of the business district as the prestige of neighboring Curtis Park declined. With Globeville, Elyria, and Highlands, Five Points helped to form a crescent of working-class housing northeast, north, and northwest of the downtown area.

Increasing population called for new or improved services. In the 1870s the city established its first public high school, organized its first uniformed police force, started work on its first sewer system, and installed its first telephones. Within three years the brisk pace of business required 563 phones and 12 operators to handle 3,500 calls per day. In the 1880s and early 1890s the city replaced volunteer firemen with paid professionals, began to develop the future Cheesman Park, acquired land for City Park and Washington Park, and switched on its first electric lights. Businesses all over the downtown area enjoyed the glow of incandescent bulbs, and 3,000-candlepower lights mounted on 150-foot steel towers flooded outlying sections like a modern sports field.

More directly important for shaping the city were improvements in water supply and public transportation. The horse-drawn railroad cars that had operated on Denver streets since 1871 were inadequate by the mid-1880s. Two corporations — the old Denver City Railroad Company and the newly organized Denver Tramway Corporation (DTC) — responded with the newest innovation of the age: the cable car. By the end of the decade the two companies were operating thirty-eight miles of cable lines on largely overlapping routes. As in other cities, however, the rapidly apparent problems of the cars convinced the DTC to convert to overhead electric trolleys in the early 1890s, a move that forced its rival out of business. For the next thirty years DTC decisions about the location of new tracks controlled the physical patterns of Denver's growth. As late as the 1920s a map of settled areas showed tentacles along the streetcar lines and gaps where transportation was unavailable.

Denver reached increasing distances into the mountains for its supply of fresh water. In 1870 the Denver City Water Company had built a downtown pumping station that fed the South Platte River directly into the city's taps. Within eight years rising use and pollution necessitated a new station and storage reservoir two miles upstream. When the great boom again stretched supplies, a second company was organized in 1889 to tap the river at the mouth of South Platte Canyon, opening a rate war in which the competitors at times piped their water free to lucky householders. After depression forced consolidation in 1894, the new Denver Union Water Company undertook the building of a massive reservoir in the mountains. Completed in 1905, Cheesman Dam and Lake were able to satisfy the needs of the growing city until the 1930s.

By the early years of the twentieth century, Denver was a mature and successful city. Businesspeople looking out their office windows in the Equitable Building on 17th Street or standing on their front porches in the Capitol Hill area could be proud of the town they had helped to build. To fill their evenings they could choose from among scores of fraternal societies, literary groups, and religious and charitable associations that represented the best impulses of Anglo-American civilization. Railroad attorney Harry May, for example, joined the Harvard Club and helped to organize the University Club soon after his arrival from the East Coast in 1890. A Discussion Club in which young adults presented essays on serious topics such as "Poetry" filled some of his evenings. Dinner engagements, theatrical performances, and late suppers of oysters and California wine filled some of the others. In 1897 middle-class Denverites could join in the new bicycle craze that was sweeping the country. In 1898 they could join the enthusiastic crowds that turned out to hear Chicago evangelist Dwight L. Moody preach at the Tabor Opera House and the Central Presbyterian Church.

Civic architecture now incorporated the classical revival styles prevalent in the East. The state capitol that businesspeople passed on their way home was the most obvious example. Begun at the end of the 1880s, occupied in an unfinished state in

Sixteenth Street, Denver, sometime during the 1910s.

1894 and 1895, and completed over the next thirteen years, it bore the full regalia of pillars and pediments. Its design was similar to at least a dozen other state capitols of the period, and its architect, E. E. Myers, in fact provided the plans for those of Michigan, Texas, Utah, and Idaho as well. The Denver Public Library building of 1909 (now used for city offices) and the original Colorado State Museum, built in 1915, also followed the classical models considered appropriate for public buildings. With the city's population passing the two hundred thousand mark, citizens could find evidence everywhere that Denver was replacing the new with the newer, the big with the better.

The same expansion that brought high wages to Denver's workers, dividends to its investors, and smiles to its boosters also fueled two decades of political controversy. Throughout the United States the 1880s and early 1890s were eras of intense urbanization. Scores of cities doubled in size, and more than 10 million people joined the nation's urban population. As a by-product, this growth created or worsened an entire range of problems concerned with the governance of cities. Massive investment in the construction of the cities' physical infrastructure —

their streets, buildings, and utilities — opened vast profit opportunities to favored businesspeople. Millions of European immigrants who crowded the urban centers failed to fit into familiar social patterns or to share accepted values at the same time that their poverty frightened affluent Americans. The Reverend Josiah Strong was scarcely alone when he warned in a best-selling book that the concentration of foreigners in the nation's cities made them centers of Romanism, intemperance, vice, and socialism and forced the conclusion that "the city has become a serious menace to our civilization."[5]

The "urban crisis" was deepened by the nature of U.S. urban politics. Most large cities by the 1880s were homes to political machines. As in the New York of "Boss" Tweed and Tammany Hall, the system required mutual give and take among three groups — political professionals, working-class voters, and business owners. Participating politicians who controlled the municipal government could provide protection for illicit businesses and favors and contracts for legitimate entrepreneurs. The contributions, kickbacks, and other payoffs with which businesspeople reciprocated helped the politicians stay in office. Most city bosses preferred to influence votes by dispensing jobs, favors, and charity to the urban poor, but they were also willing to buy or steal elections if necessary. The result was a perpetual-motion machine. Political authority flowed from voter to boss to businessperson, and economic power returned along the same path.

Although machine rule in Denver brought immediate benefits to some of the individuals involved, it had the same weakness as that in other cities: an inability to deal with the basic problems of urbanization. It added an extra dimension to the social and physical isolation of the inner-city poor by tying them to a corrupt system abhorred by middle-class suburbanites. It also ignored the need for long-range planning by encouraging businesses to direct expenditures on the basis of immediate profits. And it condoned lawlessness and immorality through cooperation with illegitimate businesses. Together, these points suggested an inclusive failure to impose pattern and direction on urban change. In book after book, article after article, contemporaries expressed their fear that unguided growth threatened to open the late nineteenth-century metropolis to moral and financial chaos.

Many Denverites thought the obvious way to combat potential anarchy was to gain control of public services. Influence over the police, for example, offered the power to mold social patterns and combat vice. Control over semipublic utilities carried power to direct physical growth and allocate profits. The result in Denver was two decades of political conflict, sporadic in the 1890s and continual after 1900. Shifting groups of reformers attempted to elect new leaders and change the legal environment in which the machine flourished. In pursuing both goals, reformers were motivated not so much by the love of office as by the hope of using municipal authority to shape the city to their own ideals.

The first challenge to the Republican machine grew out of the legislature's establishment of a Denver Fire and Police Board in 1891. Appointed directly by the governor, board members had the power to grant saloon licenses and run the public safety departments. Although designed to give the state Republican party more direct control over its Denver organization, the change opened an opportunity for reform that was seized by Populist Governor Davis Waite. It is unclear how well he understood Denver politics, but in early 1893 he moved to increase Populist influence by filling the Police Board with his own appointees. Implicit in the change was a threat to revolutionize local politics by breaking the Republican bosses and cleaning up city politics.

In June, only a few months after his initial action, Waite removed two of his own appointees for failing to investigate reported police corruption and neglecting their duty to "prohibit and suppress dance houses, tippling houses, dram shops, opium houses, gaming and gambling houses."[6] Within six months Waite was equally upset with the new board. In a hearing held in his office, Waite charged Commissioners Jackson Orr and D. J. Martin with protecting gambling housing and brothels ("Prosecutor, Judge and Executioner — Waite the Presiding Poo Bah!" screamed an opposition newspaper). The commissioners replied that their policy was to control and contain vice, not to attempt the impossible task of total suppression. Arguing that their methods had lowered crime by 25 percent, they refused to vacate their posts. Although a special session of the legislature called to deal with the economic crisis distracted Waite soon after the hearing, he returned to the issue on March 7 with a new removal order. The board countered with a district court injunction restraining Waite from taking any action for ten days.

Peace lasted for a week before an impatient governor ordered out the First Regiment of Colorado Infantry and the Chaffee Light Artillery. At noon on March 15, 1894, four hundred militiamen, with two field pieces and two Gatling guns, filed into place in front of the Denver City Hall, in which the old Police Board members had barricaded themselves. On the surrounding streets twenty thousand Denverites waited for the "entertainment" to begin. Armed with guns and dynamite, loyal police officers and Denver gamblers deputized by the sheriff of Arapahoe County guarded the entrances to the building from its windows and nearby rooftops. A detachment of regular troops from Fort Logan waited for orders at the railroad station. Most important, a committee of businesspeople led by William Byers and David Moffat worked frantically to prevent physical damage to the city and to preserve its reputation as a stable community attractive for investment. Waite had the militia marched back to its armory at dusk and agreed to submit the dispute to the Colorado Supreme Court. Its even-handed ruling held that the governor had every right to appoint new commissioners but that he had no right forcibly to remove the old ones, who finally left office in response to a direct court order.

The City Hall War has usually been treated as comic relief or as an illustration of the incompetence of Populist leadership. The opposition to Waite's actions, however, also revealed the connections between Denver's local politicians, its saloonkeepers, and its business community. The "15,000 gamblers and lewd women" on whom Waite blamed his defeat in the fall were only a part of the alliance he had unsuccessfully challenged, for it was the respectable Republican party that crushed his re-election bid with a fierce campaign.[7] Denver provided Waite's margin of defeat by voting 2 to 1 against an incumbent who threatened both licit and illicit business.

Waite's defeat brought five years of relative calm to Denver. With the Republicans in disarray over the silver issue, Independent candidate T. S. McMurray was elected mayor on a platform of economy and efficiency. Despite his good intentions, he made no fundamental changes, and it was clear by the turn of the century that a powerful new element had joined the Denver machine. The newly consolidated utility monopolies — the water, streetcar, telephone, and gas and electric companies — were in a position to make huge profits if they could guard their interests from the municipal and state governments. As a matter of "self-defense," the executives of these firms intervened more and more directly in local politics. Reformers identified a cabal including E. B. Field, director of the telephone monopoly, Walter Cheesman, owner of the Union Water Company, Daniel Sullivan, comptroller of the Gas and Electric Company, and capitalist David Moffat. William Gray Evans, son of the territorial governor and president of the Tramway Company, earned a reputation as the Tramway king and emperor of Denver. Far from denying their activities, Field and Evans offered the explanation that was popular among all of the era's respectable manipulators: they were in politics only to counter "unfair acts" by officeholders. The system was summed up by Cheesman: "Mr. Evans represents our interests in politics and of course, you understand, politics with us is a matter of business."[8] At the state level, as another water company official put it, "the people have nothing to do with nominations and elections. We rule and we're going to continue to rule."[9]

Within Denver the utilities worked through Mayor Robert Speer. Former president of the Fire and Police Board, Speer held office as mayor from 1904 through 1912 and again from 1916 to 1918. Although Denver's government was legally nonpartisan, Speer built a personal machine on the base provided by the local Democratic organization. To Evans, Cheesman, and their colleagues, Speer gave support for business interests and votes for the Republican state ticket. Smaller businesspeople found abundant opportunities for petty graft and lucrative contracts. Republicans put up nonentities against Speer or withheld effective support from their own candidates. Through the police department, Speer assured the loyalty of liquor dealers and vice interests. Crowds of eager repeaters at the ballot boxes and vote sellers could easily be assembled at downtown saloons run by city council members, and machine control of election judges and clerks allowed voting fraud to go unpunished.

Speer tried to gain the loyalty of the middle class by drawing upon the new ideas of city planning. At the start of the century, planning meant the development of physical facilities that met the needs of growing cities with new elegance and style. The informal "City Beautiful" movement was an effort to make U.S. cities impressive and inspiring. In an important sense, the intention was to catch up to Europe in urban design. The origins of the movement are often traced to the Columbian Exposition in Chicago in 1893, but its real impetus was the revitalization of L'Enfant's plan for Washington in 1901 and 1902. At the behest of Congress, a committee composed of Daniel Burnham, Frederick Law Olmsted, Jr., Charles McKim, and Augustus St. Gaudens toured Paris, Rome, and Venice before submitting plans for

LET HIM FINISH HIS WORK!

A cartoon of Robert W. Speer published in the *Denver Republican*, May 1, 1908.

filling out the "magnificent distances" of the capital. In the same years Charles Mulford Robinson codified these ideas of civic art. *The Improvement of Towns and Cities* (1901) and *Modern Civic Art* (1903) advocated the coordination of street plans, civic centers, architecture, sculpture, and landscaping to uplift city living.

In Denver, as elsewhere, much of the impetus for civic improvement came from the middle-class women of "the garden club crowd." The Woman's Club of Denver, organized in the early 1890s, had organized a Clean City Club for children in 1894 and a Civic Improvement Society in 1896. Club women used the Civic Improvement Society to mobilize both men and women in pursuit of a "cleaner, healthier, and more beautiful environment." It prodded the city administration to water trees and cut the weeds in public parks, to sweep the streets, to set out trash cans down-town, and to install park benches. It also spun off a Municipal Art League to work for large-scale public beautification.

Speer pursued both civic art and urban design out of a genuine concern for the character of the city. If public improvements also lifted the value of real estate, so much the better. The mayor invited a $100,000 contribution from the widow and family of Walter Cheesman for the refined adornment of the Grecian pavilion and renamed Congress Park in Cheesman's memory. He oversaw new parkways and built the wide boulevard along the banks of a tamed Cherry Creek. He gave away one hundred thousand elm and maple trees at the rate of three per household. He also pushed through the creation of the Denver Civic Center. Early in his first term, he had the new Denver Art Commission select Charles M. Robinson to draw up plans for the area west of the capitol. When voters turned down the elaborate scheme in 1906, the mayor kept the idea alive by appointing a Civic Center Committee and acquiring some of the necessary land. In 1909 the city library, financed both by a $200,000 donation by steel tycoon Andrew Carnegie and by the city, was completed in the northwest quadrant of the proposed site. That neoclassical gray sandstone building, used as a library until the mid-1950s, long set the architectural tone for nearby buildings and memorials. Three years later Speer obtained new proposals from Frederick Law Olmsted, Jr., the leader of U.S. landscape architecture, and Arnold Brunner, who had previously worked on the Cleveland Civic Center. Speer secured a final set of plans from Edward H. Bennett after he returned to office in 1916 and commenced development of the central park. Since his death in 1918, it has taken two generations to fill out the original concept with a city and county building, modern library, art museum, and historical center.

Unfortunately for Speer, boulevards and a civic center were not enough to fend off political outrage. Speer's electoral system worked to satisfy the disparate needs of professional politicians, big business tycoons, and working-class voters in downtown wards. For the latter in particular, his administration provided playgrounds, contributions to charities, and support for crafts unions. It also violated the sensibilities of middle-class voters, who paid high taxes not only to build parks and sewers but also to support boodling council members and incompetent administrators. The protection of vice further challenged middle-class ideas about the proper character of the city. The hundreds of saloons clustered around the central business district seemed an open invitation to "debauchery, licentiousness, depravity and wickedness."[10] Linked to the bars were the "policy shops" of Denver gambling syndicates and scores of brothels and cribs. Denver's suburbanites had reason to feel like strangers in their own city, fearing it the way many white Americans fear the central city of the 1990s.

In the first years of the twentieth century it was these alienated citizens who swelled the ranks of Denver's reformers. As progressives in the Progressive era, their participation transformed reform politics. Change in the early 1890s had been imposed upon the city by a partisan legislature and a moralizing governor. By the turn of the century Denverites were divided among themselves, engaging in a sort of civil war for control of the metropolis. Waite's ineffectualness and McMurray's failure to limit the utilities also threw doubts on the value of voting for an honest person without changing the system. Local progressives began to focus on the structure of the machine, looking for vital props whose removal might topple the entire system.

Their first campaign, begun in 1898, was for home rule, the permanent delegation of government powers from the state to the municipality. By ending state interference, home rule was expected to make local administration more efficient and reduce the hold of the state parties. The first step, the adoption of a constitutional amendment cutting Denver loose from Arapahoe County, came in 1902. Reformers wrote a city charter that reduced the number of patronage appointments and allowed the close regulation of city utilities. Threatened politicians and businesspeople mobilized to defeat the charter in November 1903, replacing it with a document that multiplied offices and made public ownership of utilities extremely difficult. As many as ten thousand fraudulent votes may have been cast and counted by the worried machine in the March 1904 election, which approved the second charter.

Blocked in their assault on the politicians, disaffected Denverites turned on the utilities. The target was well chosen, for the companies were accustomed to low tax assessments, tax rebates, and rates that allowed profits of 20 or 30 percent on actual investment. Because its original franchise had carried no specific time limit, the Denver Tramway Company, in addition, claimed a perpetual right to operate its streetcars. In 1906, however, it decided to seek a new franchise as insurance, at the same time that the Gas and Electric Company was asking voters to approve a twenty-year renewal of its privileges. Even though reformers challenged the voting lists of taxpayers eligible for the May 15 election, the results gave the Gas and Electric Company a margin of 615 out of 16,000 votes cast and the DTC a margin of 183 votes. In an ensuing investigation eventually blocked by the Colorado Supreme Court, Judge Benjamin B. Lindsey was able to show that Frank W. Frueauff, general manager of the Gas and Electric Company, had distributed several hundred worthless building lots among company employees to "qualify" additional voters. A few months later facsimile pages of Frueauff's pocket diary appeared in the *Denver Times*. Under biblical verses such as "blessed are the meek," the diary listed a total of $67,690 paid out during the franchise campaign, including $4,500 for Mayor Speer, $1,600 for the president of the Board of Supervisors, and lesser amounts for judges, state and county officials, and prominent clergy.

Continued agitation by reformers made election fraud increasingly difficult. By 1910 reformers were able to vote municipal takeover of the Union Water Company, the staunch ally of Speer and Evans. Victory led to an attack on Speer himself. The campaign was opened in the *Rocky Mountain News* by editorial writer George Creel, a single-minded "sin slayer," whose loud attacks on "shameless venality and depraved servility" were practice for his later job as head of the Office of Public Information and the nation's chief anti-German propagandist during World War I.[11] Although initial efforts centered on a campaign to abolish Speer's office through adoption of the businesslike commission system of city government, the reformers altered their tactics in December 1911. Henry Arnold, county assessor for the past eighteen months, had made a shining reputation by lowering taxes on private homes and noisily raising the valuations on properties held by banks, utilities, Simon Guggenheim, and William G. Evans. When Speer dismissed Arnold, middle-class Denverites braved December winds and assembled twenty thousand strong on the capitol grounds to hear praise for the new martyr. Denver reformers quickly scared Speer out of the mayoral race with a Citizens' party ticket headed by Arnold. Carefully concentrating on the city's residential wards, Arnold carried 58 percent of the vote in the May election against 18 percent for the Republican candidate and 24 percent for Speer's stand-in. He served as mayor for one year, until Denver tried a brief experiment with the commission form of city government between 1913 and 1916.

Denver's liquor and vice industries, a third component of the municipal machine, also felt progressive pressures. As early as 1907 moralists forced the closing of dozens of policy shops and scores of backroom poker and crap games in cigar stores and saloons. The cribs and parlor houses of Market Street were shut down in 1914, and their several hundred residents scattered to run-down hotel rooms in Denver and to friendlier cities. Defeat of the saloon took a better-organized crusade, for gambling and prostitution were, in a sense, only offshoots of the whiskey business. The Colorado Anti-Saloon League had won a small victory in 1901 when Judge Lindsey ruled that women must be excluded from Denver's bars. Stronger measures, however, awaited the General Assembly's approval of a local option law that allowed the voters of any political unit to prohibit the sale of alcohol. In 1908 four of Denver's residential wards overwhelmingly voted themselves dry, but the limits of prohibitionist strength were shown two years later when the city as a whole voted down the local option, 32,221 to 16,579.

Denver was not the only city to feel the reform impulse. Colorado Springs adopted commission government in 1909. Grand Junction in the same year voted for prohibition and changed its charter after a heated battle. Under the old government, argued reformer James Bucklin, the saloonkeepers and utility companies could use their stranglehold on the two wards south of Main Street to veto city council actions desired by a majority of citizens. The new charter provided for a special form of commission government with preferential voting in which voters marked their first, second, and third choices. The reform, said a Harvard professor, made Grand Junction "the freest city in the world," even though reformers never succeeded in pushing through a city buyout of the gas and electric company.

One of the sources for middle-class reform in Grand Junction as well as Denver was the participation of women. As historian Kathleen Underwood has pointed out, the settled city of the early twentieth century offered women far more chances for civic involvement than had the pioneer town of the 1880s. By the start of the new century, Grand Junction women had plunged headlong into community activities. The Mesa County Political and Social Science Club worked at "educating and fitting the ladies for the duties and rights of equal citizenship" after Colorado extended voting rights to women. The Twentieth Century Club and the Grand Mesa Women's Club turned talk of a public library into reality.

Given the interlocking alliance among the utilities, railroads, and manufacturing corporations, it was only a matter of time before reformers took their battles into state politics. When blocked on the municipal level, their logical response was to seek a larger constituency. Many state politicians were glad to hitch a ride, for the end of the silver crusade had left Colorado politics without clear party positions or exciting issues other than law and order. What could be more convenient than to seize onto programs that had already proved popular in Denver and Colorado Springs. In the process, the relation between city and state came full circle. The development of Denver's hinterland in the 1880s had triggered the growth of a commercial metropolis, which forced the expansion of public services whose control became the central issue in city politics. In turn, the concerns of Denverites came to determine the content of state politics and the objects of government. As in other parts of the country in the same years, the city set the issues and the state followed.

As early as 1905, frustrated Denver reformers, led by Edward Costigan and Ben Lindsey, formed a State Voters' League to act as legislative lobby and "publicity bureau of complete candor and fearlessness."[12] Although patterned after successful Denver organizations, the league failed to gain support from the bunchgrass and aspen counties. Statewide annoyance with Denver corruption, however, convinced the Republicans to award their 1906 gubernatorial nomination to the Reverend Henry Buchtel, a Methodist minister who was chancellor of the University of Denver and whose public respectability cast a shining aura over the entire ticket. Damned by Ben Lindsey as a hypocrite willing to lend his good name to cover political rottenness, Buchtel's two-year administration did bring a state civil service law, a long-needed railroad commission, and a grudging acknowledgment of the political middle by the Republican command, as well as the appointment of Simon Guggenheim to the U.S. Senate.

In 1908 it was the Democrats' turn. Backed by Thomas Patterson of the *Rocky Mountain News,* reformers captured tenuous control of the state party from the "City Hall Machine" and elected Denver Congressman John Shafroth as governor. In his two terms Shafroth presided over enactment of a broad range of labor legislation, including a child labor law and a factory inspection law, and paved the way for coal mine inspection and eight-hour work laws for women and miners. Striking more directly at the Denver machine, Shafroth also convinced the legislature to adopt the direct primary, regulate voter registration, and submit to the voters a measure allowing direct legislation by initiative and referendum. Approved by a margin of 3 to 1 in 1912, the latter measure proved extremely useful to reformers throughout the decade.

Republican liberals met with less success in changing their party. Led by Edward Costigan and J. S. Temple of Denver and Phillip Stewart of Colorado Springs, in 1910 the insurgents adopted a ringing "Declaration of Principles," which championed the cause of "the people" against "the encroachment of special interests" but failed to dent control by the regulars of the state convention. The possible presidential candidacies of Senator Robert La Follette of Wisconsin and Theodore Roosevelt occupied the organizational efforts of the Colorado Republican progressives through 1911 and 1912. After Taft regulars froze the insurgents out of the Colorado delegation to the national convention, Ben Lindsey led protesters to Chicago and endorsed Roosevelt's third party. By the end of September leading Republican liberals had united behind Roosevelt's Progressive party and a state ticket headed by Costigan. Costigan ran second to Democrat Elias Ammons, who split the "progressive" votes from Denver, Colorado Springs, and the small cities of the Western Slope by running on Shafroth's liberal record.

The decline of Colorado progressivism came quickly. After their Denver defeat, Women's Christian Temperance Union crusaders took their fight to the state, using the new initiative procedure to offer a prohibition amendment to the Colorado electorate. Falling forty thousand votes short in 1912 because of poor organization and Denver opposition, temperance advocates renewed their efforts in 1914, confusing the gubernatorial battle between Costigan, old reformer Thomas Patterson, and regular Republican George Carlson. By running on a platform of law and order in the wake of the Ludlow Massacre and monopolizing the prohibition issue, Carlson won easily and helped to carry the amendment that made Colorado a dry state as of January 1, 1916. Much of the margin came from old-stock middle-class voters in Denver's newer neighborhoods, who still saw elimination of the saloon as a way of imposing order on the chaotic inner city. Nearly thirty thousand "dry" votes were counted

Edward and Mabel Costigan in the 1930s.

in the city, up from twelve thousand in 1912. In effect, a highly conservative candidate had used the liquor issue to steal the reform vote from two of the state's most committed liberals. The heart of Colorado's Progressive constituency found the appeal of law and order in its broad sense more compelling than further commitment to humanitarian reform.

The reform alliance proved impossible to reconstruct. The Republicans soon reabsorbed the Progressives, who had been damaged by Costigan's role as attorney for the Ludlow miners. The Democrats, still shaken by the Ludlow incident and seeking a more solid image, gave their gubernatorial nomination to Julius Gunter, a gracious nonentity whose chief accomplishment in office was to direct a smooth wartime mobilization. In the same year — 1916 — Speer returned to power in Denver on his deserved reputation as a builder of parks, boulevards, sewers, and civic monuments. His re-election involved the replacement of Denver's short-lived commission government with a more traditional mayor-council form. By the time the Great War distracted public attention, the old alliance between illicit business and politics was again in operation. In 1919 a Denverite might have thought he or she was back in 1899, as newspapers opposed to the election of Republican Dewey C. Bailey accused him of failing to enforce prohibition as director of public safety. Newspaper headlines — "200 Peddlers of Liquor Busy in Denver and All Are Boosting for Bailey" — might almost have made disillusioned reform veterans feel young again.[13]

Politics in Colorado between 1900 and 1914 illustrates many of the conclusions historians have drawn about the U.S. Progressive era. The reform impulse was a new movement, arising out of the problems created by the rapid growth of Denver. Most of its leaders were middle-aged, middle-class business and professional men from Denver and smaller cities who sought to control and improve their communities through municipal and state politics. Only a scattering of veteran Democrats such as John Shafroth and Thomas Patterson had participated previously in the Populist revolt. The two movements, moreover, spoke for different constituencies. Whereas populism had appealed to mine workers, the reformers of the 1900s and 1910s found their best response in Colorado Springs and Denver.

It is also clear that in Colorado, as in the rest of the nation, the terms "Progressive movement" and "progressivism" are misleading in their implication of a coherent drive for well-defined goals. The middle-class reform movement was itself overlaid on the state's labor movement, which peaked in the same years, on the campaign to secure political rights for women, and on efforts by

Hispanics of southern Colorado to defend their social institutions. Nor was middle-class reform a single, unified movement. Moralizing prohibitionists, crusading journalists, ambitious politicians, and outraged private citizens all followed their own consciences and pursued their own concerns. Their story has been told in terms of efforts to unite against the influence of the Denver machine and the Republican establishment. With equal accuracy it could be presented as a list of reforms — scores of often unrelated proposals to regulate the state's economy, alter its government, and improve the well-being of its people. The only certain generalization is that each Progressive was reacting in some way to Colorado's transformation from a rural to an urban state, a transformation officially recognized when the 1910 census reported that more than 50 percent of Colorado's inhabitants lived in cities.[14]

# COLORADANS IN 1917

Colorado went to war in 1917 before the rest of the nation. A glance through the *Denver Post* on April 1 could have convinced anyone that the nation was already fighting a week before Congress declared war on the German Empire. Governor Julius Gunter had appointed the nation's first State War Council and called out thousands of members of the National Guard. Clergy used their Sunday to make "virile prayers" and to urge their congregations to put honor before peace. The previous night ten thousand Denverites had gathered for a "vociferous, unanimous upheaval of frenzied patriotism." Elsewhere in the city the Navy League proposed to recruit women for the Naval Coast Defense Reserve, the Board of Education promised a demonstration by thirty-five thousand school children at 10 o'clock Monday morning, and police officials worked on plans to clamp a "lid on Pacifism" by prohibiting traitorous acts in public places.[1]

Colorado's eagerness for war was part of a national frenzy. It was also an expression of a special desire for acceptance by the nation. What most Americans remembered in 1917 was not the state's thriving cities or its imposing resources but the Ludlow Massacre and the preceding history of industrial warfare. To many residents the state's greatest need was to demonstrate its maturity. How better to earn respect than to lead the way in a great patriotic venture? How better to assure future stability than to expose European minorities to massive Americanization programs and to centralize control of economic activity in the hands of business leaders?

Volunteers such as Robert Rockwell were those who made the mobilization work. A 1909 Princeton graduate, he had come to western Colorado to be a rancher. Seven years later Rockwell had won enough respect to secure election to the Colorado House of Representatives. When the United States entered the war, he had just completed his first term as a legislator who

Robert Rockwell photographed for his gubernatorial
campaign in 1924.

worked conscientiously for the stock raisers and farmers of Delta County, soliciting their opinion on bills before the agriculture,
forestry, and fish and game committees on which he served and
writing a weekly letter for home newspapers. At the end of the
session in March he had shipped his typewriter and Victrola
home to Paonia, changed the address on his subscriptions to

*Outlook* and *National Geographic,* and started to bring his business correspondence up to date, with the feeling of a job well done. As he wrote in his last open letter, "Every vote I have cast and everything I have done has been for what I considered the best interest of the majority of the people."[2]

Although the War Council assured Rockwell a month later that Delta County was already well organized, the complex bureaucracy for the home front was, in fact, as hard to mobilize as Pershing's American Expeditionary Force in France. Governor Gunter interrupted Rockwell's summer in July with a special session of the general assembly, although he gave the legislators few specific recommendations. Not until September did organization pick up with the implementation of federal programs. Rockwell accepted appointment to the Home Guard in order to protect coal mines and feedlots from saboteurs. He was also made the Paonia representative of the U.S. fuel and food administrations. In the latter post he received orders from national food administrator Herbert Hoover through Colorado and Delta County administrators. In turn, he recruited teams of women to obtain food conservation pledges from local housewives. Any woman who refused to sign a pledge card after reading a pamphlet on the Prussian system could expect continued pressure from the five-layer bureaucracy. As the state administrator wrote to Rockwell, "The time has come when we must investigate all lack of cooperation with the Government, and the failure to sign a food conservation card is just as serious . . . as failure to conform to any of the other laws designed to end the war speedily."[3]

As he overextended himself financially to buy Liberty bonds and set up a prize to encourage patriotism among Paonia high school students, it was clear that Robert Rockwell believed in the U.S. war. So did Ellis Meredith, a Denver newspaperwoman and a twenty-five-year veteran of reform politics. Born in 1865, she had become a reporter for the *Rocky Mountain News* in the early 1890s while helping to plot the successful strategy for women's suffrage in Colorado. By the turn of the century she was combining the composition of romantic novels with reform work in the Democratic party. A delegate to the national convention in 1900, vice chair of the state party, and member of the first charter revision commission in Denver, Meredith fully earned her election as president of the Denver Election Commission. In the post from 1911 to 1915, she defended the causes of reform

Ellis Meredith in the picture she preferred to use for publicity.

and women's suffrage. According to one of her opponents, she was skilled both as a writer and an organizer: "She is a fine woman, of excellent ability, clever, reliable, patriotic and dependable, and knows too damn much about politics."[4]

Whereas Rockwell did his part in the organization of the home front, Ellis Meredith helped to fight the war from Washington.

She had moved east in 1916 as director of publicity and organization for the Women's Bureau of the Democratic party. With the declaration of war in 1917, she found herself drawn again to journalism. She wrote about German atrocities and the American crusade for the *Denver Post,* looking for human-interest stories about life in the trenches and the sufferings of the Belgians. When possible, her theme was women and what they could do — the patient endurance of the women of France, the capabilities of the women of the United States.

For most of her political career, Ellis Meredith must have found Edward Keating a firm ally. Protégé of Senator Tom Patterson and managing editor of the *Rocky Mountain News* for which Meredith wrote, Keating had led the fight for primary elections in the Colorado Democratic party. In 1911 he had quit politics and moved to Pueblo to run his own newspaper, but a year later he found himself campaigning for Congress. In his first term he successfully battled the congressional power structure to secure investigations of the coal strike and the Ludlow Massacre. The miners and workers of southern Colorado reelected him by landslides in 1914 and 1916. His campaign platform was a single sentence: "I believe in Woodrow Wilson and his policies."[5]

On April 6, 1917, Edward Keating changed his career by voting against U.S. entry into a European war. Along with Representative Ben Hilliard of Denver, he led the *Post*'s "Role of Dishonor" because he refused to break his party's campaign pledge of peace. Three weeks later he was one of an even smaller minority who voted against conscription, having first introduced an unpopular amendment to exempt conscientious objectors. The *Rocky Mountain News* had already written that his presence in Congress shamed Colorado. "We Bow Our Heads" was the title of the editorial. Keating misrepresented the state, the paper wrote, "when he gave aid and comfort to the enemy by his official act." The only explanation, continued the editorialist, was Keating's desire to assure re-election votes among the immigrants of the coalfields, for surely no "American voter" could approve his actions.[6]

Upon his return to Colorado in the summer of 1918, Keating found a primary challenge within his own party. According to Major John Martin, Ed Keating was a yellow-blooded slacker who had never voted correctly on a war measure. No wonder, said the major, that Keating's backers included "every Bolshevist,

Edward Keating (center) as president of the Colorado Land
Commission, 1911.

Sinn Feiner, pro-German, Debs socialist and pacifist" in southern
Colorado.[7] Skill as a debater won Keating the primary, but he lost
the election when conservative newspapers used the issue of patriotism to get rid of a troublesome reformer. Not even the last-
minute publication of a telegram from President Wilson praising
Keating's record on labor legislation was enough to sway the outcome of the election.

Keating's defeat symbolized a change in Colorado politics. By
1918 there were few progressives left. The Democratic party ran
a statewide campaign that emphasized domestic reform instead
of patriotism and lost the election. The contest between democracy and plutocracy was of little interest to voters who turned to mil-
lionaires such as Oliver Shoup for governor and Lawrence Phipps
for senator. Keating was out of electoral politics for good, and he
returned to Washington to edit a newspaper for the railroad

unions. Ellis Meredith also remained in the East to help organize women newly enfranchised by the Nineteenth Amendment. The nation's future belonged to men such as Calvin Coolidge and Herbert Hoover, not to the old Progressives. Colorado belonged to men like Robert Rockwell, who rose to the office of Colorado state senator in 1920 and lieutenant governor in 1922 and ran for the statehouse in 1924 as a regular Republican. His literature called him "a practical businessman . . . a successful stockman . . . a taxpayer in four Colorado counties" — in short, a willing participant in the new age of Henry Ford.[8]

# CHAPTER 13

# COLORADO'S GREAT DETOUR: THE 1920s AND 1930s

In 1930 most Coloradans — or at least most of the official spokespersons — would have denied that their state was suffering from the Great Depression. "Look at the *Denver Post* and *Rocky Mountain News*," they might have told a visitor, "as fat as ever with advertising. Does that show a state in trouble? Look at the employment rate, higher than in the rest of the country. The starving poor? Our own welfare officials can't find them. The Depression may be a problem for the overindustrialized East, but it isn't for us. Governor Adams is right. Our resources protect us. Our climate protects us. It won't happen here."

This widespread pride was mistaken. The crash in 1929 soon hurt Colorado's hard-rock miners, who produced for the national market. By late 1931 the entire state knew it was in trouble, as farm commodity prices fell and trade slowed. By 1932 Denver's bank clearings were less than half of what they had been in 1929. The economic disaster of the 1930s hit Coloradans especially hard because they had not enjoyed good times during most of the 1920s. As in other parts of the interior West, agriculture and mining had been economically depressed since the end of World War I. By 1930 many people had little surplus wealth to fall back on; many others lost all or part of their nest eggs when banks failed in 1931 and 1932. The twenty years between 1920 and 1940, two decades of reduced income and limited opportunities, helped to shape a society that was like a hibernating bear: torpid and resentful of change.

The armistice in 1918, for example, spelled disaster for eastern Colorado. War-inflated grain and livestock prices fell 60 percent within three years. Large wheat growers and cattle raisers on the high plains could survive by expanding their production at slight marginal cost, but the smaller farmers were squeezed between falling receipts and fixed mortgages. In the state's dry

Keota, Weld County, 1939, a town left on the brink of economic ruin by agricultural depression and drought.

farming areas it was the 1890s all over again, with adverse markets substituting for weather to force tax sales and foreclosures and to drive the rate of tenancy from 23 percent to 35 percent. The further decline of prices and farm incomes in the early 1930s simply deepened the existing problems of wheat growers and ranchers. At the same time, it crippled Western Slope fruit and vegetable producers, who had protected themselves in the previous decade through cooperative marketing associations. Agricultural statistics for the 1930s continued the grim story: the population was down in all but one of the plains counties; less land was irrigated, and over 1 million acres were taken out of cultivation; thirty thousand agricultural jobs were lost for the state as a whole.

The report was the same for Colorado mining. The end of the Great War brought an abrupt decline to the demand for industrial metals, which cut copper and zinc production by 70 percent and forced the new molybdenum mines to shut down completely in the early 1920s. Cheap tungsten from China and vanadium from the Belgian Congo ruined Colorado producers, and increased use of natural gas and petroleum damaged Colorado's coal industry. The value of gold and silver mined in the state also fell by 75 percent. A flurry of interest in exploiting deposits of oil-bearing shale rock in far-western Colorado had appeared in the late 1910s. Two hundred fifty companies sold stock, but only a dozen or so actually tried to produce oil by heating the shale in huge retorts. By 1925 a combination of technical problems and cheap oil from Texas had ended the brief boom. Jobs for a few hundred riggers and roustabouts in the Craig and Fort Collins oil fields, a revival of gold and silver mining in the 1930s, and a growing demand for the state's molybdenum failed to prevent a 25 percent drop in the number of mine workers during the two decades.

Factories failed to fill the gap. Because much of Colorado's manufacturing involved the processing of foodstuffs and minerals, it suffered in proportion to the problems in agriculture and mining. The closing of smelters in Denver, Salida, and Pueblo after the war and the abandonment of the state's pioneer sugar factory at Grand Junction were symptomatic of the problem. Only two smelters remained in limited operation at Leadville and Durango after 1921, reworking old slag dumps and serving a few miners in the San Juans. Nor was Colorado more successful than other parts of the West in attracting new industries. By 1940 only thirty-five thousand factory workers were bringing home paychecks, down 30 percent from a peak in the late 1910s. Manufacturing, mining, and farming, which together had provided over half of Colorado's jobs in 1920, accounted for only one-third of the state's jobs by 1940.[1] The decline of these export industries dropped Colorado's per capita income below the national average for the first time in the state's history and brought an actual fall in total employment, from 366,000 in 1920 to 350,000 in 1940.

Life in Colorado became quieter as the age of bonanzas passed. Like the Clear Creek diggings, by the 1920s its people were played out. Tired of speculators, boosters, and gambling prospectors, most Coloradans wanted to age gracefully while enjoying the institutions created over the past sixty years. The commonwealth was a huge museum in which the passwords were "protect," "conserve," and "maintain." As observers reported from the 1920s through the mid-1940s, it was a state that "does not budge an inch for anybody or anything unless pinched and pushed."[2]

One sign of change was a slowing in the rate of population growth. After posting an increase of 74 percent in the first two decades of the century, Colorado added less than 20 percent to its population in the next two decades together. For the first time it lost rather than gained by migration, as both westward migrants and its own children found life more exciting and jobs easier to come by in Los Angeles. Even its cities barely held their own. Their share of the state's population rose by only 2 percent from 1910 to 1940, and by the 1930s the state had fallen behind the nation in its level of urbanization.

Failure to attract newcomers affected other social indicators. From 1860 through 1910 recurring booms had attracted a higher proportion of European immigrants, men, and people in their twenties and thirties than was the case in the United States as a whole. Over the next thirty years, however, Colorado lost these demographic patterns characteristic of a developing region. As early as 1920 the percentage of foreign-born fell below the national average. The sex ratio approached equality over the same period. Figures on age distribution show the maturing of the generation that had arrived at the start of the century. Whereas Colorado had more than its share of people between ages twenty and fifty in 1910, the population bulge spanned ages thirty to sixty by 1920, forty to seventy by 1930, and fifty to eighty by 1940. The family structure also showed the aging of the population. With more married adults than the national average, the state had significantly smaller families.

As Colorado became a mature state, it began to live off of its accumulated capital. Much of the wealth was controlled by the children and grandchildren of the old magnates. Living at ease in Denver and Colorado Springs, these descendants formed a business elite that appeared from the outside to be "self-sufficient, isolated, self-contained and complacent." A procession of journalists found Denver a "reluctant capital" of the West, a city "prematurely gray."[3] Boosters in the Chamber of Commerce praised past achievements rather than current projects, and 17th Street, the Denver banking and investment community, was more interested in a safe return than a promising risk. Investment in local manufacturing was considered dangerously venturesome, as was too-rapid industrialization that might threaten the equilibrium. Life itself was a comfortable routine in which the call of civic duty could be satisfied through campaigns for charities and annual contributions to the University of Denver.

Politics offered little guidance. An alliance of old liberals, farmers, and labor unionists did elect a long-time progressive as governor in 1922, but William Sweet's two years in office had little impact on the state's politics. The largely Republican legislature in the 1920s represented absentee-ownership of industries, local bankers, the Farm Bureau, cattlemen's associations, and American Federation of Labor craft unions. Cooperating out of a shared respect for the status quo, members of the assembly declined to reorganize the outmoded state administration or support the minimal public welfare programs found in many eastern states. During the next decade both parties hesitated to raise taxes and balanced the state budget at the expense of public schools and the unemployed. In the Colorado tradition, the legislators were willing to act only when state action could aid private enterprise. The paving of roads; the negotiating of interstate compacts dividing the waters of the Colorado, South Platte, and Rio Grande; and completing the Moffat Tunnel to shorten the rail route to the west — these were the proud accomplishments of twenty years. Indeed, the Moffat Tunnel had the special justification of being not an innovation but a project left over from the previous generation.

Without direction from forward-looking leaders, frustrated Coloradans in the decade after Versailles were vulnerable to negative politics. In the first year of the peace, they joined in the national case of jitters known since as the Red Scare. Spiraling prices and high unemployment among veterans built resentments during the first months of 1919. At the same time, Bolshevik successes in Russia and Hungary, radical agitation at home, and the bombing of homes of prominent capitalists and government officials seemed to portend revolution. In the West, as Gerald Nash has suggested, where the basic structure of society was less than firmly planted and where the Industrial Workers of the World (IWW) was active, the inevitable unease that accompanied postwar readjustments was especially likely to focus on the Bolshevik menace.[4]

A wave of severe strikes also held the headlines through most of 1919. "Bolshevik Reign Looms in Seattle Strike" shouted the *Rocky Mountain News* when Seattle unions called a general strike to back underpaid shipyard workers. Although broken within five days by a red-baiting mayor, the strike signaled a new era in industrial warfare in the minds of worried patriots.

Among the thousands of other walkouts by workers made desperate by unchecked inflation, the Boston police strike and nationwide steel and coal strikes, held in defiance of federal courts, appeared to epitomize the rule of lawlessness. The last two conflicts, which crippled local industries, particularly added to the hostility of the average Coloradan. Many would have agreed with the *Denver Post* that a federal injunction against the coal workers was "a necessary and timely rebuke to the anarchists, to bolshevists, and to the foreign labor leaders who have come to this country to destroy it."[5]

Employers anxious to break the labor movement and ambitious politicians hoping to ride the issue of Americanism into higher office worked public nervousness into hysteria. Western lawmakers scrambled to prohibit membership in any organization (including radical unions) designed to subvert their self-serving concept of the American system — a gilded-age view one wag described as socialism for the rich and capitalism for the poor. In Washington, Attorney General A. Mitchell Palmer appointed young J. Edgar Hoover as head of a new General Intelligence Bureau with instructions to root out Bolsheviks. With his eye on the Democratic presidential nomination, Palmer directed mass arrests and the deportation of 249 radicals in November and December. To greet the new year, he staged coordinated raids in thirty-three cities, detaining 4,000 suspected Communists.

Colorado did not lag in the defense of the republic. A worried state legislature as early as March 1919 determined that "the display of the Red Flag, the emblem of anarchy . . . tends to foment and cause trouble . . . encourages riots and lawlessness and inculcates disrespect for the laws of the United States and the state of Colorado, as well as for the flag of our Country, and thus endangers the peace and safety of our people." In December 1919 the same body acceded to Governor Oliver Shoup's recommendation in passing an emergency Act for the Suppression of Anarchy and Sedition that provided jail terms of up to twenty years.[6] Despite the opposition of organized labor, the Denver City Council had already forbidden public speech designed to incite rebellion against the United States or the state of Colorado. By the time of the Palmer raids — January 2, 1920 — federal agents could find only eight radicals in Denver. Two months before, Denver and Pueblo police had raided local headquarters of the IWW, seized radical literature, and run IWW organizers out of town.

Official concern about radicals opened the way for an outburst of militant patriotism in the closing months of 1919. "One-hundred-percent Americanism" was the watchword. Whereas the *Denver Catholic Register* warned that the Soviets had infiltrated the city with paid agents, the *Post, Times,* and *News* campaigned against foreigners who clung to old ways or stubbornly spoke with accents. The Sons of Colorado and the Society of Sons of the Revolution joined clergy and politicians in warning that the gravest crisis in U.S. history could be met only with "the spirit that declares it is a joy to live in the USA, it is a privilege to live in Colorado."[7] Members of the rapidly growing American Legion, recently organized in behalf of law, order, and patriotism, took on the responsibility to break up radical meetings. The *Denver Post* paid the initiation fee for all its qualified workers and urged other employers to do the same.

By the spring of 1920 fear of the Red menace was beginning to slacken across an increasingly prosperous United States. When loudly heralded rioting and demonstrations failed to materialize on May 1, the *Rocky Mountain News* joined the *Denver Express* and other journals throughout the nation in pleading, "Mr. Palmer . . . please give us a rest."[8] Even as pure xenophobia relaxed, however, the Denver Employers Association continued to exploit scare tactics in its open-shop campaign. The climax came in the summer of 1920, with a pitched battle between the Amalgamated Association of Street and Electrical Railroad Employees and the Denver Tramway Company (DTC). The union, which had organized the company's one thousand workers two years before but had failed to secure recognition, met a May wage cut with a decision to strike in defiance of an injunction. In response to the actual walkout on August 1, management imported strikebreakers and offered limited service on streetcars protected by armed guards and armored windows. On August 5 an attempt to block the cars set off rioting in which two people were killed, thirty-three injured, and the ground floor of the *Denver Post* building sacked. The next day nervous strikebreakers fired into a crowd of union members who had surrounded their barracks. Five more died and twenty-five were wounded before American Legion volunteers used their military training to restore one-sided order. The *Post* and the DTC together made certain Colorado placed the blame on the anarchists of the IWW.

> From every harvest field they came. From the mining dis-
> tricts, from faraway Montana . . . flocking to Denver like the
> vulture swamps toward carrion. . . . From the south, from
> the north and east they came, gaunt men, narrow-eyed
> men, bearded men, treacherous men — all with a purpose.
> There was a strike. There was trouble brewing — and they
> could help in the spilling of blood.[9]

The target of the Red Scare was specific. Disturbed by inflation, unemployment, and strikes, Coloradans attempted to repair their economic system in the best way they knew. They did
not fear foreigners as such but did fear radicals. The opposite of
the "one-hundred-percent American" had been the Bolshevik,
not simply the immigrant. Within a few months of the transit
strike, however, Imperial Wizard William J. Simmons of the
Knights of the Ku Klux Klan slipped quietly into the Brown Palace to initiate a movement less discriminating in its search for
scapegoats. Meeting with prominent Denverites, he set in mo-
tion the organization of a local Klavern under the name the
Denver Doers Club. After several months of slow growth, the local Klan announced itself in the *Denver Times* of June 17: "We
proclaim to the lawless element of the City and County of Denver and the State of Colorado that we are not only active now,
but we were here yesterday, we are here today, and we shall be
here forever."[10]

The Denver Klavern was a branch of an organization rapidly
growing to national power. Founded by Simmons in 1915 under
the inspiration of D. W. Griffith's movie *The Birth of a Nation,* for
half a decade the Klan was an unsuccessful fraternal organization for "high class men of intelligence and character." In 1920,
however, Simmons hired professional publicists to direct an organized membership drive. Scores of "Kleagles" were soon recruiting through the cities and towns of the South, playing on
Protestant fears of strange religions and nativist fears of alien
ways. Centering first in the Gulf South and Texas, by 1921 the
Klan moved into the Middle West, the southern plains, and the
western states where the imprint of the Mississippi Valley was
strong. From two thousand members at the beginning of 1920,
the Invisible Empire grew to one hundred thousand by the time
Simmons visited Denver and to more than 2 million by 1924.

Factory workers, professionals, small business owners, and
clerks — the 2 million were united by their fear of change. In the
age of motor cars and mechanized production, movies and mass

The Ku Klux Klan assembled at Brighton, near Denver, in 1924.

merchandising, Klan members shared a commitment to an earlier way of life and saw the organization as a reaffirmation of American values. Membership in the Invisible Empire was a blow against outsiders who were pushing their way into positions formerly held by native-born citizens. Jews and African-Americans with a modicum of self-respect were bad enough. Roman Catholics were worse — they represented the spearhead of a conspiracy against the Puritan civilization that had made the country great. At the same time, the average Klan member worried about the peace of his community and the honor of his daughter. Bootlegging, crime, loose morals, and the traveling brothels made possible by Henry Ford threatened the morality of small-town America. "Pure Womanhood!" "Crap Shooters Beware!" "Booze Must Go!" "Our Little Girls Must Be Protected!" — slogans such as these from a Texas Klan parade touched the heart of the movement.

In its first year Denver's Klan followed the national pattern, mixing petty violence and harassment with conviviality. For Friday night entertainment, Klan members routed auto caravans through the Jewish neighborhood on West Colfax, honking their horns and shouting insults. The local chapter of the NAACP suffered Klan threats, and at least one African-American who allegedly failed to observe the code of interracial contact was driven out of town. Klan members also boycotted Catholic merchants and adopted the Cyana as their official cigar (Catholics, you are not Americans). More seriously, motorists attempted half a dozen times to run down the editor of the *Denver Catholic Register*. Simultaneously, the Denver Klan displayed the trappings of a popular fraternal society. Its membership of some seventeen thousand, half of Colorado's total, supported a two-hundred-piece Imperial Klan No. 1 band, a ladies' auxiliary, a Junior Klan, and an associate chapter of the Royal Riders of the Red Robe for foreign-born Protestants. Regular Klonklaves were held on Table Mountain above Golden, and tens of thousands attended Klan initiations in Cotton Mills Stadium and Klan parties at Lakeside Park.

Brass bands were enough for a start, but by 1923 Colorado Grand Dragon John Galen Locke found the political potential of the Klan too great to waste. In May Democratic mayoral candidate Benjamin F. Stapleton denounced religious bigotry and asserted that "true Americanism needs no mask or disguise." Privately, he welcomed Locke's backing. Within a month of his victory over incumbent Dewey Bailey, Stapleton revealed his affiliation by allowing Klan members to use the civic auditorium and appointing Klan leader Rice Means director of public safety. By the following March Klan members also occupied the offices of city attorney and chief of police and several judgeships, and Stapleton had vowed renewed allegiance to Locke after a brief effort at independence.

Five months later Klan power was tested in a special mayoral election initiated by a petition from twenty-six thousand of Stapleton's opponents. Repudiating the mayor, the Denver County Democratic Assembly denounced the Invisible Empire and "any administration that permits itself to become the working tool of the Klan." According to the *Denver Post* the issue was simple: "Shall the KKK, an anonymous, secret, masked society, rule Denver, or shall the people rule Denver?" Stapleton, in turn, willingly deferred to Locke, allowing the Grand Dragon to run his campaign and vowing at a Klan rally: "I have nothing to say, except that I will work with the Klan and for the Klan in the coming election, heart and soul. And if I am reelected, I will give the Klan the kind of administration it wants."[11]

The results showed the frightening strength of the Klan. Seven of ten voters backed Stapleton, who carried every election district in the city. Although the Klan drew partisans from a broad base of Denver's Protestants, it was particularly attractive to rootless newcomers, to homeowners — such as the residents of Berkeley in northwest Denver, who felt threatened by nearby ethnic enclaves — and, in general, to those best described as middle class and lower class. Methodists and Baptists, Disciples of Christ and Presbyterians contributed many members, as did the Masons. Episcopalians and Lutherans seemed far less interested. Recognizing the extent of Klan support after the election, the *Post* reversed its previous position and admitted that the Invisible Empire was "the largest, most cohesive and most efficiently organized political force in the state of Colorado today."[12]

Even before the returns were in, Locke had offered Klan support to wealthy Republican Senator Lawrence Phipps. In return for votes he vitally needed, Phipps, although not a Klan member, contributed heavily to the Invisible Empire's campaign coffers. In August 1924 Klansmen easily secured the endorsement of the powerful Denver Republican County Convention for their candidates, Clarence J. Morley for governor and Rice Means for United States senator. At the state convention pro-Klan delegates from eastern Colorado and Fremont County joined Denverites to assure Morley and Means spots on the primary ballot. Morley opposed Robert Rockwell and Earl Cooley; Means contested a short senate term with Charles Moynihan and Charles Waterman. Because their opponents split the anti-Klan vote and pro-Klan Democrats crossed over to vote in the Republican contest, both Morley and Means won the September primary, although neither had a majority of ballots cast. In November, after a campaign fought largely on the question of Klan influence, Morley defeated the incumbent Democrat William Sweet, Phipps stood off the Adams challenge, and Means bested Democrat Morrison Shafroth. Klansmen were also selected for lieutenant governor, auditor, attorney general, secretary of state, and Supreme Court justice. The Republican party controlled both houses of the legislature, and the new governor hesitated to make a decision without consulting the Grand Dragon by telephone or exchanging notes by special messenger. The leaders of the Klan could well believe they owned the state.

In fact, 1924 marked the Klan's peak of influence in Colorado. As with the Know-Nothing party of seventy years before, the Invisible Empire found it hard to translate fear into legislation. Governor Morley's inaugural address proposed to exclude certain aliens from residence in the state and to prohibit the sacramental use of intoxicating liquors — measures aimed directly at the state's foreign-born and Catholics. Two other measures — an amendment of the primary election law and the abolition of a number of state boards and agencies — were designed to strengthen the Klan's hold on the Republican party and Colorado's government. Although the Republican majority in the house quickly responded to directions, a coalition of fourteen Democrats and six insurgent Republicans adamantly blocked the administration bills in the senate. When adjournment came after 101 days of maneuvering, Morley had suffered a political rout, and the Klan had felt its first major humiliation.

Internal dissension also plagued the Klan. Mayor Stapleton bridled at Locke's rule, as did Senator Means. At first Stapleton tried to outmaneuver Locke by organizing a sham paper Klan designed to preempt the national organization's charter in Colorado. This stratagem failed, but when Locke and his minions kidnapped a nineteen-year-old unwed father-to-be and threatened him with castration unless he married his sometime-sweetheart, the resultant publicity tarnished the Grand Dragon's image, as did the notoriety surrounding his indictment for income tax evasion. On Good Friday, April 10, 1925, Stapleton brilliantly circumvented the Klan chief of police, William Candlish, by using American Legion members to stage surprise raids on underworld dens. These blitzes unearthed a labyrinth of police connections with the demimonde and led to the suspension of a dozen Klan members from the force. Prodded by Stapleton, the national Klan made Locke resign. He retaliated by forming a rival, less rabid group, the Minutemen of America, which attracted some five thousand former Klansmen. Most of the rest of the embarrassed empire's Denver membership disappeared, although a few remained loyal.

As in Denver, Klan cells in other parts of the state used careful organization and adroit manipulation of local fears to build substantial memberships. In Colorado Springs the Empire drew members from moderate-income and lower-income neighborhoods on the city's south and west sides, whereas more affluent northern districts contributed few recruits. Staunch opposition ensured that the El Paso County contingent, although it claimed some two thousand adherents, would not become an effective political force. Cañon City, however, was well represented by the Klan. There, many middle-class Protestants chafed at the political power of the town's blue bloods and feared that the elite's alleged ally, the pope, would soon establish his summer residence at the nearby Benedictine abbey. Translating anxieties into votes, the Klan quickly dominated both political parties. Because they controlled the Fremont County sheriff, Klansmen in Cañon City were not particularly worried about law-and-order issues, but in Pueblo the specter of bootleggers and vice-infested roadhouses loomed so large that thousands donned sheets. Similar concerns spawned Klan groups in Walsenburg and Trinidad. Even in Grand Junction, where Catholics, Jews, African-Americans, and foreigners were few, hundreds of Protestant Americans were drawn — perhaps more out of boredom than bigotry — to a brotherhood that promised excitement and camaraderie.

The persistence of out-of-state Klans slowed the organization's demise, but scattered units could not effectively repair the damage done by disarray in Denver and by mounting public opposition. Ruling the empire from a garage in Cañon City, the new Grand Dragon, Fred Arnold, sat and watched as his fiefdom fizzled. Incumbents Morley and Means lost the September 1926 Republican primary, and in November voters gave the governorship to Democrat William "Billy" Adams and Rice Means's senate seat to Republican Charles Waterman.

The collapse of the Invisible Empire freed Colorado of a threat to its stability but did not introduce more progressive leadership. Adams's administration was marked (in the kindest terms) by "economy and conservatism."[13] The major local event was a three-month coal strike that began in late 1927. Although he refused to mobilize the National Guard, the governor withheld recognition from the IWW leadership and contributed to an atmosphere in which local officials harassed strikers and the mayor of Trinidad organized antiunion vigilantes. More ominously, Adams formed a "State Law Enforcement Agency" of former servicemen and gave its command to a veteran of the Ludlow Massacre. The troopers killed six workers near Lafayette on November 21 and two more in Walsenburg on January 21, breaking the strike in a manner reminiscent of an earlier era. Adams's reaction was not surprising, for twenty

A Denver automobile showroom in 1927 was as glamorous as a movie palace.

years earlier Ben Lindsey had described him in the state senate as the skilled opponent of "any reform measure that threatens the 'plum tree' of the corporations."[14]

Denver in the same years remained safely in the care of Ben Stapleton, a man more remarkable for his political longevity than for his vision. At odds with state leaders in his party, Stapleton built a personal machine based on both the law of inertia and the mayor's power to hire and fire most city employees. Holding office until 1947, with one four-year vacation, he pleased businesspeople of both parties by keeping taxes low. In the process he gave the city an administration that was stodgy, slow, and increasingly inefficient. The patronage appointees running city services gave Denver a national reputation for understaffed departments and dirty streets. The city's newspapers surrendered their opportunity to lash out at the inertia and instead indulged in an uproarious circulation battle.

The *Denver Post* was already notorious. It carried neither syndicated columnists nor local editorials, and its front page, according to John Gunther, looked like "a confused and bloody railroad accident."[15] The *Rocky Mountain News*, acquired by the Scripps-Howard chain in 1926, wasted $3 million trying to beat the *Post* at the game it had virtually invented. For all of 1927 and most of 1928, the two papers countered stunt with stunt, premium with premium. Flagpole sitters, free gasoline, expanded sports coverage, illustrated serial novels of flaming youth, limerick contests, fireworks, comic strips, and screaming headlines about local crime substituted on all but a few occasions for solid, investigative reporting. Serious *News* campaigns for reform of outmoded statutes and improvement of Denver's physical plant were all but lost in the racket.

Colorado's public leadership, in short, was unprepared for the Great Depression. Unlike many of the industrialized states of the East or the Great Lakes region, where the reform impulse of the Progressive era had carried over with some vigor, Colorado in the 1920s had rejected direct responsibility for the welfare of its citizens. As the commonwealth entered the 1930s, care for its elderly, assistance to its unemployed, and schooling for its children were provided when available by sixty-three sets of county commissioners. As late as January 1933 the legislature reaffirmed that public relief was the province of county and municipal authorities. Supported by the philosophy of self-help, legislators struggled toward a balanced budget aided by neither a state sales tax nor an income tax. The fifteen hundred citizens who converged on Denver in 1932 to agitate for the reduction of real estate assessments merely reinforced the desire for low taxes shared by the state's elite.

President Franklin D. Roosevelt's "New Deal" gave Coloradans hope not offered by local politicians. In the one hundred days between March 9 and June 16, 1933, Congress created the Civilian Conservation Corps (CCC) to employ young men; the Agricultural Adjustment Administration (AAA) to stabilize farm prices; the National Recovery Administration (NRA) to revive business by fixing prices and wages; and an adjunct to the NRA, the Public Works Administration (PWA) to prime the economy by spending billions on public projects. To provide immediate relief lawmakers established the Federal Emergency Relief Administration (FERA), which gave states grants for make-work projects and for small doles to the indigent. Beginning in mid-1935 the Works Progress Administration (WPA), which eventually spent more than $100 million in Colorado, replaced FERA as the principal job-making arm of the federal government.

Curtiss Field gave Denver big city airs in the 1920s.

Uncle Sam's dollars accomplished much. The CCC constructed both Denver's Red Rocks Amphitheater and a smaller open-air theater on Flagstaff Mountain above Boulder. In Colorado National Monument CCC workers helped carve out the spectacular Rimrock Drive; south of Pueblo corpsmen dammed the St. Charles River to make Lake San Isabel. By 1938 the corps had planted more than 9 million trees, constructed 86,887 check

Employment agencies in Denver during the 1930s.

dams, and stocked more than 2 million fish in Colorado's lakes and streams. By the time the agency ceased operations in the state in 1942, more than thirty thousand Coloradans had enrolled. One of them, Orlando Romero of Trinidad, visited Lake San Isabel decades after he had created it: "I took my wife and my son and his wife and our grandson to show them where I had been and what I had done. And I felt rather comfortable in showing them that. It is something that people are still using."[16]

WPA workers could also boast. Under the local direction of Paul Shriver, WPA became the largest single employer in the state by March 1936, when it paid more than forty-three thousand workers. After that it trimmed its rolls, but even as late as January 1942 it enrolled more than ten thousand. By then WPA had undertaken more than five thousand Colorado projects. It had built 400 structures including 63 schools, 124 recreation buildings, 26 sewage disposal plants, and 28 dams. Ault got tennis courts, Center a community center, Monte Vista a hospital, Holly a city administration building. Eads and Olathe, among many other towns, enjoyed new schools thanks to WPA.[17]

A Pueblo area known as "Hooverville."

WPA refused to hire married women whose husbands, in theory, were expected to support them. Unattached women, who made up 20 percent of WPA's workers in 1936, were generally assigned typing, filing, sewing, canning, food serving, and housekeeping chores. Reacting to charges that African-American women were segregated on a Denver sewing project, Shriver reported that at one time "colored women were segregated as a result of their own desire." But he declared that Colorado's WPA had made "a particular effort . . . to avoid any possibility of racial discrimination."[18] Hispanic farmworkers also had cause to complain, for they were often dropped from WPA in order to provide farmers with cheap labor to tend and harvest sugar beets. Sometimes the agency simply eliminated persons with Hispanic surnames from its rolls, apparently assuming that such a name condemned its bearer to back-breaking labor, which one state investigator described as "industrial slavery far worse than the chattel slavery of old." Removed from WPA, Estanislado Valverde pleaded for reinstatement: "I got a wife and six children. I was unable to send them to school because none of them has any shoes."[19]

Civil Works Administration workers at Pueblo in 1934.

The federal government seemed more attuned to the needs of out-of-work professionals. The Federal Theater Project, which offered plays at the Baker Theater in Denver, gave hungry actors a chance to eat. It also gave Denverite Mary Coyle Chase a place to produce her first play, *Me Third*. This helped advance her career and led to her Pulitzer-Prize–winning play *Harvey*. The Federal Music Project employed musicians in Denver, Colorado Springs, and Pueblo. The Federal Writers Project compiled *Colorado: A Guide to the Highest State*. Artists on the government's payroll decorated post offices and other public buildings. Taos artist Ernest L. Blumenschein gave Walsenburg's post office a sensitive rendition of the Spanish Peaks. Archie Musick of Colorado Springs, who painted a mural for the Manitou Springs post office, argued that per taxpayer the program cost little, "and it gives the artist a more solid footing in the social scheme, converting him from a precious parlor monkey to a useful tradesman, so that he may walk on the sidewalk with respectable people."[20]

The Public Works Administration required more matching money from local entities than did WPA, thus ensuring that it would have more community support than WPA. PWA helped to finance Denver's diversion of Western Slope water through the pioneer bore of the Moffat Tunnel and provided much of the money for the city's new police building. At the University of Colorado, President George Norlin finagled PWA money to build or enlarge fifteen buildings, including the library, which was named after him. Federal loans made possible the Colorado–Big Thompson irrigation-power scheme, and Washington's largesse supported massive expansion of Colorado's paved highway network.

Farmers, whose income fell from nearly $213 million in 1929 to less than $82 million in 1932, needed the water and benefited from the improved roads. Not only did commodity prices plummet but a drought, which bedeviled the decade, destroyed the crops and blighted the hopes of many growers, particularly those on the plains. Dust followed drought. Mayme Stagner, who lived near Campo in southeastern Colorado, recalled one storm: "Like a great big black wall coming in. There were brown spots in it and sort of greenish-looking spots, and it looked like a million whirlwinds all right in each other . . . and rabbits were running in front of it and birds were flying and even a coyote went across our place. Everything was horrified."[21]

Resettlement advocates encouraged a few farmers to move — the Stagners relocated to a federally sponsored agricultural colony near Alamosa. Federal agents bought marginal farmland in eastern Colorado and put it to grass, laying the basis for the Comanche and Pawnee National Grasslands. Mainly, however, Washington relied on price supports, production controls, and soil conservation to bail out the growers. Even so, most plains counties suffered during the 1930s. Kit Carson County lost nearly a quarter of its residents. Baca County declined by 41 percent. Denver picked up some of the dispossessed, as did Western Slope counties including Mesa, which grew by 30 percent. Some of the others moved to California, which reported an influx of twenty-seven thousand Coloradans during the decade. "Just what has become of the people is not known," the *Holyoke Enterprise* observed, "but the number of empty houses and business buildings is evidence that the people are not here."[22]

Mayme Stagner gave thanks to Franklin Roosevelt for helping ordinary people: "To me it [the resettlement program] was the best thing that ever happened to us."[23] Her gratitude was not without foundation. Between 1933 and 1939 Uncle Sam allocated Colorado $362.06 per capita in nonrepayable grants, making Colorado tenth among the states and giving it more than twice

The WPA claimed that it treated blacks fairly, but African-Americans complained of segregation on this sewing project at Denver's Whittier School.

as much money as it sent to Washington in taxes. New York received only $205.76 per person; California received $266.28; Kentucky, typical of the South, got less than half as much per resident as did Colorado.[24] Yet, many Coloradans were less than grateful. The "haves" resented increased taxes; the "have-nots" regretted their loss of independence. Even a pro-Roosevelt newspaper such as Fred M. Betz's *Lamar Daily News* complained that "we are still a proud people. We do not want a continuation of the dole, nor of work that is merely wasted work."[25]

State legislators initially ducked the Federal Emergency Relief Administration's demands that they match some of the funds it was spending. To pressure the lawmakers, Harry Hopkins, FERA's national administrator, cut needy Coloradans off relief at the end of 1933, refusing to reopen the federal spigot until the state put up its share. Hopkins's bravura, coupled with that of a group of angry Denverites who invaded the state capitol in early

January 1934, convinced the general assembly to provide matching funds.[26]

The debate over the New Deal — particularly over the extent, expense, and control of relief and work programs — shaped Colorado politics during the decade. When conservative Republican Lawrence C. Phipps, Sr., declined to seek re-election to the U.S. Senate in 1930, voters replaced him with Edward P. Costigan, a reformer and one-time leader of Colorado's Progressives, who, even before Franklin Roosevelt popularized the term, proposed a "new deal" for the American people.[27] After Herbert Hoover established the Reconstruction Finance Corporation to make loans to big business, Costigan damned the approach as "billions for big business, but no mercy for mankind."[28] Upon Roosevelt's election, Costigan became one of the new president's most ardent supporters.

William "Billy" Adams, having thrice been elected governor, decided not to run again in 1932. Trapped in the morass of the Depression and blamed by some for failing to properly regulate the state's savings institutions, many of which failed in 1932, he lost the backing of the powerful *Denver Post*. By stepping aside he helped to assure the election of his nephew Alva B. Adams to the U.S. Senate and opened the governorship to his lieutenant governor and personal secretary, Edwin C. Johnson. The Kansas-born Johnson possessed impeccable political credentials: boyhood on a cattle ranch, football player, work as telegrapher and railroad section hand, homesteader near Craig, state legislator, Mason, Elk, Lutheran. Tall and charming, "Big Ed" won more votes in Colorado in 1932 than did Roosevelt.[29]

Briefly, Johnson seemed to be — although not in Costigan's circle — at least within a light-year or two of Roosevelt's wide orbit. The governor, for example, privately urged FERA administrator Hopkins to deny Coloradans relief in order to pressure legislators into providing matching money.[30] But in early 1934 one of Hopkins's field agents reported that Johnson had "slipped over to the other side" and allied himself with conservative Democrats.[31] It was a homecoming, if one were needed, for Johnson had grown up in the political shadow of the conservative Billy Adams. Convinced that the governor was no friend of the New Deal, in mid-1934 Costigan supported Josephine Roche, who challenged Johnson in the Democratic gubernatorial primary.

Roche sipped tea with Eleanor Roosevelt in Washington, D.C., shortly before she announced her intention to unseat Johnson.

The message was clear: she enjoyed the blessing of the New Dealers; Big Ed did not. By 1934 Roche was well known in Colorado for her pro-labor leanings. Daughter of the founder of the Rocky Mountain Fuel Company, the state's second-largest coal producer, she took control of the firm in 1928 after her father died. With degrees from Vassar and Columbia and with wide experience in social work, including a stint as a probation officer for Denver judge Benjamin Barr Lindsey, she differed from other mine owners. They disliked paying high wages; she rewarded her workers. They hated unions; she urged miners to unionize. "Capital and labor," she declared, "have equal rights."[32]

Roche could count on considerable labor support and on the backing of liberal Democrats, who applauded her "Roche, Roosevelt, and Recovery" rhetoric. Nonetheless, party bigwigs, perhaps sensing a Johnson victory, shunned her. John A. Carroll, a Denver Democrat and one of Costigan's lieutenants, recalled: "By God, they [the Costigan forces] couldn't get anybody of any stature to nominate her so they asked me to do that." Roche trailed Johnson at the state Democratic convention but won sufficient support to force a primary election. Energetically campaigning in August, she called for a progressive state income tax and faulted Johnson for failing to cooperate with the New Deal. "To countless workers," said Costigan, "she is a new Joan of Arc." When some doubted the ability of a woman to be the state's chief executive, John Carroll, now Roche's campaign manager, retorted that "a wide-awake woman is better than a drowsy man." When the *Denver Post* attacked Roche, Costigan branded the paper "Public Enemy Number One."[33]

In the September 1934 primary Roche beat Johnson by a wide margin in Denver and also took Boulder, Grand, Gunnison, and Mesa counties, but she trailed in every other county. The *Denver Post* celebrated Big Ed's victory, which, it argued, "halted the Red march."[34] Roosevelt rescued Roche by appointing her assistant secretary of the treasury, making her the second-highest-ranking woman in his administration. In November Johnson bested his Republican rival, Nate Warren, to gain his second two-year term as governor. Fortune again favored Johnson in 1936 when ill health kept Costigan from seeking re-election to the U.S. Senate. Liberal Democrats ineffectively backed former governor William E. Sweet. Johnson, favored by conservative Democrats and palatable to many Republicans, easily beat Sweet to take Costigan's senate seat.

County officials, whose freedom of action Johnson preserved, continued to emphasize economy. Reducing expenditures and purging the welfare rolls of chiselers were more important than alleviating poverty and fighting starvation. In part, such failings were a direct function of the ongoing obsession with a balanced budget. Local and state officials were caught between rising obligations, legal barriers against deficit spending, and a continued unwillingness to raise taxes. At the end of the decade, indeed, Governor Ralph Carr diverted two-thirds of the revenues earmarked for public education to operating expenses in order to equalize income and expenditures. Only $392 million of New Deal recovery funds and $92 million from other federal programs — all money Colorado leaders claimed to scorn — enabled the state to weather the Depression.

Colorado's voters compounded the fiscal problems in 1936 when they approved an extravagant old-age pension plan. Promising $45 per month to retired Coloradans over age sixty, the program monopolized 85 percent of the revenues from the state's new sales tax and took three-quarters of its total relief payments.

Acceptance of the constitutional amendment, which merely shifted the burden of poverty from older Coloradans to younger, was an expression of the deep frustrations felt throughout the United States in 1935 and 1936. As economic recovery all over the nation slowed after brief improvement, and as Roosevelt's administration appeared to flounder, Americans turned to a series of well-publicized saviors, each of whom offered a panacea to a particular segment of the public. Catholics in the Northeast listened to the broadcasts of Father Charles Coughlin, the "radio priest" who advocated a political order similar to that of Mussolini. Voters in the Mississippi Valley applauded Huey Long in his loud battles against the plutocrats and joined his Share Our Wealth clubs by the millions. In California, land of retired farmers, Dr. Francis Townsend organized Old Age Revolving Pensions, Limited, promising $200 per month to everyone over age sixty. This Townsendite movement and its many offshoots swept through the West in 1935 and 1936, capturing two governorships and several legislatures and winning the support of a majority of Colorado's electorate. For the next decade the state's forty thousand militant pensioners formed a block strong enough to prevent more imaginative use of state money.

President Franklin Roosevelt, Eleanor Roosevelt, Ed Johnson, and Ben Stapleton in Denver, October 1936.

At the close of the 1930s, Colorado's voters followed its politicians and bureaucrats in rejecting the New Deal. When Republican Ralph Carr won the governorship in 1938, he not only carried normally Republican areas of the Western Slope and South Platte Valley but also the Democratic stronghold of Pueblo County. Two years later the state's two Democratic senators — Alva B. Adams and "Big Ed" Johnson — showed their annoyance with Roosevelt by supporting the presidential candidacy of Wendell Willkie. His fourteen-thousand-vote edge confirmed the trend that maintained Republican dominance until the late 1940s.

Colorado business organizations also emerged from the 1930s with their faith in the traditions of self-help and their opposition to high taxes and federal intervention in the economy unaltered. A congressional proposal for an Arkansas Valley Authority (AVA) modeled on the successful Tennessee Valley Authority, for example, met fierce opposition in 1941. The Denver Chamber of Commerce, Colorado representatives, the State Water Conservation Board, and Governor Carr all feared the loss of local control over vital water supplies as much as they saw the AVA as another tentacle of the federal octopus to be lopped off before it did damage.

In their reactions Coloradans joined with other westerners who replaced Roosevelt's supporters with Republicans or conservative Democrats. To most of the area between the Missouri River and the California coast, the New Deal was an alien program actuated by an alien philosophy. There was little welcome for the FERA, the Agricultural Adjustment Administration, the Wagner Labor Relations Act, and other measures in Roosevelt's program. Unlike Michigan, Minnesota, Wisconsin, or New York, no western state implemented its own "Little New Deal." Unwilling to amend time-honored values of self-help and individualism, western politicians in general failed to recognize the passing of the era of frontier booms when natural resources could be skimmed off without thought. Most would probably have applauded Ed Johnson in his assertion that "the New Deal has been the worst fraud ever perpetrated on the American people."[35]

More broadly, Colorado politics was typical of the West for the entire interwar period. When creative responses were required for rapidly changing conditions, the area's leaders reacted with rigid moralizing, which made the state an unaccustomed laggard in social innovation. Gerald Nash has politely noted the dominance of a politics of "moderation" — a placid tendency to consolidate previous changes and reject further action. Earl Pomeroy has more bluntly found the key to politics between the world wars to be "fundamentalism."[36] From 1919 to 1940, westerners faced new problems by reiterating small-town values. They voted for Coolidge, joined the Klan, damned Roosevelt's socialistic meddling, and continued to believe government's only function was to provide the individual with the opportunity to strike it rich. Clinging to the past, they failed to realize that the West for the moment was no longer the nation's great adventure.

CHAPTER 14

# GROWTH AND POLITICS
# IN THE NEW COLORADO

In 1867 Frank Hall wrote that Denver looked as if someone had dropped it from a balloon and forgotten to pick it up. Over a century later a reporter for the *New York Times* described the city as being sprawled over the valley of the South Platte like a "lumpy pancake."[1] Both descriptions were accurate. Decades of tree planting and lawn sprinkling have failed to alter the fact that visually Denver is an open town. Unlike the suburbs of Philadelphia or Chicago, its housing tracts and apartment complexes can be viewed in almost a single glance. Whether observers look from the Jefferson County foothills or the highlands south in Arapahoe County, from the Boulder Turnpike or Interstate 70 to the east, they can see nearly the entire metropolis, whose buildings dot the sloping prairies like herds of buffalo from an earlier age.

The city that sprawls along the foothills reflects the transformation of Colorado in the middle decades of the twentieth century. Between 1940 and 1970 the population of Colorado nearly doubled, from 1,123,000 to 2,207,000. The proportion of Coloradans living in cities rose in those same years from 53 to 79 percent. Most of the new urbanites settled in Denver proper, in its suburban counties, in Colorado Springs to the south, or in Boulder, Greeley, and Fort Collins to the north. Together, the urbanized areas in this 120-mile corridor accounted for almost all of the state's growth in the postwar years and for two-thirds of its people by 1970.

World War II revived flush times in Colorado. As early as 1938 Denver officials had fought the economic slump by purchasing the Agnes Sanatorium for $750,000, adding additional acreage, and donating it to the Army Air Corps for Lowry Field. The military buildup that began in 1940 and the mass mobilization of 1942 brought additional military facilities — Buckley Field east

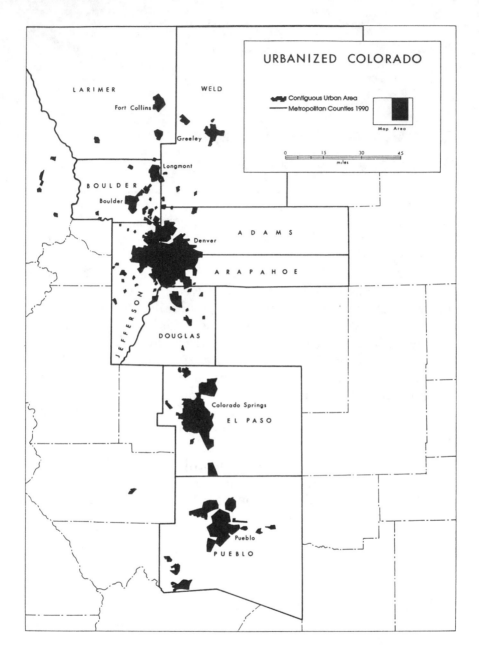

URBANIZED COLORADO

Contiguous Urban Area
Metropolitan Counties 1990

Map Area

0    15    30    45
miles

LARIMER

WELD

Fort Collins

Greeley

Longmont

BOULDER

Boulder

ADAMS

Denver

ARAPAHOE

JEFFERSON

DOUGLAS

Colorado Springs

EL PASO

Pueblo

PUEBLO

of Denver and Fort Carson and Peterson Field near Colorado
Springs. Fitzsimons Army Hospital was modernized for a new
war. The army also built Fort Hale near Leadville as a training
site for the predecessor of the Tenth Mountain Division. A few
hundred experienced skiers and mountaineers trained thousands of volunteers in the skills necessary for fighting in high

Soldiers stationed in Denver in 1942. After World War II many
servicemen returned to make Colorado their home.

mountains such as the Alps, training that was eventually put to
use in northern Italy. In total, military payrolls climbed from $3
million in 1940 to $152 million in 1944, to account for 12 percent
of all personal income in the state.

Mobilization meant military production as well as military
personnel. In the mountains the war renewed demand for industrial metals, especially Climax molybdenum, Boulder County
tungsten, and southwest Colorado vanadium used in steel manufacturing. For the plains counties the war meant good markets
for grain, meat, and beet sugar. The bulk of war contracts, however, went to Denver, whose population grew by 20 percent from
1940 to 1945. Denver factories turned out prefabricated parts
and sections for destroyer escort ships and landing craft. The
Union Pacific then hauled the sections to Vallejo, California, for
assembly at the Mare Island shipyard. Gates Rubber expanded
production for war contracts. Fourteen thousand workers at the
new Rocky Mountain Arsenal manufactured chemical weapons
and incendiary bombs.

Demand for molybdenum soared during World War II, bringing prosperity to Climax.

The largest single operation was the Denver Ordnance Plant, eagerly sought by the Chamber of Commerce and other civic organizations. Built by the federal government and operated by the Remington Arms Company, the plant was a complex of low buildings located on three square miles of cattle range on the western fringe of the city. Remington employed as many as twenty thousand workers — half of them women — to turn out millions of rounds of .30-caliber ammunition a day. Toward the end of the war, industrialist Henry J. Kaiser took over a portion of the Ordnance Plant to manufacture 155-millimeter and eight-inch artillery shells. After the war the Ordnance Plant was converted into the Denver Federal Center with regional offices for dozens of federal agencies.

World War II brought prisoners and detainees to Colorado. Several thousand German and Italian prisoners of war worked on northern Colorado farms from 1943 to 1945. After President Roosevelt signed Executive Order 9066 in February 1942, Colorado found itself with several thousand Japanese-American residents. Order 9066 authorized the relocation of 110,000 Japanese-

The War Transport Exchange helped Denverites carpool in the midst of wartime rubber and gasoline rationing.

Americans from Washington, Oregon, California, and Arizona. Denver's tiny Japanese-American community grew, as friends and relatives moved voluntarily from the deportation zone. Unlike political leaders in most western states, Governor Ralph Carr took the politically courageous stand of reminding his constituents that Americans of all ancestries deserved the same rights as citizens. Because most of the West Coast Japanese-Americans lacked the resources to quickly abandon their homes and businesses, the army forcibly uprooted them and shipped them to ten detention camps in the interior of the United States, including Amache near Granada in southeastern Colorado. At its

Camp Hale, north of Leadville, trained special mountain troops for service in Europe.

peak in October 1942, Amache housed 7,567 Japanese-Americans in wooden barracks inside high, wire fences. As the internees were gradually released toward the end of the war, about 2,000 stayed in Colorado. With anti-Japanese hysteria easing, in 1944 Colorado voters rejected a constitutional amendment that would have barred Japanese aliens from owning land.

The problems of wartime growth invigorated efforts to plan for rational land uses and economic development. Since the 1920s Denver had benefited from a relatively active planning commission that enjoyed the support of major banks and real estate firms. The end of the 1930s had seen efforts to extend physical planning to the metropolitan area through the five-county Upper Platte Valley Regional Planning Commission, and the Denver Planning Commission stepped forward to deal with housing and construction problems in the peak growth years before and after Pearl Harbor. A further step came with the establishment of the Denver Metropolitan Planning Project in August 1942. The new agency was a cooperative effort by the Denver Planning Commission, the Colorado State Planning

Commission, the National Resources Planning Board, and the University of Denver to preserve the city's expanded manufacturing base. Reorganized as the Denver Regional Association with Rockefeller Foundation funds in 1943, the group directed its attention to land use, employment, industrial development, and economic reconversion. Its pamphlet "Facing the Challenge of War and Post-War Problems" stressed the need to provide adequate electric power and to claim scarce water supplies in order to prepare for postwar growth.

Prosperity continued in the two decades after 1945. Colorado became an important participant in the new atomic age during the Cold War of the late 1940s and the 1950s. The Rocky Flats facility north of Denver turned plutonium into triggers for thermonuclear bombs. The Atomic Energy Commission (AEC) coordinated a uranium mining boom in the Four Corners region from offices in Grand Junction. Eager amateurs made the Colorado plateau "the land of the weekend prospector." Prospectors could send 55 cents to the U.S. Government Printing Office for a how-to pamphlet, buy a geiger counter in Grand Junction or Moab, Utah, and set out in search of yellow carnotite ore. Until the 1960s the AEC subsidized production with finding bonuses and premiums based on quality of ore. Towns such as Uravan and Durango boomed with uranium-processing mills. Like Grand Junction, Durango stressed its atomic reputation and welcomed the five hundred jobs at the Vanadium Corporation of America mill. The character of Durango life also changed with the arrival of several hundred geologists, engineers, and other professionals with the high salaries and sophisticated tastes of the postwar middle class. The end of the uranium boom in 1962, when the Vanadium Corporation withdrew, coincided with the promotion of Fort Lewis College into a four-year institution.

As the state found new activities to replace those damaged by the 1920s and 1930s, its steady growth pushed personal income above the national average. A comparison of income figures shows the change from the Colorado of 1930 to the Colorado of the 1960s. In 1930 farming and mining accounted for 32 percent of total employment, manufacturing for 9 percent, and government, trade, and services for 40 percent. By 1962 the figures were 9 percent, 14 percent, and 60 percent, respectively. Comparison with national patterns leads to the same conclusion — that Colorado made the jump from an extractive economy to a sophisticated service economy without going through the intermediate stage of heavy industrialization.

The economic transformation was the result of a revaluation of the amenities of the Colorado environment. Its attractions for outdoor living brought tens of thousands of new residents excited by the chance to pursue a career in a setting more pleasant than Indianapolis or Akron. In addition, the landscape offered special inducements for special industries — snow for ski resorts, clear skies for aeronautical industries and military training facilities, and empty land for the manufacture and storage of atomic explosives and nerve gas. As University of Colorado economist Morris Garnsey wrote, "The very factors which were formerly inhibitors of economic activity — climate, vast spaces, mountains, government administered reserves of forest and wilderness areas — have become major stimulants of the new kind of economy."[2]

The tourist industry has been the most obvious means for exploiting Colorado's resources of climate and location. The Denver Chamber of Commerce, the state Economic Development Council, and other promotional agencies helped to make tourism the third-ranking industry through most of the 1950s and 1960s. Different indicators give different results, but by a rough estimate, the number of tourists doubled and their expenditures in the state tripled from 1948 to 1960, with slower growth in the next decade. The Front Range counties felt the greatest benefits, for most tourists have been midwesterners or southerners who have entered the state across the eastern border and headed for Denver, Estes Park, and Pikes Peak.

With more difficult access and fewer famous attractions, Western Slope counties depended initially on the established industries of camping, hunting, and fishing. They also grew with the ski boom of the 1960s and 1970s. A map of the Colorado mineral belt, which stretches diagonally from Central City to Telluride, looks remarkably like the ski belt of the 1970s, with Steamboat Springs the only major ski center outside the old mining heartland. By 1980 the new resort complex of Vail made Eagle County the third-ranking recipient of tourist dollars after Denver and El Paso counties. Fourth place went to Pitkin County, where the old mining town of Aspen was recycled with a boost from Chicago industrialist Walter Paepcke, who established the Aspen Institute for Humanistic Studies in 1949 and assembled an all-star cast for a Goethe Bicentennial Convocation and Music Festival in the same year. Development of ski areas in the 1950s and regular summer music festivals made the old town a year-round resort. The condominium boom of the 1960s and the opening of new ski areas such as Snowmass completed Aspen's transformation into a recreational annex of California, Illinois, and New York.

Postwar Colorado also attracted "footloose" industries, firms whose inputs and outputs carry a high enough value relative to weight that transportation costs are not a major factor of production. Because their managers need not worry about sites close to markets or raw materials, they can choose locations appealing to their workers. The most spectacular example for Colorado was the decision of the Martin Marietta Aerospace Corporation in 1956 to build a plant for Titan missiles in Littleton, a suburb of Denver, in part because the location would ease the job of recruiting highly trained scientific and engineering personnel. IBM, Honeywell, Sunstrand, Ball Brothers Research, and Beech Aircraft were some of the other high-technology firms attracted by life near the mountains.

From defense industries and science-oriented corporations it is a short step to the research divisions of the Universities of Colorado and Denver and to federal research agencies — the National Bureau of Standards, the National Oceanic and Atmospheric Administration, and the National Center for Atmospheric Research. By 1963 the Denver-Boulder area ranked tenth among metropolitan areas in federal research and development funds. The metropolitan area ranked third to Washington and San Jose in the percentage of adult residents with college degrees, and some of Colorado's business and political leaders dreamed that an expanded technical complex along the Front Range might soon rival those of Massachusetts and the San Francisco Bay area.

The expansion of the high-technology sector of the Colorado economy continued in the late 1960s and the 1970s. Johns-Manville Corporation constructed a huge world headquarters against the foothills southwest of Denver because of the state's superior air service, telecommunications, universities, and scientific industries. In a heated competition, Golden gained the new federal Solar Energy Research Institute. Kodak and Hewlett-Packard located large plants in the Loveland–Greeley–Fort Collins triangle and helped to spread the Denver metropolitan boom to Larimer and Weld counties. The arrival of Hewlett-Packard and Ampex in Colorado Springs in the late 1960s helped to extend the high-tech center around Denver-Boulder into a Silicon Mountain corridor along the Front Range.

After World War II, the Denver Ordnance Plant became the Denver Federal Center, home to the host of federal agencies shown in this photo from the 1950s.

The social effects of the growing industrial-scientific-educational complex were as striking as the economic effects, for the new industries furthered the dispersal of metropolitan Denver. Few of the establishments located in the old industrial core along the Platte River within Denver city limits. Some settled in suburbs to the south and north, others in nearby cities such as Boulder, Longmont, Loveland, or Colorado Springs. Affluent Denverites have followed the high-paying jobs into the new communities that arc three-quarters of the way around the city. During the 1950s the median income in the suburban counties surpassed that in the central city for the first time. The gap widened in the 1960s, as Denver increasingly became an island of old people, poor people, and minority group members surrounded by a sea of middle-class white families who found that suburban living allowed the greatest enjoyment of Colorado's space and climate. The total population of the suburbs grew by two and a half times between 1950 and 1970, whereas that of the city of Denver itself increased by only 26 percent.

Warm air and Cold War together keyed much of the postwar growth in the Front Range metropolis. Both its central location

The National Center for Atmospheric Research, one of several federal research agencies located in Boulder near the University of Colorado, typifies the growth of Colorado's high-tech sector.

and its distance from other major cities simultaneously helped Denver dominate the Rocky Mountain Empire staked out seventy-five years before. The heart of its economic territory is Colorado, along with most of Wyoming and the edges of Kansas and Nebraska — areas served by its large trucking, warehousing, and wholesaling industries. The metropolitan area has substantially more wholesaling employment than would be expected in a city of its size. The convenience of Denver's location within the mountain West, its focal position for air transportation, and its attractiveness to college graduates also have made the city a favored site for corporate branch offices. Denver's role as the largest commercial banking center between Kansas City and the Pacific aids it as both a distributing and an administrative center and extends its influence into parts of New Mexico, Utah, and South Dakota. Equally, Denver became a secondary capital for the national government, housing state or regional offices for approximately 150 federal agencies with a civilian employment of thirty-five thousand workers in 1980.

Colorado Springs became the chief outpost for the Department of Defense in Colorado. Fort Carson, the North American Air Defense Command (NORAD) headquarters commanding North American air defenses, and the Air Force Academy, which opened in 1958, brought thousands of civilian jobs and tens of thousands of military personnel. The Air Force Academy in particular symbolized the connection between the state's defense economy and its growing research and education sectors. Military retirees were also an increasingly prominent component of the Colorado Springs and state populations. For the period 1952–1962, economist Roger Bolton has estimated that more than 20 percent of income in Colorado resulted from defense spending, making it one of the eight states most heavily dependent on the defense budget.

The expansion of metropolitan functions in the 1950s triggered a building boom that kept Denver's central business district one of the more vital in the nation. Early in the decade, out-of-state investors discovered the lucrative possibilities inherent in Denver real estate. Clint Murchison of Dallas built the Denver Club and First National Bank buildings, and William Zeckendorf constructed the Mile-Hi Center office tower, the Denver Hilton, and a department store for the merged May Company–Daniels and Fisher (May D&F). Local banks and utilities followed with more new buildings, which pushed the focus of the financial and shopping districts "up the hill" toward the capitol. A massive urban renewal program attempted to revitalize the older parts of downtown. The Skyline Project, approved in a referendum in 1967 by a 5 to 2 margin, covered thirty-seven blocks along Larimer, Lawrence, Arapahoe, and Curtis streets between Speer Boulevard and 20th Street. The Auraria Project approved two years later cleared twenty-two additional blocks west of Cherry Creek for the Auraria Educational Complex housing Denver Community College, Metropolitan State College, and the University of Colorado campus at Denver. The project aroused

Demolition of Interstate Trust Building in the 1970s, part of the rebuilding of downtown Denver.

greater debate because it required the dislocation of Chicano residents and the demolition of old houses. Despite erosion of African-American and Chicano support, however, two out of three voters approved the project.

The rebuilding of the downtown in the 1950s and 1960s was one of the tangible results of a small political revolution in Denver. Ambitious young businesspeople and lawyers eager to take advantage of new economic opportunities after World War II found the city still under the control of Mayor Ben Stapleton. As he had for more than twenty years, "interminable Ben" ruled in the interest of bankers and utility companies, which were indifferent to change. If the city's notoriously bumpy streets and illegible street signs failed to tell newcomers they were not welcome, Mayor Stapleton could be more direct. "If all those people would only go back where they came from," he responded in answer to postwar complaints, "we wouldn't have a housing shortage."[3] His attitude mirrored that of the conservative business community, which had turned a cold shoulder to ambitious postwar plans by Henry Kaiser.

The drive for a new politics came in 1947. One of the leaders was Palmer Hoyt, the new editor of the *Denver Post*. The other was James Quigg Newton, a thirty-five-year-old native returned after years at Yale and in Washington and the navy. In a city starved for leadership and fearful of losing out in the national boom, Newton ran an energetic campaign for mayor on the issue of inefficiency and won the office with the highest plurality in Denver's history.

In his eight years in office Newton ran the sort of business-like government that turn-of-the-century progressives had dreamed about. With the help of a "Michigan Mafia" of young professional administrators, he implemented competitive purchasing and civil service, pushed through a sales tax, and reorganized city health services and Denver General Hospital. Although Newton reached to broaden his coalition by appointing George Cavender of the Colorado Education Association to a City Council vacancy, his sympathies clearly lay with the very successful growth of Denver as a white-collar metropolis. The two mayors who followed Newton were the heirs of the same reform ideology. Will Nicholson was a real estate man who had been Newton's chief lieutenant on the Republican side. Richard Batterton, deputy mayor and manager of public works, carried on business-oriented government with an easy victory in 1959.

Denver's mayors in the 1960s carried on the alliance of professional administrators and downtown businesspeople. Tom Currigan followed Batterton and was succeeded in turn by Bill McNichols, a nominal Democrat with bipartisan support. For a generation city government in Denver has meant modern management and a receptive climate for growth. Renewal of the city's downtown, for example, was initiated as a private enterprise by outside investors but was taken up in the late 1950s by local businesspeople through the Downtown Denver Improvement Association. In 1962 the City Council created a Downtown Denver Master Plan Committee with both public and private members to develop a basic urban renewal plan and sell it to the electorate. A short walk through downtown Denver will show that the unified action of important business interests through these organizations and through the Chamber of Commerce had more effect on the shape of the city than the well-publicized hostility between its "old" and "new" money factions could have had.

Denver's postwar politics was in many ways a miniature of Colorado's. Despite a strong Democratic edge in registration, city voters turned repeatedly to business-oriented Republicans. Statewide, voters showed the same willingness to switch from one party to the other. Political organizations have been little more than personal followings, and, except in working-class Pueblo, regular partisanship has been considered the refuge of a lazy citizen. Colorado's white-collar voters have preferred to choose politicians in their own image. Either Democrat or Republican, the typical state legislator of the 1950s and 1960s was a white, Protestant male in his forties, college-educated as a businessman or lawyer, a newcomer to politics, and a town or city dweller. The only sure Republican areas were the rich farmlands of the Platte Valley; the only Democratic strongholds were Pueblo, Adams County, and the Hispanic south. Party balance was evidenced by the split in the eighty-eight contests for governor, senator, and member of congress held from 1940 through 1970, of which forty-six went to Republicans and forty-two to Democrats.

The leaders within both parties were advocates of growth. In a manner reminiscent of the 1870s and 1880s, agreement on the basic mission of state government meant that the elections from 1945 to 1970 turned on personalities as much as issues. The choice for governor in 1946 was Democrat Lee Knous, who excited Coloradans with his promise to maintain the economic momentum of the war years. In 1950 and 1952 the choice was Gunnison cattleman Dan Thornton, who won the state with the colorful campaign style of a former Texan. In 1954 it was Big Ed Johnson, who had tired of the United States Senate after three terms and, thus, recaptured the statehouse he had dominated in the 1930s. Johnson combined efforts with Will Nicholson to gain the addition of a Denver–Salt Lake City link to the Interstate Highway System, with the intention of assisting Denver commerce and Western Slope tourism.

When liberal Democrat John Carroll defeated Thornton for the senate in 1956 and Steve McNichols won the governorship, some political observers thought they were witnessing the start of a Democratic trend. McNichols had a head start on the job because Johnson's health problems had McNichols acting as governor for much of the previous two years. McNichols tried to reinvigorate state government in somewhat the same way Newton revitalized Denver. He later recalled that in the early 1950s, "the state was languishing. It was institutionally dead, public buildings were deteriorating, and nobody cared much about it." Rural interests dominated the legislature, and "unless there was a cow's head on it, it was hard to get a bill through."[4] McNichols's accomplishments included more funding for education, quick participation in the Interstate Highway program, and reorganization of state agencies.

In 1958 Republicans fought back by pushing a state right-to-work law but managed only to cement a statewide alliance between the AFL-CIO and the Farmers Union. A heavy voter turnout defeated the right-to-work initiative by a margin of 3 to 2, helped to re-elect McNichols to the state's first four-year gubernatorial term, and consolidated Democratic control of the general assembly. Four years later, however, Republicans duplicated the Democratic sweep, overthrowing Democratic incumbents with a ticket led by Peter Dominick and John Love. Love in particular was perfectly suited to the state's new immigrants: a political amateur who called himself a pragmatic moderate and who vowed to cut state spending. It was as much a recognition of the political temper of Colorado as an assessment of the new governor when the editor of *Cervi's Rocky Mountain Journal* called Love "the greatest suburb of all."[5]

The fine line between beneficial and damaging growth was most apparent on the Western Slope. The most lasting legacy of the uranium boom for Grand Junction was the radioactive mill tailings the Atomic Energy Commission allowed to be used in house and school foundations. The renewed interest of energy corporations in the coal and oil shale deposits of the northwest counties in the 1970s seemed to some to promise all of the benefits of another boom to towns such as Craig and Rifle — more jobs, higher wages, and new investment. Other residents anticipated the costs of prosperity — the devastation of the landscape, the disruption of ranching and tourism, the rapid growth of population, and the imposition of demands for new roads, schools, and other community services on underfinanced local governments. In either case there was growing determination that local residents should share substantially in planning and decision-making and that fairly apportioned state revenues from oil shale development be used for local needs.

A ski boom as much as a mineral boom could bring the worst features of a colonial economy to Western Slope communities. Speculation became a business of its own in many sectors of the state during the 1960s. It put money in the pockets of real estate investors and made paper fortunes for outsiders. It also priced real estate beyond the reach of most residents, locked up agricultural land, and fragmented holdings to an extent that makes orderly development impossible. As the profits from an Aspen or a Steamboat Springs went to the large developers, county and municipal governments faced staggering bills for the new services required by the exploding populations. Frequently, the influx of cocktail waitresses and ski lift operators lowered the per capita income and created miniature slums. The charm of old mountain towns was easily ruined by overcrowded dormitories, roads bulldozed through spruce forests, and strip development of condominiums and motels. In Aspen the number of skiers grew by 50 percent a year from 1967 to 1973. By the early 1970s Aspen's permanent residents had elected county commissioners pledged to preventing the narrow Roaring Fork Valley from becoming a huge smog trap. Other communities such as Steamboat Springs saw a developing alliance of established ranchers and young environmentalists against the inroads of "Texans," Colorado shorthand for aliens with money. In newer resorts yet — Telluride in the southwest San Juans — old-timers watched land prices and tax assessments quadruple and tried to decide whether the town, filling with hippies and California entrepreneurs, was really where they wanted — or could afford — to stay.

Western Slope Colorado worried about losing its water as much as its land. More than 90 percent of the population and 63 percent of the state's surface area is east of the Continental Divide, but 69 percent of its water flows to the west. By the early 1970s there was little margin not already appropriated for farming, ranching, mineral processing, recreation, or cities. Two decades previously, Denver had fought a long court battle against Western Slope interests before building the Dillon Reservoir and the Roberts Tunnel to divert Blue River water into Denver water mains. The issue surfaced again in 1973, when the Denver Water Board proposed new water processing and storage facilities requiring the flooding of a wilderness valley in the Gore Range above Vail. Voters rejected a $160 million bond issue in June and approved it only after a massive campaign in the fall. Opposition came from both environmentalists and the western counties. Each group argued that to increase Denver's water supply would guarantee the further concentration of population and political power in the overly large metropolitan area. Given the necessity to allocate a limited quantity of water among valid and competing uses, proposals for diversion from one watershed to another raised a basic question about Colorado's future — "the extent that the Denver area, and the whole state for that matter, can stop, or curtail, or at least redistribute its growth."[6]

Suburbanites were no more trusting of Denver than were Routt County ranchers. Sprawling growth in the postwar generation incited fears as far away as Loveland and Fort Collins, where residents envisioned a Denver grown as large as Los Angeles. Nearby suburbanites have often seen the city as both arrogant and aggressive. Severe drought in the early 1950s brought the independent Denver Water Board into open conflict with the growing ring of suburbs. On August 23, 1951, the board agreed to assure Denver's supplies by allowing no new water hookups beyond a "blue line" penciled on a map in its downtown Denver headquarters. By the height of the drought in 1954 and 1955, when the entire metropolitan area faced a serious crisis and suffered through stringent water rationing, the board's caution worked to the detriment of surrounding communities, which faced a fee of $2,000 per acre to cover the cost of all city services if they desired annexation to Denver. Out of necessity, suburban towns such as Englewood, Littleton, and Westminster expanded or created separate water systems. Aurora turned to Colorado Springs to develop a joint water diversion at a cost of over $50 million.

Annexation was another source of hostility. The start of an active annexation drive by Denver in the late 1960s incited fears that suburbia was about to be conscripted into the war over inner-city problems. The incorporation of Lakewood and Wheat Ridge was a direct response in Jefferson County, and Aurora competed with its own growth campaign. The final outcome of the conflict was the adoption in 1974 of two state constitutional amendments that made annexation of new territory by Denver virtually impossible.

Mutual suspicions as heavy as traffic on the Valley Highway crippled attempts at intergovernmental cooperation throughout the mid-1960s. The Inter-County Regional Planning Commission was organized in 1955 but could do little to coordinate actions by the variety of independent governments. Indeed, the ease of creating special districts in Colorado meant that by 1969 the metropolitan area counted 215 such districts for handling water, sanitation, and fire protection, in addition to 22 school

Downtown Denver in the early 1980s showing the 16th Street Mall under construction.

districts and 44 municipalities. Proposals to create an "Urban County," an area government providing six basic services, failed to pass in the legislature in 1965, 1966, and 1967 because of the opposition of the Republican party in Arapahoe and Jefferson counties. Opponents argued that Denver's complaints about an inadequate tax base were a ploy to extend its political control.

The record on metropolitan government continued to be mixed in the 1970s. The Denver Regional Council of Governments (DRCOG, the successor to the Inter-County Regional Planning Commission) gained the cooperation of suburban offi-cials in need of technical aid for their increasingly complex ad-ministrations. The DRCOG has allowed the development and acceptance of metropolitan plans for transportation and parks and the distribution of low-income housing among member cit-ies. Voters also indicated a willingness to assume new responsi-bilities in 1973, when they authorized creation of a Regional Transportation Authority and the expenditure of $1.56 billion on mass transit. They sent a contradictory signal in the same elec-tion by rejecting an Urban Service Authority for the metropoli-tan area. When the idea was revived in 1977, the indifference of

Metropolitan expansion after World War II. Tract houses near I-25 north of Denver.

suburban politicians had hardened into firm opposition. In November 1980 voters in the five-county area rejected a ballot measure that would have implemented the idea through a multiservice Metropolitan Council.

In its pattern of growth and its political values, the history of postwar Colorado has been part of the emergence of a new American region. In the past, Colorado followed patterns common to the Great Plains and the Rocky Mountain West. By 1970, however, it was more useful to look at the state as part of the new Sunbelt. From Florida to California, twentieth-century Americans have molded a new region to their liking. The horizontal "automobile cities" of Denver and Colorado Springs have their counterparts in Los Angeles and San Diego, Phoenix and Albuquerque, Dallas and Houston, Atlanta and Orlando. The growth of each has depended on climate, scenery, and location. Industries in search of cheap land for one-floor plants and residents in search of suburban landscapes have built thirty-mile and fifty-mile complexes with little resemblance to cities in Massachusetts and Michigan. Convenience to shopping centers, access to freeway interchanges, and proximity to lakes and parklands have been the factors shaping the new environment in an entire region given over to the lifestyle of white-collar America. In the process of growth during the postwar decades, old and new Coloradans transformed their state from a quiet backwater to a U.S. trendsetter.

# CHAPTER 15

# PLURAL SOCIETY IN MIDCENTURY

On May 20, 1969, more than 108,000 Denverites turned out to vote on candidates for two positions on the Denver School Board. The issue that brought out more than half of the registered voters in the city was the plan for racial integration the board had adopted by a margin of 5 to 2 in March. The proposal had called for busing 3,000 African-American students from inner-city elementary and junior high schools to the predominantly white schools in southwest Denver. Incumbent Ed Benton and newcomer Monte Pascoe, both backers of the plan, together spent an unprecedented $35,000 on their campaigns. Challengers Frank Southworth and James Perrill spent more than $90,000 in their effort to save the status quo. Nearly every organization in Denver had taken a position during the campaign, and local television stations had aired pre-election specials in prime time. When the votes were counted, Perrill and Southworth had a victory margin of 2.5 to 1 over Benton and Pascoe. Precincts with substantial African-American populations gave the pro-busing candidates their only majorities.

The 1969 election was not the end of a controversy but, rather, the beginning. The cancellation of the busing program by the new anti-busing majority on the board was met with a suit in U.S. District Court asking that the program be reinstated. Trial of the suit in 1970 before Judge William Doyle revealed impressive evidence that during previous decades the Denver School Board had systematically segregated both students and teachers by race, but three more years of litigation passed before the U.S. Supreme Court declared, on June 21, 1973, that Denver had "the affirmative duty" fully to desegregate its schools. The actual plan, as determined by Judge Doyle after weeks of expert testimony, went into effect in September 1974, with the anti-busing school board elements still outraged. The program involved shifting several thousand children by redrawing school district boundaries and busing some eighteen thousand additional schoolchildren for either full or half days to achieve citywide school integration.

In the six years of bitter debate that saw the bombing of school buses and homes, as well as legal arguments, the integration of Denver's schools remained an issue of deep emotion. Denver Republicans in particular used the cry of "forced busing" in their efforts to build up a base of support in the heavily Democratic city. In 1970 Republican District Attorney James McKevitt came from behind to defeat Craig Barnes for a seat in the U.S. House of Representatives, using Barnes's ties to the pro-busing forces as his main campaign contention. In 1971 Democratic Mayor Bill McNichols beat Dale Tooley in a runoff election with the aid of Republican voters and the integration issue. Three years later school board member Frank Southworth challenged incumbent Congresswoman Pat Schroeder on the same grounds, implementing his campaign during the first months of the integration experiment. Although peaceful implementation quieted the issue and allowed Schroeder to win with 58 percent of the votes cast, Denver newspapers noted a clear trend of white migration to the suburbs.

If nothing else, the judicial briefs and political slogans helped to define the tensions among Colorado's major ethnic groups. After 1969 three positions emerged. One might be called "white isolationism." Its strength measured by the 69 percent approval in November 1974 of a state anti-busing resolution, it represented the majority viewpoint of Anglo-Coloradans who wished racial problems would stop bothering them. For Colorado isolationists, African-Americans and Hispanos threatened both to destroy their distance from the problems facing the rest of the nation and to turn Denver into "one big city like Detroit or Newark."[1] "Separate but equal" in relation to residence, jobs, or schools was, for them, a philosophy of great appeal, sanctioned by successful practice over long decades. At the other extreme were the "integrationists," the African-Americans and liberal whites who raised the school question and who have seen the assimilation of racial minorities as a goal both practicable and desirable. The third group, which stood to the side, consists of "Hispanic separatists." In 1969 few Chicanos in Denver voted for busing, and survey interviews showed the large majority of Spanish-speaking residents saw no positive benefit from it. In fact, many Hispanic leaders saw school integration as a form of cultural assault, forced assimilation that is breaking up the development of their growing community power based on self-awareness and independence.

Fifty years earlier, examination of Colorado schools provided an equally good index to the pattern of racial relations. In the school year 1925–1926, 60 percent of the 789 African-American children enrolled in Denver's elementary schools attended either Gilpin or Whittier. When Mitchell, Ebert, and 24th Street schools were added, their combined African-American enrollment accounted for 80 percent of the total. Cole Junior High enrolled 85 percent of the African-American students at that level, and Manual had 75 percent of the African-Americans in senior high. Spanish-speaking children in the same year were also segregated, with 80 percent of 1,004 pupils attending five elementary schools. On the high school level the statistics show an additional limitation on the educational status of Spanish-speaking children: only seven were enrolled in junior high and just two in daytime high school. In the 1920s Pueblo had a similar dropout rate, with Spanish-speaking students constituting 12 percent of lower school enrollment and only 3 percent of senior high students.

In the 1920s three-fifths of the state's twelve thousand African-Americans lived in Denver, and most of the remainder lived in Pueblo and Colorado Springs. The majority of the Spanish-speaking residents, however, lived in the traditionally Hispanic counties of the south or in the agricultural zone of the piedmont, where recent immigration of farmworkers from Mexico had introduced a new element into the population. Here, along the Platte and the Arkansas, Anglo residents used their schools to define the relationship between ethnic groups. Few were as outspoken as the county school superintendent who believed "the respectable people of Weld County do not want their children to sit along side of dirty, filthy, diseased, infested Mexicans."[2] More subtle pressures from Anglo pupils who enjoyed taunting the "greasers" and from teachers who assumed Mexican children had no capacity for learning, however, made the local schools unattractive. When Mexican parents took their children as young as age eight or ten to work with them in the fields, few authorities worried about the violation of school attendance laws.

It had taken only a decade for rural Colorado to fix the position of Mexican-Americans. The Colorado Fuel and Iron Corporation had brought in the state's first Mexican immigrants to work in its steel mills soon after the turn of the century, thereby raising Pueblo's Mexican-born population from twenty-eight in 1900 to twenty-five hundred by 1920. Simultaneously, the sugar beet companies sent agents into the Spanish-American settlements along the Rio Grande to satisfy their need for laborers to do the stoop labor of bunching, thinning, hoeing, and harvesting. By 1909 twenty-six hundred Hispanics accounted for a quarter of the state's beet workers.

Around 1916 the Great Western Sugar Company, the Holly Sugar Company, and the American Sugar Beet Company began to reach farther south to replace German-Russian workers with workers recently arrived from Mexico. For the next decade Great Western and other firms maintained offices in San Antonio, Fort Worth, and especially El Paso to recruit Mexican immigrants for work in the beet fields. By the 1910s they were targeting families rather than single men as they searched for a stable labor force. A company such as Great Western spent as much as $360,000 in a single year on offices, public meetings, handbills, and train fares.

In the recruitment process the large companies acted as agents for individual farmers who had contracted to supply them with beets. The company supplied the workers needed by each grower, who in turn agreed to provide habitable houses and good water and to pay the going wage per acre for beets. In practical terms, individual laborers were at the mercy of each farmer's sense of fair play when it came to figuring the acreage worked or to interpreting what was "habitable." Although daily wages were reasonably high, migrants worked only forty-five to ninety days over the course of a five-month or six-month season. During the summer they might fill in their time with work on other crops, and in the winter they might work in the coal mines or on railroad section gangs. Even so, the average family in the boom years of 1920–1923 earned little more than $1,000 annually. With dropping wage rates and depression, the yearly average family income fell to probably half that in the mid-1930s.

The number of workers brought in from the south each year varied with the size of the crop, ranging from two thousand to fifteen thousand between 1915 and 1930. Because of the high costs of recruitment and the value of experienced workers, the sugar companies in the 1920s encouraged Mexicans to settle permanently in Colorado. Agents talked up the advantages of permanent residence, encouraged local farmers to provide year-round

The sugar beet harvest near Rocky Ford in the late 1920s.

work, and offered credit for groceries during the winter. In the Arkansas Valley the Holly and American Companies built rent-free labor colonies that offered two rooms per family, and Great Western provided land and materials for workers to build their own houses. The Great Western colonies increasingly resembled the villages of New Mexico and southern Colorado, with dances, fiestas, and intense interaction among kinship and community networks. By 1927 Spanish-speaking workers constituted 60 percent of the labor in the beet fields. In the South Platte Valley the permanent Mexican population had increased from three thousand to eleven thousand since 1920. Several thousand more spent the winters in Denver and other piedmont cities and worked the crops in summer. By the 1930 census, Colorado counted thirteen thousand residents born in Mexico and twenty-eight thousand from New Mexico, most of whom were Hispanos; twenty years before, comparable figures had been twenty-five hundred and twelve thousand, respectively.

At best, small-town Coloradans regarded Mexican immigrants as a "necessary evil." One Platte Valley resident put it simply:

"We wish the Mexicans were not there."[3] The neutral opinion in 1910 gave way to virulent prejudice by the early 1920s. Restaurants, movie theaters, and other public places excluded or segregated Mexican customers, and newspapers and police officials felt they were natural criminals. Mexican-American smelter workers in Durango faced similar discrimination in jobs and housing, living south of Sixth Street and across the Animas River in "Chihuahua" and "Mexican Flats." When asked, Anglos usually agreed that Spanish-Americans whose ancestors had lived in Colorado for several generations were superior to Mexican newcomers in intelligence and character. In practice, however, most did not distinguish between the two groups. Despite their efforts to preserve a distinct identity, Hispano Coloradans found their status reduced in Anglo eyes.

The Depression of the 1930s interrupted the evolution of Anglo-Hispanic relations. The heavy immigration of the 1920s ceased, and the number of Mexican-born Coloradans dropped by half during the decade. If lack of jobs was not discouragement enough, public officials harassed Spanish-speaking workers who entered the state in search of work. In April 1936 Governor Ed Johnson declared a state of martial law on the southern border and ordered the Colorado National Guard to refuse entry to any indigent Mexicans seeking to take jobs away from U.S. voters. Although Johnson withdrew his order within days, he carried the same attitude into other incidents as well, encouraging local authorities to detain and deport any Spanish-speaking persons they wished. Other farmworkers drifted into cities as the Depression wore on. The permanent "Mexican" population of Denver climbed from two thousand or three thousand in the early 1920s to more than six thousand by 1930 and twelve thousand by 1940.

Population totals from the census mask the reality of the vital Hispanic neighborhoods that developed in Denver in the 1920s and 1930s. An example was the old Auraria neighborhood across Cherry Creek from downtown Denver. Spanish-speaking newcomers began to replace the area's German residents in the 1920s. St. Cajetan's Church and School served the growing Hispanic community after 1926. Residents looked out for their own interests through self-help aid organizations such as the Sociedad Mutualista Mexico and the Sociedad Protectora Hispana Americana. Fifty years later Lupe Ramos fondly recalled that "the neighborhood was like one big family and everyone got along real good. Once people moved into the neighborhood, they usually stayed. The biggest event of the year was the celebration of Mexican Independence Day. . . . The other big event of the year was the bazaars at St. Cajetan's."[4]

Mexicans in Denver found they had to compete with another racial minority already established within the fabric of the city. Most whites in the 1920s and 1930s viewed the African-American community as a sort of enclave, an entity apart from the rest of the city free to operate as it wished within firm limits. African-American workers, for example, found jobs in a list of trades traditionally reserved for them — janitor, railroad porter, waiter and restaurant keeper, unskilled laborer, servant. Three-quarters of the African-American population lived in Five Points, east of the central business district, where two thousand families crowded into two of the city's forty-four census tracts. Despite civil rights legislation on the statute books, private businesspeople and public officials excluded African-Americans from facilities considered to be outside their neighborhood or beyond their social status. Neither the Brown Palace nor the Cosmopolitan hotels, for example, would accommodate them. The Denver Parks Department forbade them the use of either the Washington Park or Berkeley Park swimming pools, allowing them instead to swim on Wednesdays at the downtown pool on Curtis Street.

Colorado whites, in short, set the boundaries for African-American life. Where they could live, play, find a job, and go to school were all predetermined. Vertical mobility within those limits, however, was acceptable. A few could buy property in Five Points and rent to other African-Americans, build businesses serving the African-American community, and organize and deliver the African-American vote. For many more the limitations meant a life lived just above the level of poverty and centered on community institutions.

At the same time, the established position of African-Americans gave them an edge over the Mexicans struggling to survive in a depressed city. Whereas the average family income for African-Americans in 1940 was only 62 percent that of whites, the average income of Spanish-speaking families was less than half that of whites. Forty-one percent of white families and 34 percent of African-American families owned their own homes, but only 11 percent of Spanish-speaking families had the income to purchase a home. Even more startling were the figures on infant mortality — 65 deaths per 1,000 live births for African-Americans, 71 for Anglos, and 205 for Mexicans.

If the move from rural to urban Colorado failed to improve the income of Mexican families, it did force their problems to the attention of public officials. In the agricultural valleys they had lived literally out of sight — in shacks on individual farms or in colonies carefully separated from Anglo towns by a railroad track or a half mile of dry fields. Residential segregation in Denver was less complete. Mexicans in the 1940s spread in substantial numbers through seven census tracts northeast and southwest of the downtown area. Eighty years previously the concentration of Irish and German immigrants in New York, Boston, and Philadelphia had made the residents of the eastern states aware of poverty as a social problem. In the era of World War II, Denver showed the same response. The large numbers of Mexican-Americans and their strangeness as a group, together with the desire to assure a united home front in the battle against the Axis, triggered the "discovery" of poverty by Anglo Coloradans.

One result was a series of official gestures in the direction of racial harmony. During the war years the federal coordinator of Inter-American Affairs sponsored several conferences on Spanish-speaking Coloradans. In 1947 Mayor Quigg Newton followed the lead of other cities by appointing a Committee on Human Relations. At the same time, social action agencies flooded the concerned citizen with reports on the status of Denver's African-American and Hispanic minorities. Whether it was the Works Projects Administration's presentation of its findings on *Housing in Denver* (1941), the Denver Unity Council's analysis of *The Spanish-Speaking Population of Denver* (1946), the Mayor's Study Committee on Human Relations's *Report of Minorities in Denver* (1947), or the Denver Area Welfare Council's report on *The Spanish-American Population of Denver* (1950), the findings were consistent on two points. Through the 1940s discrimination against African-Americans and Spanish-Americans was part of the operating system in every area studied — health care, recreation, schooling, law enforcement, housing, employment. Denver's African-Americans fared significantly better than Spanish-speaking residents by all statistical indicators. In the immediate postwar years, for example, twice as many Mexicans as African-Americans lived in substandard housing, and

## TABLE 15.1   POPULATION DISTRIBUTION

| | Total | White | African-American | Asian, Native American, Pacific Islander | Other * | Hispanic † |
|---|---|---|---|---|---|---|
| **Colorado** | | | | | | |
| 1950 population | 1,325,089 | 1,296,663 | 20,177 | 8,259 | — | 118,715 |
| % of state total | | (97.9) | (1.5) | (0.6) | | (9.0) |
| 1960 population | 1,753,947 | 1,700,700 | 39,992 | 13,255 | — | 157,173 |
| % of state total | | (97.0) | (2.3) | (0.8) | | (9.0) |
| 1970 population | 2,207,259 | 2,112,352 | 66,411 | 28,496 | — | 286,407 |
| % of state total | | (95.7) | (3.0) | (1.3) | | (13.0) |
| 1980 population | 2,889,964 | 2,591,270 | 101,695 | 55,272 | 141,727 | 341,435 |
| % of state total | | (89.7) | (3.5) | (1.9) | (4.9) | (11.8) |
| 1990 population | 3,294,394 | 2,909,438 | 131,223 | 87,955 | 165,778 | 419,322 |
| % of state total | | (88.3) | (4.0) | (2.7) | (5.0) | (12.7) |
| **Denver** | | | | | | |
| 1950 population | 415,786 | 397,534 | 15,059 | 3,193 | — | 24,950 |
| % of city total | | (95.6) | (3.6) | (0.8) | | (6.0) |
| 1960 population | 493,887 | 458,626 | 30,251 | 5,010 | — | 43,147 |
| % of city total | | (92.9) | (6.1) | (1.0) | | (8.7) |
| 1970 population | 514,678 | 458,187 | 47,011 | 9,480 | — | 86,345 |
| % of city total | | (89.0) | (9.1) | (1.8) | | (16.8) |
| 1980 population | 492,365 | 375,628 | 59,095 | 13,252 | 44,390 | 92,257 |
| % of city total | | (76.3) | (12.0) | (2.7) | (9.0) | (18.7) |
| 1990 population | 467,610 | 337,623 | 60,319 | 16,077 | 53,591 | 106,554 |
| % of city total | | (72.2) | (12.9) | (3.4) | (11.5) | (22.8) |

*Other: race not otherwise classified.
†Hispanic: Spanish surname population for 1950 and 1960; Spanish language or Spanish surname population for 1970; Spanish origin population for 1980; Hispanic origin population for 1990. Hispanic population can be of any race.
Source: Data from U.S. Bureau of the Census, decennial censuses of population.

the per capita income for Spanish-speaking Denverites was only half that of African-Americans.

Since 1950 patterns of population and economic position can be traced most easily by a kind of social archaeology. Like the relics found in each stratum of a dig, the data in each decennial census allow an examination of the status of African-Americans, Anglos, and Spanish-surnamed Coloradans at intervals in the past. The most obvious changes, as shown in Table 15.1, are the accelerating growth rates of minority populations and their increasing shares of the state total population. A simultaneous trend has been the rapid shift of Spanish-surnamed residents to urban places, especially to Denver.

Broad population patterns conceal differences in the social evolution of the minority communities. The major theme of the recent history of Colorado African-Americans is progress toward middle-class status, which dates from World War II. To protect their contracts, many local war industries set quotas for African-American employment, which opened skilled factory jobs for the first time. Government offices and military facilities that were established in the 1940s have also continued to employ African-Americans at a rate higher than their share of the state's population. New jobs meant that the average income for African-American families rose from three-fifths of the Anglo level in 1940 to three-quarters of that level in 1960. Educational gains were another result. In the state as a whole, the median years of school completed by African-American adults climbed from 9.8 to 12.2 between 1950 and 1970, whereas the median for whites only rose from 10.9 to 12.4.

What economic gains did not equate to was social integration. Whether as police officers cruising Colfax Avenue or householders watering their lawns in southeast Denver, white Coloradans still set the limits within which African-Americans enjoyed their relative success. Perhaps the best example was the changing residential patterns in Denver, where African-Americans in the late 1950s and early 1960s overflowed the Five Points neighborhood and moved into newer and better housing to the east. Churches, neighborhood groups, and white liberals in the Park Hill region east of Colorado Boulevard organized the Park Hill Action Committee in an attempt to further the growth of a stable interracial community. Despite its efforts, African-American housing demand and white fears combined to reduce the white share of housing in North Park Hill (north of 26th Street) from 97 percent in 1960 to 27 percent in 1970.

Expansion of the African-American middle class left Spanish-speaking residents as the central city minority in Denver, geographically and economically occupying the position held by African-Americans in many other cities. In 1967 the Office of Economic Opportunity analyzed Denver's "urban poverty area." In twenty-eight census tracts along both sides of the Platte River in the northern half of the city, a fifth of Denver's population accounted for two-thirds of its public welfare, public health, and criminal court costs and for most of its families below the poverty level. Although the incidence of poverty and unemployment in the area was almost equal among African-Americans and Hispanics, there were twice as many members of the latter group. Indeed, only 37 percent of the city's African-Americans, but 72 percent of its Hispanics, lived within this poverty area, as new Hispanic residents filled the houses left by upward-bound Anglos and African-Americans who had moved outward.

Emphasis on the concentration of Chicanos in the central areas of Denver should not obscure a second trend of increasing importance. In comparison with African-Americans, Mexican-Americans have been more easily assimilated into Anglo society. When they moved into white working-class neighborhoods west and north of downtown, they encountered indifference or grudging accommodation more often than flying bricks. During the 1960s they also showed a larger gain in average family income than did African-Americans. Viewed from one perspective, Mexican-Americans in urban Colorado can be seen as members of an immigrant minority slowly adjusting to a dominant culture. The process was set back for a generation by the Great Depression and has been slowed by Anglo prejudice. Its pace now, however, will be determined by Spanish-speaking Coloradans in their teens and twenties. The children and grandchildren of Mexican farmworkers who settled in Denver or of Spanish-Americans who abandoned the farms of southern Colorado to move into town, they are almost all natives of the state, and most are natives of the city in which they live. They are the equivalent of the second generation among European immigrant groups: the men and women who must bridge the gap between their ancestors' culture and their urban environment.

Considered urban immigrants, the Chicanos' problems can be analyzed in different terms from those of African-Americans. Their need is less to break long-established racial barriers than to mediate conflicts between clashing cultures. As a number of sociologists have pointed out, Spanish-speaking Americans were historically reluctant to use the social institutions and encounter the bureaucracy Anglo culture takes for granted. As one example, Spanish-surnamed Coloradans are only one-sixth as likely to file official complaints of job discrimination as are African-Americans. As with European migrants of previous generations, many prefer to take their problems to intermediaries, informal

Pueblo school teacher Jim Gutierrez with students.

community leaders who can mediate between Hispano and Anglo ways. Layered with this pattern of behavior was the persistence of Spanish as a native tongue and a lack of access to schooling. An increase of 3.4 years in the median educational level for adult males between 1950 and 1970 still left them an average of 2.5 years behind Anglos.

In the 1960s younger and more politically active Chicanos reacted to pressures from an alien and domineering culture with a search for group identity. In state universities this involved a drive for programs in Chicano studies and for special facilities for Chicano students. In Denver in March 1969, this cultural awareness led to a violent clash between police and Mexican students who were protesting insulting remarks made by a teacher at West High School. The riot preceded by a few days the Chicano Youth Liberation Conference sponsored by La Crusada Para la Justicia (the Crusade for Justice) at which fifteen hundred Mexican activists gathered in Denver to discuss the past and future of the Mexican-American people. The result was a festival of Chicano solidarity, a proclamation of the virtues of La Raza, designed to counter Anglo assumptions of racial superiority and to revive pride in themselves as an ethnic group.

The same desire to secure recognition as equals meant an emphasis on community control of governmental institutions and the development of indigenous leadership. Here, too, the Crusade for Justice has led the way in Colorado. Founded by Rodolfo (Corky) Gonzales in 1965, it asserted that "to best serve our particular ethnic and cultural group our organization must be independent, and must not be dependent on the whims and demands of private agencies which are establishment-controlled and dominated."[5] The program Gonzales presented at the Poor People's March in 1968 was representative of the activist attitude. His "Plan of the Barrio" demanded community ownership of local businesses; neighborhood school boards to control local schools, which would teach Mexican-American history and Spanish as a first language; and publicly assisted housing designed around plazas and parks in the fashion of Hispano villages "to fit the needs of the family and cultural protection." The second National Chicano Youth Conference in March 1970 adopted a similar program originated by Gonzales and called "the Spiritual Plan of Atzlan" after the supposed northern homeland of the Mexican Indians. At the same time, the Crusade for Justice organized La Raza Unida as a Chicano political party that advocated the same issues of community control. Although its candidate for governor received only 2 percent of the state vote in 1970, its existence forced the major parties into more active competition for the Hispanic vote.

The problems of cultural incompatibility, which have been highly evident and highly charged in concentrated ethnic sections of Denver, were equally present in southern Colorado. In the territory from Lamar to Cortez, Anglos held tenaciously to the dominant position they gained in the nineteenth century. Daily frictions in the small towns may be relatively minor, but Anglos keep a firm grip on local offices and businesses. In rural areas the lack of capital, expertise, and good land all handicap Spanish-speaking farmers. In the larger towns such as Trinidad and Walsenburg, continued cultural isolation and low educational levels meant that Spanish-Americans were able to contribute little to economic revitalization after World War II. As late as 1960 the result was that over half of the Spanish-surnamed families in

Rodolfo "Corky" Gonzales in 1980.

counties such as Rio Grande, Conejos, Costilla, and Huerfano
subsisted on annual incomes below the poverty level of $3,000.

Colorado's Native Americans share many of the problems of
the Spanish-Americans. Denver gained a substantial Native
American population in the 1950s and 1960s when the Bureau of
Indian Affairs urged and assisted members of the large western
tribes to leave their reservations for western cities. By 1970 the
census counted 4,104 Native Americans in the Denver area,
most of whom were migrants from out of state. Their median annual family income of $7,163 was less than that of Spanish-sur-
named Denverites, even though the average adult had
completed 11.9 years of school. Other Colorado cities accounted
for 1,300 Native Americans. Twenty years later the census
counted 14,000 Native Americans in the Denver-Boulder metropolitan area, 3,000 in Colorado Springs, and 1,000 elsewhere in
the state. With Denver's Native Americans drawn from the Navajo, Sioux, and more than a dozen other tribes, social support
and social services have been provided by several multitribal
agencies. The White Buffalo Council dated to 1955 and the Denver Indian Center of Denver Native Americans United to 1971.

Denver's central location between the southwestern and the plains tribes has made the city a logical headquarters for a number of national organizations concerned with the interests and rights of Native Americans.

Few of Colorado's Utes joined the exodus to the big city. About 800 Southern Utes and 1,200 Ute Mountain Utes live in Montezuma, La Plata, and Archuleta counties. Farming and stock raising remain important occupations, but tourism, small manufacturing, and public service jobs have been growing sources of employment. The town of Ignacio on the Southern Ute reservation developed in the twentieth century as a tricultural community of Native Americans, Hispanos, and Anglo-Americans. Since the start of the 1940s, both Ute groups have governed themselves through elected tribal councils that administer law enforcement, land management, health, and welfare programs.

Dominant attitudes among the major racial segments of Colorado's population were substantially incompatible through most of the twentieth century. Tensions among the several groups have also produced divisions within each. The outward movement of middle-class African-Americans in Denver, for example, left the poorer members of the group to their own poverty and built resentment toward those who "left the Points."[6] Chicanos in the mid-1970s engaged in fierce struggles over the control and use of the power base offered by Spanish-speaking voters, and white liberals and conservatives fought over the integration issue. Colorado could be thankful that Denver, Pueblo, and Colorado Springs escaped full-scale rioting during the hot summers of the 1960s, but the potential for conflict was certainly there. Recent electoral success by Hispanic and African-American leaders is heartening, but Coloradans, like all Americans, are still challenged to lessen the covert violence racial discrimination inflicts on human lives.

CHAPTER 16

# MEASURING THE LIMITS: COLORADO SINCE 1970

On the eve of the Colorado centennial celebration in 1976, a stationary summer storm with thunderheads towering sixty-two thousand feet poured twelve inches of water within a few hours on the upper reaches of the Big Thompson watershed near Estes Park. On the steep, rocky slopes there was little to retain or absorb the rainfall. Flowing broadly across mountain meadows, down gullies, and into tributaries, the debris-laden runoff quickly filled the usually benign Big Thompson River and turned it into a raging torrent. Amid a black, rumbling night punctuated with blinding, horizontal lightning cracking down the canyon walls, the river overran its banks with a series of rapid rises. There was little warning as the flash flood surged downstream, uprooting trees, rolling ten-foot boulders in its bed, and destroying almost everything in its path.

Claiming 145 lives, the Big Thompson flood was the worst natural disaster in the state's history. Deputy coroners identified 139 victims; 6 more were listed as missing. The river was brutal and indiscriminate. The turbulent stream tumbled men, women, and children underwater, battered them against rocks, and in some cases carried their bodies miles onto the floodplain around Loveland. The Larimer County Sheriff's Office, state police, National Guard, and rangers from Rocky Mountain National Park, however, reacted efficiently to rescue stranded people, protect property, and restore order.

Over the next three years the national, state, and county governments restored Highway 34 through the canyon, established a park in the floodway, and extended financial aid to people in need. As a result of research conducted among survivors, the state highway department erected green and white warning signs in Colorado canyons that read "Climb to safety in case of flash flood." People who remained in their motor vehicles and

The aftermath of the Big Thompson flood in 1976.

homes often died when the flood waters struck. The anniversary disaster demonstrated the necessity for Coloradans to live in harmony with nature and to pay attention to the limits imposed on life by the environment in the Rocky Mountain West.[1]

The flood underscored the environmentalist stance of Governor Richard D. Lamm, who played a central role in defining Colorado's public issues in the 1970s and who rose to prominence in 1972 by leading the fight against holding the 1976 Winter Olympics in Colorado. The business community and established politicians such as Governor John Love and Denver Mayor William McNichols saw presentation of the games as a symbol of progress capable of "breaking Denver from the shell of provincialism . . . and catapulting it before the world as a truly international city."[2] Bumbling leadership by the Denver Olympic Committee and rising cost estimates, however, raised popular doubts about the undertaking. Rapidly building citizen resistance during the summer of 1972 provided seventy-seven thousand signatures to place on the November ballot a state constitutional amendment and a Denver city charter amendment forbidding use of public funds for the Olympics. During the fall campaign the Citizens for Colorado's Future reiterated these points: that the primary beneficiaries of the Olympics would be the construction and recreation industries, that the costs would be borne by the citizens through higher taxes, and that irreparable harm would be done to the environment. Counterattacks against the anti-Olympics coalition had little impact, and the amendments carried by 3 to 2 margins.

The battle over the Olympics had an immediate spillover into other races in the 1972 election. Liberal Floyd Haskell won a narrow victory over three-term Republican Senator Gordon Allott, and Patricia Schroeder captured Denver's seat in the U.S. House of Representatives. Two months earlier, in the Democratic primary, environmentalist Alan Merson defeated Congressman Wayne Aspinall, a man who for twenty-four years had epitomized the national commitment to exploit western resources. Ironically, Aspinall's defeat opened the way for Western Slope voters to choose a conservative Republican in the general election.

The 1974 elections continued to reflect ecological concerns. Republican John Vanderhoof, who had inherited the governor's chair after John Love resigned to become the "Energy Czar" of the Nixon administration, represented the "growth is good" school of politics. Richard Lamm ran a successful Populist campaign against "Johnny Van" by walking the state with a message of environmental protection. National events such as the war in Vietnam, the Watergate scandal, and recognition of the self-containment of "spaceship earth" sharpened voter interests. Lamm's image as a young, liberal, idealistic superenvironmentalist suited the political temper of the time. He rolled up majorities not only in traditionally Democratic areas but also in conservative Colorado Springs and the rural counties of the plains and mountains. Voters in 1974 added Democrat Tim Wirth to the state's congressional delegation and chose Democrat Gary Hart as senator over two-term incumbent Peter Dominick. This gave Colorado two Democratic senators.

The 1974 elections thus diminished the control of the Republican party. They signaled, moreover, a shift to younger, activist politicians, began a move toward greater participation by women and minorities, and decreased the hold of political organizations in favor of semi-independent personalities. Through reapportionment in the 1970s and 1980s, Colorado gained two new U.S. House seats, and voters began narrowly or evenly to split their national house delegations between the two parties. Republicans redressed their loss in the U.S. Senate by electing William Armstrong in 1978. After Lamm's election the governor's mansion remained a Democratic domain, whereas the Republicans ruled the state legislature. It would seem Colorado voters preferred to challenge their politicians with a balance of party affiliations.

Politics and other areas of society as never before, however, provided room for women and minorities. The civil rights and women's rights movements strongly influenced this liberalization. In 1973, for example, under pressure from the federal government, women began to work in Colorado mines, thus breaking the age-old superstition that a female underground brought bad luck. The federal offices that employed thirty-one thousand nonmilitary people in Denver became a prime employment area for women and minorities. In 1978 the Women's Bank of Denver opened with the thought that women preferred to deal with other women concerning financial matters.[3] Joyce Meskis, another example, in 1974 bought a small bookshop called The Tattered Cover and by 1993 had built it into a five-story enterprise with close to half a million volumes. It was the finest bookstore between the coasts and gave Denver a cultural lift.

Yet, politics remained the quickest route to the top, as exemplified by the career of Geraldine Bean. "I got up one morning," she stated, "and I got my kids off to school. I went in to comb my hair and wash my face, and I stood in front of the bathroom mirror crying for thirty minutes because at eight-thirty in the morning I had my children off to school. I had my housework all done. There was absolutely nothing for me to do the rest of the day." Bean returned to school at the University of Colorado and earned a doctorate in history. Then, unable to find a teaching position, she campaigned statewide for the post of regent of the university and won. She was the sixth woman regent in the history of the school and, thus, through politics came in at the top to help direct the organization from which she could not obtain a job.[4]

Pat Schroeder, one of the most important women in national politics in the early 1990s, began her career in 1972 at the suggestion of her husband. The Democrats were looking for someone, almost anyone, to compete in the first district. Schroeder ran, won, and became the first woman elected to national office from Colorado. Her outspoken wit — she dubbed Ronald Reagan the "Teflon-coated president" — and assertive stance helped open the way for women to succeed in Congress. Other women gained political success: Mary Estill Buchanan as Colorado secretary of state, Nancy Dick as lieutenant governor, Arie Taylor as an African-American legislator, Judith Albino as president of the University of Colorado, Gale Norton as attorney general, and Ann Gorsuch as head of the Environmental Protection Agency during the Reagan administration. Male dominance continued in politics, but in 1980 one-fifth of the Colorado assembly was female; this figure had risen to over one-fourth by 1990.

Minorities also made an advance in politics. George Brown, the first African-American lieutenant governor in the nation since the days of Reconstruction, served with Lamm until he was replaced by Nancy Dick in 1978. Penfield Tate, the third African-American graduate of the University of Colorado School of Law in seventy-five years, became mayor of Boulder in the early 1970s. He endured controversies over growth and homosexuals before leaving in 1975 to practice law in Denver. Norman Early served for ten years as Denver district attorney before losing the mayor's race to a fellow African-American, Wellington Webb, in 1992. Emphasizing minority employment and better city services, Webb, after working as city auditor for nine years, thus became Denver's first African-American mayor.

Webb replaced Federico F. Peña, a Hispanic who inspired Denver voters to "imagine a great city" during his first campaign in 1983. In spite of the oil recession Peña led Denver to build a convention center, contract for a new international airport, and solicit a National League baseball team. He left Denver in 1993 to become secretary of transportation in the Clinton administration. Although Peña encouraged Hispanic hiring in government, he generally thought of himself as a politician and an attorney who happened to be Hispanic.[5] This contrasted with the militancy of Rodolfo "Corky" Gonzales, who founded the Denver chapter of La Raza Unida and a local Crusade for Justice. His followers consummated his efforts in a midnight shootout with police in 1973. Such militancy fractured the Hispanic community.[6]

Representing the much smaller Native American minority — twenty-eight thousand in 1990 — Ben Nighthorse Campbell, who was from a ranch on the Western Slope near Ignacio, entered Colorado politics in 1982 as a member of the legislature and became a member of the U.S. House of Representatives in 1986 and a U.S. senator in 1992. He was three-eighths Northern Cheyenne, and, although generally moderate in politics, Campbell became a national advocate for Native American rights. The breakthrough for women and minorities in Colorado since 1974 can be counted in the 1990 statistics of elected officials — 364 women, 208 Hispanics, 14 African-Americans.[7]

These changes in the complexion of Colorado politics, however, did not signal an unlimited victory for liberals. The triumph over the old elites in the Olympics battle designated only a limited shift. Voters rejected proposals to ban throwaway containers and to impose a comprehensive severance tax on mineral extractions. Lamm had to speak in soft tones in order to maintain a working arrangement with his Republican legislature. Although almost everyone favored doing something about land use, for example, infighting in the general assembly in 1974 killed efforts to establish strong state controls on the development of real estate. During the quarrelsome 1977 session, Lamm vetoed thirty-one bills and let twenty others become law without his signature.

During his twelve-year tenure Lamm developed into Colorado's most outspoken leader. He supported the right to abortion, opposed national defense spending, promoted recycling efforts, urged immigration control, de-emphasized bilingual education, and argued for "triage ethics." Because of limited resources he concluded it was wasteful to put wheelchair lifts on every bus or to sustain dying people with expensive medical techniques. People had a "duty to die," he argued, in order to avoid societal costs and to make room for others. For thoughts of this sort Lamm earned the nickname "Governor Doom."

In 1986 Lamm made way for another Democratic governor, Roy Romer, who to an extent relaxed the growth concerns of his predecessor. Engineers punched through the western portions of Interstate 70 and hung roadways on the walls of the spectacular twelve-mile Glenwood Canyon. This completed the most environmentally controversial segment of Interstate 70. Earlier, in 1973, the Eisenhower Tunnel, sixty miles west of Denver, opened on the interstate to funnel traffic under the Continental Divide. Romer, moreover, approved portions of Interstate 470, a Denver highway loop withdrawn by Lamm, and thus encouraged expansion to the south and east of the city. This coincided with Mayor Peña's growth initiatives for the capital and encouraged a steady increase of tourists.

The reinstatement of the growth ethic resulted in part from the economic downturn of the 1980s, which affected various parts of the West, and in part from a swing back to conservatism during the Reagan years. In the November 1992 elections, although Coloradans supported Clinton on the national level, they passed constrictive state constitutional amendments. Voters made certain that revenues from the state lottery, which began in 1983, went to support parks and recreation facilities, placed severe restrictions on public budgets, and attacked homosexuality.

Amendment 2 banned any law "which provides that homosexual, lesbian, or bisexual orientation, conduct or relationships constitute or entitle a person to claim any minority or protected status, quota preference or discrimination." It was promoted as an "equal rights amendment" by the Colorado for Family Values political action group led by Will Perkins, a Colorado Springs car dealer. Fifty-three percent of the electorate approved, but the amendment immediately started a nationwide boycott of Colorado by people supporting gay and lesbian rights. It was popularly interpreted as a means to remove protective rights of homosexuals and to open a door of discrimination based upon sexual orientation. A court injunction barred its enforcement as the question of its constitutionality wound its way through the federal court system — a process that is ongoing in 1994.

Amendment 1 was promoted as a "Taxpayer's Bill of Rights" by Douglas Bruce, a Colorado Springs landlord. Such an amendment had been defeated twice before, but in November 1992 fifty-four percent of the electorate approved. The amendment froze spending by public agencies at current levels with increases allowed only for population growth and inflation. Any expenditure beyond those limits required a vote of the taxpayers, and any excess revenues were to be returned to the taxpayers. As with Amendment 2 there were challenges in the courts, but by late 1993 school districts were beginning to feel pinched. There was a consensus that Amendment 1, for better or worse, would have an effect in Colorado somewhat like the older Proposition 13 had had in California. Amendment 1 signified a retreat from representative government and a movement toward participatory democracy.

Another disturbing issue for the state was the development of nuclear power. Lamm and other environmentalists attempted without success to halt the Rulison experiments in Rio Blanco County in 1973, which sought to release pent-up natural gas

Protesters being arrested for blocking the railroad tracks leading into the Rocky Flats Nuclear Weapons Plant, 1978.

with atomic blasts one mile deep in the earth. Scientists detonated a thirty-kiloton device, but the experiment failed, and no further experimentation occurred. At Rocky Flats, however, there was sporadic agitation in the late 1970s into the 1980s. Here, at a plant twenty miles northwest of Denver, Rockwell International, under contract from the U.S. Department of Energy, manufactured plutonium triggers for hydrogen bombs. By the 1980s six thousand employees were working in one hundred buildings at this most expensive complex in Colorado.

Higher than normal cancer rates reported for the period 1969–1971 brought an investigation in 1975 that indicated downwind peoples in Arvada, Wheat Ridge, Westminster, and northwest Denver had been exposed to plutonium. A raid by federal officers in 1989 exposed illegal storage and disposal of radioactive wastes. Over a three-year span Rockwell had sprayed wastewater over a seventeen-acre site and had hoped it would evaporate. The waste, however, drained into the watershed, and the Department of Energy did not object. After the raid Rockwell pleaded guilty to ten pollution violations, but no one was indicted. EG&G, a Massachusetts company, consequently replaced Rockwell, and, under the need for defense cutbacks, the Clinton administration ordered the Rocky Flats installation to clean up and close down.[8]

The nuclear electric generating plant at Fort St. Vrain run by the Public Service Company of Colorado attracted much less attention, but it was also shut down. The 330-megawatt station utilized the nation's only high-temperature, gas-cooled reactor. Planning began in 1965, and, after numerous delays, the reactor became operational in late 1974. In 1981, because of irregularities, the Nuclear Regulatory Commission allowed it to work at only 80 percent capacity. Although Colorado voters rejected an effort to ban such operations, no other nuclear power plants have been built, and Public Service decommissioned the Fort St. Vrain installation in 1988. Coal-fired electric generation, such as that at the Rawhide plant north of Fort Collins, has proven to be less expensive and more reliable.

In spite of an undercurrent about the need to control growth and the use of resources, there has been little restriction. Governor Lamm once grumbled in frustration, "But we can't just sit here rearranging the deck chairs on the Titanic." Meanwhile, the state population grew from 2.210 million in 1970 to 3.294 million in 1990. Although the rate of state growth in the 1980s was the smallest since the 1930s, it was still larger than the growth rate of the nation, as people moved in search of economic success and quality of life. In 1990 the state ranked 26th in the United States in size of population, 14th in per capita income, 4th highest in college-level education, 23rd in poverty, 21st in number of public libraries, and 39th in number of people per square mile. Other Colorado statistics are similar to those elsewhere in the nation. The leading causes of death, for example, were heart attacks, cancer, and strokes. In 1990, however, AIDS entered the top ten causes of death at the ninth position.

There has been a slow shifting of racial characteristics over the past two decades, with small gains made by minorities. In 1990 Colorado was 3 percent Hispanic, 4 percent African-American, 2 percent Asian, and 1 percent Native American. The Mexican-Americans have remained the largest minority in the state, maintaining a majority ethnic position in the San Luis counties of Conejos and Costilla. The most interesting aspect of the population statistics, however, was that 82 percent of the citizens lived in the urban fringe along the eastern face of the Rockies. During the 1980s the Front Range counties of Arapahoe, El Paso, Jefferson, Larimer, Boulder, and Douglas experienced the bulk of the population growth. Denver County population decreased by 5 percent, but the Denver Consolidated Metropolitan Statistical Area (Denver/Boulder) expanded to 1.848 million people in 1990 — over half of the people of the state. This ends the long-term rural-to-urban shift of population that marked the twentieth century.[9]

Denver has remained the central city of Colorado, although it experienced a flight by the white population — impelled by antibusing sentiment and violence in the early 1970s — to the suburban towns of Aurora, Arvada, Lakewood, and Westminster. Aurora, to the east, developed its own water system and became the state's third-largest city by 1980. Buoyed earlier by Lowry Air Force Base, a base slated for closure in 1994, the new Denver International Airport, scheduled to open in May 1994, will likely continue the Aurora boom. Because the people who left Denver were mainly Anglo, the central city has undergone an ethnic shift. The 1990 statistics indicate an African-American population of nearly 13 percent and a Hispanic concentration of 20 percent.

As the political and financial center of the state, Denver experienced a building boom in the 1970s and a slowdown in the 1980s. During the boom, demand by energy companies created a wall of high-rise office towers along the eastern edge of the business district and inspired the television series "Dynasty." Urban renewal projects cleared much of the older section near the South Platte River valley, and J. Robert Cameron, the renewal director, commented in 1979, "What's happening now is what we dreamed of when we sent the bulldozers in . . . a new era, a twenty-four hour lifestyle in downtown Denver is taking shape."[10] I. M. Pei's graceful Mile High Center and other buildings of the 1960s that cracked through Denver's 1908 twelve-story height limitation were succeeded by new skyscrapers, such as the red granite United Bank Building, which reminded observers of a giant cash register. Meanwhile, Dana Crawford managed to preserve and renovate a block of old Denver, Larimer Square, as a downtown shopping and dining area. On the periphery Cherry Creek grew as an upscale shopping area, and on south Interstate 25 the Denver Tech Center expanded to create a small imitation of the downtown.[11]

During the recession of the 1980s, much of the building stopped. In 1982 there were twenty-eight thousand oil-related employees and entrepreneurs in Denver, but six years later only half remained. Indicators of the shift in Colorado came when Exxon abandoned its oil shale project at Parachute in 1982 and when Marvin Davis, a flamboyant billionaire oil tycoon, sold a large portion of his petroleum production operation in 1981. The international price slide brought an oil depression to Denver, and the layoffs within the oil business hurt the rest of the local economy. Hometown Frontier Airlines floundered and became part of Continental Airlines in 1986, and bankruptcies coursed the state, reaching eighteen thousand in 1988 and seventeen thousand in 1989.

The most spectacular failure involved Silverado Banking Savings and Loan. It began its rise under the leadership of Michael Wise in 1979 and expanded by making loans on raw land, office buildings, and shopping malls after the relaxation of rules for savings and loan institutions under the Reagan administration. Neil Bush, son of President George Bush, was a director of the company, which gave its crash added notoriety. Silverado began to fall apart in August 1988, with reported losses and depositors scrambling to rescue their money. Federal agents raided and closed Silverado in December of that year. The fallout continues, but an estimated cost of the failure amounts to $1 billion.[12]

Such economic problems eventually affected Denver's leadership in the arts. The capital had been the Colorado pacesetter in cultural matters, as indicated by the opening of the new art museum in 1971. Designed by architect James Sudler in association with Gio Ponti of Italy, the "fortress-like" walls used a specially

Christo Javacheff's "Valley Curtain" proved, among other things, that Colorado's geography has continued to be an inspiration to artists.

manufactured tile to reflect the ever-shifting light intensity and give the building a "live" effect. Although the museum provided continual high-quality exhibits, the most sensational art effort occurred in 1972, when Christo Javacheff strung an orange curtain, 1,300 feet long and 365 feet high, across Rifle Gap. It lasted for about thirty-six hours before being shredded by forty-mile-per-hour winds. Christo had hoped it would last a month, but he was nonetheless satisfied with the effort.

The Heritage Center — a new home for the Colorado Historical Society, with vast exhibition space — opened shortly after the centennial year near the state capitol. In 1978 the new Denver Center for the Performing Arts became available for use. This $13 million structure, financed with public and private funds, combined a theater complex with the Boettcher Concert Hall. It was meant as a home for the Denver Symphony Orchestra, as well as a site for various theatrical productions. The orchestra, nevertheless, suffered a rocky ten years during the 1970s. Brian Priestman, the conductor from 1970 to 1977, tried to expand the season and raise standards, but costs also rose. In 1977 management locked out the musicians, and Priestman resigned. The orchestra limped through the 1978–1979 season without a conductor, and then a musicians' strike in 1980–1981 almost ended the organization. Inflation, high costs, dissatisfaction, and economic recession finally killed the orchestra in 1989. With the encouragement of Barry Fey, a rock concert promoter, however, a new orchestra was formed in October 1989. Unusual because it is managed by the musicians, the Colorado Symphony Orchestra has proven successful.

The 1970s saw the end of the Denver Lyric Opera and the Civic Ballet, and the 1980s brought problems to the Denver Public Library, the eighth largest in the United States. The legislature stopped supplemental funding, which forced the library to charge user fees for non-Denver visitors and to close on Thursdays and Sundays. Fortunately, a successful bond issue in 1990 allowed for restoration of hours and expansion of the institution through outlying branches.

An offsetting, happy cultural development for Coloradans came with the growing success of their beloved Denver Broncos professional football team. Even during the losing seasons of the early 1970s, Mile High Stadium was filled to capacity on football weekends. During the 1977 season the state rallied behind the "Orange Crush" defense, coach Red Miller, and the passing ability of quarterback Craig Morton. Unfortunately, the team lost to the Dallas Cowboys in the Super Bowl, 27 to 10. The Broncos went to the Super Bowl three more times under the leadership of quarterback John Elway and coach Dan Reeves. They lost in 1987 to the New York Giants 39–20, in 1988 to the Washington Redskins by a score of 42–10, and in 1989 to the San Francisco Forty-Niners 55–10. The losses gave the fans a certain hesitancy — they cherish a successful season but wince at the prospect of suffering another Super Bowl loss. The potential of Denver as a sports town, however, was not lost, and the Colorado Rockies major league baseball team, organized by part-owner Jerry McMorris, began play in 1993. Despite its expected dismal first season, the fans set a Major League attendance record.

The economic reverses of the 1980s tempered attitudes toward growth. In the early 1970s Colorado Springs and Fort Collins elected no-growth council members. Boulder rejected a proposal to limit population to one hundred thousand in 1971 but approved a housing limit in 1977. Boulder also bought thousands of outlying acres of rural land to establish a greenbelt buffer as it expanded toward Denver. Concern for historic preservation grew in the 1970s, with the establishment of business and residential cores as historic districts in Central City, Georgetown, Silverton, Telluride, Lake City, Crested Butte, and Cripple Creek. Historic Denver, Incorporated, became one of the nation's largest preservation organizations. Preservation projects served not only to satisfy a love of the past but also as a means to attract tourists. Several well-preserved towns in the mountains — Cripple Creek, Central City, and Blackhawk — however, almost became well-preserved ghost towns and agitated for limited-stakes gambling. Voters agreed to this request in 1990. Twenty-eight percent of the gambling tax revenues go back into historic preservation.

Tourism has slowly gained recognition as a major Colorado industry, even though it is sometimes difficult to calculate precisely the motivation and spending of travelers. The Colorado Tourism Board, however, was started in 1983 through a law that also provided that a two cent tax be collected on every $10 expenditure on lodging, restaurants, transportation, private attractions, and ski lift tickets. The purpose was to promote visits to Colorado and also to analyze the tourist trade. In 1988 the board estimated spending by travelers at $4.6 billion; in 1992 the figure was $6.4 billion. The Denver Chamber of Commerce claimed that 11 percent of Denver employment and 13 percent of Colorado employment was tourist-related in 1990.

The most noted tourist business has been the ski industry. During the good snow year of 1992–1993, over 10.5 million lift tickets were sold, compared with 6.6 million in 1977–1978. In the 1970s the ski business became an important balance to the summer tourist trade. Copper Mountain and Telluride opened ski runs in 1972; Mary Jane, next door to Winter Park, began operation in 1975. The leading resort, however, was Vail, popularized in part by the visits of President Gerald Ford. In the 1980–1981 season Vail Associates opened Beaver Creek. It is located on almost five thousand acres ten miles west of Vail and was constructed at a cost of over $500 million. The area has twenty-five miles of ski trails, six chairlifts, a village, and expensive homesites. *Sports Illustrated* writer William O. Johnson suggested that Beaver Creek might well be the last such resort because of high expense, slow returns, and bureaucratic obstacles. The developers had to fight off environmentalists and win fifty-two separate official approvals.

Drought, a fact of life in the West, can also strike in wintertime, and it affected the ski industry in 1976 and 1980. Beaver Creek opened its season with a gala celebration, for example, but then closed the next day for lack of snow. For this reason, however, most areas have installed snow-making equipment to fill in where nature fails. Shortages of water combined with rationing have turned lawns brown in Denver and caused Coloradans to jealously guard their supplies. The massive Fryingpan-Arkansas water diversion plan, for instance, angered the people of Aspen and the Western Slope to the point that they brought a court action to stop it. Authorized by the federal government in 1962 and again in 1974, the $474 million project diverted sixty-nine thousand acre-feet of water eastward across the Continental Divide for urban, industrial, and agricultural use. Although it had recreational and flood control benefits, protesters said the project would injure the wilderness areas, increase salinity in the Colorado River, and encourage urbanization on the Eastern Slope, particularly at Pueblo. By 1980, despite legal actions, the project was substantially complete, and the adverse predictions have yet to be proven.

Elsewhere, the city of Thornton, a northern suburb of Denver, bought twenty-one thousand acres of farmland in Larimer and Weld counties starting in 1986. The township did not want the land; it wanted the water from irrigation rights on the Poudre River. After seven years of legal wrangling Thornton got the water, enough to double the number of urban customers and keep them supplied for forty years. Thus, it has become more important to water city lawns than to irrigate rural crops. Yet, it should be noted that 79 percent of Colorado water is used for farming and only 3 percent for homes. Denver's ambition to create a great reservoir system, Two Forks, was blocked in 1989 by the Environmental Protection Agency and various environmental groups.

On the eastern plains, meanwhile, farmers began to install center-pivot irrigation systems to use subsurface water. The method produced circular fields of grain sorghum, wheat, and corn on the semiarid land. Between 1959 and 1974 almost half a million acres of irrigated land opened in the area around

Burlington, Wray, and Holyoke. Land owners have so heavily mined the Ogallala aquifer, however, that government experts predict exhaustion in forty years. Farmers at that time may have to revert to dry-land techniques.

Rising fuel prices in the 1970s inspired a nationwide farmers' protest in 1977 and 1978. It started at Springfield in southeastern Colorado with a demand for federal support. The American Agricultural Movement, as it came to be called, organized protests at state capitols and in Washington, D.C. In Colorado some five thousand tractors encircled the capitol, as protestors quoted the famous lines of William Jennings Bryan: "Burn down your cities and leave our farms, and your cities will spring up again as if by magic; but destroy our farms and the grass will grow in the streets of every city in the country." After long negotiations in Washington, D.C., the movement failed and faded. Farmers were unable to carry through with their threat of a boycott, and, eventually, the declining petroleum prices that so injured the oil business in Denver brought relief to the farmers of the prairie.

There was some fear in the 1970s that foreign investors were buying up Colorado farmland. However, foreign ownership amounted to only 1.3 percent of land in 1984, and such fears abated. Agriculture is still considered an important factor in the Colorado economy, amounting to about $3 billion in cash receipts annually. Sugar beet production, however, declined to almost nothing in the 1970s under the impact of world sugar prices. Both Great Western and Holly Sugar closed their processing plants. Of the current agricultural receipts, livestock — mainly cattle — accounts for two-thirds. Farmers and ranchers comprise about 2 percent of the workforce, and most newcomers — around 95 percent — enter nonagricultural employment.

Another 2 percent of workers are found in the mines, particularly coal, molybdenum, uranium, sand and gravel for construction, oil, and a little gold and silver. Coal production, mainly in Routt and Moffat counties, set records in 1979 and 1980, and, with the abandonment of oil shale, coal became the state's most important mineral. Kenneth Boulding, an economist at the University of Colorado, commented on this situation: "It's really a fantastically central location. And when you think that this is going to be the Saudi Arabia of the 21st century in coal. . . . What we have in the Rocky Mountain states is the largest reserve of fossil fuel in the world. When everything else is gone, we're going to have it."[13] Most of the working people

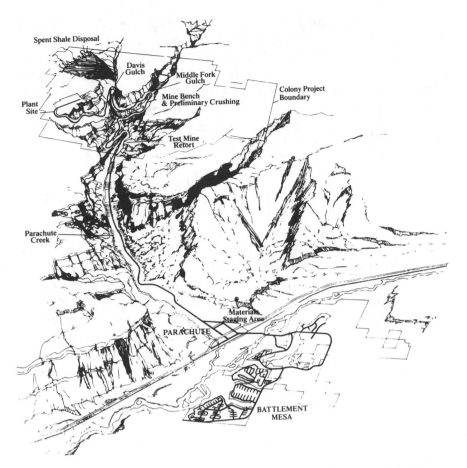

The oil shale boom briefly transformed west-central Colorado before collapsing in the early 1980s.

in Colorado are employed in manufacturing, trade — retail and wholesale — and government. The best-known industries involve rubber, luggage, and beer. Gates Rubber Company of Denver is the world's largest producer of rubber hoses and V-belts. With sales close to $1 billion per year, it is one of the largest family-owned companies in the United States. In contrast, Samsonite, another Denver family business that grew to national fame, became a part of Beatrice Foods in 1973. Monfort of Colorado, the world's largest cattle feedlot operation, grew from a family effort near Greeley in the 1930s. The company is now involved in meat packing and processing. Perhaps the most famous Colorado industry is Coors Brewery in Golden. The regional beer of the 1970s gained such a favorable mystique among tourists that it did not need to advertise. The company, however, after a twenty-month strike, moved to public ownership and national distribution. Other companies have placed installations in Colorado, such as IBM near Boulder, Martin Marietta and AT&T in Denver, Hewlett Packard in Loveland, Eastman Kodak in Windsor, and Anheuser Busch in Fort Collins. Another major employer has been the federal government, with spending in 1988 that ranked Colorado eleventh per capita, up from twenty-fifth in 1976.

In the process of development, any society, nation, or individual must seek, discover, and respect the limits of capability. During the 1970s Coloradans questioned the "growth is good" attitude as environmental concerns raised questions about the quality of life. The economic stress of the 1980s tempered the strong opposition to growth, and the attitude shifted to "growth is not necessarily bad." There was a decided promotion of tourism and an endorsement by the voters to support outdoor recreation. Politics has become more conservative, with voters notably concerned about control of government spending. All of this indicates an adjustment to the limits explored in the previous decade. How many more people, how much more water, how much exploitation can be tolerated? These questions are still being answered.

# CHAPTER 17

# MIRROR FOR AMERICA

"What, then, shall be said of this country so grandly organic and so interesting in its cosmical history?" The question was posed in 1890 in Hubert Howe Bancroft's history of Colorado. The book itself was undistinguished, a mass-production item from the shelf of Bancroft's western history factory, but the issue it raised has concerned Colorado historians for at least a century. In the 1800s local writers such as W. B. Vickers and Jerome Smiley were accustomed to introducing the growth of the state with page after page of geological history, to shaping the rocks out of chaos, uplifting the mountains, and building up the plains. Other historians have tried to discover the effects of the landscape on the character of society and the attitudes of its people. In the nineteenth century Frank Hall claimed Colorado's "superior attractions of life and environment" would make it the center for the development of western art and literature.[1] Four decades later James H. Baker prefaced an official five-volume chronicle of the state with his own reactions to the Colorado scenery and argued that the mountains gave distinctive traits to the institutions and inhabitants of the commonwealth.

From Bancroft to Baker, historians have been aware that Coloradans maintain a special relationship with their environment. Nearly every resident feels the landscape as a special presence in the state. Like an independent voice it supports a set of attitudes that are not so much different from those of other Americans as they are exaggerated. Perhaps because the land itself is extreme — higher, drier, more rugged than elsewhere — Coloradans, in response, have magnified the American experience in a way that more clearly shows our national strengths and weaknesses.

The state's unbroken soils and unsettled valleys, for example, beckoned newcomers from west, north, south, and east. The adoption of horses for hunting made Colorado a land of plenty for eighteenth-century Utes and brought the Cheyennes from the northern plains to the South Platte and Arkansas valleys.

Jeanette and Edward Eyetos, Ute Mountain Reservation. Photo by Myron Wood.

Hispanic New Mexicans in the early nineteenth century found economic opportunity in the valleys on both sides of the Sangre de Cristo Mountains. The northward movement of Hispanos anticipated the westward movement of English-speaking Americans by a generation.

In Colorado, as on other frontiers, these Anglo-American pioneers took care in packing their cultural baggage. The institutions Colorado's settlers reestablished were those the majority consciously desired, not simply those tradition dictated. One consequence in the early years was a willingness to experiment with spontaneous self-government, utopian colonies, and controlled equality of the sexes. As Baker described the 1870s and 1880s, "One was impressed with the new things, the spirit and the hope. The people believed this would be the land of broader chests and brighter brains."[2] Not until the twentieth century did this inclination toward social innovation fade, with the entrenchment of Colorado institutions and customs among its third generation of citizens.

A sense of personal alternatives has been one of the results of social freedom. European visitors to the United States have always been impressed by the ease with which Americans move from place to place, from job to job. Confronted by the range of economic opportunities offered by Colorado's topography, its settlers became actors skilled at moving from one role to another. The typical resident in the first half century of Anglo-American settlement might have tried half a dozen ways to tap the commonwealth's natural resources. A small farmer might have doubled as stockman, surveyor, construction contractor, or commission merchant. An entrepreneur with capital might have promoted irrigation ditches, opened a bank, platted a town, or bought ranch land for security. Visitors found the same freedom. The adventure contained in British travel accounts such as Isabella Bird's *A Lady's Life in the Rocky Mountains* and R. B. Townsend's *A Tenderfoot in Colorado* lies in their authors' delighted encounters with the fluidity of U.S. society. The otherwise proper Bird found it perfectly respectable in Colorado to make a solo ride two hundred miles to be wooed by a mountain man. The energetic Townsend tried his hand at hunting and ranching and participated in the deliberations of a people's court with an ease he had never dreamed of in a more established society.

This openness to any new scheme, especially to any new scheme for making money, has meant Coloradans have used their land hard. From the beginnings of Anglo-American activity, Colorado was a resource frontier that invited exploitation. Its pioneers did not come just to undertake subsistence farming or to winter in snowbound cabins; rather, they came in search of their life's main chance. They were expectant capitalists looking for commodities in demand on national and international markets. Once they found a suitable export — whether buffalo hides, gold, or beet sugar — the settlers used their initial profits to expand production and lower the costs of trade in what they hoped would be a self-propelling cycle of prosperity.

The result has been a Colorado economy dominated by the cycle of local booms. Historians can focus on the individuality of specific booms, finding some that have ended with a crash, some that have faded away, and others that have settled into permanent industries. For some decades they can distinguish simultaneous frenzies of exploitation for a range of resources — from the wheat, silver, and health booms of the 1880s to the ski, real estate, and oil shale booms of the 1970s and 1980s. Equally, historians can smooth the small disturbances into a long curve as though they were mathematicians, describing, first, a long wave of growth from 1859 to the 1910s, next a shorter interlude, and then a second growth wave from 1940 to the present.

No matter how they are described, Colorado's booms have followed closely the general pattern analyzed by historian Charles Gates. As the boom at Cripple Creek during the great depression of the 1890s and the hard times in Gilpin County during the flush years of the Civil War era suggest, the state economy has been partially independent of the national business cycle. The timing of local booms has been a function of the supply-and-demand curves for specific products — how much it costs to produce and market a resource, and how much the outside wants to buy and at what price. In Colorado the reduction of transportation costs has been the most frequent trigger for new development, as evidenced by the impact of railroads on mining and of railroads, interstate highways, and reliable air service on tourism. In their normal life cycle, the booms have faded out only when the richest resources have been skimmed off or incorporated into established businesses and the rate of return on capital has fallen to levels comparable to those in established sections of the country. For a summary of the boom process, it is hard to improve upon the description penned by Frank Hall in 1869: "All new states are born in an outburst, a sort of tempest of speculative passion, which burns and surges until the material it feeds upon is exhausted and then the substantial foundations of the state are laid."[3]

Development booms have often had irreversible environmental consequences. Overgrazing of native grasses has opened the way for invasion by sagebrush. In a land of limited summer rainfall, natural water systems have been particularly vulnerable. Minerals leaching from mines and tailing piles have damaged both surface streams and groundwater and forced expensive mitigation programs on modern mining companies. Irrigation brought immediate economic gains, but it has also damaged soils through the accumulation of salt and has changed the vegetation along the banks of eastern Colorado streams. In the last generation Coloradans purchased enough automobiles to put every adult in a driver's seat at the same time. The proliferation of cars has built a dome of dust and smog over Denver and allowed builders to scar the Front Range with a gargantuan case of second-home smallpox.

Even as they have worked, worried, and altered their landscape for its wealth, Coloradans have been in love with their land. Travelers from the green East have always found Colorado hard to get used to. Facing a drier and browner terrain than they are accustomed to, they are likely to sympathize with the comment made by Sergeant Luke Cahill when he first saw the Arkansas in 1866: "It looks like a funny river that has no water in it." The nineteenth-century booster was correct when he wrote that "it requires a residence of at least twelve months to enable any ordinary observing man to form a comparatively correct opinion of the country." The migrants who have lasted, however, have learned that the silence of the plains and the vastness of the mountains are open secrets accessible to anyone willing to learn a new visual language. Coloradans come to appreciate the sense of distance and to enjoy the gradations of blues and browns. One author verbalized their common reaction when he commented that "to write of such a wonderland can only be a labor of love for those to whom its rare beauties . . . have been revealed."[4]

During the nineteenth century artists and photographers crowded each other in their eagerness to capture this new landscape, recording in their diaries their efforts to deal with scenery on a scale previously unknown to them. In the twentieth century conservationists and naturalists have claimed Colorado as their own province. The idea of wilderness preservation, for example, was first tested as a public policy in Colorado in the 1920s. In the 1950s the successful fight to prevent the inundation of Dinosaur National Monument by Echo Park Dam signaled the revival of active conservationism in the second half of the century. Affection for the state has counterbalanced the development drive, softening the economic impulse among the turn-of-the-century generation and convincing thousands of contemporary Coloradans that "we don't want to take anything from the mountains we love."[5]

There is a final dimension to the relationship between Coloradans and their land. Political issues, now and in the past, have often been stated in geographical terms. Like William Gilpin, Colorado's citizens have tended to read its problems and its future from a map. In the 1870s the basic divisions set southern Colorado against northern Colorado and Denver against the mountain counties. A century later important disputes center on Denver's metropolitan sprawl, the allocation of water, and the regional distribution of wealth and influence. Only twice have

The suburban landscape. Jefferson County in the 1970s.

political divisions cut across regional lines to split the state into nonregional factions. At the turn of the century, conflict between businesspeople and miners and the related antagonism between old-stock Americans and recent immigrants raised the danger of class warfare everywhere in the state. Coloradans chose sides on the basis of their position on the social ladder rather than on their place of residence. The 1960s and 1970s saw the emergence of a similar horizontal division, as Coloradans increasingly identified themselves as Anglo, Chicano, Asian-American, African-American, or Native American.

Colorado's political system has shown itself to be poorly equipped to cope with issues of class and race. As with the nation as a whole, the commonwealth has been reluctant to recognize horizontal stratification. According to U.S. ideology, the hope of everyone is to "grow up with the country," to ride regional development to personal success. In Colorado there has been an added assumption, a belief that the land itself can solve almost all problems. A century ago boosters believed they needed only to point out the available resources and growth would follow automatically. Today, many environmental crusaders feel the salvation of the landscape and the curtailment of unplanned growth will be sufficient to save the state from crisis. For citizens with these points of view, problems of economic growth invite quick action and offer solutions based on the control of people's relations with their environment. Tensions within the social structure, in contrast to problems with the landscape, offer difficulties that cannot always be eased by acting upon external factors. Like Americans elsewhere Coloradans have sometimes tried to ignore questions of class and race because simple answers do not solve the problems.

For considerably more than a century, Colorado has displayed both the failures and promise of American growth. Even now, the state may be a preview of the nation in the twenty-first century. It has prospered since the 1940s as an alternate for Americans trying to avoid the mistakes of the East and California, but its very pace of growth has brought the problems of other states. We hope that our book helps Coloradans face the challenge of their future more effectively by better understanding both the mistakes and successes of the past.

# COLORADO BIOGRAPHIES

## Wayne Aspinall

Wayne Aspinall was born on April 3, 1896, and moved at age eight to Palisade, where his father operated a peach orchard. After education at the University of Denver, Aspinall practiced law in Mesa County, operated an orchard, and served in the Colorado legislature from 1930 to 1948. A Democrat, Aspinall defeated Robert Rockwell in the congressional election of November 1948, earning the first of twelve consecutive terms representing Colorado's Western Slope in Washington. A liberal on many issues, he was a firm advocate of active development of natural resources. In 1959 he became chair of the House Interior and Insular Affairs Committee, a position in which he could influence national policy on land and water, the two issues of overriding concern to his district. In Congress he pushed legislation that authorized the Glen Canyon, Navajo, Flaming Gorge, and Curecanti dams on the Colorado River and its tributaries; backed the Fryingpan-Arkansas water diversion project; and supported the interests of the mining, oil shale, and cattle industries. He also used his committee position to weaken the Wilderness Act of 1964. Changing attitudes toward the environment led to his defeat in the Democratic primary in 1972. He retired to Palisade, where he died October 9, 1983.

## Felipe Baca

Felipe Baca was born in northern New Mexico in 1829. He cleared land along the Purgatoire River in Colorado in 1860 and led twelve families north from Guadalupita to start a permanent settlement in 1862. During the next decade the small settlement grew into the town of Trinidad. Baca's personal wealth grew at the same time because of an extensive sheep raising business. He was a dominant figure in the new town, opening the first general store, donating land for a Catholic church, and presiding over the first school board in 1866. He was elected to the territorial legislature as a Republican in 1870, opposing statehood because he feared its effects on Colorado's Hispanic minority. He died in 1874.

## Casimiro Barela

Casimiro Barela was the most prominent Hispanic leader in Colorado in the first decades of statehood. Born in New Mexico on March 4, 1847, he moved with his family to southern Colorado in 1867, where he started a farm about twenty miles from Trinidad. He became wealthy from stock raising, freighting, and merchandising businesses during the 1870s and built an imposing mansion. Barela served in the territorial legislature, participated in the state constitutional convention, and represented Las Animas County in the Colorado Senate from 1876 to 1916. Barela's overriding concern as a politician was to represent and protect the lands and interests of Hispanic Coloradans, particularly as coal companies found the lands of southern Colorado increasingly valuable. He began his career as a Democrat but switched to the Republican party in 1901 in order to work on behalf of his constituents within the state's stronger party. After a series of increasingly close elections, Barela finally lost in 1916. He died on December 18, 1920.

## William Bent

Born in St. Louis on May 23, 1809, William Bent began trapping in the upper Arkansas Valley of Colorado at age fifteen. In 1830 he joined his brother Charles and Ceran St. Vrain as a partner in a new fur trading company. In 1834 and 1835 he built and began to manage a trading post on the Arkansas River while his partners lived in New Mexico. Bent's Old Fort became the major trading center of the south plains and was a stopping point for the U.S. army, which occupied New Mexico in 1846. After the United States made an insultingly low purchase offer for the fort, Bent abandoned it in 1849 and built a new post thirty-eight miles downriver. From 1854 to 1860 he was the Indian agent who dealt with the Arapaho, Cheyenne, Comanche, and Kiowa tribes for the federal government. Marriages to women of the

Cheyenne and Blackfoot tribes gave him an understanding of Native American concerns. Bent's trading empire collapsed in the 1860s with the gold rush and Native American wars, and he turned to ranching at the confluence of the Purgatoire and Arkansas rivers. He died on May 19, 1869, in a territory vastly changed from the land he had known in the 1820s and 1830s.

## Charles Boettcher

German-born Charles Boettcher (April 8, 1852) arrived in the United States in 1869. He engaged in mercantile business in Cheyenne, Wyoming, and in Greeley, Fort Collins, and Boulder in the 1870s and in banking and mercantile activity in Leadville from 1879 to 1890. He then settled in Denver and participated in organizing the Great Western Sugar Company in 1900. He was also involved in meat packing and cement manufacturing. One of the leaders in the industrialization of Colorado agriculture, Boettcher died July 2, 1948.

## Frederick Gilmer Bonfils

The colorful newspaper publisher Frederick Bonfils was born in Missouri on December 31, 1860. After engaging in both legal and questionable businesses in the Midwest, he came to Colorado in 1895 to buy the *Denver Post*. With his partner Harry Tammen, an experienced publisher and showman, Bonfils turned the *Post* into Denver's "Paper with a Heart and Soul." The editorial page targeted official corruption and advocated selected progressive causes. Meanwhile, the front page was covered with screaming headlines, sometimes in red ink, and the news columns were filled with lurid crime reports, human-interest stories, and local news. An editorial policy that placed more emphasis on "a dog fight in a Denver street" than on wars in Europe pushed circulation from 6,000 to 150,000, making Bonfils a millionaire who could afford to own and operate a circus on the side. Circulation wars with the *Rocky Mountain News* led him to physically assault *News* publisher Thomas Patterson on a Denver street. Although the two papers temporarily buried the hatchet in the late 1920s, at the time of his death on February 2, 1933, Bonfils was characteristically engaged in another bitter libel suit with the *News*.

## William N. Byers

Born in Ohio on February 22, 1831, William Byers worked as a land surveyor in Iowa, Oregon, Washington, and Nebraska. In the spring of 1859 he hauled a printing press from Omaha to the new settlement of Denver, where on April 23 he published the initial issue of the *Rocky Mountain News,* Colorado's first newspaper. Byers was a Republican and a firm advocate of statehood. He boosted the growth of Denver and promoted agriculture and tourism as ways to diversify Colorado's economy, guiding many famous visitors on trips through the Rockies. After selling the *Rocky Mountain News* in 1878, he pursued investment and business interests in Denver and compiled materials on Colorado history until his death in 1903.

## Ben Nighthorse Campbell

Ben Nighthorse Campbell was born April 13, 1933, in Auburn, California. His father was three-fourths Cheyenne, and his mother was a Portuguese immigrant. With a tubercular mother and an alcoholic father, Campbell spent time in and out of foster homes. Although he dropped out of high school, after service in the air force he graduated from San Jose State University in 1957. He learned judo and became the captain of the U.S. Olympic Judo Team in 1964. Campbell took up jewelry-making, a skill learned from his father, and developed a new technique for Native American jewelry called the Painted Mesa process. He became interested in Democratic politics after attending a meeting in Durango. As a representative of the Western Slope living in Ignacio, he was elected to the Colorado legislature in 1982, to the U.S. House of Representatives from 1987 to 1993, and to the U.S. Senate in 1992. Generally a moderate in politics, Campbell has supported the Head Start program, national health care, tax cuts, abortion rights, and Native American rights. IIe takes pride in wearing his hair in a ponytail, using scarves rather than neckties, and dressing in a Northern Cheyenne costume for ceremonial occasions.

## Ralph Carr

Ralph Carr was born in the small town of Rosita in Custer County on December 11, 1887. Educated in the public schools of

Cripple Creek and at the University of Colorado, he followed graduation by working as a lawyer and a newspaper editor in Victor, Trinidad, and Antonito. He was a specialist in irrigation law and assisted Colorado delegations in the negotiation of interstate river compacts during the 1920s. Carr was elected governor in 1938 and again in 1940. During his second term he was the only western governor who welcomed Japanese-Americans who relocated voluntarily from the Pacific states after U.S. entry into World War II and who accepted relocation camps without protest. He is warmly remembered for this stand on behalf of civil rights.

## John M. Chivington

Born in Ohio on January 27, 1821, John Chivington converted to Methodism and became an itinerant preacher in Ohio and on the Missouri Valley frontier. His active support of the antislavery "free soil" cause during the bloody north-south conflict in Kansas in 1854 through 1856 earned him the nickname "the fighting parson." Moving to Denver in 1860, he established the city's first Methodist Sunday school. The outbreak of the Civil War gave Chivington a military career. As a major (later a colonel) with the 1st Colorado Volunteers in 1861 and 1862, he played a prominent role in defeating a small Confederate army at Glorieta Pass in northern New Mexico. He became commander of the Colorado Military District in 1863 and was primarily responsible for the massacre of Native Americans at Sand Creek in November 1864. Away from Colorado from 1865 to 1883, he died in Denver on October 4, 1894.

## Edward P. Costigan

Edward P. Costigan was born in Virginia on July 1, 1874, was educated at Harvard, and opened a law practice in Denver in 1900. He quickly became a mainstay of movements for social and political reform in Denver. He was attorney for the Anti-Saloon League and helped to organize the Honest Elections League, the Law Enforcement League, the Direct Primary League, and the Direct Legislation League. He helped to turn Robert Speer out of office as mayor of Denver in 1912 and successfully defended miners accused of murder because of incidents during the Ludlow strike. An active supporter of Theodore

Roosevelt and Woodrow Wilson, he was appointed by the latter to the U.S. Tariff Commission (1917–1928). He represented Colorado in the U.S. Senate from 1931 to 1937, giving strong support to labor legislation. He died January 17, 1939.

## David Frakes Day

Born in Ohio on March 7, 1847, David Day served with distinction in the Civil War and then failed in business in Missouri. Not until he arrived in Ouray in 1879 did he find his calling as "a journalist by profession, a rabble-rouser by avocation," to quote John Monnett and Michael McCarthy. He named his small Ouray newspaper the *Solid Muldoon,* presumably to honor an unsuccessful but honest prizefighter who kept on battling no matter how often he was knocked down. Day made the paper a bubbling fountain of sharp attacks on corrupt politics and exploitation of the public by railroad and mining companies. "What is a legislature?" he asked in one issue. "In Colorado it is a conglomeration of rural and metropolitan asses elevated by misguided suffrage to positions intended by the Constitution for brains, honor, and manhood." He moved his newspaper to Durango in 1882 and kept up the fight until his death in June 1914.

## William Harrison "Jack" Dempsey

The prizefighter Jack Dempsey was born June 24, 1895, in Manassa, Colorado. As a child he followed his family from one Colorado town to another — Creede, Leadville, Denver, Steamboat Springs, Craig, Meeker, Rifle, Delta, Montrose. In his teens he worked in Colorado mines and sugar beet fields. Between 1911 and 1916 he fought a hundred bouts in Colorado and nearby states. He headed east in 1916 with the nickname "the Manassa Mauler" and earned his successful shot at heavyweight champ Jess Willard in 1919. Dempsey held the heavyweight boxing title until 1926, when he lost to Gene Tunney. He operated restaurants in New York and engaged in personal appearances until his death on May 31, 1983. In the 1920s the spread of the mass media turned U.S. sports figures into stars who could rival movie actors and politicians for public attention. The biggest of these stars were Babe Ruth in baseball, Red Grange in football, and Jack Dempsey in boxing.

## John Denver

Henry John Deutschendorf, Jr., son of a U.S. Air Force colonel, was born in Roswell, New Mexico, December 31, 1943. He acquired his first guitar while in the seventh grade, graduated from high school in Fort Worth, and earned part of his tuition to Texas Tech by singing. With his parents' blessing he dropped out of school in 1964 to pursue a musical career in California. Although he had only passed through the city on a bus, he chose the stage name "John Denver" and became a part of the Chad Mitchell Trio. In 1969 he began solo performances, and his plaintive song "Leaving on a Jet Plane" became nationally popular. His life in Aspen, Colorado, combined with another hit song, "Rocky Mountain High," inspired tourists, hippies, and others to experience the mountains. By 1990, in sales of records, Denver had become one of the top five singers of all-time. In his music he has expressed a global concern for the environment and nature.

## Anne Evans

Anne Evans was one of Colorado's leading advocates of the arts. Born in London on January 23, 1871, the daughter of former governor John Evans, she grew up in Denver and studied art in Berlin, Paris, and New York. Her contributions to the state include service on the Denver Art Commission (1904–1914 and 1932–1937) and the Denver Public Library Commission (1907–1940). She was a founding director of the Denver Art Museum in 1923 and gave the museum much of her collection of Native American and Hispanic art from the Southwest. In 1931 and 1932 she was the moving force behind the refurbishing of the Central City Opera House and the establishment of a Central City summer theater festival. Anne Evans died January 6, 1941.

## John Evans

John Evans was the epitome of the nineteenth-century community builder (or "frontier capitalist," to use the words of his biographer). Born in Ohio on March 9, 1814, he received a medical degree in Cincinnati (1838) and played a leading role in medical practice in Indiana and then in Chicago, where he taught at Rush Medical College from 1845 to 1857. He became a successful railroad promoter and real estate investor in the booming Chicago of the 1850s. He was also an active Methodist and the founder of Northwestern University in the Chicago suburb of Evanston, a town named in his honor. In 1862 he succeeded William Gilpin as territorial governor of Colorado. He was replaced in 1865, in part because of the overall responsibility of his administration for the Sand Creek massacre. He spent the next thirty years, until his death on July 3, 1897, as a Denver booster and businessman. He was the prime mover behind the Denver Pacific and the Denver, South Park and Pacific railroads; he organized the Denver Tramway Company and other local businesses; and he founded Colorado Seminary (1864), the predecessor of the University of Denver. His children — William Gray Evans and Anne Evans — continued the family tradition of business and civic leadership.

## Barney Ford

Born into slavery, Barney Ford learned about gold mining in the northern Georgia gold rush before the Civil War. He came to the Colorado gold fields as a fugitive slave in 1860. Relocating to Denver, he opened a barber shop, then a restaurant, and then the highly succesful Inter-Ocean Hotel. He was prominent in Denver business and politics and died in 1902.

## William Gilpin

William Gilpin, the first territorial governor of Colorado in 1861 and 1862, was one of the state's most unusual political leaders. Born in Pennsylvania on October 22, 1822, he spent half a year at West Point, fought the Seminole Indians in Florida, and accompanied John C. Fremont's 1843 expedition to the West Coast, where he assisted American settlers in organizing a territorial government for Oregon. In 1847 and 1848 he led forces to protect the Santa Fe trail through Kansas and Colorado from hostile Native Americans. Settling in Missouri in the 1850s, Gilpin boosted the interests of the Kansas City area. In these same years he began to develop his vision of a fully developed North America as the climax of world history. Appointed territorial governor of Colorado in 1861, in part because of his political support of President Lincoln in a strongly Democratic county, he took office with grand plans for Colorado's growth. He also offended his political opponents (especially editor William Byers) and overcommitted the U.S. Treasury while raising troops to defend Colorado and the Union. Removed from office in 1862, he stayed in Colorado until his death on January 19, 1894, filling his days as a land speculator, railroad promoter, and visionary who continued to proclaim the unique future of the American West.

## Rodolfo "Corky" Gonzales

Rodolfo Gonzales was born June 18, 1928, in Denver and grew up in a migrant labor family. A talented boxer, he won the Amateur Athletic Union national bantamweight championship in 1947 and later turned professional. On retiring from the ring in 1953 he became a Democratic political activist. Appointed to head the Denver Neighborhood Youth Corps in 1965, Gonzales was forced out the next year amid charges that he discriminated against African-Americans, allegations he denied. In mid-1966 he founded the Crusade for Justice, dedicated to organizing Chicanos and to focusing their power. By the early 1970s the crusade was running a school, publishing a newspaper, and even supporting a ballet company. The "St. Patrick's Day Massacre" of March 17, 1973, saw crusade member Luis Martinez killed by a policeman and a dozen police officers hurt. That debacle, coupled with the crusade's inflammatory rhetoric, deepened the belief of many Denverites that Gonzales was a radical. In the mid-1970s and early 1980s, the Crusade for Justice and Gonzales faded as other Hispanic leaders rose to prominence.

## Emily Griffith

Emily Griffith was born in Cincinnati on February 10, 1880. As her family moved westward to Nebraska and then Denver, she became a schoolteacher while still in her teens. From 1904 to 1908 she served as deputy state superintendent of schools before returning to teach in an immigrant neighborhood at Denver's Twenty-Fourth Street School. In 1916 she persuaded the school board to support a new, free, day and evening school for adults as well as children. The Public Opportunity School was aimed at immigrants and working people who needed to fill in gaps in their education, with particular emphasis on English and vocational training. The school grew steadily in the 1920s and 1930s, recording 8,670 students when Griffith resigned as principal in 1933. She retired to Pinecliffe, where she was killed by an intruder on June 19, 1947.

## William D. Haywood

"Big Bill" Haywood was born in Salt Lake City on February 4, 1869, and worked in his teens and twenties as a miner and cowboy. He joined the Western Federation of Miners (WFM) in Idaho in 1896 and quickly became a stalwart of the labor movement. From 1901 to 1906 he lived in Denver while serving as secretary-treasurer of the WFM. In 1906 and 1907, he was put on trial in Idaho for plotting to kill that state's former governor, Frank Steunenberg. Haywood was acquitted with the help of the famous lawyer Clarence Darrow. He also received sixteen thousand votes for governor of Colorado while in jail in Idaho. Frozen out of leadership in the WFM in 1908, Haywood continued to live in Denver until 1917, devoting his energies to the Socialist party and to the Industrial Workers of the World, the militant union he had helped to establish in 1905. Convicted of sedition for opposing U.S. involvement in World War I, he jumped bail in 1921 and fled to the Soviet Union, dying in Moscow on May 18, 1928.

## Nathaniel Hill

Born in New York on February 18, 1832, Nathaniel Hill graduated from Brown University and remained on the faculty as a professor of chemistry from 1856 to 1867. He first visited Colorado in 1864 and moved to the state permanently in 1867. He pioneered scientifically sophisticated methods for extracting gold from low-grade ores in the Central City region as manager of the Boston and Colorado Smelting Company. Hill served in the U.S. Senate from 1879 to 1885, looking after the interests of his state by strongly advocating the continued coinage of silver. He returned to Colorado, where he published the Denver *Republican* and continued to manage the Boston and Colorado Smelter, now relocated to Argo at the northern edge of Denver. Hill died May 22, 1900.

## John Wesley Iliff

John Wesley Iliff was born in Ohio on December 18, 1831. After a brief mercantile career in Kansas, he followed the gold rush to Colorado in 1859. Two years later he moved to Cheyenne and entered the cattle business, returning to live in Denver in 1874. Iliff was the cattle king of the central plains in the 1870s. By purchasing land with good water, he was able to control vast amounts of adjacent grasslands in eastern Colorado and southern Wyoming. He died on February 9, 1878.

## William Henry Jackson

Born in New York state on April 4, 1843, William Henry Jackson learned and practiced the new craft of photography in New York, Vermont, and Nebraska. From 1870 to 1878 he served as the official photographer for Ferdinand Hayden's geological survey of the western territories, taking the first photographs of what became Yellowstone Park, as well as Colorado cliff dwellings, the Mount of the Holy Cross, and other scenes from the Colorado Rockies. From 1879 to 1897 he operated the William H. Jackson Photograph and Publishing Company in Denver, helping to publicize the scenic wonders of the state. He then engaged in the publishing business in Detroit and retired to Washington, D.C., where he became a painter of western historical scenes. He published an autobiography, *Time Exposure,* in 1940 at age ninety-seven and died on June 30, 1942.

## Edwin C. Johnson

Edwin C. "Big Ed" Johnson was born in Scandia, Kansas, on January 1, 1884, and died in Denver on May 30, 1970. He homesteaded near Craig in 1910 and entered Colorado politics as a Democrat in 1923, serving as a state representative (1923–1931), lieutenant governor (1931–1933), governor (1933–1937), U.S. senator (1937–1955), and again as governor (1955–1957). An advocate for rural Colorado and a tepid supporter of the New Deal, he fought for local control of federal relief programs in the 1930s and opposed the re-election of Franklin Roosevelt in 1940. As a senator he strongly favored U.S. noninvolvement in world affairs before and after World War II. He is remembered for a short-lived attempt to use the Colorado National Guard to close Colorado's southern border to Hispanic migrant workers in 1936.

## Richard D. Lamm

Born in Madison, Wisconsin, August 3, 1935, the son of a coal company executive, Lamm grew up in Illinois and Pennsylvania. Educated as an attorney and an accountant, he moved to Colorado in the early 1960s, passed the bar exam in 1962, and became a member of the legislature from 1966 to 1974 as a Democrat. He supported no-fault insurance, the right to abortion, zero population growth, and protection of the environment. He gained a reputation for forthrightness and led the fight to defeat the 1976 Winter Olympics being held in Colorado. In 1974, after walking the state, he won the governor's position and served for three terms (1975–1987). He had to contend with Republican domination in the legislature, and, in time, became a national spokesperson for "triage ethics." Lamm became a leading advocate for the concerns of the changing mountain states and coauthored a book, *The Angry West: A Vulnerable Land and Its Future* (1982). After serving longer than any other governor, Lamm retired from politics to a career of teaching, writing, and speaking.

## Benjamin Barr Lindsey

Born in Tennessee on November 25, 1869, Ben Lindsey moved to Denver as a child. Early experience as a lawyer made him an advocate of special legal treatment for children. He helped to create a juvenile court for Denver and served as a judge from 1900 to 1927. In addition to his work with young offenders, he worked to improve legal protections, education, and recreation for young people. Lindsey was a strong supporter of political reform in Denver, taking on the Denver political establishment in election campaigns and in books, including *The Rule of Plutocracy in Colorado* (1903) and *The Beast* (with Harvey O'Higgins, 1910). He moved to Los Angeles in 1928 after political opponents removed him from his judicial position. He was elected to the Los Angeles Superior Court in 1934 and again pursued his work on children and family law until his death on March 26, 1943. Among his fifty books and pamphlets is an autobiography, *The Dangerous Life,* published in 1931.

## John A. Love

John Love broke into the 1962 governor's race as an unknown Republican candidate from Colorado Springs. Born in 1916 in Illinois, his family moved to Colorado Springs when he was four. Love graduated from the University of Denver Law School in 1941, became a navy pilot in World War II, and practiced law in Colorado Springs. Feeling the vulnerability of the Democrats, Love decided to run in 1962, and the Republicans agreed. Love had little political experience, but he was fresh, handsome, and articulate. When elected he somewhat paradoxically worked for air and water pollution control, as well as promoting the growth of the state. He resigned the governorship in 1973 to become the "Energy Czar" in the Nixon administration. Following Nixon's resignation a few months later, Love returned to Denver to work in the private sector.

## William A. H. Loveland

Born in Massachusetts on May 30, 1826, William Loveland served in the Mexican War, participated with little success in the California gold rush, and returned to New England to engage in business. In 1859 he sold out and headed for Colorado, where he built the first house and opened the first store in the tiny community of Golden. As leader of the "Golden crowd" in the mid-1860s, he stoutly pushed the interests of his town in competition with Denver. Loveland helped to make Golden the territorial capital from 1862 to 1867 and built the Colorado Central Railroad to the Clear Creek mines. When the Union Pacific bought out the Colorado Central in 1877, he moved to Denver and purchased the *Rocky Mountain News,* which he owned from 1878 to 1886. He died on December 17, 1894.

## Joseph Projectus Machebeuf

Joseph Machebeuf was born in France on August 11, 1812. After training for the Roman Catholic priesthood, he crossed the Atlantic in 1839. He served the church in Ohio (1839–1849) and New Mexico (1849–1860) before coming to the new settlements in Colorado. Before the end of the decade he had built eighteen churches, established convents, and opened schools. He became titular bishop in 1868 and the first bishop of Denver in 1887, two years before his death on July 10, 1889. His thirty years of work laid firm foundations for Catholicism in Colorado.

## Martha Maxwell

As with many writers and artists who were her contemporaries, Martha Maxwell was both a student of Colorado and a publicist for the new territory. Born in Pennsylvania on July 21, 1831, she attended the innovative coeducational Oberlin College and Lawrence University. She married James Maxwell in 1854 and accompanied him to Colorado in 1860. She spent the years 1862–1868 in the Midwest and New Jersey. Rejoining her husband in Colorado in 1868, she began to practice taxidermy on a collection of the birds and animals of Colorado. She exhibited her work in natural-looking displays in her own Rocky Mountain Museum in Boulder (1874) and Denver (1876) and at the Centennial Exposition in Philadelphia (1876). She continued to exhibit her collection in the East until she died on May 31, 1881.

## Otto Mears

Born in Russia on May 3, 1840, Otto Mears arrived in Colorado by way of gold rush San Francisco and Santa Fe. First operating a sawmill and gristmill at Conejos in 1865, he opened the first road over Poncha Pass in 1867 to supply flour to the mines of California Gulch. Over the next eighteen years he built three hundred miles of toll roads through the San Juan Mountains, linking Silverton, Ouray, and Lake City (a town he helped develop). He published newspapers in Saguache and Lake City. In 1873 he was also involved in drafting the Brunot Agreement with the Utes, which opened the San Juans to Anglo-American settlement. Between 1887 and 1904 he expanded his transportation empire by constructing railroads from Silverton to nearby mining districts and the Rio Grande Southern from Ridgway to Telluride and Durango. After spending the years 1907–1917 in Silverton, he spent his last years in California, where he died on June 24, 1931.

## Nathaniel Meeker

Like many nineteenth-century Americans, Nathaniel Meeker found it difficult to settle down. Born in Ohio on July 12, 1817, he graduated from Oberlin College (1840) and began a career of short-term newspaper jobs and sporadic attempts at storekeeping. In 1844 he participated in the "Trumbull Phalanx," a utopian community that tried to put into practice the popular theories of Francois Fourier. After learning there "how much cooperation people would bear," he resumed his peripatetic life until 1865, when he joined the staff of the *New York Tribune*. As agricultural editor for this widely circulated newspaper, he continued to write about cooperative agricultural settlements. Between 1869 and 1878 he put his theoretical ideas into practice as founder and guiding force of the Union Colony in Greeley, Colorado. In 1878 he moved to a new challenge as Indian agent for the Utes at White River. His strenuous efforts to "Americanize" the Utes and his disregard for their customs and values led them to kill Meeker on September 29, 1879.

## Enos A. Mills

Enos Mills left his home state of Kansas for Colorado fourteen years after his birth on April 22, 1870. Educating and supporting himself, he built a cabin near Longs Peak in 1886. He became a leading guide for climbs of the mountain and also worked in Butte, Montana. Between the 1890s and his death on September 21, 1922, he built a career as a nationally known speaker and writer on the natural history of the Rockies. He built the Longs Peak Inn in 1902, a popular resort and a base for climbs of the mountain. He played a central role in the campaign that resulted in the creation of Rocky Mountain National Park in 1915. Mills was sharp and intense in personality, deeply committed to broadening the public's appreciation of the Rocky Mountains, and impatient with any disagreement with his ideas.

## David Halliday Moffat

David Moffat was a central figure in the business development of Colorado. Born in New York on July 22, 1839, he learned the banking business in New York, Iowa, and Nebraska. He came to Denver in 1860, opening a store that sold books, stationery, groceries, and wallpaper, among other products. He became cashier of the First National Bank of Denver in the mid-1860s and its president in 1880. His investments and business involvements included Leadville, Creede, and Cripple Creek mines, Denver real estate and utility companies, and Colorado farmlands. Moffat is best known, however, for his railroad investments. He backed the Denver and Pacific Railroad and the Denver, South Park and Pacific in the 1860s and 1870s. He was president of the Denver and Rio Grande for several years during the 1880s. He invested much of his fortune in the Denver, Northwestern and Pacific ("the Moffat road"), which was intended to provide a direct line from Denver to Salt Lake City. The line was only partially finished when he died on March 18, 1911. It was completed as the Denver and Salt Lake Railroad and included the famous Moffat Tunnel.

## William Jackson Palmer

William Palmer was born in Delaware on September 18, 1836, and learned the railroad business as secretary to the president of the Pennsylvania Railroad from 1858 to 1861. Following a distinguished career as a cavalry officer during the Civil War, he became treasurer of the Kansas Pacific Railroad in 1865. With completion of the Kansas Pacific in 1870, Palmer founded his own railroad company — the Denver and Rio Grande — to realize a grand vision of connecting Denver with southern Colorado and the Southwest. Between 1870 and 1883 he built the Denver and Rio Grande into the primary transportation system in southern Colorado. He also founded the city of Colorado Springs, established the predecessor of the Colorado Fuel and Iron Company, and helped to organize Colorado College (1873). In 1883 he resigned the presidency of the Denver and Rio Grande and assumed leadership of the Rio Grande Western, which connected Colorado to Salt Lake City, selling that line to the Denver and Rio Grande in 1901. He died March 13, 1909.

## Thomas MacDonald Patterson

Thomas Patterson was born in Ireland November 4, 1839, and came to the United States in 1849. He grew up in Indiana, where he began to practice law, and he moved to Denver in 1872. He became city attorney and a delegate to the last territorial legislature, and he served a term in Congress (1877–1879). In 1890 he became publisher of the *Rocky Mountain News* and later published the *Denver Times*. He left the Democratic party in 1892 over the issue of silver and was elected to a term in the U.S. Senate (1901–1907) with a combination of Democratic, Populist, and Silver-Republican votes. He returned to his newspaper career until 1913 and died in Denver on July 23, 1916. Patterson was a millionaire who was also an outspoken advocate of the interests of working people, using the *Rocky Mountain News* to crusade for progressive reforms and against large corporations.

## James H. Peabody

James Peabody represented the opposite end of Colorado's political spectrum from Davis Waite. Born in Vermont on August 21, 1852, Peabody came to Colorado in 1871, working in dry goods stores in Pueblo, Denver, and Cañon City after 1875. He became a prosperous Cañon City merchant and banker and a leader in local politics as a Republican. Elected governor in 1902, he enlisted the state government on behalf of management in its contest with labor unions. The opposition Democrats fought the bitter election of 1904 with the slogan "Anybody But Peabody." Because the honesty of the election results was disputed, Peabody agreed to hold office in his second term for only one day before resigning in favor of Lieutenant Governor Jesse McDonald. Peabody died November 23, 1917.

## Federico F. Peña

Federico Peña was born in Laredo, Texas, March 15, 1947, the son of a cotton broker who moved the family to Brownsville, Texas, where Peña grew up. Peña graduated from the law school of the University of Texas and served briefly as a legal-aid lawyer in El Paso before moving to Denver in 1973, where he worked in private practice and as an attorney for the Mexican-American Legal Defense and Education Fund. In 1979 Peña won election to the Colorado legislature; he became the leader of the minority Democrats, and in 1983, became mayor of Denver. During his two terms (1983–1991) Peña pushed economic growth through downtown redevelopment and inspired recession-ridden Denverites to revitalize the city with a new convention center, airport, library, and major league baseball team. Although he was popular because of his fairness in hiring and his personal style, Peña decided against a third term. In

1993 he became secretary of transportation in the Clinton administration.

## Spencer Penrose

Spencer Penrose was a mining engineer turned tourism impresario. Born on November 2, 1865, to a prominent Philadelphia family, he came to Colorado in 1892. He struck it rich in the Cripple Creek mining boom and organized the United States Reduction and Refining Company at Colorado City, gradually gaining control of the other plants that processed Cripple Creek ore. In 1904 he was a cofounder of the Utah Copper Company, which developed one of the most lucrative mines in the West at Bingham Canyon and eventually consolidated with the Kennecott Copper Company. Penrose used his mining wealth to purchase, modernize, and expand the Broadmoor Hotel into a lavish mountain resort, which officially opened in 1918. He spent $3 million to upgrade the old road to the top of Pikes Peak for automobiles and promoted the Pikes Peak Hill Climb. Penrose generally updated the appeal of Colorado Springs as a tourist destination in the flamboyant 1920s. A man who enjoyed the limelight and the company of celebrities, Penrose died in Colorado Springs on December 7, 1939.

## Lewis Price

Lewis Price was born a slave in Missouri in 1849. After serving in an African-American regiment in the last year of the Civil War, he began a freighting business between Kansas and Colorado, followed by a business in Cheyenne. He moved to Denver in 1870. Price gradually built business success, operating a laundry and investing in real estate. In 1880 he started the *Denver Star,* the first African-American newspaper west of the Mississippi River, advocating for civil rights and the advancement of African Americans. After the newspaper folded, Price returned to real estate speculation, riding the Denver boom of the 1880s to amass a sizable fortune by 1890 and 1891. He bought a mansion at Sherman and 18th, at the edge of the fashionable Capitol Hill neighborhood, and lived the life his wealth allowed until he was ruined in the economic crash of 1893. He died in 1913, remembered as a man who had the ambition "to show white people that a Negro could outwit them," according to his obituary in the *Denver Post*.

## Josephine Roche

Josephine Roche was one of Colorado's leading voices for social reform in the first half of the twentieth century. Born in Nebraska on December 2, 1886, and educated in the East at Vassar College and Columbia University, she came to Denver in 1910 and joined the ranks of political reformers. She fought against the exploitation of women, first as Denver's first female police officer, with a beat in the city's vice district, then as director of the girl's department of Denver Juvenile Court (1915–1918). From 1918 to 1925 she worked on women's and family welfare issues in New York and Washington, returning to Colorado in 1927 when she inherited ownership of the Rocky Mountain Fuel Company, which operated coal mines in northern Colorado. As president she raised wages, invited the United Mine Workers to organize her employees, and kept the company afloat until 1944 despite fierce opposition from other coal companies. She ran unsuccessfully for governor in 1934 as a New Deal reformer and served as assistant secretary of the treasury under President Franklin Roosevelt from 1934 to 1937. After the failure of her company she worked for the United Mine Workers' pension fund and retired to Washington, where she died July 29, 1976.

## Roy Romer

Roy Romer was born in Garden City, Kansas, October 31, 1928, and was educated at Colorado State University and the University of Colorado Law School. Romer began private practice in 1955 and entered the legislature as a member of the house in 1958 and of the senate in 1966. He was Richard Lamm's chief of staff from 1975 to 1977 and was Colorado state treasurer for the period 1977–1986. In 1986 he was elected governor. Romer has modified antipathy toward growth and has sought to explain through town meetings the implications of Amendment 1 for the state budget. Agitated by gang strife, drive-by shootings, and urban violence in 1993, Romer initiated the nation's first laws prohibiting persons under age eighteen from carrying guns.

## Patricia Schroeder

Patricia Scott Schroeder was born in Portland, Oregon, on July 30, 1940. After obtaining a law degree from Harvard, she moved to Denver and began work for the National Labor Relations Board (1964–1966), later teaching law at Regis College. In 1972 Schroeder defeated Congressman James McKevitt with a grassroots campaign. She has represented Denver in the U.S. House of Representatives continuously since 1973, achieving substantial seniority on the Armed Services Committee and prominence as one of the most powerful women in national politics. She sees herself as a Jeffersonian with concerns about child care, women in politics, the oppressive seniority system of Congress, and the excesses of defense spending.

## John F. Shafroth

John Shafroth was an important figure in Colorado politics for more than thirty years. Born in Missouri on June 8, 1854, he came to Denver in 1879. He was Denver city attorney from 1887 to 1891 and represented Denver in Congress from 1895 to 1904. He was one of the state's leading proponents of political reform, supporting the vote for women, the adoption of the initiative and referendum for direct legislation, and the direct primary for choosing party nominees. The substantial social legislation passed during his two terms as governor (1909–1913) marked the high tide of progressivism in Colorado. He followed his four years in the statehouse with a term in the U.S. Senate, where he supported the programs of President Woodrow Wilson. He died on February 20, 1922.

## Robert W. Speer

Few civic leaders have had as great an impact as Robert Speer, perhaps the most influential mayor in the history of Denver. Born in Pennsylvania on December 1, 1855, Speer moved to Denver in 1877 in search of better health. He entered politics as city clerk in 1880, followed by four years as postmaster (1885–1889) and by service on the Fire and Police Board and the Board of Public Works. He was elected mayor of Denver in 1904 and served until 1912, when progressive reformers succeeded in changing the structure of the city's government.

Speer was re-elected in 1916 and served until his death on May 14, 1918. Robert Speer was simultaneously a political boss and a civic visionary. He built a powerful political organization through alliances with large corporations and the vice industries, but he used much of his power for social and physical improvements to the city. His administration recognized the needs of labor unions and working people. It also brought Denver into the twentieth century by developing parks, boulevards, and the Civic Center; erecting public buildings such as the Museum of Natural History; expanding the sewer system; and planting trees throughout the city.

## Benjamin F. Stapleton

Ben Stapleton was the longest-serving mayor in the history of Denver. Born in Kentucky on November 12, 1869, he began a law practice in Denver in 1899 and moved into public service as a police magistrate (1904–1915) and postmaster (1915–1921). Taking office as mayor in 1923, he welcomed the support of the Ku Klux Klan before later repudiating the organization. He served until 1931 and again from 1935 to 1947, presiding over an increasingly inactive administration. He was defeated by the reform campaign of Quigg Newton, Stapleton died May 22, 1950.

## Horace Austin Warner Tabor

Born in Vermont on November 30, 1830, Horace Tabor arrived in Colorado by way of Kansas. Between 1860 and 1878 he earned his living as a miner and merchant in the Leadville area. He struck it rich in the great Leadville silver boom, selling a one-third interest in the Little Pittsburgh mine for $1 million and reinvesting in other mines and real estate. He became one of Leadville's most prominent civic leaders, was elected lieutenant governor (1878–1884), and served one month in the U.S. Senate, filling out the term of Henry Teller. He continued to increase his fortune by building Denver hotels and office buildings and investing in real estate but lost his wealth in the crash of 1893. His divorce from his first wife, Augusta, and remarriage to Elizabeth McCourt Doe was notorious in Victorian Colorado. Tabor died April 10, 1899, in Denver.

## Edward T. Taylor

Edward Taylor played a major role in the development of Colorado's Western Slope. Born in Illinois on June 19, 1858, he came to Leadville in 1881, where he served as principal of the high school. After receiving a law degree from the University of Michigan, he moved to Glenwood Springs in 1887. He filled a series of local and state political offices from 1887 to 1908 and served in Congress from 1909 until his death on September 3, 1941. He is best known for the Taylor Grazing Act, which set up the system through which ranchers could secure the use of public lands for their herds.

## Henry Moore Teller

New York–born Henry Teller (May 30, 1830) practiced law in Illinois before coming to Colorado in 1861. A confirmed antislavery Republican, he became a mining lawyer in Central City, where he also helped to organize the Colorado Central Railroad. He represented Colorado in the U.S. Senate from 1876 to 1882, served as secretary of the interior from 1882 to 1885, and returned to the Senate from 1885 to 1909. He was a firm supporter of western economic development and the unlimited purchase of silver for coinage. He left the Republican party in 1896 because of its endorsement of the gold standard. Teller was better known for his oratory than for specific legislation, but the Teller Amendment at the start of the Spanish-American War in 1898 did pledge the United States to the goal of an independent Cuba. Teller died February 23, 1914.

## Davis H. Waite

Davis Waite came to Colorado politics late in life. Born April 25, 1825, in New York state, he earned a living in business, law, and editing in Pennsylvania, Missouri, Wisconsin, and Kansas, serving one term in the legislature of each of the last two states. He moved to Leadville in 1879 and to Aspen in 1881, where he edited small newspapers including the *Aspen Union Era*. Waite was a member of the Knights of Labor and a strong idealist about state politics. Elected governor on the Populist ticket in 1892, he introduced a broad reform agenda that he was unable to push through the legislature. He fought the Denver Police

Board in an effort to curtail the city's gambling and liquor trades and favored workers over management in labor disputes. He also earned a reputation as a radical and the acquired nickname "Bloody Bridles Waite" for a 1893 speech in which he declared that "it is better, infinitely better, that blood should flow to the horses' bridles, rather than our national liberties should be destroyed." Defeated after one term in office, Waite remained a firm Populist and died in Aspen on November 27, 1901.

## Wellington E. Webb

Educated at Manual High School in Denver, Colorado State College, and the University of Northern Colorado, where he earned a master's degree in sociology in 1972, Wellington Webb served in the state legislature from 1973 to 1977. He was Denver city auditor from 1982 to 1991 and then won election as mayor in a victory over Norman Early. Webb, a Democrat, became the first African-American mayor of the city; he emphasized city services, such as residential snow removal and neighborhood police patrols, rather than the "big ticket" items of his predecessor, Federico Peña. Early in his tenure, however, Webb was called to defend Denver against the boycott that resulted from the passage of the antihomosexual Amendment 2 in 1992. He traveled to New York and appeared on national television talk shows in an effort to retain convention business for the capital city. As a result of the visit of Pope John Paul II, World Youth Day, and the attendance of fans at Rockies baseball games, the tourist business has been maintained.

# COLORADO CHRONOLOGY

1598    Spain establishes settlements in New Mexico.

1706    Juan de Ulibarri claims Arkansas River Valley for Spain.

1720    Pedro de Villasur explores Platte River Valley.

1765    Juan Maria de Rivera explores San Juan Mountains and Gunnison River.

1776    Francisco Dominguez and Silvertre Escalante explore western Colorado.

1779    Juan Bautista de Anza defeats Comanche leader Cuerno Verde.

1803    The United States acquires northeastern Colorado through the Louisiana Purchase.

1806    Zebulon Pike explores headwaters of Arkansas River and Rio Grande.

1810s    U.S. fur trappers penetrate Colorado.

1820    Stephen Long explores Colorado.

1821    William Becknell opens trade between Missouri and Santa Fe along the Santa Fe Trail.

1830s    John Gantt, William Bent, Louis Vasquez, Lancaster Lupton, and other Americans establish trading posts on Arkansas and South Platte rivers.

1848    Treaty of Guadalupe Hidalgo transfers southern and western Colorado from Mexico to the United States.

1851    Treaty of Fort Laramie signed with the Cheyennes, Arapahos, and other tribes of the northern plains
First permanent Hispanic settlement in Colorado is established at San Luis.

1853    John Gunnison surveys railroad routes through central Rockies.

1858  Russell party discovers gold
      Auraria founded.

1859  Thousands join in the Pikes Peak Gold Rush
      Gold discovered along Clear Creek
      William Byers establishes *Rocky Mountain News*
      Settlers form Jefferson Territory.

1860  Auraria and Denver City merge.

1861  Colorado Territory established.

1862  Colorado volunteers help to defeat a Confederate army
      at Glorieta Pass.

1863  Denver connected to telegraph.

1864  Cherry Creek flood devastates Denver
      Third Regiment of Colorado Volunteer Cavalry
      massacres Cheyenne and Arapaho Native Americans at
      Sand Creek.

1865  Native Americans attack Julesberg in retaliation.

1867  Denver named territorial capital.

1868  Nathaniel Hill opens smelting operations at Blackhawk
      Utes sign treaty and promise to move to reservation
      Forsyth party undergoes nine-day siege at Beecher
      Island.

1869  Southern Cheyenne defeated at Summit Springs.

1870  Union Colonists establish Greeley under leadership of
      Nathan Meeker
      Denver Pacific and Kansas Pacific railroads connect
      Denver to the eastern states
      William Jackson Palmer organizes Denver and Rio
      Grande Railroad.

1871  Palmer establishes Colorado Springs
      Chicago-Colorado Colony establishes Longmont.

1872  Colorado Board of Immigration formed.

1873  Utes agree to Brunot Treaty, ceding mining regions to
      whites.

1874  Value of silver produced in Colorado exceeds that of gold
      Territory opens Colorado School of Mines.

1876  Colorado becomes a state
      Atchison, Topeka and Santa Fe Railroad reaches Pueblo.

1877 First students enter University of Colorado
Leadville becomes a silver boomtown.

1879 Utes at White River Agency kill Meeker and others,
attack troops led by Thomas Thornburgh
Agricultural College of Colorado opens.

1880 Leadville miners go on strike
Denver and Rio Grande and Santa Fe railroads agree
that DRG will be primary line in Colorado
University of Denver begins classes.

1882 Ute lands in western Colorado opened to settlement
Colorado Coal and Iron in Pueblo begins manufacture of
Bessemer steel.

1890 Gold discovered at Cripple Creek.

1891 President Harrison sets aside the first federal forest
reserves (national forests).

1892 City and county of Denver merge.

1894 Women vote for first time in Colorado elections.

1896 Leadville's Ice Palace and Ice Carnival lure tourists.

1899 First sugar beet factory opens in Grand Junction
American Smelting and Refining Company absorbs
major Colorado smelters.

1901 Miners strike the Smuggler-Union Company of
Telluride.

1902 Constitutional amendment permits legislature to
establish eight-hour workday
Newlands Act signals start of federal water projects.

1903 Miners strike at Cripple Creek.

1906 Mesa Verde National Park created.

1909 State Highway Commission established.

1914 Coal miners' strike in southern Colorado triggers Ludlow
Massacre.

1915 Rocky Mountain National Park created.

1916 Colorado votes for prohibition.

1920 State's first radio station broadcasts from Colorado
Springs.

1922 Colorado River compact allocates use of Colorado River
waters among seven states.

1925 Oil fields near Craig go into production.

1934  Taylor Grazing Act regulates ranchers' use of public lands.

1936  Voters approve state income tax.

1937  Congress authorizes Colorado–Big Thompson water project.

1942  Rocky Mountain Arsenal established.

1948  Walter Paepcke begins to transform Aspen into cultural and tourist center
Uranium prospectors rush to southwestern Colorado.

1957  Colorado Springs selected as site for North American Air Defense Command.

1958  First students enter Air Force Academy.

1960  Denver Broncos begin play.

1965  Rodolfo Gonzales founds Crusade for Justice.

1971  Denver Art Museum opens new building.

1972  Colorado rejects the 1976 Winter Olympics.

1973  The first bore of the Eisenhower Tunnel opens.

1976  Big Thompson River floods.

1977  Denver Broncos reach Super Bowl for first time.

1978  Denver Performing Arts Center opens.

1982  Exxon terminates Western Slope oil shale project.

1993  Amendment 1 limits state spending.

# COLORADO STATISTICS

## Governors of Colorado

*"Jefferson Territory"*
Robert W. Steele, 1859–1861

*Colorado Territory*
William Gilpin, 1861–1862
John Evans, 1862–1865
Alexander Cummings, 1865–1867
A. Cameron Hunt, 1867–1869
Edward McCook, 1869–1873
Samuel H. Elbert, 1873–1874
Edward McCook, 1874–1875
John L. Routt, 1875–1876

*State of Colorado*
John L. Routt (R), 1876–1879
Frederick W. Pitkin (R), 1879–1883
James B. Grant (D), 1883–1885
Benjamin H. Eaton (R), 1885–1887
Alva Adams (D), 1887–1889
Job A. Cooper (R), 1889–1891
John L. Routt (R), 1891–1893
Davis H. Waite (P), 1893–1895
Albert W. McIntire (R), 1895–1897
Alva Adams (D), 1897–1899
Charles S. Thomas (D), 1899–1901
James B. Orman (D), 1901–1903

James H. Peabody (R), 1903–1905
Jesse F. McDonald (R), 1905–1907
Henry A. Buchtel (R), 1907–1909
John F. Shafroth (D), 1909–1913
Elias M. Ammons (D), 1913–1915
George A. Carlson (R), 1915–1917
Julius C. Gunter (D), 1917–1919
Oliver H. Shoup (R), 1919–1923
William E. Sweet (D), 1923–1925
Clarence J. Morley (R), 1925–1927
William H. Adams (D), 1927–1933
Edwin C. Johnson (D), 1933–1937
Teller Ammons (D), 1937–1939
Ralph Carr (R), 1939–1943
John Vivian (R), 1943–1947
Lee Knous (D), 1947–1949
Walter Johnson (D), 1949–1951
Dan Thornton (R), 1951–1955
Edwin C. Johnson (D), 1955–1957
Stephen McNichols (D), 1957–1963
John A. Love (R), 1963–1973
John Vanderhoof (R), 1973–1975
Richard D. Lamm (D), 1975–1987
Roy Romer (D), 1987–

## U.S. Senators From Colorado

Jerome B. Chaffee (R), 1876–1879
Henry M. Teller (R), 1876–1882
Nathaniel P. Hill (R), 1879–1885
George M. Chilcott (R), 1882
Horace A.W. Tabor (R), 1883
Thomas M. Bowen (R), 1883–1889
Henry M. Teller (R and D), 1885–1909

Edward O. Wolcott (R), 1889–1901
Thomas M. Patterson (D), 1901–1907
Simon Guggenheim (R), 1907–1913
Charles J. Hughes, Jr. (D), 1909–1911
John F. Shafroth (D), 1913–1919
Charles S. Thomas (D), 1913–1921
Lawrence C. Phipps (R), 1919–1931

S. D. Nicholson (R), 1921–1923
Alva B. Adams (D), 1923–1925
Rice W. Means (R), 1925–1927
Charles W. Waterman (R), 1927–1932
Edward P. Costigan (D), 1931–1937
Walter Walker (D), 1932
Karl C. Schuyler (R), 1932–1933
Alva B. Adams (D), 1933–1941
Edwin C. Johnson (D), 1937–1955
Eugene Millikin (R), 1942–1957
Gordon Allott (R), 1955–1973

John Carroll (D), 1957–1963
Peter Dominick (R), 1963–1975
Floyd Haskell (D), 1973–1979
Gary Hart (D), 1975–1987
William Armstrong (R), 1979–1991
Tim Wirth (D), 1987–1993
Hank Brown (R), 1991–
Ben Nighthorse Campbell (D), 1993–

## Delegates and Representatives to Congress

### Delegate for "People of Pikes Peak"
Hiram J. Graham, 1858–1859

### "Jefferson Territory"
Beverly D. Williams, 1859–1860

### Colorado Territory
Hiram P. Bennet, 1861–1865
Allen A. Bradford, 1865–1867
George M. Chilcott, 1867–1869
Allen A. Bradford, 1869–1871
Jerome B. Chaffee, 1871–1875

### State of Colorado
James B. Belford (R), 1876–1877
Thomas M. Patterson (D), 1877–1879
James B. Bedford (R), 1879–1885
George G. Symes (R), 1885–1889
Hosea Townsend (R), 1889–1893
Lafe Pence (P), 1893–1895
John C. Bell (P and D), 1893–1903
John F. Shafroth (R and D),
    1895–1904
Herschel M. Hogg (R), 1903–1907
Franklin E. Brooks (R), 1903–1907
Robert W. Bonynge (R), 1904–1909
George W. Cook (R), 1907–1909
Warren A. Haggot (R), 1907–1909
Atterson W. Rucker (D), 1909–1913
John A. Martin (D), 1909–1913
Edward T. Taylor (D), 1909–1941
George J. Kindel (D), 1913–1915
H. H. Seldomridge (D), 1913–1915
Edward Keating (D), 1913–1919

B. C. Hilliard (D), 1915–1919
Charles B. Timberlake (R), 1915–1933
William N. Vaile (R), 1919–1927
Guy U. Hardy (R), 1919–1933
S. Harrison White (D), 1927–1928
William R. Eaton (R), 1928–1933
John A. Martin (D), 1933–1939
Fred Cummings (D), 1933–1941
Lawrence Lewis (D), 1933–1943
William E. Bundy (D), 1940–1941
Robert Rockwell (R), 1941–1949
Edgar Chenoweth (R), 1941–1949
William S. Hill (R), 1941–1959
Dean Gillespie (R), 1944–1947
John Carroll (D), 1947–1951
John Marsalis (D), 1949–1951
Wayne Aspinall (D), 1949–1973
Edgar Chenoweth (R), 1951–1965
Byron Rogers (D), 1951–1971
Byron Johnson (D), 1959–1961
Peter Dominick (R), 1961–1963
Don Brotzman (R), 1963–1965
Roy H. McVicker (D), 1965–1967
Frank Evans (D), 1965–1979
Don Brotzman (R), 1967–1975
James McKevitt (R), 1971–1973
William L. Armstrong (R), 1973–1979
James P. Johnson (R), 1973–1981
Patricia Schroeder (D), 1973–
Tim Wirth (D), 1975–1987
Ray Kogovsek (D), 1979–1985
Ken Kramer (R), 1979–1987

Hank Brown (R), 1981–1991
Dan Schaefer (R), 1983–
Mike Strang (R), 1985–1987
Ben Nighthorse Campbell (D),
    1987–1993

Joel Hefley (R), 1987–
David Skaggs (D), 1987–
Wayne Allard (R), 1991–
Scott Meines (R), 1993–

## Denver Mayors From the Legal Beginnings of the City

Charles A. Cook, 1861–1863
Amos Steck, 1863–1864
H. J. Brendlinger, 1864–1865
George T. Clark, 1865–1866
Milton M. DeLano, 1866–1868
William M. Clayton, 1868–1869
Baxter B. Stiles, 1869–1871
John Harper, 1871–1872
Joseph E. Bates, 1872–1873
Francis M. Case, 1873–1874
William J. Barker, 1874–1876
Richard G. Buckingham, 1876–1877
Baxter B. Stiles, 1877–1878
Richard Sopris, 1878–1881
Robert Morris, 1881–1883
John L. Routt, 1883–1885
Joseph E. Bates, 1885–1887
William Scott Lee, 1887–1889
Wolfe Londoner, 1889–1891
Platt Rogers, 1891–1893
Marion D. Van Horn, 1893–1895

Thomas S. McMurray, 1895–1899
Henry V. Johnson, 1899–1901
Robert R. Wright, Jr., 1901–1904
Robert W. Speer, 1904–1912
Henry J. Arnold, 1912–1913
J. M. Perkins, 1913–1915
William H. Sharpley, 1915–1916
Robert W. Speer, 1916–1918
William F.R. Mills, 1918–1919
Dewey C. Bailey, 1919–1923
Benjamin F. Stapleton, 1923–1931
George D. Begole, 1931–1935
Benjamin F. Stapleton, 1935–1947
J. Quigg Newton, Jr., 1947–1955
Will F. Nicholson, 1955–1959
Richard Y. Batterton, 1959–1963
Thomas G. Currigan, 1963–1968
William H. McNichols, Jr., 1968–1983
Federico F. Peña, 1983–1991
Wellington E. Webb, 1991–

## POPULATION GROWTH

|  | 1870 | 1880 | 1890 | 1900 | 1910 |
|---|---|---|---|---|---|
| State of Colorado | 39,864 | 194,327 | 413,249 | 539,700 | 799,024 |
| Denver (Metropolitan area)* | 4,759 | 35,629 | 106,713 | 133,859 | 213,381 (219,314) |
| Colorado Springs (Metropolitan area)* | — | 4,226 | 11,140 | 21,085 | 29,078 |
| Pueblo (Metropolitan area)* | — | 3,127 | 24,558 | 28,157 | 41,747 |

| (Continued) | 1920 | 1930 | 1940 | 1950 | 1960 |
|---|---|---|---|---|---|
| State of Colorado | 939,629 | 1,035,791 | 1,123,296 | 1,325,089 | 1,753,947 |
| Denver (Metropolitan area)* | 256,491 (264,232) | 287,861 (330,761) | 322,412 (384,372) | 415,786 (563,832) | 493,889 (929,383) |
| Colorado Springs (Metropolitan area)* | 30,105 | 33,237 | 36,789 | 45,472 | 70,194 (143,742) |
| Pueblo (Metropolitan area)* | 43,050 | 50,096 | 52,162 (62,039) | 63,685 (90,188) | 91,181 (118,707) |

| (Continued) | 1970 | 1980 | 1990 |
|---|---|---|---|
| State of Colorado | 2,207,259 | 2,888,834 | 3,294,394 |
| Denver (Metropolitan area)* | 514,678 (1,227,529) | 491,396 (1,619,921) | 467,610 (1,848,319) |
| Colorado Springs (Metropolitan area)* | 135,060 (235,972) | 215,150 (317,458) | 281,140 (397,014) |
| Pueblo (Metropolitan area)* | 97,453 (118,238) | 101,686 (125,972) | 98,640 (123,051) |

* 1910–1940: metropolitan district; 1950: standard metropolitan area; 1960–1980: standard metropolitan statistical area; 1990: metropolitan statistical area or consolidated metropolitan statistical area.

|  | 1870 | 1880 | 1890 | 1900 | 1910 |
|---|---|---|---|---|---|
| Number of farms | 1,738 | 4,506 | 16,389 | 24,700 | 46,170 |
| Acres irrigated | — | — | 890,735 | 1,611,271 | 2,792,032 |
| Employment in agriculture | 7,353 | 16,336 | 43,552 | 49,457 | 85,704 |
| Number of manufac-turing establishments | 256 | 599 | 1,518 | 1,323 | 2,034 |
| Employment in manufacturing | 937 | 4,393 | 12,729 | 20,007 | 29,581 |
| Employment in mining | 2,478 | 34,675 | 24,195 | 34,936 | 28,376 |
| Miles of railroad | 157 | 1,570 | 4,176 | 4,587 | 5,532 |
| Motor vehicle registration | — | — | — | — | — |

| (Continued) | 1920 | 1930 | 1940 | 1950 | 1960 |
|---|---|---|---|---|---|
| Number of farms | 59,934 | 59,956 | 51,436 | 45,578 | 33,183 |
| Acres irrigated | 3,348,385 | 3,393,619 | 2,467,548 | 2,872,348 | (1959) 2,684,757 |
| Employment in agriculture | 100,153 | 104,413 | 73,911 | 72,419 | 48,653 |
| Number of manufac-turing establishments | 2,631 | 1,545 | (1939) 1,298 | (1947) 1,602 | (1958) 2,274 |
| Employment in manufacturing | 35,673 | 34,266 | 32,687 | 56,700 | 84,000 |
| Employment in mining | 23,382 | 20,702 | 15,897 | 10,275 | 14,250 |
| Miles of railroad | 5,389 | 4,928 | 4,552 | 4,273 | 3,786 |
| Motor vehicle registration | 120,000 | 309,000 | 352,000 | 564,000 | 924,000 |

| (Continued) | 1970 | 1980 | 1990 |
|---|---|---|---|
| Number of Farms | 27,950 | 26,500 | 27,000 |
| Acres irrigated | (1969) 2,894,984 | (1978) 3,458,031 | (1987) 3,013,773 |
| Employment in agriculture | 36,826 | 37,200 |  |
| Number of manufac-turing establishments | (1969) 2,461 | 3,880 | 5,004 |
| Employment in manufacturing | 118,061 | 181,400 | 187,476 |
| Employment in mining | 13,733 | 35,600 | 20,685 |
| Miles of railroad | 3,576 | 3,459 | 3,279 |
| Motor vehicle registration | 1,442,000 | 2,342,000 | 3,155,000 |

# NOTES

## 1: Mountains and Plains

1. Donald Jackson, ed., *The Journals of Zebulon Montgomery Pike, With Letters and Related Documents* (Norman: University of Oklahoma Press, 1966), 1:345 (emphasis in original).

2. Edwin James, *Account of an Expedition From Pittsburgh to the Rocky Mountains . . . Under the Command of Maj. S. H. Long, of the U.S. Top. Engineers,* vols. 14–17 of *Early Western Travels, 1748–1846,* ed. Reuben Gold Thwaites (New York: Ams Press, 1966), 15:232, 248–251, 262; 17:133, 147 (extract is from 17:147).

3. Donald Jackson and Mary Lee Spence, eds., *The Expeditions of John Charles Fremont,* vol. 1: *Travels From 1838 to 1844* (Urbana: University of Illinois Press, 1970), p. 435; Thomas Farnham, *Travels in the Great Western Prairie, The Anahuac and Rocky Mountains, and in the Oregon Territory,* vol. 27 of *Early Western Travels,* ed. Thwaites, pp. 108–109, 114; Francis Parkman, *The Oregon Trail,* ed. E. N. Feltskog (Madison: University of Wisconsin Press, 1969), p. 318; Horace Greeley, *An Overland Journey From New York to San Francisco in the Summer of 1859,* ed. Charles T. Duncan (New York: Knopf, 1964), pp. 81, 85; Rufus Sage, *Rocky Mountain Life, or Startling Scenes and Perilous Adventures in the Far West* (Boston: Wentworth, 1857), pp. 205–208.

4. Samuel Bowles, *Our New West* (Hartford: Hartford Publishing Co., 1869), p. 42.

5. Albert Richardson, *Beyond the Mississippi: From the Great River to the Great Ocean* (Hartford: American Publishing Co., 1867), p. 177; Samuel Bowles, *Across the Continent* (Springfield, Mass.: S. Bowles, 1865), p. 30.

6. Greeley, *An Overland Journey,* p. 108.

7. *Journals of Zebulon Montgomery Pike,* 1:286.

8. Demas Barnes, *From the Atlantic to the Pacific, Overland* (New York: D. Van Nostrand, 1866), p. 22; Harold Nicolson, *Diaries and Letters, 1930–1939,* ed. Nigel Nicolson (New York: Atheneum, 1966), p. 143; John I.H. Baur, ed., *The Autobiography of Worthington Whittredge* (New York: Brooklyn Museum, n.d.), p. 45.

9. Jackson and Spence, *Expeditions of John Charles Fremont,* 1:711.

10. Jackson and Spence, *Expeditions of John Charles Fremont,* 1:712–718.

11. Lewis Mumford, *The Culture of Cities* (New York: Harcourt, Brace, 1938), p. 367.

12. Theodore Roosevelt, *Outdoor Pastimes of an American Hunter* (New York: Charles Scribner's Sons, 1905), p. 78.

13. Jean Stafford, *The Mountain Lion* (New York: Harcourt, Brace, 1947), p. 127.

14. James H. Baker and Leroy R. Hafen, eds., *History of Colorado,* 5 vols. (Denver: State Historical Society of Colorado, 1927), 1:14.

## 2: The First Coloradans

1. Clark Wissler, *The American Indian* (New York: Oxford University Press, 1938), p. 34.

2. George E. Hyde, *Indians of the High Plains: From the Prehistoric Period to the Coming of Europeans* (Norman: University of Oklahoma Press, 1959), p. 20.

3. Rupert N. Richardson, quoted in Ernest Wallace and E. Adamson Hoebel, *The Comanches: Lords of the South Plains* (Norman: University of Oklahoma Press, 1952), p. 12.

4. Alfred B. Thomas, *After Coronado: Spanish Exploration Northeast of New Mexico, 1696–1727* (Norman: University of Oklahoma Press, 1936), p. 69.

5. George Hyde, *The Life of George Bent, Written From His Letters,* ed. Savoie Lottinville (Norman: University of Oklahoma Press, 1968), p. 17.

6. Donald J. Berthrong, *The Southern Cheyennes* (Norman: University of Oklahoma Press, 1963), p. 43.

7. Walter Prescott Webb, *The Texas Rangers* (Boston: Houghton, Mifflin, 1935), p. 13.

## 3: New Mexico's Northern Frontier

1. Lewis Garrard, *Wah-to-Yah and the Taos Trail* (Palo Alto: American West Publishing Co., 1968), p. 134; Josiah Gregg, *The Commerce of the Prairies* (Chicago: Lakeside Press, 1926), p. 89.

2. David J. Weber, *The Taos Trappers* (Norman: University of Oklahoma Press, 1971), p. 91.

3. There is no end of argument over the timing and location of the several posts built by Gantt and Bent. This account follows in part that of Janet LeCompte, "Gantt's Fort and Bent's Picket Post," *Colorado Magazine* 41 (April 1964):111–125, and in part that of Samuel P. Arnold, "William W. Bent," in *The Mountain Men and the Fur Trade of the Far West,* vol. 6, ed. Leroy Hafen (Glendale, Calif.: Arthur H. Clark, 1968).

4. Garrard, *Wah-to-Yah,* p. 35.

5. Thomas Farnham, *Travels in the Great Western Prairie, The Anahuac and Rocky Mountains, and in the Oregon Territory,* vol. 28 of *Early Western Travels, 1748–1846,* ed. Reuben Gold Thwaites (New York: Ams Press, 1966), p. 163.

6. Donald Berthrong, *The Southern Cheyennes* (Norman: University of Oklahoma Press, 1963), p. 124; David Lavender, *Bent's Fort* (Gloucester, Mass.: Peter Smith, 1968), pp. 339–361.

7. Donald Meinig, *Southwest: Three Peoples in Geographical Change, 1600–1970* (New York: Oxford University Press, 1971), p. 27.

8. William B. Taylor and Elliott West, "Patron Leadership at the Crossroads: Southern Colorado in the Late Nineteenth Century," *Pacific Historical Review* 42 (August 1973):339.

9. William E. Pabor, *Colorado as an Agricultural State* (New York: Orange Judd, 1883), pp. 117–118; Samuel S. Wallihan and T. O. Bigney, eds., *The Rocky Mountain Directory and Colorado Gazetteer for 1871* (Denver: S. S. Wallihan, 1870), p. 112.

10. William Bell, *New Tracks in North America* (London: Chapman and Hall, 1869), 1:81.

11. Samuel Bowles, *Our New West* (Hartford: Hartford Publishing Co., 1869), p. 194; Pabor, *Colorado,* p. 131.

12. Hubert Howe Bancroft, *History of Nevada, Colorado and Wyoming, 1540–1888* (San Francisco: History Company, 1890), p. 593.

## 4: The Pikes Peak Gold Rush

1. Albert Richardson, *Beyond the Mississippi: From the Great River to the Great Ocean* (Hartford: American Publishing Company, 1867), p. 187.

2. Jerome Smiley, *History of Denver, With Outlines of the Earlier History of the Rocky Mountain Country* (Denver: Denver Times, 1901), p. 293; Leroy Hafen, ed., *Overland Routes to the Gold Fields,* vol. 11, Southwest Historical Series (Glendale, Calif.: Arthur H. Clark, 1942), p. 185.

3. Leroy Hafen, ed., *Colorado Gold Rush: Contemporary Letters and Reports,* vol. 10, Southwest Historical Series (Glendale, Calif.: Arthur H. Clark, 1942), pp. 30, 33, 41, 42, 53, 57, 63, 68.

4. Henry Villard, *Past and Present of the Pike's Peak Gold Region,* ed. LeRoy Hafen (Princeton: Princeton University Press, 1932), pp. 11–12.

5. William Larimer to family, June 29, 1859, quoted in *Reminiscences of General William H. Larimer and of His Son William H.H. Larimer* (Pittsburgh: Press of the New Era Printing Company, 1918), p. 107.

6. Letter of A. A. Brookfield, January 26, 1859, in Hafen, *Colorado Gold Rush,* p. 221.

7. Hafen, *Colorado Gold Rush,* pp. 238, 278; Leroy Hafen, ed., *Pike's Peak Gold Rush Guidebooks of 1859* (Glendale, Calif.: Arthur H. Clark, 1941), p. 286.

8. *Missouri Republican,* May 25, 1859, in Hafen, *Colorado Gold Rush,* p. 286.

9. *Missouri Republican,* June 15, 1859, in Hafen, *Colorado Gold Rush,* p. 371; Villard, *Past and Present,* p. 37.

10. *Missouri Republican,* August 26, 1859, and *Missouri Democrat,* November 22, 1859, in Leroy Hafen, ed., *Reports from Colorado, 1859–1865,* vol. 13, Far West and Rockies Series (Glendale, Calif.: Arthur H. Clark, 1954–1961), pp. 150, 193.

11. *Missouri Republican,* November 17, 1859, in Hafen, *Reports from Colorado,* p. 199.

12. *Missouri Republican,* November 10, 1859, in Hafen, *Reports from Colorado,* p. 186; Frederick Jackson Turner, "The West and American Ideals," in *Frontier and Section,* ed. Ray A. Billington (Englewood Cliffs, N.J.: Prentice-Hall, 1961), pp. 100–101.

13. Hafen, *Colorado Gold Rush,* p. 211.

14. Sidney B. Morrison, letter of September 16, 1860, in "Letters From Colorado, 1860–63," *Colorado Magazine* 16 (May 1939):92.

15. Thomas M. Marshall, ed., *Early Records of Gilpin County, Colorado, 1859–1861,* vol. 11, University of Colorado Historical Collections (Boulder, Colo., 1920), p. 124.

16. Villard, *Past and Present,* p. 124.

17. *Rocky Mountain News,* May 7, 1859, quoted in Frederick L. Paxson, "The Territory of Colorado," *American Historical Review* 12 (October 1906):53–65.

18. *Missouri Republican,* November 10, 1859, in Hafen, *Reports from Colorado,* p. 187.

19. Charles Henderson, *Mining in Colorado,* United States Geological Survey Professional Paper no. 138 (1926), pp. 29–30.

20. Howard Lamar, *The Far Southwest, 1846–1912: A Territorial History* (New Haven: Yale University Press, 1966), p. 234.

21. W. R. Vickers, *History of the City of Denver, Arapahoe County, and the State of Colorado* (Chicago: O. L. Baskin, 1880), p. 267.

22. Demas Barnes, *From the Atlantic to the Pacific, Overland* (New York: D. Van Nostrand, 1866), p. 24.

23. Samuel Bowles, *Across the Continent* (Springfield, Mass.: S. Bowles, 1865), p. 34; Lynn Perrigo, "Law and Order in Early Colorado Mining Camps," *Mississippi Valley Historical Review* 28 (June 1941):51.

24. Richardson, *Beyond the Mississippi,* p. 177; Earl Pomeroy, "Toward a Reorientation of Western History: Continuity and Environment," *Mississippi Valley Historical Review* 41 (March 1955):579–600; Diary of Charles C. Post, June 27, 1859, in Hafen, *Overland Routes,* p. 54.

## 5: The Era of the Booster, 1863–1876

1. William Larimer to family, February 1859, quoted in *Reminiscences of General William H. Larimer and of His Son William H.H. Larimer* (Pittsburgh: Press of the New Era Printing Company, 1918), p. 168; *Cincinnati Commercial,* June 5, 1855.

2. Junius Wharton, *History of the City of Denver* (Denver: Byers and Dailey, 1866), p. 1.

3. Samuel S. Wallihan and T. O. Bigney, eds., *The Rocky Mountain Directory and Colorado Gazetteer for 1871* (Denver: S. S. Wallihan, 1870), p. 245.

4. Bayard Taylor, *Colorado: A Summer Trip* (New York: G. P. Putnam and Son, 1867), p. 61; Samuel Bowles, *Our New West* (Hartford: Hartford Publishing Co., 1869), p. 183; William Brewer, *Rocky Mountain Letters, 1869* (Denver: Colorado Mountain Club, 1930), p. 51; *Engineering and Mining Journal,* July 13, 1869.

5. Demas Barnes, *From the Atlantic to the Pacific, Overland* (New York: D. Van Nostrand, 1866), p. 8.

6. George F. Hyde, *The Life of George Bent, Written from His Letters,* ed. Savoie Lottinville (Norman: University of Oklahoma Press, 1968), p. 140.

7. *Rocky Mountain News,* August 10, 1864; Colonel John Chivington to Major Edward Wynkoop, May 31, 1864, quoted in Donald Berthrong, *The Southern Cheyennes* (Norman: University of Oklahoma Press, 1963), p. 189.

8. Berthrong, *Southern Cheyennes,* p. 203.

9. Hyde, *Life of George Bent,* pp. 152, 155.

10. Pueblo *Colorado Chieftain,* June 1, 1869.

11. Chicago *Democratic Press, Review of Commerce for 1857,* p. 47; Caleb Atwater, *A History of the State of Ohio* (Cincinnati: Glazen and Shepard, 1838), p. 283.

12. William Gilpin, *The Mission of the North American People: Geographical, Social and Political* (Philadelphia: J. B. Lippincott, 1874), especially pp. 31, 69, 77, 89.

13. Gilpin, *Mission,* pp. 108, 119–120, 127; Jerome Smiley, *History of Denver, With Outlines of the Earlier History of the Rocky Mountain Country* (Denver: Denver Times, 1901), pp. 439–440.

14. *Rocky Mountain News,* November 24, 1859; Smiley, *History of Denver,* pp. 439–440.

15. R. B. Townsend, *A Tenderfoot in Colorado* (Norman: University of Oklahoma Press, 1968), pp. 107–108; W. R. Vickers, *History of the City of Denver, Arapahoe County, and the State of Colorado* (Chicago: O. L. Baskin, 1880), pp. 221–223.

16. William Bell, *New Tracks in North America* (London: Chapman and Hall, 1869), 2:261.

17. Smiley, *History of Denver,* p. 439; William J. Palmer to Queen Mellen, January 17, 1870, quoted in John S. Fisher, *A Builder of the West: The Life of General William Jackson Palmer* (Caldwell, Idaho: Caxton Printers, 1939), pp. 177–178.

18. *The Pueblo Colony of Southern Colorado* (Lancaster: Inquirer Printing and Publishing, 1879), p. 19.

19. Michael Beshoar, "All About Trinidad and Las Animas County, Colorado" (1882), p. 59.

20. William Jackson Palmer to Robert A. Cameron, December 1871, quoted in George L. Anderson, "General William Jackson Palmer: Man of Vision," *Colorado College Studies,* no. 4 (Colorado Springs: Spring 1960), p. 15.

21. Herbert O. Brayer, *William Blackmore: Early Financing of the Denver and Rio Grande Railway and Ancillary Land Companies* (Denver: Bradford-Robinson, 1949), p. 265.

22. Frank Fossett, *Colorado: Its Gold and Silver Mines, Farms and Stock Ranges, and Health and Pleasure Resorts* (New York: C. G. Crawford, 1879), p. 151.

## Interlude: Coloradans in 1876

1. *Daily Central City Register,* February 9, 1876.

2. Frank Hall to mother, January 20, 1867, Hall Manuscripts, State Historical Society of Colorado, Denver, Colo.

3. *Daily Central City Register,* June 2, 1874.

4. Frank Hall to mother, June 28, 1868, Hall Manuscripts.

5. Frank Hall to mother, May 2, 1869, Hall Manuscripts.

6. Frank Hall to mother, July 3, 1876, Hall Manuscripts.

7. H. H. (Helen Hunt Jackson), *Bits of Travel at Home* (Boston: Roberts Brothers, 1886), pp. 224, 227.

## 6: The Bonanza Years

1. Frank Fossett, *Colorado: Its Gold and Silver Mines, Farms and Stock Ranges, and Health and Pleasure Resorts* (New York: C. G. Crawford, 1879), pp. 219–220.

2. Duane Smith, *Horace Tabor: His Life and the Legend* (Boulder: Colorado Associated University Press, 1973), pp. 40, 42.

3. David Lavender, "This Wondrous Town; This Instant City," *American West* 4 (August 1967):6.

4. Fossett, *Colorado*, p. 413.

5. Robert Atheam, *Westward the Briton* (New York: Charles Scribner's Sons, 1953), p. 51; Fossett, *Colorado*, p. 415.

6. Athearn, *Westward*, p. 52; William W. Howard, "The Modern Leadville," *Harper's Weekly*, December 1, 1888, p. 928; Ernest Ingersoll, *The Crest of the Continent* (Chicago: R. R. Donnelley and Sons, 1885), p. 224.

7. Duane Smith, *Rocky Mountain Boom Town: A History of Durango* (Albuquerque: University of New Mexico Press, 1980), p. 90.

8. Smith, *Rocky Mountain Boom Town*, p. 56.

## 7: The Businessman's State

1. Howard Lamar, "Colorado: The Centennial State in the Bicentennial Year," *Colorado Magazine* 53 (July 1976):120.

2. Gunther Barth, *Instant Cities: Urbanization and the Rise of San Francisco and Denver* (New York: Oxford University Press, 1975), p. 129.

3. Samuel S. Wallihan and T. O. Bigney, eds., *The Rocky Mountain Directory and Colorado Gazetteer for 1871* (Denver: S. S. Wallihan, 1870), p. 251; *History of the Arkansas Valley, Colorado* (Chicago: O. L. Baskin, 1881), pp. 34–37.

4. *Tenth Census of the United States: 1880, Statistics of the Population of the United States* (Washington, D.C.: Government Printing Office, 1883), p. xx.

5. Governor Frederick Pitkin, Annual Message, 1881, quoted in Donald Hensel, "A History of the Colorado Constitution in the Nineteenth Century" (Ph.D. diss., University of Colorado, 1957), p. 308.

6. G. Michael McCarthy, "Retreat From Responsibility: The Colorado Legislature in the Conservation Era, 1876–1908," *Rocky Mountain Social Science Journal* 10 (April 1973):34; Elmer Ellis, *Henry Moore Teller: Defender of the West* (Caldwell, Idaho: Caxton Printers, 1941), p. 373.

7. Silas W. Burt and E. L. Berthoud, *The Rocky Mountain Gold Regions* (Denver: Rocky Mountain News Printing Company, 1861), p. 29.

8. *Boulder County News,* May 8, 1874, quoted in Frederick S. Allen et al., *The University of Colorado: 1876–1976* (New York: Harcourt Brace Jovanovich, 1976), p. 26.

9. *Gunnison News-Champion,* quoted in Michael McGiffert, *The Higher Learning in Colorado: An Historical Study* (Denver: Sage Books, 1964), p. 5.

10. Isaac Marcossen, "The Millionaire Yield of Denver," *Munseys* 47 (May 1912):167; Jerome Smiley, *History of Denver, With Outlines of the Earlier History of the Rocky Mountain Country* (Denver: *Denver Times,* 1901), pp. 493–494.

## 8: The Other Side of the Coin:
## A Generation of Industrial Warfare

1. Emma F. Langdon, *The Cripple Creek Strike* (Denver: Great Western Publishing Company, 1904–1905), p. 94.

2. Ray Stannard Baker, "The Reign of Lawlessness: Anarchy and Despotism in Colorado," *McClure's* 23 (May 1904):52–53; James E. Wright, *The Politics of Populism: Dissent in Colorado* (New Haven: Yale University Press, 1974), p. 234.

3. Jewell Wolcott, ed., *My Dear Friend Chas.*, Essays and Monographs in Colorado History, Monograph 5 (1990), p. 28.

4. *Labor Enquirer,* June 16, 1883, and October 2, 1886, quoted in Wright, *Politics of Populism,* pp. 25, 28.

5. Letter of B. O'Driscoll to Davis Waite, November 10, 1892, quoted in Wright, *Politics of Populism,* p. 157.

6. Vernon Jensen, *Heritage of Conflict: Labor Relations in the Nonferrous Metals Industry up to 1930* (Ithaca: Cornell University Press, 1950), p. 67.

7. Charles E. Strangeland, "Preliminaries to the Labor War in Colorado," *Political Science Quarterly* 23 (March 1908):7.

8. *Denver Times,* January 31, 1901.

9. Jensen, *Heritage of Conflict,* p. 112.

10. Gene M. Gressley, ed., *Bostonians and Bullion: The Journal of Robert Livermore, 1892–1915* (Lincoln: University of Nebraska Press, 1968), p. 92.

11. Strangeland, "Labor War in Colorado," pp. 2–3.

12. George G. Suggs, Jr., *Colorado's War on Militant Unionism* (Detroit: Wayne State University Press, 1972), p. 74.

13. Ray Stannard Baker, "The Reign of Lawlessness: Anarchy and Despotism in Colorado," *McClure's* 23 (May 1904):48.

14. Suggs, *Militant Unionism,* p. 104; Baker, "Reign of Lawlessness," p. 43.

15. George G. Suggs, Jr., "The Colorado Coal Miners' Strike of 1903–1904: A Prelude to Ludlow," *Journal of the West* 12 (January 1973):47.

16. Colin B. Goodykoontz, ed., *Papers of Edward P. Costigan Relating to the Progressive Movement in Colorado, 1902–1917* (Boulder: University of Colorado Press, 1941), p. 307.

17. Graham Adams, Jr., *Age of Industrial Violence, 1910–1915: The Activities and Findings of the United States Commission on Industrial Relations* (New York: Columbia University Press, 1966), p. 149.

18. Goodykoontz, *Papers of Edward P. Costigan,* p. 307.

19. *The Military Occupation of the Coal Strike Zone of Colorado by the Colorado National Guard, 1913–1914: Report of the Commanding General to the Governor for the Use of the Congressional Committee* (Denver, 1914), pp. 7, 10.

20. Walter H. Fink, *The Ludlow Massacre* (Denver: Williamson-Haffner, 1914), p. 13.

21. George P. West, *Report on the Colorado Strike* (Washington, D.C.: United States Commission on Industrial Relations, 1915), p. 99.

22. West, *Colorado Strike,* p. 20.

## 9: Farming and Ranching in the American Desert

1. Samuel Bowles, *Our New West* (Hartford: Hartford Publishing Co., 1869), p. 189; *Rocky Mountain News,* July 11, 1866, quoted in Deryl V. Gease, "William Byers and the Colorado Agricultural Society," *Colorado Magazine* 43 (Fall 1966):335.

2. William E. Pabor, *Colorado as an Agricultural State* (New York: Orange Judd, 1883), p. 11.

3. Pabor, *Colorado,* p. 13.

4. *Daily Colorado Tribune,* October 15, 1870, quoted in *The Union Colony at Greeley, Colorado, 1869–1871,* ed. James F. Willard, vol. 1, University of Colorado Historical Collections (Boulder, Colo., 1918), p. 287.

5. Pabor, *Colorado,* p. 33; "The Chicago-Colorado Colony," pamphlet of 1871, quoted in *Experiments in Colorado Colonization, 1869 1872,* eds. James F. Willard and Colin B. Goodykoontz, vol. 3, University of Colorado Historical Collections (Boulder, Colo., 1926), p. 141.

6. Colorado Mortgage and Investment Company, *Farmlands in Colorado* (Denver, 1879), subtitle.

7. Article XVI, Sections 5 and 6, *Constitution of the State of Colorado,* 1876.

8. William Gilpin, *The Mission of the North American People* (Philadelphia: J. B. Lippincott, 1874), pp. 71–72; Junius Wharton, *History of the City of Denver* (Denver: Byers and Dailey, 1866), p. 175; Ovando Hollister, *The Mines of Colorado* (Springfield, Mass.: Samuel Bowles, 1867), p. 426; *Daily Colorado Tribune,* December 16, 1869, quoted in Willard and Goodykoontz, *Experiments,* p. 11.

9. Clifford Westermeier, "The Legal Status of the Colorado Cattleman, 1867–1887," *Colorado Magazine* 25 (July 1948):159; Luke Cahill, "Recollections of a Plainsman," manuscript at the State Historical Society of Colorado, p. 40.

10. *Colorado Live Stock Record,* quoted in Ernest S. Osgood, *The Day of the Cattleman* (Minneapolis: University of Minnesota Press, 1929), p. 94; *Boulder County News,* quoted in Ora B. Peake, *The Colorado Range Cattle Industry* (Glendale, Calif.: Arthur H. Clark, 1937), p. 273.

11. Pabor, *Colorado,* p. 12.

12. David Emmons, *Garden in the Grasslands* (Lincoln: University of Nebraska Press, 1971), pp. 158–160.

13. Clarice Richards, *A Tenderfoot Bride: Tales From an Old Ranch* (Lincoln: University of Nebraska Press, 1988), pp. 198–199.

14. Julie Jones-Eddy, ed., *Homesteading Women: An Oral History of Colorado, 1890–1950* (New York: Twayne, 1992), pp. 16–17.

15. Carl F. Kraenzel, *The Great Plains in Transition* (Norman: University of Oklahoma Press, 1955), p. 153.

16. H. H. Finnell, "Pity the Poor Land," *Soil Conservation* 12 (September 1946):27.

17. William E. Smythe, *The Conquest of Arid America,* ed. Lawrence Lee (Seattle: University of Washington Press, 1969), p. vii; Pabor, *Colorado,* p. 137.

18. Grand Junction *Daily Sentinel,* September 15, 1899, quoted in William J. May, Jr., "The Colorado Sugar Manufacturing Company: Grand Junction Plant," *Colorado Magazine* 55 (Winter 1978):28.

19. Chicago *Democratic Press, Review of Commerce for 1856,* p. 19.

20. Pabor, *Colorado,* p. 18.

## 10: The People of Colorado, 1876–1916

1. Pueblo *Colorado Chieftain,* July 4, 1876.

2. *Rocky Mountain News,* July 6, 1876.

3. Elizabeth Cady Stanton et al., eds., *History of Woman Suffrage* (Rochester, N.Y.: Charles Mann, 1886), 3:720, 723.

4. Ellis Meredith, "Women Citizens of Colorado," *The Great Divide* 11 (February 1894):53.

5. Carrie Chapman Catt to Ellis Meredith, June 12, 1893, and Meredith to Catt, June 30, 1893, in Ellis Meredith Papers, State Historical Society of Colorado, Denver, Colo.

6. Ellis Meredith to Carrie Chapman Catt, June 14, 1893, and Meredith to Susan B. Anthony, June 14, 1893, Meredith Papers.

7. Ellis Meredith to Carrie Chapman Catt, June 3, 1893, Meredith Papers.

8. Susan B. Anthony to the women of Denver, July 16, 1893, Meredith Papers.

9. Carrie Chapman Catt to Ellis Meredith, July 16, 1893, Meredith Papers.

10. William McLeod Raine, "Truth About Women Suffrage," *The Circle* (October 1907):220, quoted in Billie Barnes Jensen, "The Woman Suffrage Movement in Colorado" (M.A. thesis, University of Colorado, 1959), p. 81.

11. Meredith, "Women Citizens," p. 53.

12. Susan B. Anthony to Ellis Meredith, October 25, 1893; November 27, 1893, Meredith Papers.

13. Susan B. Anthony to Martha Conine, June 24, 1902, in Conine Papers, Western History Department, Denver Public Library.

14. Denver Women's Law and Order League to Lyman Abbott, June 13, 1914, Meredith Papers.

15. Sheryll Paterson-Black, "Women Homesteaders on the Great Plains Frontier," *Frontiers: A Journal of Women Studies* 1 (Spring 1976):67–88; interview with Donald Wall conducted by Stephen J. Leonard, October 8, 1993.

16. Civil Works Administration, Logan and Phillips counties, Mrs. S. S. Wormley interview, p. 105, typescript in Colorado Historical Society collection, hereafter

cited as CWA. CWA, Yuma County, Mrs. Hans Christensen interview, p. 60; CWA, Morgan and Sedgwick counties, Mrs. W. H. Clatworthy interview, p. 243.

17. Ruth Moynihan et al., eds., *So Much to Be Done: Women Settlers on the Mining and Ranching Frontier* (Lincoln: University of Nebraska Press, 1990), p. 146; CWA, Larimer County, Mrs. William B. St. Clair interview, p. 164.

18. Lillian Schlissel et al., eds., *Far From Home: Families of the Western Journey* (New York: Schocken Books, 1989), p. 139; Michael B. Husband, ed., "The Recollections of a Schoolteacher in the Disappointment Creek Valley," *Colorado Magazine* 51 (Spring 1974):144–145.

19. Katherine Harris, "Women and Families on Northeastern Colorado Homesteads, 1873–1920" (Ph.D. diss., University of Colorado–Boulder, 1983), p. 174.

20. Nell Brown Probst, *Those Strenuous Dames of the Colorado Prairie* (Boulder: Pruett Publishing, 1982), pp. 25–40.

21. Sarah Deutsch, *No Separate Refuge: Culture, Class, and Gender on an Anglo-Hispanic Frontier in the American Southwest, 1880–1940* (New York: Oxford University Press, 1987), pp. 61, 200.

22. Leanne L. Sander, "'The Men All Died of Miners' Disease': Women and Families in the Industrial Mining Environment of Upper Clear Creek Colorado, 1870–1900" (Ph.D. diss., University of Colorado–Boulder, 1990), p. 299.

23. Janet Robinson, *The Magnificent Mountain Women: Adventures in the Colorado Rockies* (Lincoln: University of Nebraska Press, 1991) covers numerous Colorado women, including Eastwood. Maxine Benson details Maxwell's life in *Martha Maxwell, Rocky Mountain Naturalist* (Lincoln: University of Nebraska Press, 1986). Elizabeth Jameson, "Women as Workers: Women as Civilizers: True Womanhood in the American West," in Susan Armitage and Elizabeth Jameson, eds., *The Women's West* (Norman: University of Oklahoma Press, 1987), p. 155, tells of Welch.

24. Elizabeth Jameson, "Imperfect Unions: Class and Gender in Cripple Creek," *Frontiers: A Journal of Women Studies* 1 (Spring 1976):106; *Queen Bee*, January 13, 1892; *Queen Bee* and *Labor Enquirer*, quoted in Stephen J. Leonard, "Bristling for Their Rights: Colorado Women and the Mandate of 1893," *Colorado Heritage* (Spring 1993):9.

25. Colorado Bureau of Labor Statistics, *Seventh Biennial Report* (Denver: Smith-Brooks, 1900), p. 78.

26. Janet Lecompte, ed., *Emily: The Diary of a Hard-Worked Woman* (Lincoln: University of Nebraska Press, 1987), p. 122.

27. Joyce Goodfriend, "The Struggle for Survival: Widows in Denver, 1880–1912," in Arlene Scadron, ed., *On Their Own: Widows and Widowhood in the American Southwest* (Urbana: University of Illinois Press, 1988), p. 178.

28. Anne M. Butler, *Daughters of Joy, Sisters of Mercy: Prostitutes in the American West, 1865–1890* (Urbana: University of Illinois Press, 1985), pp. 63–64; Phil Goodstein, *The Seamy Side of Denver* (Denver: New Social Publications, 1993), pp. 42–43; Philip S. Van Cise, *Fighting the Underworld* (Cambridge, Mass.: Riverside Press, 1936), p. 21.

29. Undated newspaper clipping in Martha Conine scrapbook, p. 53, Conine Papers; Lawrence Lewis, "How Women Suffrage Works in Colorado," *Outlook* 82 (January 27, 1906):175; Salida *Record*, January 1, 1911.

30. *Rocky Mountain News,* July 14, 1865.

31. Unattributed manuscript page filed in Denver Public Library, Western History Department's clipping collection, under the heading "Italians."

32. Interview with John and Sam Rougas conducted by Edith Edson, August 1, 1978, in Oral History Collection, Pueblo Regional Library.

33. Interview with Jane Edelstein conducted by Ruth Stein, July 20, 1978, in Oral History Collection, Pueblo Regional Library.

34. *Rocky Mountain News,* weekly ed., June 25, 1865; Edward McCook, "Message to the State Legislature," Colorado Territory, Legislative Assembly, Council, *Council Journal: Eighth Session, 1870* (Central City: D. C. Collier, 1870), p. 21.

35. J. P. Spanier, *L'Agricotore Italiano negli Stati Uniti di America* (Naples: Tipi Angelo Trani, n.d.), p. 51.

36. *Denver Times,* February 18, 1899.

37. *Rocky Mountain News,* May 19, 1876.

38. *Rocky Mountain News,* July 15, 1890.

39. *Rocky Mountain News,* December 5, 1883.

40. From a speech delivered by a Mrs. Thomas to a meeting in Washington, D.C., May 21, 1914, Meredith Papers.

41. Speech by J. Kier Hardy, Denver ca. March 1912, newspaper clipping in John R. Lawson, Scrapbook, vol. 1:17, in John R. Lawson Collection, Western History Department, Denver Public Library.

42. *Rocky Mountain News,* May 2, 1874.

43. Hilko de Beers to his wife, July 6 and 27, 1908; August 24, 1908, in Hilko de Beers Manuscripts, Western History Department, Denver Public Library.

44. Frances Xavier Cabrini letter of February 18, 1902, quoted in Anon., *Our Lady of Mount Cannel* (Hackensack: Custombook, 1975), p. 10.

45. Henry Denman, *Tenth Biennial Report of the Inspector of Coal Mines of the State of Colorado, 1901–1902* (Denver: Smith-Brooks, 1903), p. 165.

46. James Dalrymple, *Fourth Annual Report of the State Inspector of Coal Mines, 1916* (Denver: Eames Bros., 1916), p. 49.

47. Henry Denman, *Ninth Biennial Report of the Inspector of Coal Mines of the State of Colorado, 1899–1900* (Denver: Smith-Brooks, 1901), p. 8.

48. J. P. C. Poulton, Scrapbook, p. 38, in Poulton Papers, Western History Department, Denver Public Library.

49. Joseph Buchanan, *The Story of a Labor Agitator* (New York: Outlook, 1903), p. 278; Myron Reed, *Denver Republican,* January 25, 1894; Mary Lathrop in *Denver Republican,* January 27, 1894; interview with Mary F. Leonard conducted by Stephen J. Leonard, July 11, 1970, in Leonard's possession.

50. Fumio Ozawa, "Japanese in Colorado," in *Colorado Times,* ed., *Japanese American Who's Who* (Denver: 1959), p. 40, quoting the *Daily Mining Record,* February 7, 1908.

51. *Rocky Mountain News,* February 3, 1907, quoted in Ozawa, "Japanese in Colorado," p. 100.

52. *Denver Republican,* July 17, 1909.

53. Colorado Bureau of Labor Statistics, *Third Biennial Report, 1891–1892* (Colorado Springs: Gazette Printing, 1892), p. 131.

54. *Denver Times,* December 29, 1908.

55. *Denver Republican,* April 1, 1889.

56. George P. Rawick, ed., *The American Slave: A Composite Autobiography* (Westport: Greenwood Press, 1977), Supplement Series 1, vol. 2:72–73.

57. Denver *Daily Tribune,* May 11, 1879, quoted in George H. Wayne, "Negro Migration and Colonization in Colorado: 1870–1930," *Journal of the West* 15 (January 1976):108–109.

58. *Rocky Mountain News,* February 11, 1885; *Denver Times,* April 3, 1899.

59. Thomas F. Dawson and F.J.V. Skiff, *The Ute War: A History of the White River Massacre* (Boulder: Johnson Publishing, 1980), p. 36; *Rocky Mountain News,* March 13, 1884.

60. *Denver Times,* October 17, 1898.

61. Rawick, *American Slave,* pp. 30–31.

62. *The Pueblo Chieftain,* July 5, 1917.

63. Yvonne Johnson, "Globeville: Denver's Melting Pot," typescript in files of the Denver Public Library, Western History Department, p. 26.

## 11: The Discovery of Scenery: The Growth of Tourism

1. Frank Fossett, *Colorado: Its Gold and Silver Mines, Farms and Stock Ranges, and Health and Pleasure Resorts* (New York: C. G. Crawford, 1879), p. 155.

2. Samuel Bowles, *Our New West* (Hartford: Hartford Publishing, 1869), p. 196; Ovando C. Hollister, *The Mines of Colorado* (Springfield, Mass.: Samuel Bowles, 1867), p. iv.

3. Fossett, *Colorado,* p. 7; A. A. Hayes, Jr., "Vacation Aspects of Colorado," *Harper's* 60 (March 1880):542; William E. Smythe, *The Conquest of Arid America* (Seattle: University of Washington Press, 1969), p. 164.

4. Richard Harding Davis, *The West From a Car Window* (New York: Harper and Brothers, 1892), p. 270.

5. Fossett, *Colorado,* pp. 36, 47.

6. *The United States, With Excursions to Mexico, Cuba, Puerto Rico, and Alaska* (Leipzig: Karl Baedecker, 1909), p. 489; Lewis Iddings, "Life in the Altitudes: The Colorado Health Plateau," *Scribner's* 19 (1896):143.

7. Samuel S. Wallihan and T. O. Bigney, eds., *The Rocky Mountain Directory and Colorado Gazetteer for 1871* (Denver: S. S. Wallihan, 1870), p. 248; Bowles, *Our New West,* p. 132.

8. James F. Meline, *Two Thousand Miles on Horseback* (New York: Hurd and Houghton, 1867), p. 85.

9. Hayes, "Vacation Aspects," p. 555.

10. Samuel Bowles, *The Switzerland of America* (Springfield, Mass.: Samuel Bowles, 1869), p. 19.

11. F. J. Bancroft, pamphlet written for Colorado Territorial Board of Immigration, quoted in Carl Ubbelohde, *A Colorado Reader* (Boulder: Pruett Publishing, 1962); Charles Denison, *The Influence of the Climate of Colorado on the Nervous System* (Denver: Richards, 1874); Samuel A. Fisk, "Colorado for Invalids," *Popular Science Monthly* 25 (July 1884):313.

12. Jerome Smiley, *History of Denver, With Outlines of the Earlier History of the Rocky Mountain Country* (Denver: *Denver Times,* 1901), p. 977.

13. William Byers, *Encyclopedia of Biography of Colorado,* quoted in Levette J. Davidson, "The Festival of Mountain and Plain," *Colorado Magazine* 25 (July 1948):146.

14. Jewell Wolcott, ed., *My Dear Friend Chas.*, Essays and Monographs in Colorado History, Monograph no. 5 (1990), p. 102.

15. "Friend of the Rocky Mountains," *Literary Digest* 55 (July 14, 1917):44.

16. John Muir, quoted in Roderick Nash, *Wilderness and the American Mind* (New Haven: Yale University Press, 1973), p. 128; Enos Mills, *Wild Life on the Rockies* (Boston: Houghton-Mifflin, 1909), p. 213.

17. Enos Mills, *Adventures of a Nature Guide* (Garden City: Doubleday, Page, 1920), pp. 245, 249.

## 12: Denver: The Rocky Mountain Metropolis

1. Emily French, *Emily: The Diary of a Hard-Worked Woman,* ed. Janet LeCompte (Lincoln: University of Nebraska Press, 1987), p. 133.

2. *Rocky Mountain News,* quoted in Duane A. Smith, *Horace Tabor: His Life and the Legend* (Boulder: Colorado Associated University Press, 1973), p. 150.

3. Jerome Smiley, *History of Denver, With Outlines of the Earlier History of the Rocky Mountain Country* (Denver: *Denver Times,* 1901), p. 483; Richard Brettell, *Historic Denver: The Architects and Their Architecture, 1885–1893* (Denver: Historic Denver, 1973), p. 30.

4. Brettell, *Historic Denver,* p. 48.

5. Josiah Strong, *Our Country: Its Possible Future and Present Crisis* (New York: Baker and Taylor, 1891), p. 172.

6. Session Laws of Colorado, quoted in Leon Fuller, "History of the People's Party in Colorado" (Ph.D. diss., University of Wisconsin, 1933), p. 147.

7. Davis Waite to Ignatius Donnelly, December 11, 1894, quoted in John R. Morris, "The Women and Governor Waite," *Colorado Magazine* 44 (Winter 1967):16.

8. Benjamin B. Lindsey and Harvey J. O'Higgins, *The Beast* (Seattle: University of Washington Press, 1970), p. 191.

9. E. K. MacColl, "John Franklin Shafroth: Reform Governor of Colorado, 1909–1913," *Colorado Magazine* 29 (January 1952):41.

10. Elliott West, "Cleansing the Queen City: Prohibition and Urban Reform in Denver," *Arizona and the West* 14 (Winter 1972):335.

11. George Creel, *Rebel at Large: Recollections of Fifty Crowded Years* (New York: G. P. Putnam's Sons, 1947), p. 98; Robert Perkin, *The First Hundred Years* (Garden City: Doubleday, 1959), p. 415.

12. Roland L. DeLorme, "Colorado's Mugwump Interlude: The State Voters' League, 1905–1906," *Journal of the West* 7 (October 1968):526.

13. *Denver Times,* May 7, 1919, quoted in James E. Hansen II, "Moonshine and Murder: Prohibition in Denver," *Colorado Magazine* 50 (Winter 1973):16.

14. In fact, the census indicated that Colorado was 50.3 percent urban in 1910. The figure dropped to 48.2 percent in 1920 as a result of the farm boom of World War I but returned to 50.2 percent in 1930 and 52.6 percent in 1940.

## Interlude: Coloradans in 1917

1. *Denver Post,* April 1 and 3, 1917.

2. Robert Rockwell, letter to constituents, March 26, 1917, in Rockwell Papers, University of Colorado Western Historical Collections (Boulder, Colo.).

3. T. B. Steams to Robert Rockwell, October 23, 1917, in Rockwell Papers.

4. Unidentified letter to Norman E. Mack, December 8, 1917, in Ellis Meredith Papers, State Historical Society of Colorado, Denver, Colo.

5. Edward Keating, *The Gentleman From Colorado* (Denver: Sage Books, 1964), p. 415.

6. *Rocky Mountain News,* July 25, 1918.

7. *Denver Weekly News,* July 25, 1918, clipping in Dawson Scrapbooks, State Historical Society of Colorado, Denver, Colo.

8. Rockwell campaign leaflet, 1922, in Rockwell Papers.

## 13: Colorado's Great Detour: The 1920s and 1930s

1. In the Mountain states as a whole, the comparable decline was from 58 to 38 percent. In the Plains states it was from 59 to 43 percent. The problems of all three industries were regional, not local.

2. John Gunther, *Inside U.S.A.* (New York: Harper and Brothers, 1947), p. 213.

3. Robert Perkin, *The First Hundred Years* (Garden City: Doubleday, 1959), p. 571; Gunther, *Inside U.S.A.,* p. 224.

4. Gerald D. Nash, *The American West in the Twentieth Century* (Englewood Cliffs: Prentice-Hall, 1973), p. 74.

5. *Rocky Mountain News,* February 24, 1919, quoted in Phillip L. Cook, "The Red Scare in Denver," *Colorado Magazine* 43 (Fall 1966):310; *Denver Post,* November 8, 1919, quoted in Cook, "Red Scare," p. 313.

6. Cook, "Red Scare," pp. 311, 316.

7. Governor Oliver Shoup, quoted in Cook, "Red Scare," p. 317.

8. *Rocky Mountain News,* May 3, 1920, quoted in Cook, "Red Scare," p. 321.

9. *Tramway Bulletin* 11 (September 1920):14, quoted in Cook, "Red Scare," p. 325.

10. *Denver Times,* June 17, 1921, quoted in Kenneth T. Jackson, *The Ku Klux Klan in the City, 1915–1930* (New York: Oxford University Press, 1967), p. 216.

11. *Denver Post,* August 3, 1924, quoted in Jackson, *Ku Klux Klan,* p. 224.

12. *Denver Post*, August 13, 1924, quoted in Jackson, *Ku Klux Klan,* p. 226.

13. Leroy Hafen, *Colorado: The Story of a Western Commonwealth* (New York: Ams Press, 1970), p. 288.

14. Benjamin B. Lindsey and Harvey J. O'Higgins, *The Beast* (Seattle: University of Washington Press, 1970), p. 233.

15. Gunther, *Inside U.S.A.*, p. 225.

16. Thomas Lyons, ed., *1930 Employment 1980: Humanistic Perspectives on the Civilian Conservation Corps in Colorado* (Boulder: Colorado Humanities Program, 1980), p. 184.

17. *Denver Post*, May 20, 1938; *Lamar Daily News*, January 30, 1939; *Limon Leader*, November 6, 1939; *Pueblo Chieftain,* January 28, 1938; January 20, 1974; *Rocky Mountain News*, December 8, 1937; January 3, 1938; November 6, 1938; May 11, 1941; May 28, 1943.

18. Paul Shriver to Alfred Edgar Smith, May 25, 1938, Record Group 69, WPA, State Central Files, Colorado, 641 in National Archives, Washington, D.C.

19. Sugar Beet Conference in Colorado as of March 19–20, 1937, Record Group 69, WPA, State Central Files, Colorado, 640; *Colorado Labor Advocate* (Denver), May 19, 1932; Estanislado Valverde to F. C. Harrington, September 21, 1939, WPA, State Central Files, Colorado, 641, both in National Archives, Washington, D.C.

20. Quoted in Gus B. Flake to Edward B. Rowan, July 15, 1942, Record Group 121, Records Concerning Federal Art Activities, Textual Records of the Section of Fine Arts, Public Buildings Administration and Its Predecessors, Case Files Concerning Embellishments of Federal Buildings, 1934–1943, Colorado, Box 11, Entry 133, in National Archives, Washington, D.C.

21. Mayme Stagner, "Resettlement — A Story of Faith and Courage, A Tape Recording Made by Mrs. Mayme (Bert) Stagner, April 8, 1981," *San Luis Valley Historian* 21, no. 2 (1989):6.

22. *Holyoke Enterprise*, January 18, 1934,

23. Stagner, "Resettlement," p. 14.

24. Donald C. Reading, "A Statistical Analysis of New Deal Economic Programs in the Forty-Eight States, 1931–1939" (Ph.D. diss., Utah State University, 1971), p. 105.

25. *Lamar Daily News*, April 10, 1935.

26. Frank Cross, "Revolution in Colorado," *The Nation* (February 7, 1934):153.

27. Edward P. Costigan, untitled transcript of a radio speech on KOA Radio (Denver), September 9, 1930, in John A. Carroll Papers, Metropolitan State College of Denver, Auraria Library, Denver.

28. *Congressional Record*, 72nd Congress, 1st Session, February 3, 1932, p. 3307.

29. *Weld County News*, October 27, 1932.

30. Edwin C. Johnson to Harry Hopkins, December 29, 1933, Record Group 69, FERA, State Series, Colorado, 400 in National Archives, Washington, D.C.

31. T. J. Edmonds to Harry Hopkins, January 20, 1934, FERA, State Series, Colorado, 400 in National Archives, Washington, D.C.

32. Josephine Roche radio speech, February 16, 1932, quoted in Marjorie Hornbein, "Josephine Roche: Social Worker and Coal Operator," *Colorado Magazine* 53 (Summer 1976):243.

33. John A. Carroll interview with Stephen J. Leonard, February 27, 1976; *Rocky Mountain News*, May 24, August 19, September 7 and 9, 1934; Edward Costigan radio address, August 24, 1934, Box 46, Costigan Papers, University of Colorado–Boulder.

34. *Denver Post*, September 12, 1934.

35. Quoted in James Wickens, "The New Deal in Colorado," *Pacific Historical Review* 38 (August 1969):291.

36. Nash, *American West*, pp. 110–118; Earl Pomeroy, *The Pacific Slope: A History of California, Oregon, Washington, Idaho, Utah and Nevada* (New York: Knopf, 1965), pp. 215–252.

## 14: Growth and Politics in the New Colorado

1. Frank Hall to family, letter of January 20, 1867, in Hall Papers, State Historical Society of Colorado, Denver, Colo.; *New York Times*, March 14, 1974.

2. Morris Garnsey, "Aridity and Politics in the West," *Colorado Quarterly* 14 (Autumn 1965):158.

3. *Time*, March 10, 1947; Robert Perkin and Charles A. Graham, "Denver: Reluctant Capital," in *Rocky Mountain Cities*, ed. Ray B. West (New York: W. W. Norton, 1949), p. 281.

4. Steve McNichols, quoted in John C. Bromley, Daniel L. Anderson, and Charles H. Ingold, "Growing Pains: Reflections on Governing Colorado," *Colorado Heritage*, no. 4 (1988), p. 38.

5. Eugene Cervi, quoted in Neal R. Peirce, *The Mountain States of America* (New York: W. W. Norton, 1972), p. 59.

6. *Denver Post*, June 23, 1974.

## 15: Plural Society in Midcentury

1. *Denver Post*, July 8, 1974.

2. Paul S. Taylor, "Mexican Labor in the United States: The Valley of the South Platte, Colorado." *University of California Publications in Economics,* 6 (1929):215–216.

3. Taylor, "Mexican Labor," pp. 211–216.

4. Quoted in Magdalena Gallegos, "The Forgotten Community," *Colorado Heritage*, no. 2 (1985), p. 14.

5. Stanley Steiner, *La Raza: The Mexican Americans* (New York: Harper and Row, 1970), pp. 384–389.

6. *Denver Post*, November 21, 1965.

## 16: Measuring the Limits: Colorado Since 1970

1. David McComb, *Big Thompson: Profile of a Natural Disaster* (Boulder: Pruett Publishing, 1980), pp. 15–17, 48–74, 98–101.

2. *Denver Post*, September 25, 1972.

3. *Denver Post*, October 2, 1977; January 1, 1980.

4. Geraldine Bean Interview, Oral History of Colorado Project, State Historical Society of Colorado, January 24, 1975.

5. Stephen J. Leonard and Thomas J. Noel, *Denver: Mining Camp to Metropolis* (Niwot: University Press of Colorado, 1990), pp. 404–405.

6. Leonard and Noel, *Denver*, pp. 386–387, 397.

7. *State and Metropolitan Area Data Book*, 1991 (Washington, D.C.: U.S. Department of Commerce, 1991), p. 302.

8. Leonard and Noel, *Denver*, pp. 320–321.

9. Statistics are taken from *Statistical Abstract of the United States, 1992*; *State and Metropolitan Area Data Book, 1991*; and *Colorado Vital Statistics* (Denver: Colorado Department of Health, 1992).

10. Quoted in Willard Hasselbush, "Denver: Activity Remains Strong in Both Downtown and Suburban Markets," *National Real Estate Investor* 21 (September 1979):85.

11. Leonard and Noel, *Denver*, pp. 247–248, 409–411.

12. Steven K. Wilmsen, *Silverado: Neil Bush and the Savings & Loan Scandal* (Washington, D.C.: National Press Books, 1991), pp. 25–28, 46–51, 59, 181, 203.

13. Kenneth Boulding Interview, Oral History of Colorado Project, March 4, 1975.

## 17: Mirror for America

1. Hubert Howe Bancroft, *History of Nevada, Colorado and Wyoming, 1540–1888* (San Francisco: History Company, 1890), p. 329; Frank Hall, *History of the State of Colorado* (Chicago: Blakely Printing, 1889–1895), 2:vi.

2. James H. Baker, "Introductory Outline," in *History of Colorado,* eds. James Baker and Leroy Hafen (Denver: State Historical Society of Colorado, 1927), 1:11.

3. Frank Hall to family, May 2, 1869, Hall Papers, State Historical Society of Colorado, Denver, Colo.

4. Luke Cahill, "Recollections of a Plainsman," manuscript at State Historical Society of Colorado, Denver, Colo.; Samuel S. Wallihan and T. O. Bigney, *The Rocky Mountain Directory and Colorado Gazetteer* (Denver: S. S. Wallihan, 1871), p. 253; W. R. Vickers, *History of the City of Denver, Arapahoe County, and the State of Colorado* (Chicago: O. L. Baskin, 1880), p. 17.

5. U.S. Department of Agriculture, *Hearings on the Uncompahgre Primitive Area,* November 15–16, 1971, p. 107, in University of Colorado Western Historical Collections (Boulder, Colo.).

# ACKNOWLEDGMENTS

The authors have benefited from the help of a number of persons in the preparation of this history. The following have provided particularly valuable ideas and suggestions: Mark Foster and Tom Noel of the University of Colorado at Denver; David Lonsdale of the University of Northern Colorado; Liston Leyendecker, James Hansen, and Dan Tyler of Colorado State University; Katherine Engles, Alice Sharp, David Halaas, David Wetzel, Rebecca Lintz, Margaret Walsh, and Eric Paddock of the Colorado Historical Society; Frank Nation and Gloria Kennison of Metropolitan State College; Enid Thompson of the University of Denver; Joseph Velikonja of the University of Washington; Mary Nation of the Colorado Supreme Court; Don Etter; Maxine Benson; Joanne Dodds, western research librarian for the Pueblo Library District; and Nancy Whistler, Fred Yonce, and Eleanor Gehres and her staff from the Denver Public Library. Carl Abbott would also like to acknowledge the opportunity he had to learn more about the Western Slope as Aspinall professor at Mesa College in 1985.

# BIBLIOGRAPHIC ESSAY

## General Works

Partly because of the centennial of Colorado statehood, several good single-volume histories are available. Marshall Sprague, *Colorado: A Bicentennial History* (New York, 1976), is a brief, personalized introduction. Robert Athearn's *The Coloradans* (Albuquerque, 1976), begins the story with the Fifty-niners. Carl Ubbelohde, Maxine Benson, and Duane Smith, *A Colorado History* (6th ed., Boulder, 1988), is more complete and systematic. Richard N. Ellis and Duane A. Smith, *Colorado: A History in Photographs* (Niwot, Colo., 1991), is an enjoyable introduction to the development of the state. Leroy Hafen, *Colorado: The Story of A Western Commonwealth* (Denver, 1933), and Percy Fritz, *Colorado: The Centennial State* (New York, 1941), lack the benefit of two generations of active historical research. Thomas E. Cronin and Robert D. Loevy, *Colorado Politics and Government: Governing the Centennial State* (Lincoln, Neb., 1993), is an up-to-date discussion of state politics in historical perspective.

Leroy Hafen, ed., *Colorado and Its People: A Narrative and Topical History of the Centennial State* (4 vols., New York, 1948), is still an excellent large reference work on Colorado. Its topical chapters were written by the leading experts in their fields. Older, and of considerably less value, are Wilbur F. Stone, ed., *History of Colorado* (4 vols., Chicago, 1918–1919), and James H. Baker and Leroy Hafen, eds., *History of Colorado* (5 vols., Denver, 1927).

The nineteenth century produced a number of histories, gazetteers, and general descriptions of Colorado in which early residents described the state as they saw it. Silas Burt and Edward Berthoud, *The Rocky Mountain Gold Regions* (Denver, 1861); Junius Wharton, *History of the City of Denver* (Denver, 1866); Ovando Hollister, *The Mines of Colorado* (Springfield, Mass., 1867); and Samuel Wallihan and T. O. Bigney, *The Rocky Mountain Directory and Colorado Gazetteer for 1871* (Denver, 1870), all date from the first years of settlement. Frank Fossett, *Colorado: Its Gold and Silver Mines* (New York, 1879), is an invaluable description of all aspects of the Colorado economy on the brink of the great boom. Frank Hall, *History of the State of Colorado* (4 vols., Chicago, 1889–1895), is a history of Colorado growth and politics written by an active politician and booster.

The closing decades of the century also saw publication of a number of specialized reference volumes designed to memorialize regions and individuals of Colorado. O. L. Baskin and Company of Chicago published three such books, all with the same introduction by W. H. Vickers: *History of Clear Creek and Boulder Valleys, Colorado* (1880), *History of the City of Denver, Arapahoe County, and Colorado* (1880), and *History of the Arkansas Valley, Colorado* (1881). Duane Vandenbusch and Duane S. Smith, *A Land Alone: Colorado's Western Slope* (Boulder, 1981), is a valuable recent addition to such regional histories. William Byers, ed., *Encyclopedia of Biography of Colorado* (Chicago, 1901), is especially useful for its historical introduction by one of the founders of Anglo-American Colorado. Jerome Smiley, *History of Denver* (Denver, 1901), is a compilation of information on that city conceived in the grand style of the nineteenth century. An up-to-date history of the city is Stephen J. Leonard and Thomas Noel, *Denver: Mining Camp to Metropolis* (Niwot, Colo., 1990).

Several other books deserve special mention. *Colorado: A Guide to the Highest State* (New York, 1941), is a volume in the American Guide Series compiled by workers for the Work Projects Administration in the 1930s. An impressive amount of original research makes the book not simply a guide and gazetteer but also an intelligent study of the state's history and social patterns. Robert Perkin, *The First Hundred Years: An Informal History of Denver and the Rocky Mountain News* (Garden City, 1959), is a pleasure to read. It relates the history of Denver's first newspaper and highlights many important points in the history of the city as well. Eleanor Gehres et al., *The Colorado Book* (Golden, Colo., 1993), is a well-chosen selection of short excerpts from Colorado writers. Bohdan S. Wynar, ed., *Colorado Bibliography* (Littleton, Colo., 1980), has nearly 9,200 unannotated entries on books relating to Colorado. Readers interested in a biographical approach to Colorado history might try Richard Lamm and Duane Smith, *Pioneers and Politicians: 10 Colorado Governors in Profile* (Boulder, 1984), and John H. Monnett and Michael McCarthy, *Colorado Profiles: Men and Women Who Shaped the Centennial State* (Evergreen, Colo., 1987).

## 1: Mountains and Plains

For introductions to the natural environment of Colorado and human alterations of that environment, see Thomas P. Huber, *Colorado: The Place of Nature, the Nature of Place* (Niwot, Colo., 1993); Kenneth A. Erickson and Albert W. Smith, *Atlas of Colorado* (Boulder, 1985); and Thomas J. Noel, Paul F. Mahoney, and Richard E. Stevens, *Historical Atlas of Colorado* (Norman, Okla., 1993).

The perceptions of early visitors to Colorado are recorded in their own accounts of their journeys. The classic reports of official explorers are found in *The Journals of Zebulon Montgomery Pike,* ed. Donald Jackson (Norman, Okla., 1966); Edwin James, *Account of an Expedition From Pittsburgh to the Rocky Mountains,* in Reuben Gold Thwaites, *Early Western Travels, 1748–1846* (New York, 1966), vols. 14–17; and *The Expeditions of John Charles Fremont,* vol. I: *Travels From 1838 to 1844,* ed. Donald Jackson and Mary Lee Spence (Urbana, Ill., 1970). Among the most widely read travelers' accounts are the following from the 1860s: Horace Greeley, *An Overland Journey* (New York, 1860); Albert Richardson, *Beyond the Mississippi* (Hartford, 1867); and Samuel Bowles, *Across the Continent* (Springfield, Mass., 1865), and *Our New West* (Hartford, 1869). Exploration and the definition of regions are also discussed in Richard Bartlett, *Great Surveys of the American West* (Norman, Okla., 1962); Carl I. Wheat, "Mapping the American West, 1640–1857," *Proceedings of the American Antiquarian Society* 64 (1954):19–194; G. M. Lewis, "Regional Ideas and Reality in the Cis-Rocky Mountain West," *Transactions of the Institute of British Geographers* 30 (1962):135–150; Clifford Westermeier, *Colorado's First*

*Portrait: Scenes by Early Artists* (Albuquerque, 1970); and William Goetzmann, *Army Exploration in the Far West* (New Haven, 1959), and *Exploration and Empire: The Explorer and the Scientist in the Winning of the American West* (New York, 1966).

Population figures in the United States Census, census atlases published regularly after 1880, and the *National Atlas of the United States* (Washington, D.C., 1969) are the best sources for beginning a study of Colorado's settlement regions. For early settlement patterns, also see Ovando Hollister, *The Mines of Colorado* (Springfield, Mass., 1867); Frank Fossett, *Colorado: Its Gold and Silver Mines* (New York, 1879); and Colin Goodykoontz, "The Exploration and Settlement of Colorado," in Junius Henderson et al., *Colorado: Short Studies of Its Past and Present* (Boulder, 1927). For recent regional patterns, Donald J. Bogue and Calvin L. Beale, *Economic Areas of the United States* (Glencoe, Ill., 1961), is valuable for its information on population and economic activities. For discussions of some of the West's larger regions, see Carl Kraenzel, *The Great Plains in Transition* (Norman, Okla., 1955); Walter Prescott Webb, *The Great Plains* (Boston, 1931); Philip L. Fradkin, *A River No More: The Colorado River and the West* (New York, 1981); Joel Garreau, *The Nine Nations of North America* (Boston, 1981); and Donald Meinig, *Southwest: Three Peoples in Geographical Change, 1600–1970* (New York, 1971), and "American Wests: Preface to a Geographical Introduction," *Annals of the Association of American Geographers* 62 (1972):159–184.

## 2: The First Coloradans

J. Donald Hughes, *American Indians in Colorado* (Boulder, 1987), is a very useful introduction. Bruce E. Ripperteau, *A Colorado Book of the Dead* (Denver, 1979); and E. Steve Cassells, *The Archeology of Colorado* (Boulder, 1983), summarize our current understanding of Native American cultures before European contact. Historians interested in western Native American peoples owe an immense debt to the University of Oklahoma Press, which has published more than a hundred monographs in its series "The Civilization of the American Indian." Among the relevant tribal histories in the series are Ernest Wallace and E. Adamson Hoebel, *The Comanches: Lords of the South Plains* (1952); Ruth Underhill, *The Navajos* (1956); Donald J. Berthrong, *The Southern Cheyennes* (1963); Virginia Cole Trenholm, *The Arapahoes, Our People* (1970); George Hyde, *Indians of the High Plains: From the Prehistoric Period to the Coming of Europeans* (1959); Robert Emmitt, *The Last War Trail: The Utes and the Settlement of Colorado* (1954); and Jack Forbes, *Apache, Navajo and Spaniard* (1960).

Relevant to Cheyenne history are the following: George Bird Grinnell, *The Fighting Cheyennes* (Norman, Okla., 1958), a reprint of a fifty-year-old classic by a pioneer anthropologist; George Hyde, *The Life of George Bent, Written From His Letters* (Norman, Okla., 1968), a reworking of the reminiscences of a man who lived in both white and Native American cultures; and John Stands In Timber and Margot Liberty, *Cheyenne Memories* (New Haven, 1967).

Facets of Ute history can be found in Marshall Sprague, *Massacre: The Tragedy at White River* (Boston, 1957); Wilson Rockwell, *The Utes: A Forgotten People* (Denver, 1956); James Jefferson, Robert W. Delaney, and Gregory Thompson, *The Southern Utes: A Tribal History* (Ignacio, Colo., 1972); and Robert Delaney, *The Ute Mountain Utes* (Albuquerque, 1989). Omer C. Stewart,

*Ethnohistorical Bibliography of the Ute Indians of Colorado* (Boulder, 1971), is an invaluable research aid.

The two animals whose use dominated the lives of the western Native American tribes have each been the subject of an excellent study. Frank Gilbert Roe, *The Indian and the Horse* (Norman, Okla., 1955), summarizes the available information about the adoption and use of that animal. Tom McHugh, *The Time of the Buffalo* (New York, 1972), has a scope worthy of its subject.

A detailed survey of Spanish frontier policy, explorations, and relations with U.S. Native Americans is John Francis Bannon, *The Spanish Borderlands Frontier, 1513–1821* (New York, 1970). His summary draws on a number of more detailed studies, among them: Max L. Moorhead, *The Apache Frontier: Jacobo Ugarte and Spanish-Indian Relations in Northern New Spain, 1769–1791* (Norman, Okla., 1968); Alfred B. Thomas, *After Coronado: Spanish Exploration Northeast of New Mexico, 1696–1727* (Norman, Okla., 1936); Henry Folmer, *Franco-Spanish Rivalry in North America* (Glendale, Calif., 1953); Noel M. Loomis and Abraham P. Nasatir, *Pedro Vial and the Roads to Santa Fe* (Norman, Okla., 1967); Alfred B. Thomas, *Forgotten Frontiers: A Study of the Spanish Indian Policy of Don Juan Bautista de Anza* (Norman, Okla., 1932); and Marc Simmons, *Spanish Government in New Mexico* (Albuquerque, 1968). Two sweeping studies that view the native peoples of the Southwest as equal actors with Europeans are Elizabeth A.H. John, *Storms Brewed in Other Men's Worlds: The Confrontation of Indians, Spanish, and French in the Southwest, 1540–1795* (College Station, Tex., 1975), and Thomas Hall, *Social Change in the Southwest, 1350–1880* (Lawrence, Kan., 1989).

## 3: New Mexico's Northern Frontier

There are two starting points for an investigation of the New Mexico–Colorado fur trade. David Lavender, *Bent's Fort* (New York, 1954 [reprint 1968]), describes the rise and fall of Bent, St. Vrain and Company. David J. Weber, *The Taos Trappers* (Norman, Okla., 1971), re-evaluates the same business from the viewpoint of New Mexico. Taken together, they show how the Colorado of 1820–1840 looked from St. Louis and Santa Fe. David Wishart, *The Fur Trade of the American West, 1807–1840: A Geographical Synthesis* (Lincoln, Neb., 1979), discusses Colorado trapping as an offshoot of the fur trade in areas to the north.

The Santa Fe Trail was a major subject for nineteenth-century U.S. writers. Two accounts of the trail, which can still be read with pleasure, are Josiah Gregg, *The Commerce of the Prairies,* and Lewis Garrard, *Wah-to-Yah and the Taos Trail;* each has been reprinted frequently. Max L. Moorhead, *New Mexico's Royal Road: Trade and Travel on the Chihuahua Trail* (Norman, Okla., 1958), is a scholarly analysis of the importance of the trail and its commerce.

There are detailed treatments of Colorado fur trading in the biographical sketches in Leroy Hafen, ed., *The Mountain Men and the Fur Trade of the Far West* (10 vols.; Glendale, Calif., 1965–1972). Janet LeCompte, *Pueblo, Hardscrabble and Greenhorn: The Upper Arkansas, 1832–1856* (Norman, Okla., 1978), gives full details of early farming and trading posts. The *Colorado Magazine* (v. 54, Fall 1977) devotes a special issue to the reconstruction effort at Bent's Fort.

Donald Meinig, *Southwest: Three Peoples in Geographical Change, 1600–1970* (New York, 1971), introduces the idea of New Mexican migration northward as a major folk movement. Jack Forbes, "Frontiers in American History," *Journal of the West* 1 (July 1962):63–72; Edward H. Spicer, *Cycles of Conquest* (Tucson, 1962); and the essays in John Francis Bannon, ed., *Bolton and the Spanish Borderlands* (Norman, Okla., 1964), all place the New Mexican frontier within a broader historical framework. Details of the northward movement into the twentieth century are traced in Sarah Deutsch, *No Separate Refuge: Culture, Class, and Gender on an Anglo-Hispanic Frontier in the American West, 1880–1940* (New York, 1987); and Richard Nostrand, *The Hispano Homeland* (Norman, Okla., 1992).

The patterns of settlement and social relations prevalent in Hispanic New Mexico are described in Marc Simmons, "Settlement Patterns of Village Plans in Colonial New Mexico," *Journal of the West* 8 (January 1969):7–21; Clark Knowlton, "Spanish Americans in New Mexico," *Sociology and Social Research* 45 (July 1961):448–454, and "Patron-Peon Patterns Among the Spanish Americans of New Mexico," *Social Forces* 41 (October 1962):12–17; Nancie L. Gonzalez, *The Spanish Americans of New Mexico: A Heritage of Pride* (Albuquerque, 1969); and Fray Angelico Chavez, "The Penitentes of New Mexico," *New Mexico Historical Review* 29 (April 1954):97–123.

For discussions of the process of migration and the adaptation of New Mexican institutions to new circumstances, see William B. Taylor and Elliott West, "Patron Leadership at the Crossroads: Southern Colorado in the Late Nineteenth Century," *Pacific Historical Review* 42 (August 1973):335–357; Alvar Ward Carlson, "Rural Settlement Patterns in the San Luis Valley," *The Colorado Magazine* 44 (Spring 1967):111–128; Hugh and Evelyn Burnett, "Madrid Plaza," *Colorado Magazine* 42 (Summer 1965):224–237; Ralph Carr, "Private Land Claims in Colorado," *Colorado Magazine* 25 (January 1948):20–40; Carey McWilliams, *North From Mexico* (New York, 1968); and Morris F. Taylor, *Trinidad, Colorado Territory* (Trinidad, 1966).

Several nineteenth-century writers paid special attention to southern Colorado: William Bell, *New Tracks in North America* (2 vols. London, 1869); William E. Pabor, *Colorado as an Agricultural State* (New York, 1883); James Meline, *Two Thousand Miles on Horseback* (New York, 1867); Helen Hunt Jackson, *Bits of Travel at Home* (Boston, 1866); and Michael Beshoar, *All About Trinidad and Las Animas County, Colorado* (Denver, 1882).

Two necessary sources for the study of Hispanic Colorado are Dorothy Woodward, "The Penitentes of New Mexico" (Ph.D. diss., Yale University, 1935); and Marta Weigle, *Brothers of Light, Brothers of Blood: The Penitentes of the Southwest* (Albuquerque, 1976). Contrast these with the missionary efforts described in Randi Jones Walker, *Protestantism in the Sangre de Cristos, 1850–1920* (Albuquerque, 1991). See also Frances L. Swadesh, *Los Primeros Pobladores: Hispanic Americans of the Ute Frontier* (South Bend, 1974).

## 4: The Pikes Peak Gold Rush

Leroy Hafen compiled most of the primary documents that deal with the Pikes Peak gold rush in the following volumes in the Southwest Historical Series (Glendale, Calif., 1941–1942): vol. 9, *Pike's Peak Gold Rush Guidebooks of 1859;* vol. 10, *Colorado Gold Rush: Contemporary Letters and Reports;* and vol. 11, *Overland Routes to the Gold Fields, 1859.* Other documents on the migration are found in "Letters From Colorado, 1860–1863," *Colorado Magazine* 16 (May 1939):90–93; and in Leroy Hafen, ed., *Reports From Colorado,*

*1859–1865, Far West and Rockies Series,* vol. 13 (Glendale, Calif., 1961). The three journalists who recorded the strike in Gregory Gulch described early Colorado in the following books: Horace Greeley, *An Overland Journey* (New York, 1860); Henry Villard, *Past and Present of the Pike's Peak Gold Region,* ed. Leroy Hafen (Princeton, 1932); and Albert Richardson, *Beyond the Mississippi* (Hartford, 1867). Agnes Wright Spring, "Rush to the Rockies, 1859," *Colorado Magazine* 36 (April 1959):82–120, summarizes the excitement of 1858 and 1859, and Doris Monahan, *Destination, Denver City: The South Platte Trail* (Athens, Ohio, 1985), describes the westward journey.

An outstanding treatment of the political beginnings of Colorado can be found in Howard Lamar, *The Far Southwest, 1846–1912: A Territorial History* (New Haven, 1966). A new interpretation of local politics in early Colorado communities is Richard Hogan, *Class and Community in Frontier Colorado* (Lawrence, Kan., 1990). For more detail on local self-government in the mountains, see Thomas M. Marshall, ed., *Early Records of Gilpin County, Colorado, 1859–1861* (Boulder, 1920); Thomas M. Marshall, "The Miners' Laws of Colorado," *American Historical Review* 25 (April 1920):426–439; and Lynn Perrigo, "Law and Order in Early Colorado Mining Camps," *Mississippi Valley Historical Review* 28 (June 1941):41–62. A typical claim club is described in George L. Anderson, "The Cañon City or Arkansas Valley Claim Club, 1860–1862," *Colorado Magazine* 16 (November 1939):201–210. Self-government in Denver is the subject of Francis Williams, "Trials and Judgements of the People's Courts of Denver," *Colorado Magazine* 27 (October 1950):294–302; and B. Richard Burg, "The Administration of Justice in the Denver People's Courts: 1859–1861," *Journal of the West* 7 (October 1968):510–521. Frederick L. Paxson, "The Territory of Colorado," *American Historical Review* 12 (October 1906):53–65, and Calvin Gower, "Gold Rush Governments," *Colorado Magazine* 42 (Spring 1965):114–132, deal with regional efforts at self-government. For another facet of territorial politics, see Eugene H. Berwanger, "Reconstruction on the Frontier: The Equal Rights Struggle in Colorado, 1865–1867," *Pacific Historical Review* 46 (August 1975):313–330.

Religious beginnings in Colorado are covered in Alice Cowan Cochran, *Miners, Merchants, and Missionaries: The Role of Missionaries and Pioneer Churches in the Colorado Gold Rush and Its Aftermath, 1858–1870* (Metuchen, N.J., 1980); Louisa Ward Arps, ed., *Faith on the Frontier* (Denver, 1976); and Thomas Noel, *Colorado Catholicism and the Archdiocese of Denver* (Niwot, Colo., 1989). Sandra Dallas, *Cherry Creek Gothic: Victorian Architecture in Denver* (Norman, Okla., 1971), describes the physical appearance of the early city, and Thomas Noel, "The Multifunctional Frontier Saloon: Denver, 1859–76," *Colorado Magazine* 52 (Spring 1975):114–136, describes the saloon institution. Gunther Barth, *Instant Cities: Urbanization and the Rise of San Francisco and Denver* (New York, 1975), analyzes the city's cultural evolution. Lyle Dorsett, *The Queen City: A History of Denver* (Boulder, 1977), is an urban biography that covers the city's entire career. Caroline Bancroft, *Gulch of Gold* (Denver, 1958), describes life in Central City in the 1860s. Liston Edgington Leyendecker, *Palace Car Prince: A Biography of George Mortimer Pullman* (Niwot, Colo., 1992), follows the career of a businessperson in Central City in the years 1860–1863. Duane Smith, *Rocky Mountain Mining Camps: The Urban Frontier* (Bloomington, 1967), places the evolution of these and other towns in a larger context. Every gazetteer and nearly every Colorado travel account of the 1860s also describes the two cities.

## 5: The Era of the Booster, 1863–1876

A general introduction to the early 1860s is Duane A. Smith, *The Birth of Colorado: A Civil War Perspective* (Norman, Okla., 1989).

The most complete biography of William Gilpin is Thomas Karnes, *William Gilpin: Western Nationalist* (Austin, 1970). Also see Gilpin's own *Mission of the North American People* (Philadelphia, 1874), and Herbert O. Brayer, *William Blackmore: The Spanish-Mexican Land Grants of New Mexico and Colorado, 1863–1878* (Denver, 1949).

Other early efforts at boosterism are discussed in the following articles: Liston E. Leyendecker, "Colorado and the Paris Universal Exposition, 1867," *Colorado Magazine* 46 (Winter 1969):1–15; Ralph Blodgett, "The Colorado Territorial Board of Immigration," *Colorado Magazine* 46 (Summer 1969):245–256; David F. Halaas, "Frontier Journalism in Colorado," *Colorado Magazine* 44 (Summer 1967):185–203; Wallace B. Turner, "Frank Hall: Colorado Journalist, Public Servant, and Historian," *Colorado Magazine* 53 (Fall 1976):328–351; and Maxine Benson, *Martha Maxwell: Rocky Mountain Naturalist* (Lincoln, 1986).

William Jackson Palmer is the subject of John S. Fisher, *Builder of the West: The Life of General William Jackson Palmer* (Caldwell, Idaho, 1939). Palmer is the central figure in Robert Athearn, *Rebel of the Rockies: A History of the Denver and Rio Grande Railroad* (New Haven, 1962), and in Herbert O. Brayer, *William Blackmore: Early Financing of the Denver and Rio Grande Railway and Ancillary Land Companies* (Denver, 1949). He is also the subject of George L. Anderson, "General William Jackson Palmer: Man of Vision," *Colorado College Studies,* no. 4 (Colorado Springs, 1960), and Brit Allan Storey, "William Jackson Palmer: The Technique of a Pioneer Railroad Promoter in Colorado, 1871–1880," *Journal of the West* 5 (April 1966):263–274.

James E. Fell, Jr., *Ores to Metals: The Rocky Mountain Smelting Industry* (Lincoln, 1979), describes the work of Nathaniel Hill. The building of other Colorado railroads is described in Glenn C. Quiett, *They Built the West* (New York, 1965); Richard Overton, *Gulf to Rockies* (Austin, 1953); Robert Athearn, *Union Pacific Country* (Chicago, 1971); Morris Cafky, *The Colorado Midland* (Denver, 1965); and Thomas J. Noel, "All Hail the Denver Pacific: Denver's First Railroad," *Colorado Magazine* 50 (Spring 1973):93–116.

Analyses of the Sand Creek Massacre are in Donald Berthrong, *The Southern Cheyennes* (Norman, Okla., 1963); Raymond Carey, "The Puzzle of Sand Creek," *Colorado Magazine* 41 (Fall 1964):314–335; Michael Sievers, "Sands of Sand Creek Historiography," *Colorado Magazine* 49 (Spring 1972):116–142; and David Svaldi, *Sand Creek and the Rhetoric of Extermination* (Lanham, Md., 1989). The continued warfare is narrated in John Monnett, *The Battle of Beecher Island and the Indian War of 1867–1869* (Niwot, Colo., 1992).

## 6: The Bonanza Years

The standard survey of western mining is Rodman Paul, *Mining Frontiers of the Far West* (New York, 1963). William Greever, *The Bonanza West: The Story of Western Mining Rushes, 1848–1900* (Norman, Okla., 1963), and Otis Young, *Western Mining* (Norman, Okla., 1970), are also valuable.

The following deal specifically with Colorado: Duane Smith, *Colorado Mining: A Photographic History* (Albuquerque, 1977); Charles Henderson, *Mining in Colorado,* United States Geological Survey Professional Paper no. 138

(1926); Rodman Paul, "Colorado as a Pioneer of Science in the Mining West," *Mississippi Valley Historical Review* 47 (July 1960):34–50.

Duane Smith, *Rocky Mountain Mining Camps* (Bloomington, 1967), is a general survey of boomtown life. C. Eric Stoehr, *Bonanza Victorian: Architecture and Society in Colorado Mining Towns* (Albuquerque, 1975), focuses on their physical appearance. John Reps, *Cities of the American West: A History of Frontier Town Planning* (Princeton, 1979), reproduces and discusses early town plans and bird's-eye views.

A recent and complete history of Leadville is Edward Blair, *Leadville: Colorado's Magic City* (Boulder, 1980). Also valuable are Elliott West, *The Saloon on the Rocky Mountain Mining Frontier* (Lincoln, 1979), which has a chapter on Leadville saloonkeepers; Don L. Griswold and Jean H. Griswold, *The Carbonate Camp Called Leadville* (Denver, 1951); and David Lavender, "This Wondrous Town; This Instant City," *American West* 4 (August 1967):5–14. Contemporaneous descriptions are Ernest Ingersoll, "Ups and Downs in Leadville," *Scribner's Monthly* 18 (October 1879):801–825; H. H. (Helen Hunt Jackson), "To Leadville," *Atlantic Monthly* 43 (May 1879):567–579; and Samuel F. Emmons, *Geology and Mining Industry of Leadville, Colorado* (Washington, D.C., 1886).

For Mary Hallock Foote, see Rodman W. Paul, ed., *A Victorian Gentlewoman in the Far West: The Reminiscences of Mary Hallock Foote* (San Marino, 1972); Wallace Stegner's fictionalized portrait in *Angle of Repose* (New York, 1971); and her own novels of Leadville: *The Led-Horse Claim* (Boston, 1883), and *The Last Assembly Ball* (Boston, 1889). Another woman's view of life in the mining towns is Anne Ellis, *The Life of an Ordinary Woman* (Boston, 1929).

For the development of other mining regions, see the following: Robert Taylor, *Cripple Creek*, Indiana University Publication: Geographic Monograph Series (Bloomington, 1966), which is a historical-geographical analysis; Marshall Sprague, *Money Mountain: The Story of Cripple Creek* (Boston, 1953); Malcolm Rohrbough, *Aspen: The History of a Silver Mining Town, 1879–1893* (Chicago, 1986); Duane A. Smith, "The San Juaner: A Computerized Portrait," *Colorado Magazine* 52 (Spring 1975):137–152; Duane A. Smith, *Rocky Mountain Boom Town: A History of Durango* (Albuquerque, 1980); Michael Kaplan, "The Toll Road Building Career of Otto Mears, 1881–87," *Colorado Magazine* 52 (Spring 1975):153–170; Stanley Dempsey and James E. Fell, Jr., *Mining the Summit: Colorado's Ten Mile District, 1860–1960* (Norman, Okla., 1986); Liston E. Leyendecker, *The Pelican-Dives Feud*, Essays and Monographs in Colorado History, no. 1 (Denver, 1985); Duane A. Smith, *When Coal Was King: A History of Crested Butte, Colorado* (Golden, Colo., 1984); and Phyllis Smith, *Once a Coal Miner: The Story of Colorado's Northern Coal Field* (Boulder, 1989). David Lavender, *Red Mountain* (Garden City, N.Y., 1963), is a vivid novel about mining in the San Juans.

Working conditions in the mines and early reactions are described in Mark Wyman, *Hard Rock Epic: Western Miners and the Industrial Revolution, 1860–1910* (Berkeley, 1979); Richard Lingenfelter, *The Hard Rock Miners* (Berkeley, 1974); Paul T. Bechtol, Jr., "The 1880 Labor Dispute in Leadville," *Colorado Magazine* 47 (Autumn 1970):312–325; and James Whiteside, *Regulating Danger: The Struggle for Mine Safety in the Rocky Mountain Coal Industry* (Lincoln, 1990).

## 7: The Businessman's State

Late-nineteenth-century boosterism is discussed in M. James Kedro, "Literary Boosterism," *Colorado Magazine* 52 (Summer 1975):200–224; Mort Stern, "Harry Tammen and His Great Divide," *Essays and Monographs in Colorado History,* Essays no. 10 (1989):1–49; and Duane Smith, "A Land Unto Itself: The Western Slope," *Colorado Magazine* 55 (Spring-Summer 1978):181–204.

Marshall Sprague, *Massacre: The Tragedy at White River* (Boston, 1957), explores the events surrounding the removal of the Utes. Kathleen Underwood, *Town Building on the Colorado Frontier* (Albuquerque, 1987), looks at the first twenty years of Grand Junction.

Political battles and the development of attitudes about the functions of state government are discussed in Elmer Ellis, *Henry Moore Teller: Defender of the West* (Caldwell, Idaho, 1941); Harry E. Kelsey, Jr., *Frontier Capitalist: The Life of John Evans* (Denver, 1969); Colin Goodykoontz, "Some Controversial Questions Before the Colorado Constitutional Convention of 1876," *Colorado Magazine* 17 (January 1940):1–16; Duane Smith, *Horace Tabor: His Life and the Legend* (Boulder, 1973); John D.W. Guice, *The Rocky Mountain Bench: The Territorial Supreme Court of Colorado, Montana, and Wyoming, 1861–1890* (New Haven, 1972); Gordon M. Bakken, "The Impact of the Colorado State Constitution on Rocky Mountain Constitution Making," *Colorado Magazine* 47 (Spring 1970):153–175; Gordon Bakken, "The Development of Law in Colorado, 1861–1912," *Colorado Magazine* 53 (Winter 1976):63–78; and Michael McCarthy, *Hour of Trial: The Conservation Conflict in Colorado and the West* (Norman, Okla., 1977). An unpublished dissertation of great value is Donald Hensel, "A History of the Colorado Constitution in the Nineteenth Century" (University of Colorado, 1957).

The development of education is treated in Michael McGiffert, *The Higher Learning in Colorado* (Denver, 1964); Frederick S. Allen et al., *The University of Colorado, 1876–1976* (New York, 1976); Robert W. Larson, *Shaping Educational Change: The First Century of the University of Northern Colorado* (Boulder, 1989); Duane A. Smith, *Sacred Trust: The Birth and Development of Fort Lewis College* (Niwot, Colo., 1991); and James E. Hansen II, *Democracy's College: A History of Colorado State University* (Fort Collins, 1977), and *Beyond the Ivory Tower: A History of Colorado State University Cooperative Extension* (Fort Collins, 1991).

A number of first-rate studies examine the financing of the mining and metals industry and the trend toward business consolidations: Clark Spence, *British Investments and the American Mining Frontier, 1860–1901* (Ithaca, 1958); Joseph King, *A Mine to Make a Mine: Financing the Colorado Mining Industry, 1859–1902* (College Station, Tex., 1977); Richard H. Peterson, *The Bonanza Kings: The Social Origins of Western Mining Entrepreneurs, 1870–1900* (Lincoln, 1977); James E. Fell, Jr., *Ores to Metals: The Rocky Mountain Smelting Industry* (Lincoln, 1979); and H. Lee Scamehorn, *Pioneer Steelmaker in the West: The Colorado Fuel and Iron Company, 1892–1903* (Boulder, 1976), and *Mill and Mine: The CF&I in the Twentieth Century* (Lincoln, 1992). William Wyckoff, "Incorporation as a Factor in the Formation of Urban Systems," *Geographical Review* 77 (July 1987):279–292, looks generally at Colorado's eastern business connections. Also relevant are Larry Schweikart, "Frontier Banking in Colorado," *Essays in Colorado History,* no. 8 (1988):15–33, and Thomas J.

Noel, *Growing Through History With Colorado: The Colorado National Banks, The First 125 Years* (Denver, 1987).

Recent biographies of important business leaders include Mark Foster, *Henry M. Porter: Rocky Mountain Empire Builder* (Niwot, Colo., 1991), and Robert C. Black III, *Railroad Pathfinder: The Life and Times of Edward L. Berthoud* (Evergreen, Colo., 1988). Richard Peterson, *Bonanza Rich: Lifestyles of the Western Mining Entrepreneurs* (Moscow, Idaho, 1991), provides a collective biographical portrait.

## 8: The Other Side of the Coin: A Generation of Industrial Warfare

Labor violence in early twentieth-century Colorado inspired much contemporary analysis. The best way to gain an understanding of the bitterness on both sides is to read some of the leading articles and pamphlets. On the Cripple Creek strike of 1903–1904, see: Ray Stannard Baker, "The Reign of Lawlessness: Anarchy and Despotism in Colorado," *McClure's* 23 (May 1904):43–57, and "Organized Capital Challenges Organized Labor," *McClure's* 23 (July 1904):279–292; William English Walling, "The Labor Rebellion in Colorado," *Independent* 57 (August 18, 1904):36–39; J. Warner Mills, "The Economic Struggle in Colorado," part 1, *Arena* 34 (July 1905):1–10, no. 2, 35 (February 1906):150–158, no. 3, 36 (October 1906):375–390; and Charles E. Strangeland, "The Preliminaries to the Labor War in Colorado," *Political Science Quarterly* 23 (March 1908):1–17. Emma F. Langdon, *The Cripple Creek Strike: A History of Industrial Wars in Colorado* (Denver, 1904–1905), is a passionate presentation of the case of the Western Federation of Miners. Benjamin Rastall, *Labor History of the Cripple Creek District* (Madison, 1908), attempts a more impartial analysis.

For the background to the coal strike of 1913–1914, Lawrence Lewis, "Colorado Fuel and Iron Company: Uplifting 17,000 Employees," *World's Work* 9 (March 1905):5939–5944, provides the company's own view of its paternalism. Walter H. Fink, *The Ludlow Massacre* (Denver, 1914), shows the outrage of Colorado unionists. Zeese Papanikolas, *Buried Unsung: Louis Tikas and the Ludlow Massacre* (Lincoln, 1991), tells the story of one of the strike leaders. George P. West, *Report on the Colorado Strike* (Washington, D.C., 1915), was a staff report for the United States Commission on Industrial Relations, which condemns company policy. John D. Rockefeller, Jr., *The Colorado Industrial Plan* (1916), contains the speeches with which Rockefeller announced and publicized his solution to labor problems. That plan is analyzed in Howard Gitelman, *Legacy of the Ludlow Massacre: A Chapter in American Industrial Relations* (Philadelphia, 1988).

James E. Wright, *The Politics of Populism: Dissent in Colorado* (New Haven, 1974), analyzes the Populist movement and places it within the context of labor unrest in Colorado. John D. Hicks, *The Populist Revolt* (Minneapolis, 1931), and Leon Fuller, "Colorado's Revolt Against Capitalism," *Mississippi Valley Historical Review* 21 (December 1934):343–360, both suffer from their age. G. Michael McCarthy, "Colorado's Populist Leadership," *Colorado Magazine* 48 (Winter 1971):30–42, is a useful study.

Several articles trace organized labor in Colorado through the 1880s and 1890s: Paul T. Bechtol, Jr., "The 1880 Labor Dispute in Leadville," *Colorado Magazine* 47 (Autumn 1970):312–325; Dennis S. Grogan, "Unionization in

Boulder and Weld Counties to 1890," *Colorado Magazine* 44 (Autumn 1967):324–341; Merrill Hough, "Leadville and the Western Federation of Miners," *Colorado Magazine* 49 (Winter 1972):19–34; and David Lonsdale, "The Fight for the Eight Hour Day," *Colorado Magazine* 43 (Autumn 1966):339–353. Michael Neuschatz, *The Golden Sword: The Coming of Capitalism to the Colorado Mining Frontier* (New York, 1986), is a recent synthesis.

The labor crisis of 1903–1904 is treated in George G. Suggs, Jr., *Colorado's War on Militant Unionism: James H. Peabody and the Western Federation of Miners* (Detroit, 1972); George Suggs, "The Colorado Coal Miners Strike of 1903–1904," *Journal of the West* 12 (January 1973):36–50; Melvin Dubofsky, *We Shall Be All: A History of the Industrial Workers of the World* (Chicago, 1969); and Vernon Jensen, *Heritage of Conflict: Labor Relations in the Nonferrous Metals Industry up to 1930* (Ithaca, 1950). The viewpoint of management is expressed in Gene M. Gressley, ed., *Bostonians and Bullion: The Journal of Robert Livermore, 1892–1915* (Lincoln, 1968).

The Ludlow Massacre is the subject of George S. McGovern and Leonard Guttridge, *The Great Coal Field War* (Boston, 1972), which is well written and insightful. Also see Graham Adams, Jr., *Age of Industrial Violence: 1910–1915* (New York, 1966), and Barron Beshoar, *Out of the Depths* (Denver, 1942). Upton Sinclair's previously unpublished sequel to *King Coal* (New York, 1917) was issued in 1976; John Graham, ed., *The Coal War* (Boulder, 1776), is a novel concerned with Colorado's coal war and with the Ludlow Massacre in particular.

Colston E. Warne and Merrill E. Gaddis, "Eleven Years of Compulsory Investigation of Industrial Disputes in Colorado," *Journal of Political Economy* 35 (October 1927):657–683, evaluates the position of labor in the 1920s. Also see Bobbalee Shuler, "Scab Labor in the Colorado Coal Fields," *Essays in Colorado History*, no. 8 (1988):55–75.

Finally, Harold V. Knight, *Working in Colorado: A Brief History of the Colorado Labor Movement* (Boulder, 1971), is a brief and readable summary of the development of Colorado labor unions.

## 9: Farming and Ranching in the American Desert

William E. Pabor, *Colorado as an Agricultural State: Its Farms, Fields and Garden Lands* (New York, 1883), is an intelligent work of boosterism by a participant in the development of irrigated farming. Two collections of documents are the standard sources for information on the colonization experiments: James F. Willard, ed., *The Union Colony at Greeley, Colorado, 1869–1871* (Boulder, 1918), and James F. Willard and Colin B. Goodykoontz, eds., *Experiments in Colorado Colonization, 1869–1872* (Boulder, 1926). John Tice reported extensively on agriculture in *Over the Plains and On the Mountains* (St. Louis, 1872).

The evolution of irrigation after its beginnings in the Platte Valley colonies can be traced in the following: Robert G. Dunbar, "The Origins of the Colorado System of Water Rights Control," *Colorado Magazine* 27 (October 1950):241–262; Alvin T. Steinel, *History of Agriculture in Colorado* (Fort Collins, Colo., 1926); William E. Smythe, *The Conquest of Arid America*, ed. Lawrence Lee (Seattle, 1969); George W. James, *Reclaiming the Arid West: The Story of the United States Reclamation Service* (New York, 1917); James E. Sherow, "Watering the Plains: An Early History of Denver's Highline Canal," *Colorado Heritage*, no. 4 (1988): 2–13; Donald A. MacKendrick, "Before the Newlands Act:

State-Sponsored Reclamation Projects in Colorado, 1888–1903," *Colorado Magazine* 52 (Winter 1975):1–22; Oliver Knight, "Correcting Nature's Error: The Colorado–Big Thompson Project," *Agricultural History* 30 (October 1956):157–169; Donald B. Cole, "Transmountain Water Diversion in Colorado," *Colorado Magazine* 25 (March and May 1948):49–63, 118–135; and Daniel Tyler, *The Last Water Hole in the West: A History of the Northern Colorado Water Conservancy District and the Colorado–Big Thompson Project* (Niwot, Colo., 1992).

James Earl Sherow, *Watering the Valley: Development Along the High Plains Arkansas River, 1870–1950* (Lawrence, Kan., 1990), is a comprehensive study of southeastern Colorado with particular attention to environmental changes. Clark C. Spence, *The Salvation Army Farm Colonies* (Tucson, 1985), describes the Fort Amity colony in the Arkansas Valley.

The Colorado cattle industry is the subject of Ora B. Peake, *The Colorado Range Cattle Industry* (Glendale, Calif., 1937); Maurice Frink, W. Turrentine Jackson, and Agnes Wright Spring, *When Grass Was King* (Boulder, 1956); William R. White, "Illegal Fencing on the Colorado Range," *Colorado Magazine* 52 (Spring 1975):93–113; and Clifford P. Westermeier, "The Legal Status of the Colorado Cattleman, 1867–1887," *Colorado Magazine* 25 (May and July 1948):109–118, 157–166. First published in 1920, Clarice Richards, *A Tenderfoot Bride: Tales From an Old Ranch* (Lincoln, 1988), describes ranch life as seen by a cultivated easterner. Developments in Colorado are placed within a broader framework in Walter Prescott Webb, *The Great Plains* (New York, 1931); Ernest S. Osgood, *The Day of the Cattleman* (Minneapolis, 1929); John T. Schlebecker, *Cattle Raising on the Plains 1900–1961* (Lincoln, 1963); and Gene M. Gressley, *Bankers and Cattlemen* (New York, 1966).

Aspects of the sugar beet business are covered in Geraldine Bean, *Charles Boettcher: A Study in Pioneer Western Enterprise* (Boulder, 1976); Dena S. Markoff, "The Sugar Industry in the Arkansas River Valley: National Sugar Beet Company," *Colorado Magazine* 55 (Winter 1978):69–92, and "A Bittersweet Saga: The Arkansas Valley Beet Sugar Industry, 1900–1979," *Colorado Magazine* 56 (Summer-Fall, 1979):161–178; and William J. May, Jr., "The Colorado Sugar Manufacturing Company: Grand Junction Plant," *Colorado Magazine* 55 (Winter 1978):15–46.

Classic examples of nineteenth-century boosterism that focus on the agricultural promise of Colorado are William Gilpin, *The Mission of the North American People* (Philadelphia, 1874), and Walter von Richthofen, *Cattle-Raising on the Plains of North America* (New York, 1885).

The evolution of attitudes toward the high plains has been thoroughly examined. See, for example, Martin Bowden, "The Perception of the Western Interior in the United States," *Proceedings of the Association of American Geographers* I (1969):16–21; G. M. Lewis, "William Gilpin and the Concept of a Great Plains Region," *Annals of the Association of American Geographers* 56 (March 1966):33–51; Deryl V. Gease, "William Byers and the Colorado Agricultural Society," *Colorado Magazine* 43 (Fall 1966):325–338; and Robert Athearn, *Union Pacific Country* (Chicago, 1971). David M. Emmons, *Garden in the Grasslands* (Lincoln, 1971), is an excellent summary of the boomer literature. For results in Colorado, see Morris F. Taylor, "The Town Boom in Las Animas and Baca Counties," *Colorado Magazine* 55 (Spring-Summer 1978):111–132.

The problems of dryland agriculture in the twentieth century are treated with great insight in Carl F. Kraenzel, *The Great Plains in Transition* (Norman, Okla., 1955). Also see Charles M. Davis, "Changes in Land Utilization on the Plateau of Northwest Colorado," *Economic Geography* 18 (October 1942):379–388; H. H. Finnell, "Pity the Poor Land," *Soil Conservation* 12 (September 1946):27–32; John R. Borchert, "The Dust Bowl in the 1970s," *Annals of the Association of American Geographers* 61 (March 1971):1–22; and Leslie Hewes, *The Suitcase Farming Frontier: A Study of the Historical Geography of the Central Great Plains* (Lincoln, 1973).

The roles and activities of women on the early twentieth-century farming frontier can be followed in Julie Jones-Eddy, ed., *Homesteading Women: An Oral History of Colorado, 1890–1950* (New York, 1992), and Katherine Harris, *Long Vistas: Women and Families on Colorado Homesteads* (Niwot, Colo., 1993).

## 10: The People of Colorado, 1876–1916

Since 1979, when Julie R. Jeffrey published *Frontier Women: The Trans-Mississippi West, 1840–1880* (New York), other studies have illuminated the once dimly lit field of women in the West. Sandra L. Myres provides a survey in *Westering Women and the Frontier Experience 1800–1915* (Albuquerque, 1982). Glenda Riley includes material on Colorado in *The Female Frontier: A Comparative View of Women on the Prairie and the Plains* (Lawrence, Kan., 1988), as does Anne M. Butler in *Daughters of Joy, Sisters of Mercy: Prostitutes in the American West, 1865–1890* (Urbana, 1985). Elizabeth Jameson and Katherine Harris focus on Colorado women in essays on working women and women homesteaders in *The Women's West* (Norman, Okla., 1987), edited by Susan Armitage and Elizabeth Jameson.

Sarah Deutsch covers Hispanic women in *No Separate Refuge: Culture, Class and Gender on an Anglo-Hispanic Frontier in the American Southwest, 1880–1940* (New York, 1987). Joyce Goodfriend scrutinizes widows in "The Struggle for Survival: Widows in Denver, 1880–1912," in *On Their Own: Widows and Widowhood in the American Southwest* (Urbana, 1988), edited by Arlene Scadron. Emily French, *Emily, the Diary of a Hard-Worked Woman*, edited by Janet LeCompte (Lincoln, 1987), chronicles the economic privation that plagued many divorced women. Ruth Moynihan et al., eds., *So Much to Be Done: Women Settlers on the Mining and Ranching Frontier* (Lincoln, 1990), reprints Annie M. Green's reminiscence of life in Greeley.

Julie Jones-Eddy concentrates on Colorado in *Homesteading Women: An Oral History of Colorado, 1890–1950* (New York, 1992), as do Nell Brown Probst in *Those Strenuous Dames of the Colorado Prairie* (Boulder, 1983) and Janet Robertson in *The Magnificent Mountain Women: Adventures in the Colorado Rockies* (Lincoln, 1991). Elliot West's *Growing Up With the Country: Childhood on the Far-Western Frontier* (Albuquerque, 1989) provides a pioneering overview. Lillian Schlissel et al., eds., *Far From Home: Families of the Westward Journey* (New York, 1989) include Byrd Gibbens's "Charles and Maggie Brown in Colorado and New Mexico."

Of Colorado women who deserve a book-length biography, few have received one. Among the exceptions are Martha Maxwell, who is given her due by Maxine Benson in *Martha Maxwell, Rocky Mountain Naturalist* (Lincoln, 1986); Clara Brown, covered by Kathleen Bruyn in *"Aunt" Clara Brown: Story of a*

*Black Pioneer* (Boulder, 1970); and Margaret Tobin Brown, revisited by Christine Whitacre in *Molly Brown: Denver's Unsinkable Lady* (Denver, 1984). John H. Monnett and Michael McCarthy devote chapters to Susan Shelby Magoffin, "Poker Alice" Tubbs, Frances Jacobs, Ann Bassett, Cornelia Baxter, Josephine Roche, and Florence Sabin in *Colorado Profiles: Men and Women Who Shaped the Centennial State* (Evergreen, Colo., 1987). Elinor Bluemel, *One Hundred Years of Colorado Women* (Denver, 1973), provides short biographies, as does Billie A. Grant, *Black Women of the West: Success in the Workplace* (Denver, 1982). Joyce Goodfriend and Dona K. Flory, "Women in Colorado Before the First World War," *Colorado Magazine* 53 (Summer 1976):201–228, suggests research opportunities, as does Nancy Whistler, ed., *Colorado Oral History Guide* (Denver, 1980). For other material, including scholarly periodical articles on women that appeared in the 1970s, see the 1982 edition of *Colorado: A History of the Centennial State.*

On equal suffrage see Joseph G. Brown, *The History of Equal Suffrage in Colorado, 1868–1898* (Denver, 1898), and for an anti-woman's suffrage view, see Lawrence Lewis, "How Woman's Suffrage Works in Colorado," *Outlook* 82 (January 27, 1906):167–178. Scholarly treatments include: Billie Barnes Jensen, "Colorado Woman Suffrage Campaigns of the 1870s," *Journal of the West* 12 (April 1973):254–271, and John R. Morris, "The Women and Governor Waite," *Colorado Magazine* 44 (Winter 1967):11–19. The Spring 1993 issue of *Colorado Heritage* is devoted to women's suffrage. In addition to essays by Lee Chambers-Schiller, Carolyn Stefanco, Stephen J. Leonard, Thomas J. Noel, and Rosemary Fetter, it contains a guide to sources on suffrage in Colorado and nationally by Marcia T. Goldstein and Rebecca A. Hunt.

The story of Colorado's ethnic groups, like that of its women, is slowly developing from the filiopietistic stage to the level of mature, integrated histories. A still useful general summary is Colin B. Goodykoontz, "The People of Colorado," in Hafen, *Colorado and Its People*, II:77–120. Several groups are covered in Stephen J. Leonard, "The Irish, English and Germans in Denver, 1860–1890," *Colorado Magazine* 54 (Spring 1977):126–154. Thomas J. Noel also synthesizes in *The City and the Saloon: Denver, 1858–1916* (Lincoln, 1982), and Therese S. Westermeier covers a number of ethnic events in "Colorado Festivals," *Colorado Magazine* 27 (April 1951):172–183. Several city and town studies, including Holly Barton, *Cokedale, 1907–1947: Anatomy of a Model Mining Community* (Cokedale, Colo., 1976); Edward Blair, *Leadville: Colorado's Magic City* (Boulder, 1980); Daniel F. Doeppers, "The Globeville Neighborhood in Denver," *Geographical Review* 57 (October 1967):506–522; Richard and Suzanne Fetter, *Telluride From Pick to Powder* (Caldwell, Idaho, 1979); and Duane Smith, *Rocky Mountain Boom Town: A History of Durango* (Albuquerque, 1980), contain information on a variety of groups. So do business and industry histories such as Dena S. Markoff, "The Sugar Industry in the Arkansas River Valley: National Beet Sugar Company," *Colorado Magazine* 57 (Winter 1978):69–92, and H. Lee Scamehorn, *Pioneer Steelmaker in the West: The Colorado Fuel and Iron Company, 1872–1903* (Boulder, 1976).

Although there are many treatments of individual groups, some contingents — even such sizeable ones as the Swedes, Irish, and Canadians — have generally been ignored. Conversely, the Chinese and Japanese are the beneficiaries of several studies, including Patricia Ourada, "The Chinese in Colorado," *Colorado Magazine* 29 (October 1952):273–284; Fumio Ozawa, "Japanese in Colorado," in

*Colorado Times,* ed., *Japanese American Who's Who* (Denver, 1959), 7–93; Gerald E. Rudolph, "The Chinese in Colorado, 1869–1911" (M.A. thesis, University of Denver, 1964); Helen Webster, "The Chinese School of the Central Presbyterian Church of Denver," *Colorado Magazine* 40 (January and April, 1963):57–63, 132–137; and Roy T. Wortman, "Denver's Anti-Chinese Riot, 1880," *Colorado Magazine* 42 (Fall 1965):275–291.

British investors and experts have received attention because of their financial and technical importance, but they have not often been viewed as immigrants. See William T. Jackson, *The Enterprising Scot: Investors in the American West After 1873* (Chicago, 1968); Clark Spence, *British Investments and the American Mining Frontier, 1860–1901* (Ithaca, 1958); Alfred P. Tiscendorf, "British Investments in Colorado Mines," *Colorado Magazine* 30 (October 1953):241–246; and Otis E. Young, "A Dedication to the Memory of Thomas Arthur Rickard, 1864–1953," *Arizona and the West* 2 (Summer 1969):105–108. On the Cornish see Lynn I. Perrigo, "The Cornish Miners of Early Gilpin County," *Colorado Magazine* 14 (May 1937):92–101, and Arthur C. Todd, *The Cornish Miner in America* (Glendale, Calif., 1967). An old work by Evan Williams, *History of the Welsh People of Colorado* (Denver, 1889), is still of some use. C. W. Hurd, "J. K. Mullen, Mining Magnate of Colorado," *Colorado Magazine* 29 (April 1952):104–118, is one of the few articles addressing the Irish.

Mildred S. MacArthur did an early laudatory pamphlet on the Germans, "History of the German Element in Colorado" (Chicago, 1917), which was followed in the same vein by W. R. Hentschel's short "The German Element in the Development of Colorado" (Denver, 1930). Of more recent vintage is Lyle Dorsett, "The Ordeal of Colorado's Germans During World War I," *Colorado Magazine* 51 (Fall 1974):277–293. Largely because of the efforts of Colorado State University's Germans From Russia project, that heretofore neglected group has recently received considerable scholarly attention. See, for example, Kenneth Rock, "Unsere Leute: The Germans From Russia in Colorado," *Colorado Magazine* 54 (Spring 1977):155–183; Timothy Kloberdanz, "People Without a Country: The Russian Germans of Logan County," in Dale Wells, *The Logan County Ledger* (n.p., 1976):226–247. Also included in Wells is Nell Brown Probst, "The New Americans: Bohemians, Italians, Japanese, Mexicans," 193–224.

Ida Uchill provided the foundation and built much of the superstructure for local Jewish history in her splendid *Pioneers, Peddlers, and Tsadikim* (Denver, 1957), which was followed by Allen D. Breck, *A Centennial History of the Jews of Colorado, 1859–1959* (Denver, 1961). Phil Goodstein also recounts Jewish history in *Exploring Jewish Colorado* (Denver, 1992). Also see Marjorie Hornbein, "Dr. Charles Spivak of Denver: Physician, Social Worker, Yiddish Author," *Western States Jewish Historical Quarterly* 11 (April 1979):195–211; Dorothy Roberts, "The Jewish Colony at Cotopaxi," *Colorado Magazine* 18 (July 1941); and Michael W. Rubinoff, "Rabbi in a Progressive Era. C.E.H. Kauver [sic] of Denver," *Colorado Magazine 54* (Summer 1977):220–239.

Many gaps are yet to be filled in the history of the state's Southern and Eastern Europeans, although some fine work has been done. See M. James Kedro, "Czechs and Slovaks in Colorado, 1860–1920," *Colorado Magazine* 54 (Spring 1977):93–125, and Stanley Cuba's detailed articles on the Polish, "A Polish Community in the Urban West: St. Joseph's Parish in Denver, Colorado," *Polish American Studies* 36 (Spring 1979):33–74, and "Poles in the Early Musical and Theatrical Life of Colorado," *Colorado Magazine* 54 (Summer 1977):240–276. Joseph Velikonja's unpublished paper, "Slovene Immigration to Colorado" (American Association for the Advancement of Slavic Studies, New Haven, October 10, 1979, in files of the Denver Public Library, Western History Department), gives much useful information. Colorado's Greeks are briefly noted in Theodore Saloutos, "Cultural Persistence and Change: Greeks in the Great Plains and Rocky Mountain West, 1890–1970," *Pacific Historical Review* 49 (February 1980):77–104. Also see George J. Patterson, "The Unassimilated Greeks of Denver" (Ph.D. diss., University of Colorado–Boulder, 1960). Some of the most recent work on Italians is among the best. See Philip F. Notarianni, "Italian Involvement in the 1903–04 Coal Miners' Strike in Southern Colorado and Utah," in George E. Pozzetta, ed., *Pane e Lavoro: The Italian American Working Class* (Toronto, 1980), pp. 47–65, and Christine De Rose, "Inside Little Italy: Italian Immigrants in Denver," *Colorado Magazine* 54 (Summer 1977):277–293. Earlier works on Italians include Marcello Gandolfo, *Gli Italiani nel Colorado: Libro Dedicato agli Italiani, 1899–1900* (Denver, ca. 1900), and Giovanni Perilli, *Colorado and the Italians in Colorado* (Denver, ca. 1922).

David P. Nelson details the history of a small Swedish group in "Ryssby: A Swedish Settlement," *Colorado Magazine* 54 (Spring 1977):184–199. Anna Poulsen tells of Brush's Danish sanitarium in *EbenEzer: The History of Seventy Years of Christian Mercy Work in Colorado* (Brush, Colo., 1979), and Dorothy Roberts chronicles the rapid rise and fall of the Dutch in southern Colorado in "A Dutch Colony in Colorado," *Colorado Magazine* 17 (November 1940):229–236.

A thesis by James Rose Harvey, "Negroes in Colorado" (M.A. thesis, University of Denver, 1941), provides the starting place for many writers on Colorado's African-Americans. Among the scholarly articles are Eugene H. Berwanger, "William J. Hardin: Colorado Spokesman for Racial Justice," *Colorado Magazine* 52 (Winter 1975):52–65; James R. Harvey, "Negroes in Colorado," *Colorado Magazine* 26 (July 1949):165–176; Harmon Mothershead, "Negro Rights in Colorado Territory," *Colorado Magazine* 40 (July 1963):212–223; and George H. Wayne, "Negro Migration and Colonization in Colorado, 1870–1930," *Journal of the West* 15 (January 1976):102–140. Book-length studies include Kathleen Bruyn, *"Aunt" Clara Brown: Story of a Black Pioneer* (Boulder, 1970), and Marion Talmadge and Iris Gilmore, *Barney Ford, Black Baron* (New York, 1973). William M. King tells of Andrew Green, an African-American, in *Going to Meet a Man: Denver's Last Legal Public Hanging, 27 July 1886* (Niwot, Colo., 1990).

## 11: The Discovery of Scenery: The Growth of Tourism

The starting point for any study of tourism in the American West is Earl Pomeroy, *In Search of the Golden West: The Tourist in Western America* (New York, 1957), a delightful and insightful guide to a subject as vast as the West itself. The evolution of American attitudes toward the outdoors can be studied in Hans Huth, *Nature and the American: Three Centuries of Changing Attitudes* (Lincoln, 1972), and Roderick Nash, *Wilderness and the American Mind* (New Haven, 1973). Dorothy Dines, Stephen J. Leonard, and Stanley Cuba, *Charles Partridge Adams* (Golden, Colo., 1993), focuses on a landscape artist active in Colorado in the late nineteenth and early twentieth centuries.

The rise of the tourism industry in Colorado and the West is the theme of J. Valerie Fifer, *American Progress: The Growth of the Transport, Tourist, and Information Industries in the Nineteenth-Century West Seen Through the Life and*

*Times of George A. Crofutt, Pioneer and Publicist of the Transcontinental Age* (Chester, Conn., 1988). Marshall Sprague has covered some of the most colorful incidents in the development of Colorado tourism in *Newport in the Rockies* (Denver, 1961), and *A Gallery of Dudes* (Boston, 1966). Billy M. Jones, *Health Seekers in the Southwest, 1817–1900* (Norman, Okla., 1967), and John E. Baur, "The Health Seeker in the Westward Movement, 1830–1900," *Mississippi Valley Historical Review* 46 (June 1959):91–110, both treat the nineteenth-century health seeker.

Every travel account of nineteenth-century Colorado offers direct or indirect evidence about the tourist business. Robert Athearn, *Westward the Briton* (New York, 1953), summarizes the reactions of dozens of British travelers. Among the more useful accounts are the following: Bayard Taylor, *Colorado: A Summer Trip* (New York, 1867); Samuel Bowles, *Our New West* (Hartford, 1869); Fitz Hugh Ludlow, *The Heart of the Continent* (New York, 1870); S. Anna Gordon, *Camping in Colorado* (New York, 1879); A. A. Hayes, Jr., "Vacation Aspects of Colorado," *Harper's* 60 (March 1880):542–557; Ernest Ingersoll, *Knocking Around the Rockies* (New York, 1883), and *The Crest of the Continent* (Chicago, 1885); Helen Hunt Jackson, *Bits of Travel at Home* (Boston, 1886); Richard Harding Davis, *The West From a Car Window* (New York, 1892); Isabella Bird, *A Lady's Life in the Rocky Mountains* (London, 1879); and R. B. Townsend, *A Tenderfoot in Colorado* (Norman, Okla., 1968).

Descriptions of Denver and Colorado Springs found in magazines of the time also give useful information on the tourist business. For example, see George R. Buckman, "Colorado Springs," *Lippincott's Magazine* 31 (January 1883):9–20; Edwards Roberts, "The City of Denver," *Harper's* 76 (May 1888):944–957; Lewis Iddings, "Life in the Altitudes: The Colorado Health Plateau," *Scribners Monthly* 19 (1896):136–151; "Denver," *Saturday Review* 53 (April 29, 1882):527; and Mabel Loomis Todd, "Pike's Peak and Colorado Springs," *Nation* 57 (October 5, 1893):245–246.

Early discussions of the effects of Colorado's climate on health can be found in the *Reports* of the Colorado Board of Immigration and the State Board of Health of Colorado for years during the 1870s and 1880s. Also see articles by Dr. Samuel A. Fisk in *Popular Science Monthly:* "Colorado for Invalids," 25 (July 1884):313–320, and "Colorado as a Winter Sanitarium," 28 (March 1886):668–679, as well as Francis S. Kinder, "The Consumptive's Chances in Colorado," *Review of Reviews* 27 (June 1903):698–702. Douglas R. McKay, "A History of the Nordach Ranch: Colorado's First Sanatorium of the Open Air," *Colorado Magazine* 56 (Summer-Fall 1979):179–195, and Jeanne Abrams, *Blazing the Tuberculosis Trail*, Colorado Historical Society Monograph no. 6 (Denver, 1990), describe the Colorado sanatorium movement.

For the development of local parks, festivals, and other tourist facilities, see Levette J. Davidson, "The Festival of Mountain and Plain," *Colorado Magazine* 25 (July and September 1948):145–157, 203–211; "Denver's Democratic Invasion," *The Colorado Magazine* 41 (Summer 1964):185–197; Seth B. Bradley, "The Origin of the Denver Mountain Parks System," *Colorado Magazine* 9 (January 1932):26–29; Leroy Hafen, "The Coming of the Automobile and Improved Roads to Colorado," *Colorado Magazine* 8 (January 1931):1–16; and Thomas J. Noel, "Paving the Way to Colorado: The Evolution of Auto Tourism in Denver," *Journal of the West* 26 (July 1987):42–49. The ski industry is described in Abbott Fay, *Ski Tracks in the Rockies: A Century of Colorado Skiing* (Louisville, Colo., 1984).

For the development of the national park system within Colorado, see C. W. Buchholtz, *Rocky Mountain National Park: A History* (Boulder, 1983); Duane A. Smith, *Mesa Verde National Park: Shadows of the Centuries* (Lawrence, Kan., 1988); Richard Beidleman, "The Black Canyon of the Gunnison National Monument," *Colorado Magazine* 40 (July 1963):161–178; Robert Shankland, *Steve Mather of the National Parks* (New York, 1970); and John Ise, *Our National Park Policy: A Critical History* (Baltimore, 1961).

Enos Mills is discussed in Carl Abbott, "The Active Force: Enos Mills and the National Park Movement," *Colorado Magazine* 56 (Winter-Spring 1979):56–73, and "To Arouse Interest in the Outdoors: The Literary Career of Enos Mills," *Montana: The Magazine of Western History* 31 (April 1981):2–15. Complementary perspectives on life in the Estes Park area can be found in Joe Mills, *A Mountain Boyhood* (Lincoln, 1990), and Janet Robertson, *The Magnificent Mountain Women: Adventures in the Colorado Rockies* (Lincoln, 1990).

## 12: Denver: The Rocky Mountain Metropolis

For statistics on the changing population and economy of Denver in the years 1880–1910, the best sources are the publications of the United States Bureau of the Census. The place to turn for descriptions of business firms, social and political institutions, utilities and services, and neighborhoods is Jerome Smiley, *History of Denver* (Denver, 1901), with more recent insights in Lyle Dorsett and Michael McCarthy, *The Queen City: A History of Denver* (Boulder, 1986). Sandra Dallas, *Cherry Creek Gothic* (Norman, Okla., 1971); Richard Brettell, *Historic Denver: The Architects and Their Architecture, 1885–1893* (Denver, 1973); Francine Haber, Kenneth R. Fuller, and David N. Wetzel, *Robert S. Roeschlaub: Architect of the Emerging West* (Denver, 1988); and Thomas J. Noel and Barbara Norgren, *Denver: The City Beautiful and Its Architects, 1893–1941* (Denver, 1987), are all valuable treatments of the physical evolution of the city and its architectural styles. George Hilton, "Denver's Cable Railways," *Colorado Magazine* 44 (Winter 1967):35–52, is the only published scholarly study of an important public service.

To discover what outsiders thought about Denver in these years, see Robert Athearn, *Westward the Briton* (New York, 1953), or William Thayer, *Marvels of the New West* (Norwich, Conn., 1887). Denverites stood for their self-portrait in James I. Day, *Our Architecture and Scenes of Denver, Colorado* (Denver, 1906); Denver Chamber of Commerce, *Denver: A Glimpse of the City and State* (1898); and *Illustrated Denver: The Queen City of the Plains* (Denver, 1892). Descriptions of daily life at two very different social levels in late-nineteenth-century Denver are found in Henry F. May, *Coming to Terms: A Study in Memory and History* (Berkeley, 1987), and Emily French, *Emily: The Diary of a Hard-Worked Woman*, ed. Janet LeCompte (Lincoln, 1987).

Early Denver neighborhoods are profiled in Thomas Noel, *Richtofens Montclair: A Pioneer Denver Suburb* (Boulder, 1976); Don Etter, *Auraria: Where Denver Began* (Boulder, 1972); William West and Don Etter, *Curtis Park: A Denver Neighborhood* (Boulder, 1980); Ruth Wiberg, *Rediscovering Northwest Denver: Its History, Its People, Its Landmarks* (Boulder, 1976); and Phil Goodstein, *Denver's Capitol Hill* (Denver, 1988), and *South Denver Saga* (Denver, 1991). Robert Autobee, *If You Stick With Barnum*, Essays and Monographs in Colorado History, Monograph 8 (1992), traces the Barnum neighborhood from its nineteenth-century beginnings to the present. Robert Tank, "Mobility and

Occupational Structure on the Late Nineteenth-Century Urban Frontier: The Case of Denver, Colorado," *Pacific Historical Review* 47 (May 1978):189–216, compares Denver to other cities; Gretchen Claman, "A Typhoid Fever Epidemic and the Power of the Press in Denver in 1879," *Colorado Magazine* 56 (Summer-Fall 1979):143–160, describes an early environmental crisis. Mark H. Rose, "Urban Environments and Technological Innovation: Energy Choices in Denver and Kansas City, 1900–1940," *Technology and Culture* 25 (July 1984):503–539, describes the changing fabric of everyday life.

Key Denver businesses are described in Ellen Fisher, *One Hundred Years of Energy: Public Service Company of Colorado and Its Predecessors, 1869–1969* (New York, 1989), and Eugene Adams, Lyle Dorsett, and Robert S. Pulcipher, *The Pioneer Western Bank — First of Denver: 1860–1980* (Denver, 1984).

Several of the participants in Denver's political life at the turn of the century wrote about their experiences. The most valuable account is Benjamin B. Lindsey and Harvey J. O'Higgins, *The Beast* (Seattle, 1970). George Creel, *Rebel at Large: Recollections of Fifty Crowded Years* (New York, 1947), and Edward Keating, *The Gentleman From Colorado* (Denver, 1964), are also useful. Clyde L. King analyzed the evolution of the Denver machine in *History of the Government of Denver With Special Reference to Its Relations With Public Service Corporations* (Denver, 1911). King's *The Regulation of Municipal Utilities* (New York, 1914), and Delos F. Wilcox, *Municipal Franchises* (Chicago, 1910–1911), place the reform movement in a national context. Lindsey's life is covered in Charles Larsen, *The Good Fight: The Life and Times of Ben B. Lindsey* (Chicago, 1972). A valuable unpublished source is John Pickering, "Blueprint of Power: The Public Career of Robert Speer in Denver" (Ph.D. diss., University of Denver, 1978).

Progressive politics in Denver has received considerable attention in recent years. Among the most informative works of scholarship are the following: Allen Breck, *William Gray Evans, 1855–1924: Portrait of a Western Executive* (Denver, 1964); J. Paul Mitchell, "Boss Speer and the City Functional: Boosters and Businessmen Versus Commission Government," *Pacific Northwest Quarterly* 63 (October 1972):156–164; J. Paul Mitchell, "Municipal Reform in Denver: The Defeat of Mayor Speer," *Colorado Magazine* 45 (Winter 1968):27–41; Elliott West, "Cleansing the Queen City: Prohibition and Urban Reform in Denver," *Arizona and the West* 14 (Winter 1972):331–346; Roland DeLorme, "Turn of the Century Denver: An Invitation to Reform," *Colorado Magazine* 45 (Winter 1968):1–15; and James E. Hansen II, "Moonshine and Murder: Prohibition in Denver," *Colorado Magazine* 50 (Winter 1973):1–23. William H. Wilson, *The City Beautiful Movement* (Baltimore, 1989), has two definitive chapters on early city planning in Denver. Also see William H. Wilson, "New Wine in Old Bottles: The Denver Mountain Parks Movement," *Colorado Heritage* no. 2 (1989):10–15.

A valuable source for reform movements on the state level is Colin B. Goodykoontz, ed., *Papers of Edward P. Costigan Relating to the Progressive Movement in Colorado, 1902–1917* (Boulder, 1941). Articles on the subject include E. K. MacColl, "John Franklin Shafroth: Reform Governor of Colorado, 1909–1913," *Colorado Magazine* 29 (January 1952):37–52; Charles Bayard, "The Colorado Progressive Republican Split of 1912," *Colorado Magazine* 45 (Winter 1968):61–78; C. Warren Vander Hill, "Colorado Progressives and the Bull Moose Campaign," *Colorado Magazine* 43 (Spring 1966):93–112; and Fred

Greenbaum, "The Colorado Progressives in 1906," *Arizona and the West* 7 (Spring 1965):21–32. Local progressivism outside Denver is discussed in Donald A. MacKendrick, "Thunder West of the Divide: James W. Bucklin, Colorado Utopian Reformer," *Essays and Monographs in Colorado History* (Denver, 1984):35–53.

## 13: Colorado's Great Detour: The 1920s and 1930s

The history of Colorado in the 1920s and 1930s of necessity begins with an analysis of the economic indicators. One can turn directly to statistics in the United States Census or the data presented in Harvey Perloff et al., *Regions, Resources, and Economic Growth* (Baltimore, 1960), and Leonard Arrington, *The Changing Economic Structure of the Mountain West, 1850–1950* (Logan, Utah, 1963).

Reactionary politics in Colorado during the 1920s is well documented. Phillip L. Cook, "The Red Scare in Denver," *Colorado Magazine* 43 (Fall 1966):308–326, treats the problems of the years 1919 and 1920. David Chalmers, *Hooded Americanism* (Garden City, N.Y., 1965), and Kenneth T. Jackson, *The Ku Klux Klan in the City, 1915–1930* (New York, 1967), include chapters on Colorado, and James H. Davis, "Colorado Under the Klan," *Colorado Magazine* 42 (Spring 1965):93–108, is detailed and well researched. John Creighton, "The Small-Town Klan in Colorado," *Essays and Monographs in Colorado History*, no. 2 (Denver, 1983):175–197, and Robert Goldberg, *Hooded Empire: The Ku Klux Klan in Colorado* (Urbana, 1981), are recent and thorough studies.

Donald J. McClurg, "The Colorado Coal Strike of 1927," *Labor History* 4 (Winter 1963):68–92, and Charles Bayard, "The 1927–28 Colorado Coal Strike," *Pacific Historical Review* 32 (August 1963):235–250, treat labor warfare. John Livingston, "Governor William Sweet: Persistent Progressive Versus Pragmatic Politics," *Colorado Magazine* 54 (Winter 1977):6–25, is also relevant.

Stephen J. Leonard's *Trials and Triumphs: A Colorado Portrait of the Great Depression, With FSA Photographs* (Niwot, Colo., 1993) covers the Depression as well as other events of the decade. James Wickens, *Colorado in the Great Depression* (New York, 1979), provides a detailed history of the economic breakdown and the New Deal. The Civilian Conservation Corps up to 1936 is treated in C. N. Allenger and L. A. Gleyere, comps., *History of the Civilian Conservation Corps in Colorado* (Denver, ca. 1936). Colorado's African-Americans during the 1930s have received little attention, but Sarah Deutsch in *No Separate Refuge: Culture, Class and Gender on an Anglo-Hispanic Frontier in the American Southwest, 1880–1940* (New York, 1987) devotes a chapter to "Depression, Government and Regional Community."

The *Pacific Historical Review* 38 (August 1969), contains three articles that place in perspective Colorado's political response to the New Deal: James T. Patterson, "The New Deal in the West," Leonard Arrington, "The New Deal in the West: A Preliminary Statistical Inquiry," and James Wickens, "The New Deal in Colorado." Also concerned with Colorado in the 1930s are James Wickens, "Tightening the Colorado Purse Strings," *Colorado Magazine* 46 (Fall 1969):271–286; Mary Farley, "Colorado and the Arkansas Valley Authority," *Colorado Magazine* 48 (Summer 1971):221–234; Marjorie Hornbein, "Josephine Roche: Social Worker and Coal Miner," *Colorado Magazine* 53 (Summer 1976):243–260; Roy E. Brown, "Colorful Colorado: State of Varied Interests," in Thomas Donnelly, ed., *Rocky Mountain Politics* (Albuquerque, 1940); Mary

Motian-Meadows, "Western Visions: Colorado's New Deal Post Office Murals," *Colorado Heritage* (Autumn 1991):15–35; and Don C. Reading, "A Statistical Analysis of New Deal Economic Programs in the Forty-Eight States, 1933–1939" (Ph.D. diss., Utah State University, 1972).

Three general histories of the West are helpful for placing interwar Colorado in context: Earl Pomeroy, *The Pacific Slope* (New York, 1965); Gerald D. Nash, *The American West in the Twentieth Century* (Englewood Cliffs, 1973); and Richard Lowitt, *The New Deal and the West* (Bloomington, 1984).

## 14: Growth and Politics in the New Colorado

John Gunther, *Inside U.S.A.* (New York, 1947); Neil Morgan, *Westward Tilt* (New York, 1963); and Neal R. Pierce, *The Mountain States of America* (New York, 1972), contain evaluations of Colorado life and politics by intelligent, perceptive journalists.

General analyses of postwar Colorado politics are found in Curtis Martin, "Colorado," in Frank Jonas, ed., *Western Politics* (Salt Lake City, 1961); Curtis Martin and Rudolph Gomez, *Colorado Politics and Government* (Boulder, 1964); and Daniel Elazar, *Cities of the Prairie: The Metropolitan Frontier and American Politics* (New York, 1970). The *Western Political Quarterly* formerly published analyses of the biennial elections in the western states. Articles on Colorado appeared in the following volumes: 4 (March 1951):72–75; 6 (March 1953):108–110; 10 (March 1957):117–121; 12 (March 1959):301–308; 14 (March 1961):327–330; 16 (June 1963):421–425; 18 (June 1965):475–480; 20 (June 1967):555–562; 22 (September 1969):475–481; and 24 (June 1971):274–281. Victor Hejm and Joseph Pisciotte, "Profiles and Careers of Colorado State Legislators," *Western Political Quarterly* 21 (December 1968):698–722, and Susanne A. Storber, *Legislative Politics in the Rocky Mountain West* (Boulder, 1967), are also useful.

For the war years, see Stephen J. Leonard, "Denver at War," *Colorado Heritage* 4 (1987):30–41; Christine Pfaff, "An Ammunition Factory in the Rockies," *Colorado Heritage* (Summer 1992):33–45; and Melyn Johnson, "At Home in Amache," *Colorado Heritage,* no. 1 (1989):2–13.

Studies of urban growth patterns in Colorado include M. John Loeffler, "Population Syndromes of the Colorado Piedmont," *Annals of the Association of American Geographers* 55 (March 1965):26–66; Leo Adde, *Nine Cities: The Anatomy of Downtown Renewal* (Washington, D.C., 1969); Mechlin D. Moore, *Downtown Denver,* Urban Land Institute Technical Bulletin no. 54 (1965); Carl Abbott, "Boom State and Boom City: Stages in Denver's Growth," *Colorado Magazine* 50 (Summer 1973):207–230; and Otis D. Duncan et al., *Metropolis and Region* (Baltimore, 1960). Stephen J. Leonard and Thomas J. Noel, *Denver: Mining Camp to Metropolis* (Niwot, Colo., 1990), provides excellent coverage of recent metropolitan growth. Histories of other communities within the metropolitan area include Phyllis Smith, *A Look at Boulder From Settlement to City* (Boulder, 1981), and Steven F. Mehls, Carol J. Drake, and James E. Fell, Jr., *Aurora: Gateway to the Rockies* (Evergreen, Colo., 1985).

Much of the information necessary for the analysis of Denver's socioeconomic development is found in reports by the Denver Planning Office, the Denver Community Renewal Program, the Denver Urban Observatory, the Downtown Denver Master Plan Committee, and the Denver Regional Council of Governments (formerly the Inter-County Regional Planning Commission). For a case study, see Thomas J. Noel, *Denver's Larimer Street: Main Street, Skid Row, and Urban Renaissance* (Denver, 1981).

Denver metropolitan politics and government are the subjects of William Charles Bernard, *Metro Denver: Mile High Government* (Boulder, 1970); George V. Kelly, *The Old Gray Mayors of Denver* (Boulder, 1974); Kenneth S. Gray, "Report on Politics in Denver" (Harvard-MIT Center for Urban Research, 1959); James L. Cox, *Metropolitan Water Supply: The Denver Experience* (Boulder, 1967); Maxine Kurtz, "The Tri-County Regional Planning Commission," *Public Administration Review* 7 (1947):113–122; Susan W. Furniss, "The Response of the Colorado General Assembly to Proposals for Metropolitan Reform," *Western Political Quarterly* 26 (December 1973):747–765; Robert Perkin and Charles A. Graham, "Denver: Reluctant Capital," in Ray B. West, ed., *Rocky Mountain Cities* (New York, 1949); Dennis R. Judd, "From Cowtown to Sunbelt City: Boosterism and Economic Growth in Denver," in Susan S. Fainstein et al., *Restructuring the City* (New York, 1986); Dennis R. Judd and Randy L. Ready, "Entrepreneurial Cities and the New Politics of Economic Development," in George E. Peterson and Carol W. Lewis, eds., *Reagan and the Cities* (Washington, D.C., 1986); and Carl Abbott, *The New Urban America: Growth and Politics in Sunbelt Cities* (Chapel Hill, 1987).

Information on aspects of Colorado's postwar economic development is found in a series of reports issued by the University of Colorado Bureau of Business Research and the University of Denver's Denver Research Institute. Denver Research Institute, *Economic Forces Behind Colorado's Growth, 1870–1962* (Denver, 1963), is especially valuable. Also see John Garwood, "An Analysis of Postwar Industrial Migration to Utah and Colorado," *Economic Geography* 29 (January 1953):79-88; Henry Lansford, "Science in Colorado: The Second Century Begins," *Science* 195 (February 4, 1977):477–479; and Jeff Miller, *Stapleton International Airport: The First Fifty Years* (Boulder, 1983). Discussions of Colorado's place within the economy of the American West are found in Morris Garnsey, *America's New Frontier: The Mountain West* (New York, 1950), and in United States National Resources Planning Board, *Mountain States Region Industrial Development* (Washington, D.C., 1941).

Booms and busts in western Colorado are discussed in Denver Research Institute, *Policy Analysis for Rural Development and Growth Management in Colorado* (1973); Michael Husband, "'History's Greatest Metal Hunt': The Uranium Boom on the Colorado Plateau," *Journal of the West* 21 (October 1982):17–23; and Andrew Gulliford, *Boomtown Blues: Colorado Oil Shale, 1885–1985* (Niwot, Colo., 1989).

For debates over directions for Colorado growth, the primary sources are the *Rocky Mountain News* and the *Denver Post*. Additionally, during the 1960s and 1970s the *New York Times* carried frequent news articles about the ongoing discussion of Colorado's future. On the subject of land use and growth policy, see Colorado Land Use Commission, A *Land Use Program for Colorado* (1974); Colorado Legislative Council, *Designing for Growth*, Report for General Assembly Committee on Balanced Population, Research Report no. 195 (1972); and the newsletters and reports of the League of Women Voters and the Colorado Open Space Council.

## 15: Plural Society in Midcentury

The primary sources for the history of Mexican-American migration into rural Colorado before World War II are Paul S. Taylor, "Mexican Labor in the United States: The Valley of the South Platte, Colorado" *University of California Publications in Economics* 6 (1929):215–216, and Robert N. McLean and Charles A. Thomson, *Spanish and Mexican in Colorado* (New York, 1929). Also helpful are Kent Hendrickson, "The Sugar Beet Laborer and the Federal Government," *Great Plains Journal* 3 (1964):44–59, and Carey McWilliams, *North From Mexico* (New York, 1968).

Ira D.A. Reid, *The Negro Population of Denver, Colorado: A Survey of Its Economic and Social Status* (Denver, 1929), includes an impressive quantity of data and is the only published source on African-American Denverites during the interwar years. Lionel Lyles, "An Historical-Urban Geographical Analysis of Black Neighborhood Development in Denver, 1860–1970" (Ph.D. diss., University of Colorado, 1977), is a useful source.

For studies of the Spanish-speaking population of rural Colorado since 1940, see R. W. Roskelly and Catherine R. Clark, *When Different Cultures Meet* (Denver, 1949); Howard E. Thomas and Florence Taylor, *Migrant Farm Labor in Colorado* (New York, 1951); John H. Burma, *Spanish-Speaking Groups in the United States* (Durham, 1954); Colorado Legislative Council, *Migratory Labor in Colorado,* Report to the Colorado General Assembly, Research Publication no. 72 (1962); Colorado Legislative Council, *Migrant Labor Problems in the 1970s* Research Publication No. 157 (1970); Wade H. Andrews, "Family Composition and Characteristics of an Economically Deprived Cross-Cultural Rocky Mountain Area," *Rocky Mountain Social Science Journal* 3 (April 1966):122–135; and Alvar W. Carlson, "Seasonal Farm Labor in the San Luis Valley," *Annals of the Association of American Geographers,* 63 (March 1973):97–108. Richard Jessor et al., *Society, Personality, and Deviant Behavior: A Study of a Tri-Ethnic Community* (New York, 1968), is perhaps the most accessible of the many monographs resulting from the University of Colorado's "tri-ethnic" research project on relations among Hispanos, Anglos, and Native Americans in southwestern Colorado.

A number of individuals and agencies studied the economic and social adjustment of African-American and Hispanic minority groups to life in Denver during the 1930s, 1940s, and 1950s. Some of their reports include: Lynn Perrigo, "Community Background of Denver Criminality," *Social Forces* 17 (December 1938):232–239; Barron Beshoar, "Report from the Mountain States," *Common Ground* 4 (Spring 1944):22–30; *Housing in Denver,* University of Denver Reports 17, no. 1 (1941); Denver Unity Council, *The Spanish-Speaking Population of Denver: Housing, Employment, Health, Recreation, Education* (Denver, 1946); Mayor's Interim Study Committee on Human Relations, *Report of Minorities in Denver* (Denver, 1947); and Denver Area Welfare Council, *The Spanish-American Population of Denver* (Denver, 1960). Also see Magdelena Gallegos, "The Forgotten Community: Hispanic Auraria in the Twentieth Century," *Colorado Heritage* 2 (1985):5–26.

Detailed analyses of the status of minority group population since 1960 can be found in Reuben A. Zubrow et al., *Poverty and Jobs in Denver* (Denver, 1969); Colorado Commission on Spanish-Surnamed Citizens, *The Status of Spanish-Surnamed Citizens in Colorado: Report to the Colorado General Assembly* (Denver, 1967); Denver Planning Office, *A Strategy for Community Renewal* (Denver,

1973); Leo Grebler, Joan W. Moore, and Ralph C. Guzman, *The Mexican-American People: The Nation's Second Largest Minority* (New York, 1970); James A. Atkins, *Human Relations in Colorado: A Historical Record* (Denver, 1969); and Christine Marin, *A Spokesman of the Mexican-American Movement: Rodolfo "Corky" Gonzales and the Fight for Chicano Liberation, 1966–1972* (San Francisco, 1977).

For other racial groups, see Russell Endo, "Japanese of Colorado: A Sociohistorical Portrait," *Journal of Social and Behavioral Research* 31 (Fall 1985):100–110, and J. Donald Hughes, *American Indians in Colorado* (Boulder, 1987).

The social friction that arose from neighborhood change is discussed in George Bardwell, *Characteristics of Negro Residents in Park Hill Area of Denver, Colorado* (Denver, 1966), and Daniel Doeppers, "The Globeville Neighborhood in Denver," *Geographical Review* 57 (October 1967):506–522. The crisis of Denver school integration is treated in Harold E. Jackson, "Discrimination and Busing: The Denver School Board Election of May, 1969," *Rocky Mountain Social Science Journal* 8 (October 1971):101–108. Stanley Steiner, *La Raza: The Mexican Americans* (New York, 1970), contains an admiring introduction to the career of Rodolfo Gonzales. Nicholas P. Lovrich, Jr., and Otwin Marenin, "A Comparison of Black and Mexican-American Voters in Denver," *Western Political Quarterly* 29 (June 1987):284–294; Nicholas P. Lovrich, Jr., "Differing Priorities in an Urban Electorate: Service Preferences Among Anglo, Black, and Mexican-American Voters," *Social Science Quarterly* 55 (December 1974):704–717; and Rodney E. Hero and Kathleen Beatty, "The Election of Federico Peña as Mayor of Denver: Analysis and Implications," *Social Science Quarterly* 70 (June 1989):300–310 deal with recent voting patterns. For detailed information on ethnic confrontation in contemporary Colorado, again refer to major urban newspapers and to the *New York Times*.

## 16: Measuring the Limits: Colorado Since 1970

Recent information, for the most part, must come from contemporary publications such as the *Denver Post, Rocky Mountain News, Colorado Business Review,* and *Colorado Women's Digest*. Few accounts by historians focus on the current scene, but the following are helpful for specific subjects: Lyle W. Dorsett, *The Queen City: A History of Denver* (Boulder, 1977); Stephen J. Leonard and Thomas J. Noel, *Denver: Mining Camp to Metropolis* (Niwot, Colo., 1990); Mark S. Foster, "Colorado's Defeat of the 1976 Winter Olympics," *Colorado Magazine* 53 (Spring 1976):163–186; David McComb, *Big Thompson: Profile of a Natural Disaster* (Boulder, 1980); Duane A. Smith, *Rocky Mountain Boom Town: A History of Durango* (Albuquerque, 1980); Erin S. Christensen and Gail L. Ukockis, *Challenge to Build: A History of Public Works and APWA in Colorado* (Fort Collins, 1987); Andrew Gulliford, *Boomtown Blues: Colorado Oil Shale, 1885–1985* (Niwot, Colo., 1989); Daniel Tyler, *The Last Water Hole in the West: The Colorado–Big Thompson Project and the Northern Colorado Water Conservancy District* (Niwot, Colo., 1992); Steven K. Wilmsen, *Silverado: Neil Bush and the Savings and Loan Scandal* (Washington, D.C., 1991).

An oral history project in the mid-1970s, conducted by David McComb under the sponsorship of Colorado State University, the Boettcher Foundation, and the State Historical Society, provided 116 transcribed interviews with elites from around the state. The interviews are available for research use at the Heritage Center in Denver. Other oral history projects that deal with specific locations and topics can be found through the Oral History Clearing House of the Denver Public Library. The interviews are useful in providing eye witness accounts of events and for adding a personal interpretation.

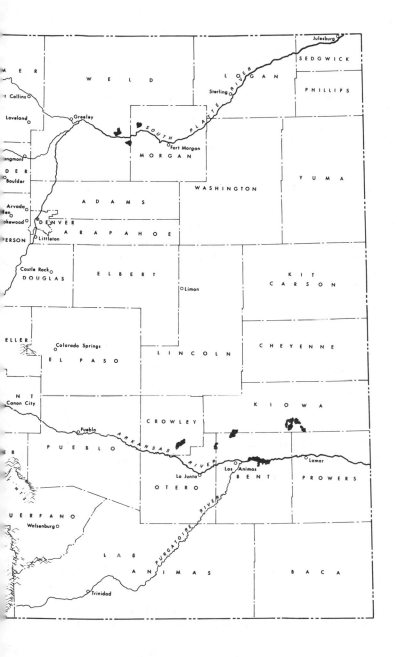

# COLORADO

## BASE MAP

0   10   20   30   40   50
miles

Julesburg

SEDGWICK

PHILLIPS

W E L D

MORGAN

South Platte River

Sterling

Fort Morgan

Greeley

Collins

Loveland

ongmont

Boulder

Arvada

lakewood

DENVER

Littleton

ERSON

D E R

A D A M S

A R A P A H O E

Castle Rock

DOUGLAS

E L B E R T

Limon

Y U M A

WASHINGTON

K I T
C A R S O N

ELLER

Colorado Springs

E L   P A S O

L I N C O L N

C H E Y E N N E

N T

Canon City

Pueblo

P U E B L O

ARKANSAS RIVER

C R O W L E Y

K I O W A

La Junta

Las Animas

Lamar

O T E R O

B E N T

P R O W E R S

UERFANO

Walsenburg

PURGATOIRE RIVER

L A S

A N I M A S

B A C A

Trinidad

# CREDITS

Grateful acknowledgment is made to the following for permission to publish the photographs and maps in this book.

THE CLEVELAND MUSEUM OF ART, Bequest of Mrs. Henry A. Everett for the Dorothy Burnham Everett Memorial Collection, for "Smelting Works at Denver."

THE STATE HISTORICAL SOCIETY OF COLORADO for Mount Sneffels; Cliff Palace; Conejos; church at Guadalupe; Francisco Plaza; William Bent; Black Hawk; John Chivington; Frank Hall; William H. Jackson; burro train; Elkton Mine; deep mining; Grand Junction; militia guarding Emmett Mine; Colorado National Guard riding trains; celery pickers; Ludlow tent colony; bicyclists, Denver picnic; camp on Roaring fork; automobile camping; flat tire; Ellis Meredith; auto showroom; Curtiss Field; Franklin Roosevelt; WPA workers; soldiers in 1942; Climax; War Transport Exchange; Camp Hale; Interstate Trust Building demolition; and Corky Gonzales.

THE DENVER PUBLIC LIBRARY WESTERN HISTORY DEPARTMENT for Helen Hunt Jackson; miners in San Juan County; advertisement; Beaumont Hotel; San Juan County Courthouse; dust storm; dining Car; Boston and Colorado smelter; Industrial Exposition building; Fort Collins; Sixteenth Street in Denver; Frederick Douglass, Jr.; W. R. Speer cartoon; Edward Costigan; and employment agencies.

THE LIBRARY OF CONGRESS for "The Rocky Mountains"; farm couple near Kersey; and Keota.

UNIVERSITY OF COLORADO WESTERN HISTORICAL COLLECTIONS for narrow gauge railroad; Baldwin's map of mining claims; Gunnison tunnel; Old main; tourists waiting for train; Robert Rockwell; Edward Keating; and sugar beet harvesting.

PUEBLO LIBRARY DISTRICT WESTERN RESEARCH ROOM for Colorado Fuel and Iron; Colorado Hungarians; Italian funeral; "Hooverville"; and CWA workers.

COLORADO STATE UNIVERSITY OFFICE OF EDUCATIONAL MEDIA for Main street of Rocky Ford; skiing; putting up hay; and sand blowing.

SOUTHERN COLORADO UNIVERSITY TEACHER CORPS for Pueblo school teacher.

AMON CARTER MUSEUM, FORT WORTH, TEXAS for Ute encampment and Ku Klux Klan.

PHOTOGRAPHICS GROUP, NATIONAL CENTER FOR ATMOSPHERIC RESEARCH, BOULDER, COLORADO, for National Center for Atmospheric Research.

Andrew Gulliford, *Boomtown Blues: Colorado Oil Shale, 1985–1985* (University of Colorado) for view of oil shale region.

And to photographers ROBERT ADAMS for Pawnee Grassland, tract houses, and suburban landscape; JOSEPH DANIEL for Rocky Flats protest; RICHARD W. KRAMER, Bureau of Reclamation, for Denver Federal Center sign; DAVID McCOMB for Big Thompson flood; HARRY SKUNK for Valley Curtain; RICHARD VAN PELT for red Rock Lake; and MYRON WOOD for Dawn on a Ranch and Jeanette and Edward Eyetos. Maps were drawn and photographed by KENNETH A. ERICKSON, Department of Geography, University of Colorado.

Permission to print poem, "The Flower fed the Buffaloes," by Vachel Lindsay, was given by Nicholas Lindsay.

The passage referenced by Note 8, Chapter 4, is reprinted by permission of the publishers, The Arthur Clark Company, from *Colorado Gold Rush* by Leroy Hafen.

# INDEX

Rocky Mountains: early reactions, 4–5; attitudes in nineteenth century, 228–29; attitudes in twentieth century, 241–43

Roeschlaub, Robert, 133

Rogers, Henry, 134

Rogers, Platt, 234

Romer, Roy, 342, 380

Romney, Caroline, 112

Roosevelt, Franklin, 296, 297, 300

Roosevelt, Theodore, 13, 128, 264

Routt, John, 125–26, 188

Royal Gorge: railroad construction, 89; tourist attraction, 227

Russell, William Green, 51–52

Sage, Rufus, 4

St. Charles. *See* Denver

St. Louis Western Colony, 164

St. Vrain, Ceran, 35–40 *passim*

St. Vrain, Marcellin, 37

Saloons, 110, 206, 260

Salvation Army farm colony, 165

San Carlos Pueblo, 28

Sanatoriums, 199, 232

Sand Creek Massacre, 76–77

Sanderlin, Ed, 214

Sangre de Cristo Grant, 41, 48, 82

Santa Fe Railroad, 89–90

Santa Fe trade, 34–36

Schools: public schools, 130; immigrant groups and, 208; racial integration, 214, 322–23, 324

Schroeder, Patricia, 323, 339, 340, 381

Seven Years' War, 27, 33

Shafroth, John: opposes conservation, 128; as governor, 263–64; as reformer, 266; biography, 381

Shafroth, Morrison, 285

Shoup, Oliver, 280

Sibley, Henry H., 67

Silver: boom at Georgetown, 87; boom at Leadville, 102–10

Silverado Banking Savings and Loan, 347

Silverton, 111, 118

Simmons, William J., 282

Simpson, George, 39

Skiing, 242(illus.), 302, 316–17, 308, 350

Smelter Trust. *See* American Smelting and Refining Company

Smelting: experiments, 85–87; at Leadville, 103; in Pueblo and Denver, 133; consolidation, 133–35; in 1920s, 277

Smiley, Jerome, 249, 355

Smith, A. J., 63

Smith, Eben, 132

Smythe, William E., 179

Snyder, Zachariah, 130

Solar Energy Research Institute, 309

Solly, Samuel E., 230

Soule, Silas, 79

Southworth, Frank, 322, 323

Spain: settles New Mexico, 22–23; frontier policy, 25–28; relations with France, 26–27, 33; relations with Indians, 32; relations with United States, 33

Spanish-Americans: in twentieth century, 14; settlement in Colorado, 41–43; cultural patterns, 43–46; relations with Anglo-Americans, 44–48, 97; religion, 45. *See also* Mexican Americans

Speer, Robert, 234, 257–61, 266, 381–82

Stafford, Jean, 13

Stapleton, Benjamin, 284–85, 288, 299(illus.), 313

State Board of Immigration, 173

State War Council, 268

Steamboat Springs, 317

Steele, R. W., 63

Stevens, William, 102

Stone, Lucy, 188, 189

Strahorn, Robert, 160

Stratton, Winfield Scott, 114

Strikes: Leadville strike of 1880, 108; Cripple Creek strike of 1903, 139, 141, 149–50; Idaho Springs strike of 1903, 140; Colorado City strike of 1903, 140, 147; Telluride strike of 1903, 140, 141, 150; coal strike of 1903, 141; Denver smelter strike of 1903, 140, 148; Telluride strike of 1901, 145, 147–48; coal strike of 1913–14, 151–54; Denver tramway strike of 1920, 281; coal strike of 1927, 287

Strong, Josiah, 254

Sublette, Andrew, 37

Sudler, James, 347

Sugar beet industry, 181–83, 325–27

Sugar City, 183

Sullivan, Daniel, 256

Summit Springs Battle, 78

Sunbelt region, 320–21

Sun dance, 30–31

Sweet, William, 279, 285

Swink, George, 165

Tabor, Horace A.W.: and Leadville boom, 102, 103, 106–07; and growth of Denver, 120, 138, 248–49; as politician, 126, 216; as typical Coloradan, 138; biography, 382

Taos, 27, 35, 38–39

Tate, Penfield, 341

Taylor, Arie, 341

Taylor, Bayard, 222, 230

Taylor, Edward, 11, 128, 183, 190, 383

Taylor Grazing Act, 179

Teller, Henry Moore: and railroads, 84; as politician, 84; opposes conservation, 129; biography, 383

Telluride, 111, 118

Telluride strike of 1901, 145, 147–48

Telluride strike of 1903, 140, 141, 150

Temple, J. S., 264

Thornburgh, Thomas, 124

Thornton, Dan, 315

Tierney, Luke, 55

Tikas, Louis, 151

Tooley, Dale, 323

Tourism: in United States, 223; in nineteenth century, 224–29, 232(illus.), 233–34; and health, 229–32; early twentieth century, 235–40; after 1940, 308–09, 317; in 1980s, 350

Townsend, R. B., 355

Tramway strike of 1920, 287

Transportation; by stage and wagon, 74–75, 111; railroads, 83–92, 233;

automobiles, 238–41, 288(illus.), 342

Treaties. *See* Indian treaties

Trinidad, 42, 46–48, 90–91

Tuberculosis, 199, 230–32

Tungsten, 276

Ulibarri, Juan de, 25–26

Union Colony, 161–63, 192

Union Pacific Railroad, 83–84, 85–86

United Mine Workers: coal strike of 1903, 141; early growth, 144; coal strike of 1913–14, 151–53; decline in Colorado, 155; in 1920s, 275

United States Commission on Industrial Relations, 154

United States Reduction and Refining Company, 134

United States Trade and Intercourse Act, 39

Upper Platte Valley Regional Planning Commission, 306

Uranium, 307

Urban Renewal, 312–13, 346–47

Urban Service Authority, 319

Urbanization: and American West, vii–viii; in United States, 253–54; in modern Colorado, 267, 278, 301–02, 310, 346; and ethnic groups in Colorado, 327, 329, 330

Utes: early migrations, 21; adoption of horses, 24; relations with Spanish, 24–25, 26, 27; relations with other tribes, 27, 28; trade with New Mexico, 34; opposition to settlement in Colorado, 41, 122; in 1860s and 1870s, 79(illus.), 123–24; attitudes of Coloradans, 124; White River Massacre, 125; removal from Colorado, 125; contemporary, 336, 356(illus.)

Ute Mountain Tribe, 125, 336

Vail, 350

Valverde (governor of New Mexico), 26

Vanadium, 276

Van Cise, Philip, 196

Vanderhoof, John, 339

Vasques, Louis, 37